America Firsthand

America Firsthand

FOURTH EDITION

Volume I
Readings from Settlement to Reconstruction

Robert D. Marcus

State University of New York College at Brockport

and

David Burner

State University of New York at Stony Brook

BEDFORD BOOKS ⚮ Boston

For Bedford Books
President and Publisher: Charles H. Christensen
General Manager and Associate Publisher: Joan E. Feinberg
History Editor: Katherine E. Kurzman
Development Editor: Charisse Kiino
Managing Editor: Elizabeth M. Schaaf
Production Editor: Tony Perriello
Production Assistant: Deborah Baker
Copyeditor: David Bemelmans
Cover Design: Hannus Design Associates
Cover Art: View Along the East Battery, Charleston, c. 1831, by S. Bernard. Yale University Art Gallery.

Library of Congress Catalog Card Number: 97–72373

Manufactured in the United States of America.

1 0 9 8 7
f e d c b a

For information, write: Bedford Books, 75 Arlington Street, Boston, MA 02116 (617-426-7440)

ISBN: 0-312-15349-X

Acknowledgments
Bracketed numbers indicate selection numbers.
[1] "Declarations of Spanish Officials" and "Declarations of Pueblo Indians" from Charles Wilson Hackett, *Revolt of the Pueblo Indians of New Mexico and Otermän's Attempted Reconquest 1680–1682* (Albuquerque: The University of New Mexico Press, 1942), pp. 207–14, 238–42 and 245–49. With the permission of The University of New Mexico Press.
[3] "Life of the Admiral Christopher Columbus" from Fernando Colón, *The Life of the Admiral Christopher Columbus by His Son Ferdinand,* translated and annotated by Benjamin Keen (New Brunswick: Rutgers University Press, 1959). Copyright © 1959 by Benjamin Keen. Reprinted by permission of the translator.

Preface

The fourth edition of *America Firsthand* aims to capture, through the variety of experiences it records, a lively picture of America and the diverse individual perspectives that comprise its history. Designed to supplement United States history survey textbooks, its two volumes give center stage to ordinary Americans who speak directly of their own lives. These include people from many groups whose experience until recently has been largely lost in mainstream history. As much as possible, individuals speak in their own words and in selections long enough to be memorable, personal, and immediate. The accounts of indentured servants, southern aristocrats, runaway slaves, factory workers, western explorers, civil rights activists, immigrants, and many others offer students opportunities to identify with a wide range of human experience.

Like their predecessors, these volumes respond to the increasing difficulty of teaching and learning American history, particularly the challenge of connecting traditional chronology with the new materials of social history. While the readings convey the experiences and force of specific personalities, *America Firsthand*, fourth edition, has retained the traditional markers of United States history by including accounts of people who acted in or responded to such events as the American Revolution, the western movement, the Civil War, Reconstruction, both World Wars, the Great Depression, the civil rights movement, and the war in Vietnam.

America Firsthand has been extensively revised in the fourth edition. We have retained readings that users wanted to continue teaching and have dropped less successful ones. Among many new readings in the first volume, students will find the diary of Hetty Shepard, a teenaged Puritan girl writing during King Philip's War, an account of the impact of the American Revolution on the slaves of Southern planter Landon Carter, and correspondence of Elizabeth Cady Stanton and Susan B. Anthony as they begin their long collaboration on women's rights. Fresh selections in the second volume include John Wesley Powell's diary of his party's dangerous exploration of the Grand Canyon, interviews of American soldiers who survived the Bataan death march during World War II, an account of how Odessa Williams raised grandchildren and great grandchildren on welfare in Philadelphia in the 1980s and 1990s, and the reflections of Katie Argyle on the death of a friend she had known only on the Internet.

The fourth edition has several new features intended to make it an even more effective teaching tool. The sections into which the book is divided have been brought closer to the typical organization of the standard American history textbook. Each part is organized around a general theme and begins with an introduction that announces the theme and briefly explains the relationship of each reading to it. Two "Points of View" then characterize the section theme by presenting an event from two different perspectives. Neither of the selections presents a simple pro or con position, nor do the critical thinking questions that follow them. By examining a single event that dramatically portrays the central theme of the section, they focus student attention, thereby allowing a deepening of perception and a more interesting probing of the past. Through the "Points of View" in Volume One, students will discover ways of thinking about the Pueblo Indian revolt of 1680, the Salem witchcraft trials, the Boston massacre, the battle of the Alamo, Nat Turner's slave rebellion, and the march of William T. Sherman's army through Georgia and the Carolinas. Volume Two "Points of View" engage students in consideration of a notorious Ku Klux Klan murder in South Carolina during Reconstruction, the battle of Little Big Horn, the Triangle Shirtwaist fire, the Scopes trial, the building of the atomic bomb, and the My Lai incident.

The headnotes preceding each selection have been revised and expanded to better prepare students for each reading by providing necessary background information without providing too much coaching. New questions immediately after the headnotes enable students and instructors to give attention to specific passages and issues that can provide points for discussion as well as material for testing or essays.

America Firsthand, fourth edition, presents the American experience through the perspectives of diverse people who have in common a vivid record of the world they inhabited and the times they experienced. We hope that the readings will serve as fertile ground in which students can begin to root their own interest in history and deepen their perception of the times in which they live.

Acknowledgments
Many fine teachers provided thoughtful criticism and good suggestions for the fourth edition of *America Firsthand*.

Our thanks to Irwin Klibaner, Madison Area Technical College; Dennis Deslippe, Shippensburg University; Norman L. Rosenberg, Macalester University; Ted Karamanski, Loyola University; Ruth Helm, University of Colorado at Boulder; Jean E. Friedman, University of Georgia; James S. Olson, Sam Houston State University; Anne S. Laszlo, Northern Essex Community

College; Jim Harper, Texas Tech University; Mark Newman, University of Illinois at Chicago; Sarah Deutsch, Clark University; Brian C. Hosmer, University of Delaware; James T. Moore, Virginia Commonwealth University; Janette Thomas Greenwood, Clark University; Margaret L. Brown, Brevard College; Rebecca S. Shoemaker, Indiana State University; Michael J. Shaff, Laramic County Community College; David Sloan, University of Arkansas; Wilma King, Michigan State University; Monys A. Hagen, Metropolitan State College of Denver; Susan Curtis, Purdue University; Gene A. Smith, Texas Christian University; David Dalton, College of the Ozarks; Nicolas Proctor, Emory University; Jeffrey S. Adler, University of Florida; and Susan Gray, Arizona State University.

We owe gratitude as well to the many people whose editorial work and judgment improved this edition. Phyllis Valentine and Charisse Kiino were both creative and good humored in keeping us in line through the long process of turning the third edition into the much altered fourth. Others at Bedford Books who played major roles have our thanks as well: Charles Christensen, Joan Feinberg, Katherine Kurzman, Elizabeth Schaaf, Tony Perriello, David Bemelmans, Susan Pace, Dick Hannuo, and Fred Courtright. Outside the Bedford organization, Beth Donaldson did fine service in picture and other research and Elizabeth Marcus in modernizing seventeenth century prose. And Tom West remains for both of us the editors' editor.

Contents

America Firsthand

Mapa 6.º

Fr Martin de Jesus.

Fr Angel

Fr. Martin de Jesus.

Ñanuma.

Aqui se demuestra que ya pasificos los naturales, obraron en la viña del Señor los Padres misioneros bautizando á unos, y predicando á otros, luchando al mismo tiempo con los Demonios, á cuya empresa, asistia fiel y fervoroso el General Na

This rendering of missionaries converting Indians to Catholicism by a contemporary Spanish artist reveals a great deal about European perceptions of native American culture.

PART ONE

Indians and Europeans

Cultural Conflict

The age of exploration added the scientific and humanist ambitions of the Re-
naissance to the older hopes of discovering the lost tribes of Israel and of gaining a westward sea route to the rich trade of the Orient. Accounts of the New
World, such as that found in Colón's life of Columbus, flooded Europe with
reports that were as much a product of the confused dreams of the age as they
were of the realities of America.

The people of this new land were named "Indians" by explorers who mis-
took the Americas for the East Indies or the Orient. These native Americans
had their own complex cultures, which rapidly came into conflict with those
of white explorers and settlers. And, much like the Europeans, they survived
among shifting allies and enemies, territorial disputes, and cultural borrowings.
European settlers, soldiers, missionaries, plants, animals, technologies, and
especially germs disrupted and fundamentally transformed this world, finally
destroying most of it. Bartolomé de Las Casas's report of the Spanish conquest
captures the full horrors of that first encounter. Yet it is important to remember that for three centuries after Columbus, various Indian nations played independent and sometimes powerful roles in the diplomacy of the western
hemisphere, that their adaptations and cultural exchanges—now including
encounters with white civilizations—continued, and that, however much diminished, many tribes have maintained their identity into the present.

The varying accounts of the Pueblo revolt of 1680 offer differing perspectives on the Spanish Empire's uneasy mix of Indian and European religions and
interests. John Smith's description of Virginia's Indians and William Bradford's account of the Pequot War show how cultural conflicts similar to those
of the Spanish conquest worked themselves out in the colonies of the British
Empire. And Father Paul Le Jeune, illustrating the French Empire in the New

1

World, suggests how little understanding existed even between friendly whites and receptive native Americans.

Indians throughout the colonial era and well into the nineteenth century provoked fear and a sense of mystery. Stories about what happened when whites were captured by Indians, beginning with John Smith's account of his supposed rescue by Pocahontas, remained popular for more than two centuries, making captivity narratives among the first best-sellers produced in this country. Mary Jemison's account of her captivity among the Seneca illustrates how Anglo-Americans domesticated their anxieties about Indians and wrapped them in an aura of romance.

Points of View:
Revolt of the Pueblo Indians (1680)

1

Declarations of Spanish Officials
Pedro de Leiva et al.

Just as Anglo-America had a western frontier, Spanish America had a northern frontier comprising northern Mexico as well as much of present-day Florida, Texas, New Mexico, Arizona, and California. The Anglo frontier was highly individualistic and secular; the Spanish frontier was closely controlled by the Spanish government and the Catholic Church. Anglo frontiersmen made Indians their enemies and were willing to see them massacred. Spanish officials and frontiersmen battled the Indians as well, subjugated what tribes they could, and often brutally exploited the Indians' labor. But they also intermixed and intermarried with them, creating a substantial caste of mestizos, while Spanish missionaries converted Indians to Catholicism, educated them to Spanish ways, and tried—with some success—to assimilate them. Christianized Indians often made up a substantial proportion of new settlements. Unlike Indians in the Anglo world, they were an integral part of the Spanish frontier movement.

The tribes of northern Mexico and New Mexico often resisted the Spanish as they had the Aztecs. Revolts followed the movement of the frontier northward throughout the seventeenth century. The greatest of these, the Pueblo revolt of 1680, had its antecedents in 1675 when the Spanish governor raided a meeting of medicine men, eventually executing three and severely punishing the rest. One of them, Popé, revived the ancient tribal religion and plotted to destroy the Spanish. Although his plan was discovered at the last moment, the uprising nonetheless devastated the Spanish settlements, forcing the abandonment of Santa Fe, the only substantial city north of El Paso.

Subsequently, most of the tribes in the region remained free of Spanish rule for six-teen years.

These official reports and proclamations from Spanish officers are products of Gov-ernor Don Antonio de Otermín's unsuccessful attempt at reconquest in 1681. After marching through many abandoned pueblos, Otermín's small army, nearly half of them Indians, found hundreds of Indians gathered at La Isleta. After a minor skirmish these Indians asked for pardon for their rebellion and provided the Spaniards with supplies.

BEFORE YOU READ

1. What do these Spanish sources suggest as the causes of the rebellion?
2. Why did the Indians make peace with the Spaniards? How many possible mo-tives can you find in the readings?
3. Did the Spanish act in ways that contributed to the Indians' decision to make peace?

PEDRO DE LEIVA, JUAN LUCERO DE GODOY, NICOLÀS RODRÍGUEZ REY, ALONSO DEL RÍO, AND LORENZO DE MADRID

On the second of December [1681] the camp marched from this place over another piece of bad road on which a difficult trail for the wagons was made, and after marching all day they halted in the place which they call the en-trance of Las Vueltas de Acomilla. On the fourth day of the said month we marched from this place toward the pueblo of Cèbolleta. His lordship went ahead with a company, reconnoitered the said pueblo, entered it, and found it depopulated, and that the apostates had left it for fear of the Apaches and had gone to join the rebels farther in the interior. Here the hermitage where the holy sacraments were administered was found entirely demolished, and the wood from it made into an underground estufa[1] of idolatry. Some of the houses of the pueblo were burned, and a short distance away from it were found some deep subterranean chambers, in four parts, full of maize — most of it spoiled — earthen jars, calabashes, and some pots. On top of everything was a very curi-ous sort of vessel made of clay, and carved on it was a figure with the face of an Indian and the body of a toad. Inside of it were many powdered idolatrous herbs, two pieces of human flesh, feathers, and other superstitious things made by the idolaters, who offer them to that figure so that it will guard their maize. We marched from here on the day of the fifth to the estancia of Las Barran-cas, where his lordship issued a proclamation which he ordered incorporated in the *autos*.[2] He arranged there to march with seventy men to the pueblo of La Isleta, because of having sent previously to the hills to ascertain whether or not there was smoke or any sign that it might be populated. Five leagues

Charles Wilson Hackett, *Revolt of the Pueblo Indians of New Mexico and Otermín's Attempted Recon-quest 1680–1682* (Albuquerque: University of New Mexico Press, 1942), pp. 207–14.
  1. **estufa:** Pueblo religious symbol.
  2. *autos:* presentation.

before reaching the said pueblo it had been seen that there was smoke and that it was occupied. He marched that night with the said seventy men, and being in sight of the pueblo at dawn, he formed four squadrons to surround and advance upon it from all directions. They took their positions, extolling the most holy sacrament in loud voices, according to the order he gave, and he led the advance with all the soldiers, completing the encirclement. The apostate traitors took up their arms, shouted loudly, and discharged some arrows, the whole pueblo being garrisoned with men. Seeing that the plaza and the dwellings were taken, they said that they would surrender peaceably, laid down their arms, and went down to offer obedience to his lordship. They excused themselves for having taken up arms by saying that they had believed themselves ambushed by the Apaches. The said señor governor and captain-general ordered that all the men, women, and children assemble in the plaza, both those of the pueblo and others from outside who were there, of the Piro nation, from the pueblos of El Socorro, Alamillo, and Sevilleta. More than five hundred souls having assembled, the governor—seeing the holy temple and convent burned and ruined, the crosses thrown down throughout the pueblo, and a cowpen inside the body of the church—was very indignant, and ordered the cows turned into the fields and gave the Indians a severe reprimand. They excused themselves, saying that they had not done it; that the Indians who led the rebellion, with all the rest from the Taos, Pecuríes, and Teguas nations, had descended to burn all the temples, images, and things of divine worship, ordering that they live as they had in their heathen days; that now they were living as they liked, without priests, governor, or Spaniards; and that they must obey the leaders of the traitors. They stated many other things, which, since there is not now time for them, his lordship decided should be given in the form of juridical statements when the occasion should present itself. He ordered the idolatrous traitors to exhibit all the things they had in their possession belonging alike to the church and to the citizens. On inspecting the houses with them, there were found the chest of the most holy sacrament from the ciborium,[3] some pieces of sashes worn by the priests, five handbells, four candlesticks, three large bells which were buried in the body of the church, a missal,[4] and two other books. Of property belonging to the Spaniards there were found three beasts, a copper ladle, a brass mortar, six ploughshares, and other trifles. Everything belonging to the church was turned over to the secretary of government, so that he might deliver it to the very reverend father visitador, Fray Francisco de Ayeta, and the other things were given to their owners who were present. The said Señor Don Antonio de Otermín at once ordered that on the same day it be proclaimed that crosses should be made for the plaza and all the houses, and other small ones for everyone to wear around their necks; and that many thanks be given to God for the happy result. Two Indians who had been outside the pueblo had escaped from the siege, and in order that the other

3. **ciborium:** covered cup holding Eucharistic wafer.
4. **missal:** book of devotions used in saying Mass.

pueblos might not be abandoned and so that the people might not fortify themselves in the sierras and mesas, two Indians of the pueblo of Sandia, which is ten leagues beyond this pueblo, were sent to require in his lordship's name of those of the pueblos of Alameda, Puaray, and Sandia, all of whom are of one nation, to give themselves up peaceably so that they might be instructed in the holy gospel, since they were Christians; and they were warned that if they did not, they would be subdued by force of arms. This being done, and the said Indians being dispatched, he immediately sent word of the event to the said reverend father visitador, who, being ill, had remained with the wagons. His reverence being encouraged by the news, he mounted on horseback and passed to the pueblo, where his lordship went out to receive him. And all the apostate Indians, men, women, and children, went out in a procession to receive his reverence, who said in a loud voice, "Praised be the most holy sacrament and the purity of our Lady, the Virgin Mary, conceived without stain of sin," and all the said apostates responded, "Forever." His reverence dismounted and everyone embraced him, and it being now the hour, the Ave María was sounded with the bugle and all of them recited the most holy prayer of the Ave María in loud voices, three times. Whereupon they went to their houses very happy, and the activities of this day ended. . . .

On the day of the 8th, which was that of the Immaculate Conception of our Lady, all the said people were assembled in the plaza of the said pueblo, the portable altar being in the middle of it, and the very reverend father visitador blessed a most holy cross of pine, very large, which he had ordered made, and raising it on his shoulders, assisted by his lordship, he placed it on the same spot in the cemetery where had formerly been the one which the apostates had hacked down. His lordship ordered a volley of musketry to be fired, and he having confessed so as to receive the sacrament at mass, the very reverend father visitador, Fray Francisco de Ayeta, also confessed. His reverence then recited a prayer, donned an alb and chasuble,[5] and, being robed, said mass with all solemnity. He preached again to the said apostates, explaining to them anew the divine commands, and that they should give infinite thanks to God for the great favors He had done them in rescuing them from idolatry and from slavery to the devil, and in having restored them to the fold of our holy mother church. His reverence and the other religious as well spoke very kindly to them. The señor governor and captain-general addressed them in the same manner, and gave them to understand the great power of his Majesty and the obedience which his vassals owe him, and how much in his debt they are for the heavy expenditures he has made from his royal treasury for the reduction of their souls and for conserving them in the holy faith for almost a hundred years. Almost the whole day was taken up with these and other activities, and the Indians were left pardoned in the royal name of his Majesty, and very well pleased. On this day an Indian named Pedro Naranjo was arrested for being a

5. **alb and chasuble:** garments worn by priests for Mass.

great sorcerer and idolater, he having come down from the upper pueblos at the order of the chiefs of the apostates to teach superstitions. In order to obtain evidence of his crimes, it was arranged to dispatch immediately the lieutenant general of cavalry with sixty picked men and a troop of Indians, to the interior pueblos, to reconnoiter them, issuing him an order of everything he was to do until his lordship should break camp and march to proceed with the pacification and reduction. . . .

Proclamation [Place of Las Barrancas, December 5, 1681]

Don Antonio de Otermín, governor and captain-general of the kingdom and provinces of New Mexico and their presidio for his Majesty, etc. Whereas on to-day, the 5th of the month of December, this army of his Majesty finds itself in this place of Las Barrancas, within the kingdom of New Mexico, twenty-three leagues beyond the pueblo of Senecú, in which district all the pueblos, four in number, and the estancias[6] are entirely deserted, burned, and destroyed, except for this estancia which, although it is deserted and lacks windows and doors, has a whole roof and a main door; and since I find myself ten leagues from the pueblo of La Isleta, where it is presumed that the treacherous Indian apostates and rebels have retired and fortified themselves, and I being disposed to advance upon the said pueblo and the others of the kingdom, attempting to reduce them and return them to the yoke of the holy gospel and to his Majesty's crown as vassals of his who have had almost a hundred years of instruction in the doctrine and of recognized vassalage to the king, our lord; and being mindful that many of the poor Spanish residents, during the convocation and general rebellion of the apostate Christians, lost their lives, and others that came out lost their property, and that in the administrations and districts of the convents they [the Indians] not only rebelliously and tyrannically killed the ministers and spiritual fathers, but, carried away by their anger and hatred of the holy faith, they burned and broke in pieces the divine images of Jesus Christ, the most holy Virgin Mary, and all the other saints and things of divine worship, not leaving a single cross or sign of the existence of Christianity—grave crimes which must be attended to with all care; and so that action may be taken in accordance with God's will and as the case demands in the service of both Majesties, I order all the men of this army, active officers, retired captains, and any other soldiers, and the Indian natives, in any advances, sieges, open warfare, or peaceful surrender that may occur, that none shall dare to sack the pueblos and houses or to take any kind of cattle that may be found in the fields, but that everything, in whatever manner it may be taken, shall be brought into my presence to be accounted for. The things pertaining to divine worship and the valuables and cattle belonging to the convents shall be delivered to the very reverend father preacher, Fray Francisco de Ayeta, commissary of the Holy Office, procurador and visitador general, so that as le-

6. **estancias:** cattle ranches.

gitimate prelate whose place it is, he may dispose at his will of that which may be thus found. In the same manner the cattle and goods belonging to the deceased who perished at the hands of the said rebels are to be disposed of for the good of their souls and to such legitimate heirs as they may have. Let there be returned to those who are now in this army the livestock which appears lawfully to be theirs, from the brands and marks, none of it being sold, and also any other things that may be found. This is to apply to Indians captured in open war and to men and women servants who fled during the said rebellion. In the same manner there is to be kept and safeguarded that which may appear to belong to the people of the presidio[7] who remained at El Paso and the plaza de armas, so that there may be taken and delivered to each one that which clearly belongs to him. The firearms which may be found shall also be brought into my presence, in order to find the blunderbusses[8] belonging to his Majesty which were in use on the frontiers, as well as the horses and livestock which were the property of the king, our lord. All the soldiers are to obey and observe the orders of their superior officers which emanate from me, and those of their squad captains. They are to be always vigilant and obedient, without leaving their posts, but all being united in the service of God and of his Majesty, for good order and government so demands, under penalty that he who does the contrary shall be condemned to death as a traitor to the king, and to the loss of all his goods. The latter will at once be applied on expenses for account of this kingdom, of which a report will be given to his Majesty through his viceroy, governor, and captain-general of the city of Mexico. This proclamation is to be made public by the secretary of government and war, he certifying to its publication, and he will insert it with the other *autos* which may be drawn up now or in the future. For this purpose I so provided, ordered, and signed before the said secretary. Done in the place of Las Barrancas on the 5th day of the month of December, 1681.

2

Testimony of Pueblo Indians
Pedro Naranjo and Josephe

Once Cortés conquered Tenochtitlán in 1519, the Spanish quickly gained control over the entire Aztec Empire. Indians accustomed to tribute and forced labor simply adapted to new masters. But as Spanish soldiers, settlers, and missionaries moved northward in search of precious metals and outposts to secure their empire from European and Indian enemies, they found that the methods that had worked farther south failed among the more independent tribes that had never been conquered by their Aztec predecessors. Franciscan and Jesuit missionaries struggled mightily to convert native Americans as

7. **presidio:** fort.
8. **blunderbusses:** firearms used at short range.

settlement inched northward; by 1670, about twenty-eight hundred Spaniards popu-
lated the valley of the Rio Grande.

The country was generally poor, punctuated only by an occasional silver mine; the
population lived largely by farming and raising livestock. Needed supplies from Mex-
ico arrived infrequently and at great cost. Governors and missionaries battled for pre-
eminence while settlers, there at the king's command, were disgruntled. And the In-
dians, however sincere their conversion to Catholicism, were at the bottom of society
bearing the brunt of these harsh circumstances. Nor were the old religions dead. The
valley was a true frontier with Apache, Hopi, and Navaho, all beyond Spanish power,
threatening the Pueblo Indians while providing a powerful example of freedom.

The uprising of the Pueblo Indians in 1680 drove the Spanish out of Santa Fe and
all the surrounding settlements. Four hundred Spaniards died during the conflict and
the rest retreated south to El Paso. Efforts at reconquest in 1681 had only temporary
success. A number of the converted Indians who made peace at La Isleta moved south
for Spanish protection against their tribal enemies. But others remained independent
and returned to the practice of their native religions. In the 1690s, a new Spanish com-
mander, Don Diego de Vargas, through skillful diplomacy and a few carefully limited
military campaigns, brought most of the Pueblo tribes back under Spanish rule. But
in the meantime, the Indian capture of Spanish horses had begun a momentous trans-
formation. Within a generation, this superweapon of the age had spread far northward
among the Indians. When it met the other superweapon—the rifle—carried west-
ward by English and French frontiersmen and traders, the plains Indian brave who
has dominated the American imagination was born.

BEFORE YOU READ

1. How did Pedro Naranjo explain the revolt? To what extent do you think he was tailoring his answer to his Spanish questioners?

2. How did Josephe explain the revolt? What differences do you notice between his account and Pedro Naranjo's?

3. What according to Josephe were the strategic objectives of the leaders of the revolt? How did they inspire the Pueblo Indians to revolt?

DECLARATION OF PEDRO NARANJO OF THE QUERES NATION

December 19, 1681

In the said plaza de armas on the said day, month, and year, for the prose-cution of the judicial proceedings of this case his lordship caused to appear be-fore him an Indian prisoner named Pedro Naranjo, a native of the pueblo of San Felipe, of the Queres nation, who was captured in the advance and attack upon the pueblo of La Isleta. He makes himself understood very well in the Castil-

Charles Wilson Hackett, *Revolt of the Pueblo Indians of New Mexico and Otermín's Attempted Recon-quest 1680–1682* (Albuquerque: University of New Mexico Press, 1942), pp. 238–42, 245–49.

ian language and speaks his mother tongue and the Tegua. He took the oath in due legal form in the name of God, our Lord, and a sign of the cross. . . .

Asked whether he knows the reason or motives which the Indians of this kingdom had for rebelling, forsaking the law of God and obedience to his Majesty, and committing such grave and atrocious crimes, and who were the leaders and principal movers, and by whom and how it was ordered; and why they burned the images, temples, crosses, rosaries, and things of divine worship, committing such atrocities as killing priests, Spaniards, women, and children, and the rest that he might know touching the question, he said that since the government of Señor General Hernando Ugarte y la Concha they have planned to rebel on various occasions through conspiracies of the Indian sorcerers, and that although in some pueblos the messages were accepted, in other parts they would not agree to it; and that it is true that during the government of the said señor general seven or eight Indians were hanged for this same cause, whereupon the unrest subsided. Some time thereafter they [the conspirators] sent from the pueblo of Los Taos through the pueblos of the custodia two deerskins with some pictures on them signifying conspiracy after their manner, in order to convoke the people to a new rebellion, and the said deerskins passed to the province of Moqui, where they refused to accept them. The pact which they had been forming ceased for the time being, but they always kept in their hearts the desire to carry it out, so as to live as they are living to-day. Finally, in the past years, at the summons of an Indian named Popé, who is said to have communication with the devil, it happened that in an estufa of the pueblo of Los Taos there appeared to the said Popé three figures of Indians who never came out of the estufa. They gave the said Popé to understand that they were going underground to the lake of Copala. He saw these figures emit fire from all the extremities of their bodies, and that one of them was called Caudi, another Tilini, and the other Tleume; and these three beings spoke to the said Popé, who was in hiding from the secretary, Francisco Xavier, who wished to punish him as a sorcerer. They told him to make a cord of maguey fiber and tie some knots in it which would signify the number of days that they must wait before the rebellion. He said that the cord was passed through all the pueblos of the kingdom so that the ones which agreed to it [the rebellion] might untie one knot in a sign of obedience, and by the other knots they would know the days which were lacking; and this was to be done on pain of death to those who refused to agree to it. As a sign of agreement and notice of having concurred in the treason and perfidy they were to send up smoke signals to that effect in each one of the pueblos singly. The said cord was taken from pueblo to pueblo by the swiftest youths under the penalty of death if they revealed the secret. Everything being thus arranged, two days before the time set for its execution, because his lordship had learned of it and had imprisoned two Indian accomplices from the pueblo of Tesuque, it was carried out prematurely that night, because it seemed to them that they were now discovered; and they killed religious, Spaniards, women, and children. This being done, it was proclaimed in all the pueblos that everyone in common should obey the commands of their father whom they did not know, which would be given through El Caydi or El Popé. This was heard by Alonso Catití, who came to the pueblo of this declarant to say that everyone must unite to go to the villa to kill the governor and the Spaniards who had remained with him, and that he who did not obey would, on their return, be beheaded; and in fear of this they agreed to it. Finally the señor governor and those who were with him escaped from the siege, and later this declarant saw that as soon as the Spaniards had left the kingdom an order came from the said Indian, Popé, in which he commanded all the Indians to break the lands and enlarge their cultivated fields, saying that now they were as they had been in ancient times, free from the labor they had performed for the religious and the Spaniards, who could not now be alive. He said that this is the legitimate cause and the reason they had for rebelling, because they had always desired to live as they had when they came out of the lake of Copala. Thus he replies to the question.

Asked for what reason they so blindly burned the images, temples, crosses, and other things of divine worship, he stated that the said Indian, Popé, came down in person, and with him El Saca and El Chato from the pueblo of Los Taos, and other captains and leaders and many people who were in his train, and he ordered in all the pueblos through which he passed that they instantly break up and burn the images of the holy Christ, the Virgin Mary and the other saints, the crosses, and everything pertaining to Christianity, and that they burn the temples, break up the bells, and separate from the wives whom God had given them in marriage and take those whom they desired. In order to take away their baptismal names, the water, and the holy oils, they were to plunge into the rivers and wash themselves with amole, which is a root native to the country, washing even their clothing, with the understanding that there would thus be taken from them the character of the holy sacraments. They did this, and also many other things which he does not recall, given to understand that this mandate had come from the Caydi and the other two who emitted fire from their extremities in the said estufa of Taos, and that they thereby returned to the state of their antiquity, as when they came from the lake of Copala; that this was the better life and the one they desired, because the God of the Spaniards was worth nothing and theirs was very strong, the Spaniards' God being rotten wood. These things were observed and obeyed by all except some who, moved by the zeal of Christians, opposed it, and such persons the said Popé caused to be killed immediately. He saw to it that they at once erected and rebuilt their houses of idolatry which they call estufas, and made very ugly masks in imitation of the devil in order to dance the dance of the cacina; and he said likewise that the devil had given them to understand that living thus in accordance with the law of their ancestors, they would harvest a great deal of maize, many beans, a great abundance of cotton, calabashes, and very large watermelons and cantaloupes; and that they could erect their houses and enjoy abundant health and leisure. As he has said, the people were very much pleased, living at their ease in this life of their antiquity, which was the chief cause of their falling into such laxity. Following what has already been stated, in order to terrorize them further and cause them to observe the diabolical commands, there came to them a pronouncement from the three demons already described, and from El Popé, to the effect that he who might still keep in his heart a regard for the priests, the governor, and the Spaniards would be known from his unclean face and clothes, and would be punished. And he stated that the said four persons stopped at nothing to have their commands obeyed. Thus he replies to the question.

Asked what arrangements and plans they had made for the contingency of the Spaniards' return, he said that what he knows concerning the question is that they were always saying they would have to fight to the death, for they do not wish to live in any other way than they are living at present; and the demons in the estufa of Taos had given them to understand that as soon as the Spaniards began to move toward this kingdom they would warn them so that they might unite, and none of them would be caught. He having been questioned further and repeatedly touching the case, he said that he has nothing more to say. . . . His declaration being read to him, he affirmed and ratified all of it. He declared himself to be eighty years of age, and he signed it with his lordship and the interpreters and assisting witnesses. . . .

DECLARATION OF JOSEPHE, SPANISH-SPEAKING INDIAN

December 19, 1681

In this said place and plaza de armas of this army on the 19th day of the month of December, 1681, for the said judicial proceedings of this case, his lordship caused to appear before him an Indian prisoner named Josephe, able to speak the Castilian language, a servant of Sargento Mayor Sebastián de Herrera who fled from him and went among the apostates. . . . Being asked why he fled from his master, the said Sargento Mayor Sebastián de Herrera, and went to live with the treacherous Indian apostates of New Mexico, where he has been until he came among us on the present occasion, he said that the reason why he left was that he was suffering hunger in the plaza de armas of La Toma [del Río del Norte], and a companion of his named Domingo urged this declarant to go to New Mexico for a while, so as to find out how matters stood with the Indians and to give warning to the Spaniards of any treason. They did not come with the intention of remaining always with the apostate traitors and rebels, and after they arrived they [the Indians] killed the said Domingo, his companion, because of the Pecos Indians having seen him fighting in the villa along with the Spaniards. He said that because his comrade was gone he had remained until now, when he saw the Spaniards and came to them, warning them not to be careless with the horses, because he had heard the traitors say that although the Spaniards might conclude peace with them, they would come to attack them by night and take away the horses. Thus he responds to this question.

Asked what causes or motives the said Indian rebels had for renouncing the law of God and obedience to his Majesty, and for committing so many kinds of crimes, and who were the instigators of the rebellion, and what he had heard while he was among the apostates, he said that the prime movers of the rebellion were two Indians of San Juan, one named El Popé and the other El Taqu, and another from Taos named Saca, and another from San Ildefonso named Francisco. He knows that these were the principals, and the causes they gave were alleged ill treatment and injuries received from the present secretary, Francisco Xavier, and the maestre de campo, Alonso García, and from the sargentos mayores, Luis de Quintana and Diego López, because they beat them, took away what they had, and made them work without pay. Thus he replies.

Asked why, since the said rebels had been of different minds, some believing that they should give themselves up peacefully and others opposing it, when the Spaniards arrived at the sierra of La Cieneguilla de Cochití, where the leaders of the uprising and people from all the nations were assembled, they had not attempted to give themselves up and return to the holy faith and to obedience to his Majesty—for while they had made some signs, they had done nothing definite—he said that although it is true that as soon as the Spaniards arrived some said that it was better to give up peaceably than to have war, the young men were unwilling to agree, saying that they wished to fight. In particular one Spanish-speaking Indian or coyote named Francisco, commonly called El Ollita, said that no one should surrender in peace, that all must fight, and that although some of his brothers were coming with the Spaniards, if they fought on the side of the Spaniards he would kill them, and if they came over to the side of the Indians he would not harm them. Whereupon everyone was disturbed, and there having arrived at this juncture Don Luis Tupatú, governor of the pueblo of Los Pecuríes, while they were thus consulting, news came to the place where the junta was being held from another Indian named Alonso Catití, a leader of the uprising, believed to be a coyote, in which he sent to notify the people that he had already planned to deceive the Spaniards with feigned peace. He had arranged to send to the pueblo of Cochití all the prettiest, most pleasing, and neatest Indian women so that, under pretense of coming down to prepare food for the Spaniards, they could provoke them to lewdness, and that night while they were with them, the said coyote Catití would come down with all the men of the Queres and Jemez nations, only the said Catití attempting to speak with the said Spaniards, and at a shout from him they would all rush down to kill the said Spaniards; and he gave orders that all the rest who were in the other junta where the said Don Luis and El Ollita were present, should at the same time attack the horse drove, so as to finish that too. This declarant being present during all these proceedings, and feeling compassion because of the treason they were plotting, he determined to come to warn the Spaniards, as he did, whereupon they put themselves under arms and the said Indians again went up to the heights of the sierra, and the Spaniards withdrew. Thus he replies to the question. . . .

. . . He said that what he has stated in his declaration is the truth and what he knows, under charge of his oath, which he affirms and ratifies, this, his said declaration, being read to him. He did not sign because of not knowing how, nor does he know his age. Apparently he is about twenty years old. . . .

FOR CRITICAL THINKING

1. John Francis Bannon observes in *The Spanish Borderlands Frontier, 1513–1821* that the revolt of 1680 resulted from a "culture clash on all levels—material, personal, religious." Discuss this statement. What culture clashes can you detect by comparing the Spanish and the Indian testimony? What was the role of religion in this conflict?

2. What picture of the Spanish Empire and its treatment of Indians do you get from the two documents? Do the Spanish appear to have been cruel masters? How sincere was their interest in converting the Indians to Christianity?

3. Compare the Spanish treatment of Indians with that by the English and Anglo-Americans.

3

Life of the Admiral Christopher Columbus
Fernando Colón

*The idea of sailing west to reach the riches of the East Indies and the Asian mainland
was much in vogue with literate Europeans during the late fifteenth century. Learned
people agreed that the earth was round; their only questions about reaching the Orient were how long and how dangerous such a voyage would be.*

*Christopher Columbus, the son of an obscure Genoese weaver, and himself a weaver
of ambitious dreams, made his historic voyage to the New World in 1492. Sailing with
a tiny fleet of three ships and a crew of ninety sailors, he found the thirty-three-day
crossing easier than his nearly decade-long effort to find royal patrons willing to support it. The trip drew not only on his own skills at seafaring but also on his ability to
plan such an expedition, obtain governmental approval and financing, and finally,
demonstrate (or advertise) its success so that such explorations could continue. (Columbus himself was to make a total of four voyages to the New World.)*

*The explorations that followed Columbus's — those of Cabot, Verrazano, Cartier,
and many others — benefited from a new maritime technology borrowed from Arab
sailors and from a variety of new vessels such as the light-weight caravels used by
Columbus. Mariners also perfected sails and various types of riggings that gave ships
added stability and greater maneuverability on the open seas. And when leaving sight
of the coast, new navigational aids — charts, compasses, and astrolabes — permitted
them to determine their position with some, though not perfect, accuracy.*

*One of the basic documents from which we know the life of Columbus, Colón's bi-
ography of the admiral, was written by a loyal son who accompanied his father on the
last of his voyages to the New World. The son literally lived on his father's legacy, for
the Crown awarded Colón income from the labors of four hundred Indian slaves.*

BEFORE YOU READ

1. How difficult (from Colón's account) would you judge Columbus's first voyage
to have been? Did the ships experience bad weather? How accurately did Columbus cal-
culate where they were?

2. How close to mutiny do you think the crew actually was? Does Colón give any
evidence of a real conspiracy to commit mutiny? Would he be liable to exaggerate, report accurately, or underplay such dangers?

3. How accurate do you suppose Colón's account of the Indians of San Salvador is?
What do you find convincing and what doubtful?

HOW THE ADMIRAL SAILED FROM THE
GRAND CANARY AND CONTINUED HIS VOYAGE OF
DISCOVERY, AND WHAT HAPPENED TO HIM
ON THE OCEAN

On the afternoon of Friday, September 1st, the ships having been made ready in all respects, the Admiral hoisted sails and set out from the Grand Canary. Next day they reached Gomera,[1] where they passed four more days in taking on meat, wood, and water. And on the morning of the Thursday following, September 6, 1492, which day may be taken to mark the beginning of the enterprise and the ocean crossing, the Admiral sailed westward from Gomera; but he made little headway on account of feeble and variable winds.

At daybreak on Sunday, he found he was nine leagues[2] west of the island of Ferro. This day they completely lost sight of land, and many sighed and wept for fear they would not see it again for a long time. The Admiral comforted them with great promises of lands and riches. To sustain their hope and dispel their fears of a long voyage he decided to reckon less leagues than they actually made, telling them they had covered only fifteen leagues that day, though they had actually gone eighteen. He did this that they might not think themselves so great a distance from Spain as they really were, but for himself he kept a secret accurate reckoning.

Continuing their voyage, at sundown of Tuesday, September 11th, about one hundred and fifty leagues west of the island of Ferro, the Admiral saw a large fragment of mast that may have belonged to a ship of 120 tons and that seemed to have been in the water for a long time. In this region and farther west the currents set strongly to the northeast. At midnight of September 13th, after the fleet had run another fifty leagues westwards, the needles were found to vary half a point to the northwest, and in the morning a little more than half a point to the northeast. From this the Admiral knew that the needle did not point to the polestar, but to some other fixed and invisible point. No one had ever noticed this variation before, so he had good reason to be surprised at it. Three days later, almost one hundred leagues west of that area, he was even more surprised to find that at midnight the needles varied a whole point to the northwest, while in the morning they again pointed directly to the polestar.

Fernando Colón, *The Life of Christopher Columbus by His Son Ferdinand*, trans. Benjamin Keen (New Jersey: Rutgers University Press, 1959).
    1. **Gomera:** one of the Canary Islands.
    2. **leagues:** unit of distance—about three miles.

HOW ALL THE SHIP'S PEOPLE,
BEING EAGER TO REACH LAND,
WERE VERY ATTENTIVE TO THE
THINGS THEY SAW IN THE SEA

As this was the first voyage of that kind for all the men in the fleet, they grew frightened at finding themselves so far from land without prospect of aid, and did not cease to grumble among themselves. Seeing nothing but water and sky all about, they paid the closest attention to all they observed, as was natural for men who had gone a greater distance from land than any had ever done before. So I shall mention all the things to which they assigned any importance (but only in telling of the first voyage), though I will not take note of those minor signs that are commonly and frequently observed at sea.

On the morning of September 19th a pelican flew over the Admiral's ship, followed by others in the afternoon. This gave him some hope of soon sighting land, for he reflected that these birds would not have flown far from land. Accordingly, when it grew calm, the ship's people sounded with two hundred fathoms[3] of line; they found no bottom, but noted that now the currents set to the southwest. Again, on Thursday, the 20th of the month, two hours before noon, two pelicans flew over the ship and a while later came another; the sailors also caught a bird like a heron, save that it was black, with a white tuft on its head and feet like a duck's, as is common with water birds. They also caught a little fish and saw much weed of the kind mentioned before. At daybreak three little birds flew singing over the ship; they flew away when the sun came out, but left the comforting thought that unlike the other large water birds, which might have come a great distance, these little birds could not have come from afar. Three hours later they saw another bird that came from the west-northwest, and next day, in the afternoon, they saw another *rabo de junco*[4] and a pelican; they also saw more seaweed than ever before, stretching northward as far as they could see. This also comforted them, since they concluded it must come from some nearby land; but at times it caused them great fright, because in places the weed was so thickly matted that it held back the ships. And since fear conjures up imaginary terrors, they even feared lest the weed grow so thick that there might happen to them what is supposed to have happened to St. Amador in the frozen sea that is said to hold ships fast. That is why they kept as clear as possible of those mats of weed.

The next day they sighted a whale, and the Saturday following, September 22d, some *pardelas*[5] were seen. During those three days the wind blew from the southwest, more westerly at some times than at others; and though

3. **fathoms:** unit of length for measuring depth of water—usually six feet.
4. *rabo de junco:* sea bird.
5. *pardelas:* sea birds.

this wind was contrary to his design, the Admiral wrote that he found it very helpful. For one of the bogeys his people had been scaring themselves with was the idea that since the wind was always at their backs, they would never have a wind in those waters for returning to Spain. Then, when they got such a wind, they would complain that it was inconstant, and that since there was no heavy sea, that proved it would never blow hard enough to return them the great distance they had come from Spain. To this the Admiral would reply that must be because they were near land, which kept the sea smooth, and he sought to convince them as well as he could. But [in his journal] he wrote that he stood in need of God's aid, such as Moses had when he was leading the Jews out of Egypt and they dared not lay violent hands upon him on account of the miracles that God wrought by his own means. So, says the Admiral, it happened with him on this voyage. For soon after, on Sunday, September 23d, there arose a wind from the west-northwest, with a rough sea such as the people wanted; also, three hours before noon, a turtledove flew over the ship, and in the afternoon they saw a pelican, a small river bird, some white birds, and some crabs among the weed. Next day they saw another pelican, and many *pardelas* flying out of the west, and some little fish, some of which the sailors caught with harpoons, because they would not bite at hooks.

HOW THE MEN GRUMBLED BECAUSE OF THEIR DESIRE TO RETURN, AND HOW CERTAIN SIGNS AND TOKENS OF LAND MADE THEM CONTINUE GLADLY ON THEIR COURSE

As these signs proved fruitless, the men grew ever more restless and fearful. They met together in the holds of the ships, saying that the Admiral in his mad fantasy proposed to make himself a lord at the cost of their lives or die in the attempt; that they had already tempted fortune as much as their duty required and had sailed farther from land than any others had done. Why, then, should they work their own ruin by continuing that voyage, since they were already running short of provisions and the ships had so many leaks and faults that even now they were hardly fit to retrace the great distance they had traveled? Certainly (said they), none would blame them for deciding to return but rather would hold them for very brave men for having enlisted on such a voyage and having sailed so far. And since the Admiral was a foreigner without favor at Court and one whose views had been rejected and criticized by many wise and learned men, none would speak in his defense and all would believe what they said, attributing to ignorance and ineptitude whatever he might say to justify himself. Others said they had heard enough gab. If the Admiral would not turn back, they should heave him overboard and report in Spain that he had fallen in accidentally while observing the stars; and none would question their story. That, said they, was the best means of assuring their safe return.

The grumbling, lamenting, and plotting went on day after day; and at last the Admiral himself became aware of their faithlessness and wicked designs against him. Therefore at times he addressed them with fair words; again, very passionately, as if fearless of death, he threatened punishment to any who hindered his voyage. By these different means he managed somewhat to calm their fears and check their machinations. To bolster their hopes he reminded them of the signs and tokens mentioned above, assuring them they would soon sight land. After that they looked most diligently for those signs and thought each hour a year until land was reached.

Finally, at sunset of Tuesday, September 25th, while the Admiral was talking with Pinzón, whose ship had come close alongside, Pinzón suddenly cried out, "Land, land, sir! I claim the reward!" And he pointed to a bulk that clearly resembled an island and lay about twenty-five leagues distant. At this the people felt such joy and relief that they offered thanks to God. The Admiral himself gave some credit to that claim until nightfall, and wishing to please them that they might not oppose continuing the voyage, he gratified their wishes and steered in that direction a good part of the night. But next morning they knew that what they had supposed to be land was nothing more than squall clouds, which often resemble land.

So, to the grief and vexation of most of his people, they again sailed westward, as they had done since leaving Spain, save when the winds were contrary. Ever vigilant for signs, they sighted a pelican and a *rabo de junco* and other birds of that kind. The morning of Thursday, September 27th, they saw another pelican flying west to east; they also saw many fish with gilded backs, and caught one of these fish with a harpoon. A *rabo de junco* flew close by; and they noted that for the last few days the currents had not been as constant and regular as before but changed with the tides; the quantity of seaweed also diminished.

Although very attentive to these signs, the Admiral did not neglect the portents of the heavens or the courses of the stars. He was much surprised to observe that in this region the Guards appeared at night directly to the west, while at daybreak they were directly northeast. From this he concluded that during one night the ships traveled only three lines or nine [astronomical] hours, and by observation he found this to be true every night. He also noted that in the evening the needles varied a whole point, while at dawn they pointed directly to the polestar. This fact greatly disquieted and confused the pilots, until he told them its cause was the circle described by the polestar about the pole. This explanation partly allayed their fears, for these variations on a voyage into such strange and distant regions made them very apprehensive.

HOW THEY CONTINUED TO SEE
THE ABOVE-MENTIONED SIGNS AND TOKENS
AND OTHERS THAT WERE EVEN MORE
HOPEFUL, WHICH GAVE THEM SOME COMFORT

At sunrise on Monday, October 1st, a pelican flew over the ship, and two hours before noon came two more; the direction of the weed was now east to west. In the morning of that day the pilot of the Admiral's flagship said they were 578 leagues west of Ferro, and the Admiral put the figure at 584; but from his secret reckoning he knew they had traveled 707 leagues, a difference of 129 between his count and the pilot's. The reckonings of the other two ships varied even more widely; in the afternoon of the Wednesday following, the *Niña's* pilot claimed they had sailed 540 leagues, while the *Pinta's* set the figure at 634. Allowing for the distance they had covered the past three days, their reckonings still fell far short of the true and reasonable total, for they had always sailed with a stiff wind at their backs. But the Admiral dissembled this error that his people might not grow even more frightened, finding themselves so far from home.

Next day, seeing no birds save some *pardelas*, the men feared they unknowingly had passed between some islands; for they thought the great multitude of birds they had seen were birds of passage bound from one island to another. The Admiral's people wished to turn off in one or another direction to look for those lands, but he refused because he feared to lose the fair wind that was carrying him due west along what he believed to be the best and most certain route to the Indies. Besides, he reflected that he would lose respect and credit for his voyage if he beat aimlessly about from place to place looking for lands whose position he had claimed to know most accurately. Because of this refusal, the men were on the point of mutiny, grumbling and plotting against him. But God was pleased to assist him with new signs, for on Thursday, October 4th, they saw a flight of more than forty *pardelas* and two pelicans which came so near the ships that a grummet hit one with a stone. They had previously seen another bird like a *rabo de junco* and one resembling a sea gull, and many flying fish fell into the ships. Next day another *rabo de junco* flew over the ship, and a pelican came from the west; many *pardelas* were seen.

But the farther they sailed the more their spirits fell. . . . God, however, was pleased to offer them some small comfort; for they saw many large flocks of birds, more varied in kind than those they had seen before, and others of small land birds which were flying from the west to the southwest in search of food. Being now a great distance from Spain, and convinced that such small birds would not fly far from land, the Admiral changed course from west to southwest, noting [in his journal] that he was making a slight deviation from his main course in imitation of the Portuguese, who made most of their discoveries by attending to the flights of birds. He did this especially because the birds they saw were flying in almost the very same direction where he always expected land to be found. . . .

But by this time the men's anxiety and desire to sight land had reached such a pitch that no sign of any kind would satisfy them. And though on Wednesday, October 10th, they saw birds passing overhead both night and day, they did not cease to complain nor the Admiral to reprove them for their small spirit, telling them that for better or worse they must go through with the enterprise of the Indies on which the Catholic Sovereigns had sent them.

HOW THE ADMIRAL SIGHTED THE FIRST LAND, THIS BEING AN ISLAND IN THE ARCHIPELAGO CALLED THE BAHAMAS

Our Lord, perceiving how difficult was the Admiral's situation because of his many opponents, was pleased on the afternoon of Thursday, October 11th, to give them clear indications that they were near land, which cheered the men greatly. First the flagship's people saw a green branch pass near the ship, and later, a large green fish of the kind that is found near reefs. Then the *Pinta's* people saw a cane and a stick; and they fished up another stick skillfully carved, a small board, and an abundance of weeds of the kind that grow on the shore. The *Niña's* crew saw other signs of the same kind, as well as a thorn branch loaded with red berries that seemed to be freshly cut.

These signs, and his own reasoning, convinced the Admiral that land must be near. That night, therefore, after they had sung the Hail Mary as seamen are accustomed to do at nightfall, he spoke to the men of the favor that Our Lord had shown them by conducting them so safely and prosperously with fair winds and a clear course, and by comforting them with signs that daily grew more abundant. And he prayed them to be very watchful that night, reminding them that in the first article of the instructions issued to each ship at the Canaries he had given orders to do no night-sailing after reaching a point seven hundred leagues from those islands, but that the great desire of all to see land had decided him to sail on that night. They must make amends for this temerity by keeping a sharp lookout, for he was most confident that land was near; and to him who first sighted it he would give a velvet doublet in addition to the annuity for life of 10,000 maravedís that their Highnesses had promised.

That same night, about two hours before midnight, as the Admiral stood on the sterncastle, he saw a light, but he says it was so uncertain a thing that he dared not announce it was land. He called Pedro Gutiérrez, butler to the King, and asked him if he saw that light. He replied that he did, so they called Rodrigo Sánchez of Segovia to have a look, but he was too slow in coming to the place from which the light could be seen. After that they saw it only once or twice. This made them think it might be a light or torch belonging to fisher-men or travelers who alternately raised and lowered it, or perhaps were going from house to house; for the light appeared and disappeared so quickly that few believed it to be a sign of land.

Being now very watchful, they held on their course until about two hours after midnight, when the *Pinta*, a speedy sailer that ranged far ahead, fired the signal for land. A sailor named Rodrigo de Triana first sighted it while they were still two leagues away. It was not he who received the grant of 10,000 maravedís from the Catholic Sovereigns, however, but the Admiral, who had first seen the light amid the darkness, signifying the spiritual light with which he was to illuminate those parts.

Land being now very near, all the ship's people impatiently awaited the coming of day, thinking the time endless till they could enjoy what they had so long desired.

HOW THE ADMIRAL WENT ASHORE
AND TOOK POSSESSION OF THE LAND
IN THE NAME OF THE CATHOLIC SOVEREIGNS

At daybreak they saw an island about fifteen leagues in length, very level, full of green trees and abounding in springs, with a large lake in the middle, and inhabited by a multitude of people who hastened to the shore, astounded and marveling at the sight of the ships, which they took for animals. These people could hardly wait to see what sort of things the ships were. The Christians were no less eager to know what manner of people they had to do with. Their wishes were soon satisfied, for as soon as they had cast anchor the Admiral went ashore with an armed boat, displaying the royal standard. The captains of the other two ships did the same in their boats with the banner of the expedition, on which was depicted a green cross with an F on one side, and crowns in honor of Ferdinand and Isabella on the other.

After all had rendered thanks to Our Lord, kneeling on the ground and kiss-ing it with tears of joy for His great favor to them, the Admiral arose and gave this island the name San Salvador. Then, in the presence of the many natives assembled there, he took possession of it in the name of the Catholic Sover-eigns with appropriate ceremony and words. The Christians forthwith ac-cepted him as admiral and viceroy and swore obedience to him as the repre-sentative of their Highnesses, with such show of pleasure and joy as so great a victory deserved; and they begged his pardon for the injuries that through fear and little faith they had done him.

Many Indians assembled to watch this celebration and rejoicing, and the Admiral, perceiving they were a gentle, peaceful, and very simple people, gave them little red caps and glass beads which they hung about their necks, to-gether with other trifles that they cherished as if they were precious stones of great price.

OF THE CONDITION AND CUSTOMS OF THOSE PEOPLE, AND WHAT THE ADMIRAL SAW ON THAT ISLAND

The Admiral having returned to his boats, the Indians followed him thither and even to the ships, some swimming and others paddling in their canoes; they brought parrots, skeins of woven cotton, darts, and other things, which they exchanged for glass beads, hawk's bells, and other trifles. Being a people of primitive simplicity, they all went about as naked as their mothers bore them; and a woman who was there wore no more clothes than the men. They were all young, not above thirty years of age, and of good stature. Their hair was straight, thick, very black, and short—that is, cut above the ears—though some let it grow down to their shoulders and tied it about their heads with a stout cord so that it looked like a woman's tress. They had handsome features, spoiled somewhat by their unpleasantly broad foreheads. They were of middle stature, well formed and sturdy, with olive-colored skins that gave them the appearance of Canary Islanders or sunburned peasants. Some were painted black, others white, and still others red; some painted only the face, others the whole body, and others only the eyes or nose.

They had no arms like ours, nor knew thereof; for when the Christians showed them a naked sword, they foolishly grasped it by the blade and cut themselves. Nor have they anything of iron, for their darts are sticks with sharpened points that they harden in the fire, arming the end with a fish's tooth instead of an iron point. Some Indians had scars left by wounds on their bodies; asked by signs what had caused them, they replied, also by signs, that the natives of other islands came on raids to capture them and they had received their wounds in defending themselves. They appeared fluent in speech and intelligent, easily repeating words that they had once heard. The only animals of any kind on the island were parrots, which they brought with the things mentioned above for barter. This traffic continued till nightfall.

Next morning, October 13th, many of these people came to the beach and paddled to the ships in their little boats, called canoes; these are made from the bole of a tree hollowed out like a trough, all in one piece. The larger ones hold forty to forty-five persons; the smaller ones are of all sizes, down to one holding but a single man. The Indians row with paddles like baker's peels or those used in dressing hemp. But their paddles are not attached to the sides of the boat as ours are; they dip them in the water and pull back with a strong stroke. So light and skillfully made are these canoes that if one overturns, the Indian rowers immediately begin to swim and right it and shake the canoe from side to side like a weaver's shuttle until it is more than half empty, bailing out the rest of the water with gourds that they carry for this purpose.

That day they brought the same things to barter as the previous day, giving all they had, in exchange for some trifle. They had no jewels or metal objects except some gold pendants which they wear hanging from a hole made through the nostrils. Asked whence came that gold, they replied by signs, from the south, where lived a king who had many tiles and vessels of gold. They added that to the south and southwest there were many other islands and large countries. Being very eager to obtain our things, and having nothing more to give in exchange, they picked up anything they could lay their hands on as soon as they came aboard, were it only a piece of broken crockery or part of a glazed bowl, then jumped into the sea and swam ashore with it. . . .

4

Destruction of the Indies
Bartolomé de Las Casas

Bartolomé de Las Casas (1474–1566) saw Columbus in 1493 when the explorer passed through Seville returning home from his first voyage. His father and two uncles sailed in that year on Columbus's second voyage. Then in 1502 Las Casas himself travelled to the New World to serve as an officer of the king. But Las Casas was a most unusual colonialist and by 1523 had become a Dominican friar, condemning his former colleagues' treatment of the New World's natives.

Las Casas spent the rest of his long life attempting to protect the native Americans against the massacres, tortures, slavery, and forced labor imposed on them by their Spanish conquerors. His powerful writings created the image of Spanish conquest often called the "Black Legend," a vision of destruction and cruelty until that time unparalleled. Modern scholars generally accept the accuracy of Las Casas's shocking portraits of devastation, many of which he personally witnessed. Today, however, many view these horrors not as the outcome of some peculiar Spanish cruelty but as characteristic of the bloody "Columbian encounter" between Europeans and other cultures in the age of exploration and conquest.

BEFORE YOU READ

1. Do you think Las Casas's view of the native Americans was accurate?
2. Do you judge his criticism of the Spanish Empire to have been fair and accurate?
3. Throughout his life Las Casas remained fiercely loyal to both the Spanish monarch and the Catholic Church and retained great respect for Columbus. Can you reconcile these feelings with his condemnation of the Spanish Empire's actions in the New World?

SHORT REPORT OF THE DESTRUCTION
OF THE WEST INDIES

The Indies were discovered in the year fourteen hundred and ninety-two. The year following, Spanish Christians went to inhabit them, so that it is since forty-nine years that numbers of Spaniards have gone there: and the first land, that they invaded to inhabit, was the large and most delightful Isle of Hispaniola [present-day Dominican Republic and Haiti], which has a circumference of six hundred leagues.

Francis Augustus McNutt, *Bartholomew de las Casas: His Life, His Apostolate, and His Writings* (New York: G. P. Putnam's Sons, 1709), pp. 314–21.

2. There are numberless other islands, and very large ones, all around on every side, that were all—and we have seen it—as inhabited and full of their native Indian peoples as any country in the world.

3. Of the continent, the nearest part of which is more than two hundred and fifty leagues distant from this Island, more than ten thousand leagues of maritime coast have been discovered, and more is discovered every day; all that has been discovered up to the year forty-nine is full of people, like a hive of bees, so that it seems as though God had placed all, or the greater part of the entire human race in these countries.

4. God has created all these numberless people to be quite the simplest, without malice or duplicity, most obedient, most faithful to their natural Lords, and to the Christians, whom they serve; the most humble, most patient, most peaceful, and calm, without strife nor tumults; not wrangling, nor querulous, as free from uproar, hate and desire of revenge, as any in the world.

5. They are likewise the most delicate people, weak and of feeble constitution, and less than any other can they bear fatigue, and they very easily die of whatsoever infirmity; so much so, that not even the sons of our Princes and of nobles, brought up in royal and gentle life, are more delicate than they; although there are among them such as are of the peasant class. They are also a very poor people, who of worldly goods possess little, nor wish to possess: and they are therefore neither proud, nor ambitious, nor avaricious.

6. Their food is so poor, that it would seem that of the Holy Fathers in the desert was not scantier nor less pleasing. Their way of dressing is usually to go naked, covering the private parts; and at most they cover themselves with a cotton cover, which would be about equal to one and a half or two ells square of cloth. Their beds are of matting, and they mostly sleep in certain things like hanging nets, called in the language of Hispaniola *hamacas*.

7. They are likewise of a clean, unspoiled, and vivacious intellect, very capable, and receptive to every good doctrine; most prompt to accept our Holy Catholic Faith, to be endowed with virtuous customs; and they have as little difficulty with such things as any people created by God in the world.

8. Once they have begun to learn of matters pertaining to faith, they are so importunate to know them, and in frequenting the sacraments and divine service of the Church, that to tell the truth, the clergy have need to be endowed of God with the gift of pre-eminent patience to bear with them: and finally, I have heard many lay Spaniards frequently say many years ago, (unable to deny the goodness of those they saw) certainly these people were the most blessed of the earth, had they only knowledge of God.

9. Among these gentle sheep, gifted by their Maker with the above qualities, the Spaniards entered as soon as they knew them, like wolves, tigers, and lions which had been starving for many days, and since forty years they have done nothing else; nor do they otherwise at the present day, than outrage, slay, afflict, torment, and destroy them with strange and new, and divers kinds of cruelty, never before seen, nor heard of, nor read of, of which some few will

be told below: to such extremes has this gone that, whereas there were more than three million souls, whom we saw in Hispaniola, there are to-day, not two hundred of the native population left.

10. The island of Cuba is almost as long as the distance from Valladolid to Rome; it is now almost entirely deserted. The islands of San Juan [Puerto Rico], and Jamaica, very large and happy and pleasing islands, are both desolate. The Lucaya Isles lie near Hispaniola and Cuba to the north and number more than sixty, including those that are called the Giants, and other large and small Islands; the poorest of these, which is more fertile, and pleasing than the King's garden in Seville, is the healthiest country in the world, and contained more than five hundred thousand souls, but to-day there remains not even a single creature. All were killed in transporting them, to Hispaniola, because it was seen that the native population there was disappearing.

11. A ship went three years later to look for the people that had been left after the gathering in, because a good Christian was moved by compassion to convert and win those that were found to Christ; only eleven persons, whom I saw, were found.

12. More than thirty other islands, about the Isle of San Juan, are destroyed and depopulated, for the same reason. All these islands cover more than two thousand leagues of land, entirely depopulated and deserted.

13. We are assured that our Spaniards, with their cruelty and execrable works, have depopulated and made desolate the great continent, and that more than ten Kingdoms, larger than all Spain, counting Aragon and Portugal, and twice as much territory as from Seville to Jerusalem (which is more than two thousand leagues), although formerly full of people, are now deserted.

14. We give as a real and true reckoning, that in the said forty years, more than twelve million persons, men, and women, and children, have perished unjustly and through tyranny, by the infernal deeds and tyranny of the Christians; and I truly believe, nor think I am deceived, that it is more than fifteen.

15. Two ordinary and principal methods have the self-styled Christians, who have gone there, employed in extirpating these miserable nations and removing them from the face of the earth. The one, by unjust, cruel and tyrannous wars. The other, by slaying all those, who might aspire to, or sigh for, or think of liberty, or to escape from the torments that they suffer, such as all the native Lords, and adult men; for generally, they leave none alive in the wars, except the young men and the women, whom they oppress with the hardest, most horrible, and roughest servitude, to which either man or beast, can ever be put. To these two ways of infernal tyranny, all the many and divers other ways, which are numberless, of exterminating these people, are reduced, resolved, or sub-ordered according to kind.

16. The reason why the Christians have killed and destroyed such infinite numbers of souls, is solely because they have made gold their ultimate aim, seeking to load themselves with riches in the shortest time and to mount by high steps, disproportioned to their condition: namely by their insatiable avarice and ambition, the greatest, that could be on the earth. These lands,

being so happy and so rich, and the people so humble, so patient, and so easily subjugated, they have had no more respect, nor consideration nor have they taken more account of them (I speak with truth of what I have seen during all the aforementioned time) than, — I will not say of animals, for would to God they had considered and treated them as animals, — but as even less than the dung in the streets.

17. In this way have they cared for their lives—and for their souls: and therefore, all the millions above mentioned have died without faith, and without sacraments. And it is a publicly known truth, admitted, and confessed by all, even by the tyrants and homicides themselves, that the Indians throughout the Indies never did any harm to the Christians: they even esteemed them as coming from heaven, until they and their neighbours had suffered the same many evils, thefts, deaths, violence and visitations at their hands.

OF HISPANIOLA

In the island of Hispaniola—which was the first, as we have said, to be invaded by the Christians—the immense massacres and destruction of these people began. It was the first to be destroyed and made into a desert. The Christians began by taking the women and children, to use and to abuse them, and to eat of the substance of their toil and labour, instead of contenting themselves with what the Indians gave them spontaneously, according to the means of each. Such stores are always small; because they keep no more than they ordinarily need, which they acquire with little labour; but what is enough for three households, of ten persons each, for a month, a Christian eats and destroys in one day. From their using force, violence and other kinds of vexations, the Indians began to perceive that these men could not have come from heaven.

2. Some hid their provisions, others, their wives and children: others fled to the mountains to escape from people of such harsh and terrible intercourse. The Christians gave them blows in the face, beatings and cudgellings, even laying hands on the lords of the land. They reached such recklessness and effrontery, that a Christian captain violated the lawful wife of the chief king and lord of all the island.

3. After this deed, the Indians consulted to devise means of driving the Christians from their country. They took up their weapons, which are poor enough and little fitted for attack, being of little force and not even good for defence. For this reason, all their wars are little more than games with sticks, such as children play in our countries.

4. The Christians, with their horses and swords and lances, began to slaughter and practise strange cruelty among them. They penetrated into the country and spared neither children nor the aged, nor pregnant women, nor those in child labour, all of whom they ran through the body and lacerated, as though they were assaulting so many lambs herded in their sheepfold.

5. They made bets as to who would slit a man in two, or cut off his head at one blow: or they opened up his bowels. They tore the babes from their

mothers' breast by the feet, and dashed their heads against the rocks. Others they seized by the shoulders and threw into the rivers, laughing and joking, and when they fell into the water they exclaimed: "boil body of so and so!" They spitted the bodies of other babes, together with their mothers and all who were before them, on their swords.

6. They made a gallows just high enough for the feet to nearly touch the ground, and by thirteens, in honour and reverence of our Redeemer and the twelve Apostles, they put wood underneath and, with fire, they burned the Indians alive.

7. They wrapped the bodies of others entirely in dry straw, binding them in it and setting fire to it; and so they burned them. They cut off the hands of all they wished to take alive, made them carry them fastened on to them, and said: "Go and carry letters": that is; take the news to those who have fled to the mountains.

8. They generally killed the lords and nobles in the following way. They made wooden gridirons of stakes, bound them upon them, and made a slow fire beneath: thus the victims gave up the spirit by degrees, emitting cries of despair in their torture.

9. I once saw that they had four or five of the chief lords stretched on the gridirons to burn them, and I think also there were two or three pairs of gridirons, where they were burning others; and because they cried aloud and annoyed the captain or prevented him sleeping, he commanded that they should strangle them: the officer who was burning them was worse than a hangman and did not wish to suffocate them, but with his own hands he gagged them, so that they should not make themselves heard, and he stirred up the fire, until they roasted slowly, according to his pleasure. I know his name, and knew also his relations in Seville. I saw all the above things and numberless others.

10. And because all the people who could flee, hid among the mountains and climbed the crags to escape from men so deprived of humanity, so wicked, such wild beasts, exterminators and capital enemies of all the human race, the Spaniards taught and trained the fiercest boar-hounds to tear an Indian to pieces as soon as they saw him, so that they more willingly attacked and ate one, than if he had been a boar. These hounds made great havoc and slaughter.

11. And because sometimes, though rarely, the Indians killed a few Christians for just cause, they made a law among themselves, that for one Christian whom the Indians killed, the Christians should kill a hundred Indians.

5

Description of Virginia
John Smith

Before he became one of the original settlers of Jamestown in 1607, Captain John Smith (1580–1631) was already experienced as a soldier and diplomat, fighting the Spanish in the Netherlands and the Turks in Hungary. At Jamestown he took part in governing the colony—leading it from 1608 to 1609—and in managing relations with the native Americans. His story, told years later, of being saved from death by the friendly intervention of Pocahontas, the daughter of Chief Powhatan, has a secure place in American legend. Historians and ethnographers continue to disagree about whether it happened and, if it did, whether Smith correctly understood its meaning in the context of the indigenous Indian culture. Some suspect that it was part of a ritual inducting Smith into the tribe rather than a rescue.

Smith returned to England in 1609. His later years were given over to promoting both himself and the settlement of the New World he had helped to colonize. His descriptions in numerous writings both of British America and of its native American inhabitants set patterns that continued for centuries.

BEFORE YOU READ

1. How would you describe Smith's account of the New World? What kind of modern writing or communication does it suggest?

2. What adjectives would you apply to Smith's description of the native Americans? How reliable does his account of the Indians seem to you?

THE COMMODITIES IN VIRGINIA
OR THAT MAY BE HAD BY INDUSTRY

The mildness of the air, the fertility of the soil, and the situation of the rivers are so propitious to the nature and use of man as no place is more convenient for pleasure, profit, and man's sustenance. Under that latitude or climate, here will live any beasts, as horses, goats, sheep, asses, hens, etc. The waters, islands, and shoals are full of safe harbors for ships of war or merchandise, for boats of all sorts, for transportation or fishing, etc.,

The Bay and rivers have much marketable fish and places fit for salt works, building of ships, making of iron, etc.

Muscovia and Polonia yearly receive many thousands for pitch, tar, soap ashes, rosin, flax, cordage, sturgeon, masts, yards, wainscot, furs, glass, and suchlike; also Swethland for iron and copper. France, in like manner, for wine,

Captain John Smith of Willoughby by Alford, Lincolnshire; President of Virginia and Admiral of New England. Works: 1608–1631. Ed. by Edward Arber, The English Scholar's Library, No. 16. (Birmingham, 1884), pp. 63–67. Modernized by Elizabeth Marcus.

canvas, and salt, Spain as much for iron, steel, figs, raisins and sherry. Italy with silks and velvets, consumes our chief commodities. Holland maintains itself by fishing and trading at our own doors. All these temporize with others for necessities, but all as uncertain as to peace or war, and besides the charge, travel and danger in transporting them, by seas, lands, storms and pirates. Then how much has Virginia the prerogative of all those flourishing kingdoms for the benefit of our lands, when as within one hundred miles all those are to be had, either ready provided by nature or else to be prepared, were there but industrious men to labor. Only copper might be lacking, but there is good probability that both copper and better minerals are there to be had if they are worked for. Their countries have it. So then here is a place a nurse for soldiers, a practice for mariners, a trade for merchants, a reward for the good, and that which is most of all, a business (most acceptable to God) to bring such poor infidels to the true knowledge of God and his holy Gospel.

OF THE NATURAL INHABITANTS
OF VIRGINIA

The land is not populous, for the men be few, their far greater number is of women and children. Within 60 miles of Jamestown there are about some 5,000 people, but of able men fit for their wars scarce 1,500. To nourish so many together they have yet no means, because they make so small a benefit of their land, be it never so fertile.

Six or seven hundred have been the most that have been seen together, when they gathered themselves to have surprised Captain Smyth at Pamaunke, having but 15 to withstand the worst of their fury. As small as the proportion of ground that has yet been discovered, is in comparison of that yet unknown. The people differ very much in stature, especially in language, as before is expressed.

Since being very great as the Sesquaesahamocks, others very little as the Wighcocomocoes: but generally tall and straight, of a comely proportion, and of a color brown, when they are of any age, but they are born white. Their hair is generally black, but few have any beards. The men wear half their heads shaven, the other half long. For barbers they use their women, who with 2 shells will grate away the hair in any fashion they please. The women are cut in many fashions agreeable to their years, but ever some part remain long.

They are very strong, of an able body and full of agility, able to endure, to lie in the woods under a tree by the fire, in the worst of winter, or in the weeds and grass, in ambush in the summer.

They are inconstant in everything, but what fear constrains them to keep. Crafty, timorous, quick of apprehension and very ingenious. Some are of disposition fearful, some bold, most cautious, all savage. Generally covetous of copper, beads and such like trash. They are soon moved to anger, and so malicious, that they seldom forget an injury: they seldom steal from one another, lest their conjurors should reveal it, and so they be pursued and punished.

That they are thus feared is certain, but that any can reveal their offenses by conjuration I am doubtful. Their women are careful not to be suspected of dishonesty without leave of their husbands.

Each household knows their own lands and gardens, and most live off their own labors.

For their apparel, they are some time covered with the skins of wild beasts, which in winter are dressed with the hair but in summer without. The better sort use large mantles of deerskin not much different in fashion from the Irish mantles. Some embroidered them with beads, some with copper, others painted after their manner. But the common sort have scarce to cover their nakedness but with grass, the leaves of trees or suchlike. We have seen some use mantles that nothing could be discerned but the feathers, that was exceedingly warm and handsome. But the women are always covered about their middles with a skin and are ashamed to be seen bare.

They adorn themselves most with copper beads and paintings. Their women have their legs, hands, breasts and face cunningly embroidered with diverse works, as beasts, serpents, artificially wrought into their flesh with black spots. In each ear commonly they have three great holes, from which they hang chains, bracelets or copper. Some of their men wear in those holes a small green and yellow colored snake, near half a yard in length, which crawling and lapping herself around his neck oftentimes familiarly would kiss his lips. Others wear a dead rat tied by the tail. Some on their heads wear the wing of a bird or some large feather, with a rattle; those rattles are somewhat like the chape of a rapier, but less, which they take from the tails of a snake. Many have the whole skin of a hawk or some strange fowl, stuffed with the wings abroad. Others a broad piece of copper, and some the hand of their enemy dried. Their heads and shoulders are painted red with the root Pocone pounded to a powder mixed with oil; this they hold in summer to preserve them from the heat and in winter from the cold. Many other forms of paintings they use, but he is the most gallant that is the most monstrous to behold.

Their buildings and habitations are for the most part by the rivers or not far distant from some fresh spring. Their houses are built like our arbors of small young springs bowed and tied, and so close covered with mats or the barks of trees very handsomely, that notwithstanding either wind, rain or weather, they are as warm as stoves, but very smokey; yet at the top of the house there is a hole made for the smoke to go into right over the fire.

Against the fire they lie on little mounds of reeds covered with a mat, borne from the ground a foot and more by a mound of wood. On these round about the house, they lie heads and points one by the other against the fire, some covered with mats, some with skins, and some stark naked lie on the ground, from 6 to 20 in a house.

Their houses are in the midst of their fields or gardens; which are small plots of ground, some 20, some 40, some 100, some 200, some more, some less. Sometimes from 2 to 100 of these houses are together, or but a little separated by groves of trees. Near their habitations is a little small wood, or old trees on the ground, by reason of their burning of them for fire. So that a man may gallop a horse among these woods anyway, but where the creeks or rivers shall hinder.

Men, women and children have their several names according to the particular whim of their parents. Their women (they say) are easily delivered of child, yet do they love children dearly. To make them hardy, in the coldest mornings they wash them in the rivers, and by painting and ointments so tan their skins that after a year or two no weather will hurt them.

The men bestow their times in fishing, hunting, wars, and such manlike exercises, scorning to be seen in any woman like exercise, which is the cause that the women be very painful and the men often idle. The women and children do the rest of the work. They make mats, baskets, pots, mortars, pound their corn, make their bread, prepare their victuals, plant their corn, gather their corn, bear all kinds of burdens and suchlike.

6

The Pequot War
William Bradford

In the late sixteenth century, a branch of the Mohican tribe from near the upper Hudson River began to migrate eastward across New England, then down the Connecticut Valley. As they conquered weaker tribes in their path, they came to be called "Pequot," an Algonquian word meaning "destroyers." By the time these invaders from the West encountered those later invaders from the East, the Puritans, the Pequot were hated by most of the many Indian tribes of New England.

Friction began in 1634 when the Pequot, in the midst of a war with the Dutch and the Narragansett Indians, killed an English trader and his crew. The colonists and the Pequot both wanted peace and soon agreed to a treaty that fixed reparations for the murders and established trade relations. But the Pequot only fulfilled a small part of what they had agreed to. Then two years later the Pequot again shed English blood and Puritan policy changed sharply. In August 1636, a Massachusetts Bay colony expedition under strict instructions to exact revenge without mercy destroyed Pequot villages on Block Island and along the Connecticut shore. The Pequot struck back just as ruthlessly, ambushing settlers in Connecticut, even roasting one alive. Both sides sought alliances with other Indian tribes, particularly the Narragansett, who under the urging of Roger Williams allied with the Europeans. The rest of the story you will read in the words of William Bradford (1590–1657), the governor of Plymouth Plantation, one of Massachusetts Bay's allies in the Pequot War.

The destruction of the Pequot came to represent Indian extermination at the hands of white settlers. But some cautions are in order. For one thing, the Pequot War did not pit all Indians against whites: Other Indian tribes and the Puritans hated the Pequots. And although the tribe appeared to have been annihilated, the Pequot have reappeared in the twentieth century, though numbering but a few hundred people. Their gambling casinos in Connecticut make them among the richest of Americans. When the Smithsonian Institution sought many millions of dollars in private funding for the restoration of the Museum of the American Indian in splendid new quarters in New York City, the largest single contribution to this monument to the Indian past came from the Pequot Indians.

BEFORE YOU READ

1. Why did other Indians cooperate with the Puritans? Was it in their long-term interest to do so?

2. What did William Bradford and John Winthrop think of their enemies? Compare this idea of the foe with views of enemies in other wars the United States has been involved in such as the Revolutionary War, World War II, and the Gulf War.

William Bradford, *Of Plymoth Plantations, 1620–1647* (London, 1637). Modernized by Elizabeth Marcus.

3. Why do you think the Narragansett played such a limited role in the battles despite their cooperation with the Puritans?

At the beginning part of this year [1637], the Pequots fell openly upon the English at Connecticut, in the lower parts of the river, and slew many of them (as they were at work in the fields), both men and women, to the great terror of the rest, and went away in great pride and triumph, with many high threats. They also assaulted a strong, well-defended fort at the river's mouth, and though they did not prevail there, it struck the fort's defenders with much fear and astonishment to see the Pequots bold attempts in the face of danger, which caused them to stand upon their guard and to prepare for resistance, while Mr. Vane, then being Governor, solicited their friends and confederates in the Bay of Massachusetts to send them speedy aid, as they waited for more forcible assaults.

In the meantime, the Pequots, especially in the winter before, sought to make peace with the Narragansetts, and used very pernicious arguments that the English were strangers and had begun to overspread their territory and would deprive them thereof in time, if they were suffered to grow and increase, and if the Narragansets did assist the English to subdue them they did but make way for their own overthrow, for if they were rooted out, the English would soon take occasion to subjugate them and if they would harken to them they should not need to fear the strength of the English, for they would not come to open battle with them, but fire their houses, kill their cattle and lie in ambush for them as they went abroad upon their occasions, and all this they might easily do without any or little danger to themselves. Which course being held, they well saw the English could not long subsist, but they would either be starved with hunger, or be forced to forsake the country, with many the like things, insomuch that the Narragansets were once wavering, and were half-minded to have made peace with them, and joined against the English. But when the Narragansets considered how much wrong they have received from the Pequots, and what an opportunity they now had by the help of the English to right themselves, revenge was so sweet to them, as it prevailed above all the rest, so as they resolved to join with the English against them and did. The court here agreed forthwith to send 50 men at their own charge, and with as much speed as possibly they could, got them armed and had made them ready under sufficient leaders, and provided a ship to carry them provisions and tend upon them for all occasions, but when they were ready to march (with a supply from the Bay), they had word to stay, for the enemy was as good as vanquished, and there would be no need.

I shall not take upon me exactly to describe their proceedings in these things, because I expect it will be fully done by themselves, who best know the carriage and circumstances of things; I shall therefore but touch them in general. From Connecticut, (who were most sensible of the hurt sustained and the present danger), they sent out a party of men and another party met them from the Bay at the Narragansets, who were to join them. The Narragansets were earnest to be gone before the English were well rested and refreshed, especially some of them which came last. It should seem their desire was to come upon the enemy suddenly and undiscovered. There was a ship of this place, newly put in there, which was come from Connecticut, which did encourage them to lay hold of the Indians' forwardness, and to show as great forwardness as they did, for it would encourage them, and expedition might prove to their great advantage.

So they went on, and so ordered their march, as the Indians brought them to a fort of the enemies' (in which most of their chief men were) before day. They approached the same with great silence, and surrounded it both with English and Indians, that they might not break out, and so assaulted them with great courage, shooting among them, and entered the fort with all speed, and those that first entered found sharp resistance from the enemy, who both shot at and grappled with them, others ran into their houses and brought out fire and set them on fire, which soon took in their mats, and standing close together, with the wind, all was quickly on a flame, and thereby more were burnt to death than were otherwise slain, it burned their bowstrings and made them unserviceable. Those that escaped the fire were slain with the sword, some hewed to pieces, others run through with their rapiers, so as they were quickly dispatched and very few escaped. It was conceived that they thus destroyed about 400 at this time.

It was a fearful sight to see them thus frying in the fire, and the streams of blood quenching the same, and horrible was the stink and the scent thereof, but the victory seemed a sweet sacrifice and they gave the prayers thereof to God, who had wrought so wonderfully for them, thus to enclose their enemies in their hands, and give them so speedy a victory over so proud and insulting an enemy. The Narraganset Indians, all this while, stood 'round about, but aloof from all danger, and left the whole execution to the English, except for the stopping of any that broke away, insulting over their enemies in this their ruin and misery, when they saw them dancing in the flames, calling them by a word in their own language, signifying O brave Pequots! Which they used familiarly among themselves in their own prayers, in songs of triumph after their victories.

After this service was thus happily accomplished, they marched to the waterside where they met with some of their vessels by which they had refreshing with victuals and other necessities. But in their march the rest of the Pequots drew into a body and accosted them thinking to have some advantage against them by reason of a neck of land, but when they saw the English prepared for them, they kept aloof so as they neither did hurt, nor could receive any. After their refreshing and repair to gather for further counsel and directions, they resolved to pursue their victory, and follow the war against the rest, but the Narraganset Indians most of them forsook them and such of them as they had with them for guides, or otherwise, they found them very cold and backward in the business, either out of envy or that they saw the English would make more profit of the victory than they were willing they should, or else deprive them of such advantage as themselves desired by having them become tributaries unto them, or the like.

For the rest of this business, I shall only relate the same as it is in a letter which came from Mr. Winthrop to the Governor here as follows.

Worthy Sir: I received your loving letter, and am much provoked to express my affections towards you, but limited time forbids me for my desire is to acquaint you with the Lord's great mercies towards us, in our prevailing against his and our enemies, that you may rejoice and praise his name with us. About 80 of our men, having coasted along towards the Dutch plantation, (sometimes by water, but most by land,) met here and there with some Pequots whom they slew or took prisoners. Two sachems[1] they took and beheaded, and not hearing of Sassacouse (the chief sachem), they gave a prisoner his life, to go and find him out. He went and brought them word where he was, but Sassacouse, suspecting him to be a spy, after he was gone, fled away with some 20 more to the Mohawks, so our men missed him. Yet, dividing themselves and ranging up and down, as the providence of God guided them (for the Indians were all gone save 3 or 4 and they knew not whether to guide them, or else would not), upon the 13th of this month they light upon a great company of them, viz. 80 strong men and 200 women and children, in a small Indian town, fast by a hideous swamp, which they all slipped into before our men could get to them.

Our captains were not then come together, but there was Mr. Ladle and Captain Mass, and Captain Patrick with some 20 or more of his, who, shooting at the Indians, Captain Task with 50 more came soon in at the noise. Then they gave order to surround the swamp, it being about a mile about, but Lieutenant Davenport and some 12 more not hearing that command, fell into the swamp among the Indians. The swamp was so thick with shrubwood and so boggy with all, that some of them stuck fast and received many shots. Lieutenant Davenport was dangerously wounded about his armhole, and another shot in the head, so as, fainting they were in great danger to have been taken by the Indians. But Sergeant Rigges, and Jeffrey, and 2 or 3 more, rescued them, and slew diverse of the Indians with their swords. After they were drawn out, the Indians desired parley, and were offered (by Thomas Standton, our interpreter) that, if they would come out and yield themselves, they should have their lives, all that had not their hands in the English blood. Whereupon the sachem of the place came forth, and an old man or 2 and their wives and children, and after that some other women and children, and so they spoke for 2 hours until it was night. Then Thomas Standton was sent into them again to call them forth, but as they said they would sell their lives there, and so shot at him so thick as, if he had not cried out, and been presently rescued, they had slain him.

Then our men cut off a place in the swamp with their swords, and cooped the Indians in so narrow a compass that they could easily kill them through the thickets. So they continued all the night, standing about 12 feet from each other, and the Indians, coming close up to our men, shot their arrows so thick that they

1. **sachems:** leaders among Indians.

pierced their hat brims, and their sleeves and stockings, and other parts of their clothes, yet so miraculously did the Lord preserve them as not one of them was wounded, save those three who went rashly into the swamp. When it was near day, it grew very dark, so as those of them which were left dropped away between our men, though 12 or 14 feet asunder, but were presently discovered, and some killed in the pursuit. Upon searching of the swamp the next morning, they found nine slain, and some they pulled up, whom the Indians had buried in the mire, so as they do think that of all this company not 20 did escape, for they after found some who died in their flight of their wounds received.

The prisoners were divided, some to those of the river, and the rest to us. Of these we send the male children to Bermuda, by Mr. William Peirce, and the woman and maid children are disposed about in the towns. There have been slain and taken, in all, about 700. The rest are dispersed, and the Indians in all quarters so terrified as all their friends are afraid to receive them. Two of the sachems of Long Island came to Mr. Stoughton and tendered themselves to be tributaries under our protection. And two of the Neepnett sachems have been with me to seek our friendship. Among the prisoners we have the wife and children of Mononotto, a woman of a very modest countenance and behavior. It was by her mediation that they the two English maids were spared from death, and were kindly used by her, so that I have taken charge of her. One of her first requests was, that the English would not abuse her body, and that her children might not be taken from her. Those which were wounded were fetched off soon by John Galop, who came with his dinghy in a happy hour, to bring them victuals, and to carry their wounded men to the ship, where our chief surgeon was, with Mr. Willson being about eight leagues off. Our people are all in health, (the Lord be praised,) and although they had marched in their arms all the day and had been in fight all the night, yet they professed they found themselves so fresh as they could willingly have gone to such another business.

That I may make an end of this matter, this Sassacouse (the Pequots' chief sachem) being fled to the Mohawks, they cut off his head, with some other of the chief of them, whether to satisfy the English or rather the Narragansets, (who, as I have since heard, hired them to do it), or for their own advantage, I well know not, but thus this war took end. The rest of the Pequots were wholly driven from their place, and some of them submitted themselves to the Narragansets, and lived under them, others of them betook themselves to the Monhiggs, under Uncass, their sachem, with the approbations of the English of Connecticut, under whose protection Uncass lived, and he and his men had been faithful to them in this war and done them very good service. But this did so vex the Narragansets, that they had not the whole sway over them, as they have never ceased plotting and contriving how to bring them under, and because they cannot attain their ends, because of the English who have protected them, they have sought to raise a general conspiracy against the English, as will appear in another place. . . .

7

Encounter with the Indians
Father Paul Le Jeune

In the sixteenth and seventeenth centuries the Society of Jesus of the Roman Catholic Church, more commonly known as the Jesuits, energetically proselytized in virtually every Portuguese, Spanish, and French colony. The first Jesuit missionaries arrived in French Canada in 1632 determined to bring Christianity to the Indians by living with them, learning their languages, educating their children, and demonstrating (sometimes at the cost of their lives) that they were as brave as the native American warriors. The Jesuits played a major role in cementing French alliances with many native American nations across Canada and into the Ohio Valley. This gave France a strategic position in the New World, hemming the colonies of British North America against the eastern seaboard until French power was destroyed in the mid-eighteenth century. The Jesuits in Canada reported regularly on their ministry. These reports form an important account of American Indian life and greatly influenced the European perception of the New World.

Father Paul Le Jeune, born in France in 1591, became a Jesuit in 1613. He had been a professor of rhetoric as well as Superior of the Jesuit House at Dieppe before he radically changed his activities by going to French North America in 1632. Le Jeune found much to admire in the native Americans, as well as much that he could neither understand nor accept. The report included here was written from Quebec in August 1634. Le Jeune worked among the Indians until 1649. He died in Paris in 1664.

BEFORE YOU READ

1. What were Father Le Jeune's impressions and assessment of native American religion?
2. What did he consider the Indians' virtues?
3. What did he consider their main vices?

CHAPTER IV. ON THE BELIEF, SUPERSTITIONS, AND ERRORS OF THE MONTAGNAIS SAVAGES

I have already reported that the Savages believe that a certain one named Atahocam had created the world, and that one named Messou had restored it. I have questioned upon this subject the famous Sorcerer and the old man with whom I passed the Winter; they answered that they did not know who was the first Author of the world, — that it was perhaps Atahocam, but that was not certain; that they only spoke of Atahocam as one speaks of a thing so far distant that nothing sure can be known about it. . . .

Reuben Gold Thwaites, ed., *The Jesuit Relations and Allied Documents: Travels and Explorations of the Jesuit Missionaries in New France* (Cleveland: The Burrows Brothers Co., 1987).

As to the Messou, they hold that he restored the world, which was destroyed in the flood; whence it appears that they have some tradition of that great universal deluge which happened in the time of Noë. . . .

They also say that all animals, of every species, have an elder brother, who is, as it were, the source and origin of all individuals, and this elder brother is wonderfully great and powerful. . . . Now these elders of all the animals are the juniors of the Messou. Behold him well related, this worthy restorer of the Universe, he is elder brother to all beasts. If any one, when asleep, sees the elder or progenitor of some animals, he will have a fortunate chase; if he sees the elder of the Beavers, he will take Beavers; if he sees the elder of the Elks, he will take Elks, possessing the juniors through the favor of their senior whom he has seen in the dream. . . .

Their Religion, or rather their superstition, consists besides in praying; but O, my God, what prayers they make! In the morning, when the little children come out from their Cabins, they shout, *Cacouakhi, Pakhais Amiscouakhi, Pakhais Mousouakhi, Pakhais*, "Come Porcupines; come, Beavers; come, Elk;" and this is all of their prayers.

When the Savages sneeze, and sometimes even at other times, during the Winter, they cry out in a loud voice, *Etouctaian miraounam an Mirouscamikhi*, "I shall be very glad to see the Spring."

At other times, I have heard them pray for the Spring, or for deliverance from evils and other similar things; and they express all these things in the form of desires, crying out as loudly as they can, "I would be very glad if this day would continue, if the wind would change," etc. I could not say to whom these wishes are addressed, for they themselves do not know, at least those whom I have asked have not been able to enlighten me. . . .

These are some of their superstitions. How much dust there is in their eyes, and how much trouble there will be to remove it that they may see the beautiful light of truth! I believe, nevertheless, that anyone who knew their language perfectly, in order to give them good reasons promptly, would soon make them laugh at their own stupidity; for sometimes I have made them ashamed and confused, although I speak almost entirely by my hands, I mean by signs. . . .

CHAPTER V. ON THE GOOD THINGS
WHICH ARE FOUND AMONG THE SAVAGES

If we begin with physical advantages, I will say that they possess these in abundance. They are tall, erect, strong, well proportioned, agile; and there is nothing effeminate in their appearance. Those little Fops that are seen elsewhere are only caricatures of men, compared with our Savages. I almost believed, heretofore, that the Pictures of the Roman Emperors represented the ideal of the painters rather than men who had ever existed, so strong and powerful are their heads; but I see here upon the shoulders of these people the heads of

Julius Caesar, of Pompey, of Augustus, of Otho, and of others, that I have seen in France, drawn upon paper, or in relief on medallions.

As to the mind of the Savage, it is of good quality. I believe that souls are all made from the same stock, and that they do not materially differ; hence, these barbarians having well formed bodies, and organs well regulated and well arranged, their minds ought to work with ease. Education and instruction alone are lacking. Their soul is a soil which is naturally good, but loaded down with all the evils that a land abandoned since the birth of the world can produce. I naturally compare our Savages with certain villagers, because both are usually without education, though our Peasants are superior in this regard; and yet I have not seen any one thus far, of those who have come to this country, who does not confess and frankly admit that the Savages are more intelligent than our ordinary peasants.

Moreover, if it is a great blessing to be free from a great evil, our Savages are happy; for the two tyrants who provide hell and torture for many of our Europeans, do not reign in their great forests, — I mean ambition and avarice. As they have neither political organization, nor offices, nor dignities, nor any authority, for they only obey their Chief through good will toward him, therefore they never kill each other to acquire these honors. Also, as they are contented with a mere living, not one of them gives himself to the Devil to acquire wealth.

They make a pretence of never getting angry, not because of the beauty of this virtue, for which they have not even a name, but for their own contentment and happiness, I mean, to avoid the bitterness caused by anger. The Sorcerer said to me one day, speaking of one of our Frenchmen, "He has no sense, he gets angry; as for me, nothing can disturb me; let hunger oppress me, let my nearest relation pass to the other life, let the Hiroquois, our enemies, massacre our people, I never get angry." What he says is not an article of faith; for, as he is more haughty than any other Savage, so I have seen him oftener out of humor than any of them; it is true also that he often restrains and governs himself by force, especially when I expose his foolishness. I have only heard one Savage pronounce this word, *Ninichcatihin*, "I am angry," and he only said it once. But I noticed that they kept their eyes on him, for when these Barbarians are angry, they are dangerous and unrestrained.

Whoever professes not to get angry, ought also to make a profession of patience; the Savages surpass us to such an extent, in this respect, that we ought to be ashamed. I saw them, in their hardships and in their labors, suffer with cheerfulness. My host, wondering at the great number of people who I told him were in France, asked me if the men were good, if they did not become angry, if they were patient. I have never seen such patience as is shown by a sick Savage. You may yell, storm, jump, dance, and he will scarcely ever complain. I found myself, with them, threatened with great suffering; they said to me, "We shall be sometimes two days, sometimes three, without eating, for lack of food; take courage, *Chihiné*, let thy soul be strong to endure suffering and hardship; keep thyself from being sad, otherwise thou wilt be sick; see how we do not cease to laugh, although we have little to eat." One thing alone casts them down,—it is when they see death, for they fear this beyond measure; take away this apprehension from the Savages, and they will endure all kinds of degradation and discomfort, and all kinds of trials and suffering very patiently. . . .

They are very much attached to each other, and agree admirably. You do not see any disputes, quarrels, enmities, or reproaches among them. Men leave the arrangement of the household to the women, without interfering with them; they cut, and decide, and give away as they please, without making the husband angry. . . .

CHAPTER VI. ON THEIR VICES
AND THEIR IMPERFECTIONS

The Savages, being filled with errors, are also haughty and proud. Humility is born of truth, vanity of error and falsehood. They are void of the knowledge of truth, and are in consequence, mainly occupied with thought of themselves. They imagine that they ought by right of birth, to enjoy the liberty of Wild ass colts, rendering no homage to any one whomsoever, except when they like. They have reproached me a hundred times because we fear our Captains, while they laugh at and make sport of theirs. All the authority of their chief is in his tongue's end; for he is powerful in so far as he is eloquent; and, even if he kills himself talking and haranguing, he will not be obeyed unless he pleases the Savages. . . .

I have shown in my former letters how vindictive the Savages are toward their enemies, with what fury and cruelty they treat them, eating them after they have made them suffer all that an incarnate fiend could invent. This fury is common to the women as well as to the men, and they even surpass the latter in this respect. I have said that they eat the lice they find upon themselves, not that they like the taste of them, but because they want to bite those that bite them.

These people are very little moved by compassion. When any one is sick in their Cabins, they ordinarily do not cease to cry and storm, and make as much noise as if everybody were in good health. They do not know what it is to take care of a poor invalid, and to give him the food which is good for him; if he asks for something to drink, it is given to him, if he asks for something to eat, it is given to him, but otherwise he is neglected; to coax him with love and gentleness, is a language which they do not understand. As long as a patient can eat, they will carry or drag him with them; if he stops eating, they believe that it is all over with him and kill him, as much to free him from the sufferings that he is enduring, as to relieve themselves of the trouble of taking him with them when they go to some other place. I have both admired and pitied the patience of the invalids whom I have seen among them.

The Savages are slanderous beyond all belief; I say, also among themselves, for they do not even spare their nearest relations, and with it all they are deceitful. For, if one speaks ill of another, they all jeer with loud laughter; if the other appears upon the scene, the first one will show him as much affection and treat him with as much love, as if he had elevated him to the third heaven by his praise. The reason of this is, it seems to me, that their slanders and derision do not come from malicious hearts or from infected mouths, but from a mind which says what it thinks in order to give itself free scope, and which seeks gratification from everything, even from slander and mockery. Hence they are not troubled even if they are told that others are making sport of them, or have injured their reputation. All they usually answer to such talk is, *mama irinisiou,* "He has no sense, he does not know what he is talking about;" and at the first opportunity they will pay their slanderer in the same coin, returning him the like.

Lying is as natural to Savages as talking, not among themselves, but to strangers. Hence it can be said that fear and hope, in one word, interest, is the measure of their fidelity. I would not be willing to trust them, except as they would fear to be punished if they had failed in their duty, or hoped to be rewarded if they were faithful to it. They do not know what it is to keep a secret, to keep their word, and to love with constancy, — especially those who are not of their nation, for they are harmonious among themselves, and their slanders and raillery do not disturb their peace and friendly intercourse. . . .

CHAPTER XII. WHAT ONE MUST SUFFER
IN WINTERING WITH THE SAVAGES

In order to have some conception of the beauty of this edifice, its construction must be described. I shall speak from knowledge, for I have often helped to build it. Now, when we arrived at the place where we were to camp, the women, armed with axes, went here and there in the great forests, cutting the framework of the hostelry where we were to lodge; meantime the men, having drawn the plan thereof, cleared away the snow with their snowshoes, or with shovels which they make and carry expressly for this purpose. Imagine now a great ring or square in the snow, two, three or four feet deep, according to the weather or the place where they encamp. This depth of snow makes a white wall for us, which surrounds us on all sides, except the end where it is broken through to form the door. The framework having been brought, which consists of twenty or thirty poles, more or less, according to the size of the cabin, it is planted, not upon the ground but upon the snow; then they throw upon these poles, which converge a little at the top, two or three rolls of bark sewed together, beginning at the bottom, and behold, the house is made. The ground inside, as well as the wall of snow which extends all around the cabin, is covered with little branches of fir; and, as a finishing touch, a wretched skin is fastened to two poles to serve as a door, the doorposts being the snow itself. . . .

You cannot stand upright in this house, as much on account of its low roof as the suffocating smoke; and consequently you must always lie down, or sit flat upon the ground, the usual posture of the Savages. When you go out, the cold, the snow, and the danger of getting lost in these great woods drive you in again more quickly than the wind, and keep you a prisoner in a dungeon which has neither lock nor key.

This prison, in addition to the uncomfortable position that one must occupy upon a bed of earth, has four other great discomforts,—cold, heat, smoke, and dogs. As to the cold, you have the snow at your head with only a pine branch between, often nothing but your hat, and the winds are free to enter in a thousand places. . . . When I lay down at night I could study through this opening both the Stars and the Moon as easily as if I had been in the open fields.

Nevertheless, the cold did not annoy me as much as the heat from the fire. A little place like their cabins is easily heated by a good fire, which sometimes roasted and broiled me on all sides, for the cabin was so narrow that I could not protect myself against the heat. You cannot move to right or left, for the Savages, your neighbors, are at your elbows; you cannot withdraw to the rear, for you encounter the wall of snow, or the bark of the cabin which shuts you in. I did not know what position to take. Had I stretched myself out, the place was so narrow that my legs would have been halfway in the fire; to roll myself up in a ball, and crouch down in their way, was a position I could not retain as long as they could; my clothes were all scorched and burned. You will ask me perhaps if the snow at our backs did not melt under so much heat. I answer, "no;" that if sometimes the heat softened it in the least, the cold immediately turned it into ice. I will say, however, that both the cold and the heat are endurable, and that some remedy may be found for these two evils.

But, as to the smoke, I confess to you that it is martyrdom. It almost killed me, and made me weep continually, although I had neither grief nor sadness in my heart. It sometimes grounded all of us who were in the cabin; that is, it caused us to place our mouths against the earth in order to breathe. For, although the Savages were accustomed to this torment, yet occasionally it became so dense that they, as well as I, were compelled to prostrate themselves, and as it were to eat the earth, so as not to drink the smoke. I have sometimes remained several hours in this position, especially during the most severe cold and when it snowed; for it was then the smoke assailed us with the greatest fury, seizing us by the throat, nose, and eyes. . . .

As to the dogs, which I have mentioned as one of the discomforts of the Savages' houses, I do not know that I ought to blame them, for they have sometimes rendered me good service. . . . These poor beasts, not being able to live outdoors, came and lay down sometimes upon my shoulders, sometimes upon my feet, and as I only had one blanket to serve both as covering and mattress, I was not sorry for this protection, willingly restoring to them a part of the heat which I drew from them. It is true that, as they were large and numerous, they occasionally crowded and annoyed me so much, that in giving me a little heat they robbed me of my sleep, so that I very often drove them away. . . .

8

Captured by Indians
Mary Jemison

Captivity narratives were popular during the entire period in which native Americans were thought to constitute a danger to white settlers on the frontier. Mary Jemison's narrative is one of the most famous, having gone through dozens of printings since its initial publication in 1824. That she fell in love with an Indian man and remained a member of the Seneca tribe all her life obviously added spice to her life story.

Although it is written in the first person, the Narrative is not really an autobiography. Jemison was eighty years old and illiterate when James E. Seaver interviewed her and wrote it. By then she was long famous in western New York as the "white woman of the Genesee" who since her abduction, probably in 1758 at the age of fifteen, had lived among the Senecas. The Narrative is an important source description of Seneca life and culture as well as a fascinating account of a white American woman's assimilation into that culture.

BEFORE YOU READ

1. What was the Seneca custom of adoption as Jemison explained it?
2. How did Jemison explain the Indians' famous cruelty?
3. Why do you think captivity narratives were such popular reading?
4. What do you think Jemison meant when she said "Indians must and will be Indians, in spite of all the means that can be used to instruct them in the arts and sciences"?

CHAPTER III

The night was spent in gloomy forebodings. What the result of our captivity would be, it was out of our power to determine, or even imagine. At times, we could almost realize the approach of our masters to butcher and scalp us; again, we could nearly see the pile of wood kindled on which we were to be roasted; and then we could imagine ourselves at liberty, alone and defenseless in the forest, surrounded by wild beasts that were ready to devour us. The anxiety of our minds drove sleep from our eyelids; and it was with a dreadful hope and painful impatience that we waited for the morning to determine our fate.

The morning at length arrived, and our masters came early and let us out of the house, and gave the young man and boy to the French, who immediately took them away. Their fate I never learned, as I have not seen nor heard of them since.

James E. Seaver, *A Narrative of the Life of Mary Jemison: Deh-He-Wä-Mis.*, 4th ed. (New York: Miller, Orton, and Mulligan, 1856), pp. 52, 53–63, 67–70, 72–74.

I was now left alone in the fort, deprived of my former companions, and of every thing that was near or dear to me but life. But it was not long before I was in some measure relieved by the appearance of two pleasant-looking squaws, of the Seneca tribe, who came and examined me attentively for a short time, and then went out. After a few minutes' absence, they returned in company with my former masters, who gave me to the squaws to dispose of as they pleased.

The Indians by whom I was taken were a party of Shawnees, if I remember right, that lived, when at home, a long distance down the Ohio.

My former Indian masters and the two squaws were soon ready to leave the fort, and accordingly embarked—the Indians in a large canoe, and the two squaws and myself in a small one—and went down the Ohio. When we set off, an Indian in the forward canoe took the scalps of my former friends, strung them on a pole that he placed upon his shoulder, and in that manner carried them, standing in the stern of the canoe directly before us, as we sailed down the river, to the town where the two squaws resided.

On the way we passed a Shawnee town, where I saw a number of heads, arms, legs, and other fragments of the bodies of some white people who had just been burned. The parts that remained were hanging on a pole, which was supported at each end by a crotch stuck in the ground, and were roasted or burnt black as a coal. The fire was yet burning; and the whole appearance afforded a spectacle so shocking that even to this day the blood almost curdles in my veins when I think of them.

At night we arrived at a small Seneca Indian town, at the mouth of a small river that was called by the Indians, in the Seneca language, She-nan-jee, about eighty miles by water from the fort, where the two squaws to whom I belonged resided. There we landed, and the Indians went on; which was the last I ever saw of them.

Having made fast to the shore, the squaws left me in the canoe while they went to their wigwam or house in the town, and returned with a suit of Indian clothing, all new, and very clean and nice. My clothes, though whole and good when I was taken, were now torn in pieces, so that I was almost naked. They first undressed me, and threw my rags into the river; then washed me clean and dressed me in the new suit they had just brought, in complete Indian style; and then led me home and seated me in the center of their wigwam.

I had been in that situation but a few minutes before all the squaws in the town came in to see me. I was soon surrounded by them, and they immediately set up a most dismal howling, crying bitterly, and wringing their hands in all the agonies of grief for a deceased relative.

Their tears flowed freely, and they exhibited all the signs of real mourning. At the commencement of this scene, one of their number began, in a voice somewhat between speaking and singing, to recite some words to the following purport, and continued the recitation till the ceremony was ended; the company at the same time varying the appearance of their countenances, gestures, and tone of voice, so as to correspond with the sentiments expressed by their leader.

"Oh, our brother! alas! he is dead—he has gone; he will never return! Friendless he died on the field of the slain, where his bones are yet lying unburied! Oh! who will not mourn his sad fate? No tears dropped around him: oh, no! No tears of his sisters were there! He fell in his prime, when his arm was most needed to keep us from danger! Alas! he has gone, and left us in sorrow, his loss to bewail! Oh, where is his spirit? His spirit went naked, and hungry it wanders, and thirsty and wounded, it groans to return! Oh, helpless and wretched, our brother has gone! No blanket nor food to nourish and warm him; nor candles to light him, nor weapons of war! Oh, none of those comforts had he! But well we remember his deeds! The deer he could take on the chase! The panther shrunk back at the sight of his strength! His enemies fell at his feet! He was brave and courageous in war! As the fawn, he was harmless; his friendship was ardent; his temper was gentle; his pity was great! Oh! our friend, our companion, is dead! Our brother, our brother! alas, he is gone! But why do we grieve for his loss? In the strength of a warrior, undaunted he left us, to fight by the side of the chiefs! His warwhoop was shrill! His rifle well aimed laid his enemies low: his tomahawk drank of their blood: and his knife flayed their scalps while yet covered with gore! And why do we mourn? Though he fell on the field of the slain, with glory he fell; and his spirit went up to the land of his fathers in war! Then why do we mourn? With transports of joy, they received him, and fed him, and clothed him, and welcomed him there! Oh, friends, he is happy; then dry up your tears! His spirit has seen our distress, and sent us a helper whom with pleasure we greet. Deh-he-wä-mis has come: then let us receive her with joy!—she is handsome and pleasant! Oh! She is our sister, and gladly we welcome her here. In the place of our brother she stands in our tribe. With care we will guard her from trouble; and may she be happy till her spirit shall leave us."

In the course of that ceremony, from mourning they became serene,—joy sparkled in their countenances, and they seemed to rejoice over me as over a long-lost child. I was made welcome among them as a sister to the two squaws before mentioned, and was called Deh-he-wä-mis; which, being interpreted, signifies a pretty girl, a handsome girl, or a pleasant, good thing. That is the name by which I have ever since been called by the Indians.

I afterward learned that the ceremony I at that time passed through was that of adoption. The two squaws had lost a brother in Washington's war, sometime in the year before, and in consequence of his death went up to Fort Du Quesne on the day on which I arrived there, in order to receive a prisoner, or an enemy's scalp, to supply their loss. It is a custom of the Indians, when one of their number is slain or taken prisoner in battle, to give to the nearest relative of the dead or absent a prisoner, if they have chanced to take one; and if not, to give him the scalp of an enemy. On the return of the Indians from the conquest, which is always announced by peculiar shoutings, demonstrations of joy, and the exhibition of some trophy of victory, the mourners come forward and make their claims. If they receive a prisoner, it is at their option either to satiate their vengeance by taking his life in the most cruel manner they can conceive of, or to receive and adopt him into the family, in the place of him whom they have lost. All the prisoners that are taken in battle and carried to the encampment or town by the Indians are given to the bereaved families, till their number is good. And unless the mourners have but just received the news of their bereavement, and are under the operation of a paroxysm of grief, anger, or revenge; or, unless the prisoner is very old, sickly, or homely, they generally save them, and treat them kindly. But if their mental wound is fresh, their loss so great that they deem it irreparable, or if their prisoner or prisoners do not meet their approbation, no torture, let it be ever so cruel, seems sufficient to make them satisfaction. It is family and not national sacrifices among the Indians, that has given them an indelible stamp as barbarians, and identified their character with the idea which is generally formed of unfeeling ferocity and the most barbarous cruelty.

It was my happy lot to be accepted for adoption. At the time of the ceremony I was received by the two squaws to supply the place of their brother in the family; and I was ever considered and treated by them as a real sister, the same as though I had been born of their mother.

During the ceremony of my adoption, I sat motionless, nearly terrified to death at the appearance and actions of the company, expecting every moment to feel their vengeance, and suffer death on the spot. I was, however, happily disappointed; when at the close of the ceremony the company retired, and my sisters commenced employing every means for my consolation and comfort.

Being now settled and provided with a home, I was employed in nursing the children, and doing light work about the house. Occasionally, I was sent out with the Indian hunters, when they went but a short distance, to help them carry their game. My situation was easy; I had no particular hardships to endure. But still, the recollection of my parents, my brothers and sisters, my home, and my own captivity, destroyed my happiness, and made me constantly solitary, lonesome, and gloomy.

My sisters would not allow me to speak English in their hearing; but remembering the charge that my dear mother gave me at the time I left her, whenever I chanced to be alone I made a business of repeating my prayer, catechism, or something I had learned, in order that I might not forget my own language. By practicing in that way, I retained it till I came to Genesee flats, where I soon became acquainted with English people, with whom I have been almost daily in the habit of conversing.

My sisters were very diligent in teaching me their language; and to their great satisfaction, I soon learned so that I could understand it readily, and speak it fluently. I was very fortunate in falling into their hands; for they were kind, good-natured women; peaceable and mild in their dispositions; temperate and decent in their habits, and very tender and gentle toward me. I have great reason to respect them, though they have been dead a great number of years.

In the second summer of my living at Wiishto, I had a child, at the time that the kernels of corn first appeared on the cob. When I was taken sick, Sheninjee was absent, and I was sent to a small shed on the bank of the river, which was made of boughs, where I was obliged to stay till my husband returned. My two sisters, who were my only companions, attended me; and on the second day of my confinement my child was born; but it lived only two days. It was a girl; and notwithstanding the shortness of the time that I possessed it, it was a great grief to me to lose it.

After the birth of my child I was very sick, but was not allowed to go into the house for two weeks; when, to my great joy, Sheninjee returned, and I was taken in, and as comfortably provided for as our situation would admit. My disease continued to increase for a number of days; and I became so far reduced that my recovery was despaired of by my friends, and I concluded that my troubles would soon be finished. At length, however, my complaint took a favorable turn, and by the time the corn was ripe I was able to get about. I continued to gain my health, and in the fall was able to go to our winter quarters, on the Saratoga, with the Indians.

From that time nothing remarkable occurred to me till the fourth winter of my captivity, when I had a son born, while I was at Sciota. I had a quick recovery, and my child was healthy. To commemorate the name of my much-lamented father, I called my son Thomas Jemison.

CHAPTER IV

In the spring, when Thomas was three or four moons (months) old, we returned from Sciota to Wiishto, and soon after set out to go to Fort Pitt, to dispose of our furs and our skins that we had taken in the winter, and procure some necessary articles for the use of our family.

I had then been with the Indians four summers and four winters, and had become so far accustomed to their mode of living, habits, and dispositions, that my anxiety to get away, to be set at liberty and leave them, had almost subsided. With them was my home; my family was there, and there I had many friends to whom I was warmly attached in consideration of the favors, affection, and friendship with which they had uniformly treated me from the time of my adoption. Our labor was not severe; and that of one year was exactly similar in almost every respect to that of the others, without that endless variety that is to be observed in the common labor of the white people. Notwithstanding the Indian women have all the fuel and bread to procure, and the cooking to perform, their task is probably not harder than that of white women, who have those articles provided for them; and their cares certainly are not half as numerous, nor as great. In the summer season, we planted, tended, and harvested our corn, and generally had all our children with us; but had no master to oversee or drive us, so that we could work as leisurely as we pleased. We had no plows on the Ohio, but performed the whole process of planting and hoeing with a small tool that resembled, in some respect, a hoe with a very short handle.

Our cooking consisted in pounding our corn into samp or hominy, boiling the hominy, making now and then a cake and baking it in the ashes, and in boiling or roasting our venison. As our cooking and eating utensils consisted of a hominy block and pestle, a small kettle, a knife or two, and a few vessels of bark or wood, it required but little time to keep them in order for use.

Spinning, weaving, sewing, stocking knitting, and the like, are arts which have never been practiced in the Indian tribes generally. After the revolutionary war, I learned to sew, so that I could make my own clothing after a poor fashion; but I have been wholly ignorant of the application of the other domestic arts since my captivity. In the season of hunting, it was our business, in addition to our cooking, to bring home the game that was taken by the Indians, dress it, and carefully preserve the eatable meat, and prepare or dress the skins. Our clothing was fastened together with strings of deerskin, and tied on with the same.

In that manner we lived, without any of those jealousies, quarrels, and revengeful battles between families and individuals, which have been common in the Indian tribes since the introduction of ardent spirits among them.

The use of ardent spirits among the Indians, and a majority of the attempts which have been made to civilize them by the white people, have constantly made them worse and worse; increased their vices, and robbed them of many of their virtues, and will ultimately produce their extermination. I have seen, in a number of instances, the effects of education upon some of our Indians, who were taken, when young, from their families, and placed at school before they had had an opportunity to contract many Indian habits, and there kept till they arrived to manhood; but I have never seen one of those but was an Indian in every respect after he returned. Indians must and will be Indians, in spite of all the means that can be used to instruct them in the arts and sciences.

One thing only marred my happiness while I lived with them on the Ohio, and that was the recollection that I once had tender parents, and a home that I loved. Aside from that recollection, which could not have existed had I been taken in my infancy, I should have been contented in my situation. Notwithstanding all that has been said against the Indians, in consequence of their cruelties to their enemies—cruelties that I have witnessed and had abundant proof of—it is a fact that they are naturally kind, tender, and peaceable toward their friends, and strictly honest; and that those cruelties have been practiced only upon their enemies, according to their idea of justice.

Judge Samuel Sewall, member of the special court that tried witches at Salem in 1692, five years later publicly repented his role in the trials.

PART TWO

The Colonial Experience

A Rapidly Changing Society

The late-seventeenth-century world of Hetty Shepard and the Salem witch-craft trials was remarkably different from the universe of Eliza Pinckney and Benjamin Franklin just a few generations later. In the interim, adherence to orthodox Christianity had declined so that it no longer was the encompassing universal view of the world; a numbers of colonists instead embraced the Enlightenment confidence in science and human reason. And the physical, economic, and social circumstances of life in British America had undergone an equally great transformation. The entire white population of British America in 1660 would have fit into Yankee Stadium; but by 1750 the colonists numbered over one million. Conflict with Indian neighbors had threatened virtually all the early colonies; but by the mid-eighteenth century the whites firmly controlled the eastern seaboard. As colonial political life had reflected the instability of seventeenth-century England's age of revolutions, so eighteenth-century colonial government reflected a maturing if still clumsy empire that would by 1763 dominate the world's diplomacy. And during the lengthy peace between the end of major European warfare in 1715 and the start of the French and Indian War in 1756, the depression of the late seventeenth century turned into a long economic boom.

African slaves, involuntary migrants to the New World, contributed enormously to the colonies' prosperity. Slaves imported through the brutal slave trade that Olaudah Equiano graphically describes became the crucial labor force for the sugar plantations of the West Indies. Supplying these islands with fish, grain, lumber, livestock, and other goods enriched the economies of the middle colonies and New England. After about 1680 African slavery became an important part of southern plantation agriculture on the mainland. Planters in South Carolina, like Charles Lucas, father of Eliza Pinckney, migrated from the Indies with their slaves so that in South Carolina by 1720 slaves outnumbered whites by almost two to one.

News of opportunity in the new land brought greater numbers of immigrants to the colonies throughout the eighteenth century. Many thousands of Germans came to the middle colonies. Like Gottlieb Mittelberger, most signed on as indentured servants to pay their passage. Harsh as their circumstances were, many eventually prospered in the New World. An even greater number of Scotch-Irish—descendants of the Scottish Protestants who had settled in northern Ireland—followed to settle in the frontier valleys of Pennsylvania, Virginia, and the Carolinas.

Prosperity, security, and political stability enabled a new kind of leadership to emerge in the British colonies. Men like Benjamin Franklin and the rare woman like Eliza Pinckney became outstanding citizens of the British Empire, moving comfortably between the colonies and the mother country while contributing to the life and culture of both. At the same time, they planted deep roots in their local environments: Pinckney's world was that of South Carolina plantations; Franklin's was that of Philadelphia, the second largest city—only London exceeded it—in the English-speaking world. From such a combination of imperial interests and colonial pride came the revolutionary generation.

Points of View: The Salem Witchcraft Trials (1692)

9

The Case Against George Burroughs

Ann Putnam et al.

In 1692 the perception of many people was that the Devil assaulted the seaport town of Salem, Massachusetts, north of Boston. Scores of warlocks and witches—men and women who had entered into a covenant with the Devil to drive little children mad, to sicken and kill livestock and people—had invaded this village of a few hundred people. The jails bulged with over a hundred prisoners awaiting trial, including a four-year-old child bound for nine months in heavy iron chains. Twenty-seven people eventually came to trial; the court hanged nineteen—fourteen women and five men—as witches. One man, refusing to enter a plea, had heavy weights laid on his body until he was pressed to death.

Only three New Englanders had ever been hanged as witches before 1692 when nine adolescent girls in Salem suddenly appeared bewitched. Under intense questioning, the shrieking and contorting girls accused some of their neighbors and even some from outside Salem of witchcraft. Cotton Mather and other leading Puritan minis-

ters carefully advised Puritan leaders that the young women's testimony was insufficient to support a conviction for witchcraft in the absence of "other, and more human, and most convincing testimonies" since the Devil could assume what shape he pleased, even that of a leading divine like Mather himself.

The leader of all the New England witches, the afflicted girls alleged, was the Reverend George Burroughs, Salem's former minister. Burroughs had left Salem village for Maine nearly twenty years earlier in the midst of controversies with several parishioners, chief among them John Putnam, whose twelve-year-old niece Ann was the first to identify Burroughs as the leader of all the witches and the murderer of at least three people by witchcraft. The magistrates issued a warrant, and he was seized and brought to Salem. His theology, local ministers discovered, had evolved in an unorthodox direction: He neither baptized infants nor did he celebrate communion. People remembered his boasting about his strength: Though small and wiry, he was extraordinarily strong and agile and had been an outstanding athlete in his student days at Harvard. And some revived ancient gossip about mistreatment of his first two wives.

The court, well aware of its awesome responsibilities in trying a minister as a witch, nonetheless easily found Burroughs guilty. Faithful to the biblical injunction not to "suffer a witch to live," they sent him to Gallows Hill, where he protested his innocence, faultlessly recited the Lord's Prayer (which folklore said witches could not do), and stood to the snap of the rope.

BEFORE YOU READ

1. What was the evidence that George Burroughs was a witch? Was it all "spectral evidence" (that is, evidence as to what his specter or shape had done to the adolescent girls)? What was the nonspectral evidence (evidence of what Burroughs himself rather than his specter had done)? Did it justify convicting Burroughs in a society that accepted unquestionably the existence of witchcraft?

2. How do you explain the young women's accusations?

3. How do you explain the elders of the community believing them? What does your textbook say on this issue?

TESTIMONY OF ANN PUTNAM

The deposition of Ann Putnam, who testifies and says that on 20th of April, 1692, at evening, she saw the apparition of a minister, at which she was grievously affrighted and cried out, oh, dreadful, dreadful, here is a minister come. What, are ministers witches, too? Whence come you, and what is your name? For I will complain of you, though you be a minister, if you be a wizard. And immediately I was tortured by him, being racked and almost choked by him. And he tempted me to write in his book, which I refused with loud outcries, and said I would not write in his book though he tore me all to pieces, but told him that it was a dreadful thing that he, which was a minister that should teach

Paul S. Boyer and Stephen Nissenbaum, *Salem-Village Witchcraft: A Documentary Record* (Belmont, CA: Wadsworth, Pub. Co., 1972), pp. 67–68, 69, 72, 74, 77–78, 80, 84–85, 86–87; Charles W. Upham, *Salem Witchcraft*, vol. 2 (New York: Ungar, 1969), pp. 300–01.

children to fear God, should come to persuade poor creatures to give their souls to the devil. Oh, dreadful, dreadful. Tell me your name that I may know who you are. Then again he tortured me and urged me to write in his book, which I refused.

And then presently he told me that his name was George Burroughs, and that he had had three wives, and that he had bewitched the first two of them to death, and that he killed Mistress Lawson because she was so unwilling to go from the village, and also killed Mr. Lawson's child because he went to the eastward with Sir Edmond [Andros] and preached so to the soldiers, and that he had bewitched a great many soldiers to death at the eastward when Sir Edmond was there, and that he had made Abigail Hobbs a witch, and several witches more. And he has continued ever since, by times tempting me to write in his book and grievously torturing me by beating, pinching, and almost choking me several times a day. And he also told me that he was above a witch, he was a conjurer.

TESTIMONY OF THOMAS PUTNAM, PETER PRESCOTT, ROBERT MORRELL, AND EZEKIEL CHEEVER

We whose names are underwritten, being present with Ann Putnam at the time above mentioned, heard her declare what is abovewritten, what she said she saw and heard from the apparition of Mr. George Burroughs, and also beheld her tortures and perceived her hellish temptations by her loud outcries, I will not, I will not write though you torment me all [the] days of my life. And, being conversant with her ever since, have seen her tortured and complaining that Mr. Burroughs hurt her and tempts her to write in his book.

Thomas Putnam
Peter Prescott
Robert Morrell

COMPLAINT AGAINST GEORGE BURROUGHS

Salem, April the 30th, 1692

There being complaint this day made (before us) by Captain Jonathan Walcot and Sergeant Thomas Putnam of Salem Village, in behalf of their Majesties, for themselves, and also for several of their neighbors, against George Burroughs, minister in Wells in the province of Maine, Lydia Dasting in Reading, widow Susanah Martin of Amesbury, widow Dorcas Hoar of Beverly, widow Sarah Murrell of Beverly, and Phillip English of Salem, merchant, for high suspicion of sundry acts of witchcraft done or committed by them upon the bodies of Mary Walcot, Marcy Lewis, Abigail Williams, Ann Putnam, and Eliz Hubert, and Susanah Sheldon (viz.) upon some or all of them, of Salem Village or farms, whereby great hurt and damage been done to the bodies of said persons above named, therefore craved justice.

Signed by both the
Complainers   } Jonathan Walcott
abovesaid   Thomas Putnam

The abovesaid complaint was exhibited before us this 30th April, 1692.

John Hathorne   }
Jonathan Corwin   } Assistants

SUMMARY OF THE EXAMINATION OF GEORGE BURROUGHS

The examination of Geo Burroughs, 9 May, 1692.

By the
Honoured
{ Wm. Stoughton
John Hathorne
Sam. Sewall
Jonath. Corwin } Esq^s

Being asked when he partook of the Lord's Supper, he being (as he said) in full communion at Roxbury, he answered it was so long since, he could not tell. Yet he owned he was at meeting one Sabbath at Boston part of the day, and the other at Charlestown part of a Sabbath, when that sacrament happened to be at both, yet did not partake of either. He denied that his house at Casco was haunted, yet he owned there were toads. He denied that he made his wife swear that she could not write to his father [-in-law] Ruck without his approbation of her letter to her father. He owned that none of his children but the eldest was baptized.

The above was in private, none of the bewitched being present. At his entry into the room, many, if not all, of the bewitched were grievously tortured.

1. Sus. Sheldon testified that Burroughs's two wives appeared in their winding sheets, and said that man killed them.
   He was bid to look upon Sus. Sheldon.
   He looked back and knocked down all (or most) of the afflicted who stood behind him. . . .
2. Mary Lewes deposition going to be read and he looked upon her, and she fell into a dreadful and tedious fit.

3. Mary Walcot

4. Eliz. Hubbard   } Testimony going to be read and they all fell into
                           fits.
   Susan Sheldon

5. Susan Sheldon   } Affirmed, each of them, that he brought the
   Ann Putman jun^r. } book and would have them write.

Being asked what he thought of these things, he answered it was an amazing and humbling providence, but he understood nothing of it. And he said, some of you may observe that when they begin to name my name, they cannot name it. . . .

INDICTMENT OF GEORGE BURROUGHS

Essex Ss. The jurors for our Sovereign Lord and Lady, the King and Queen, presents that George Burroughs, late of Falmouth within the province of the Massachusetts Bay in New England, clerk, the ninth day of May, [1692] . . . and divers other days and times as well, before and after, certain detestable arts called witchcraft and sorceries, wickedly and feloniously hath used, practiced, and exercised at and within the Township of Salem in the County of Essex and aforesaid, in, upon, and against one Ann Putnam of Salem in the County of Essex, singlewoman, by which said wicked arts the said Ann Putnam . . . was, and is, tortured, afflicted, pined, consumed, wasted and tormented. Also for sundry other acts of witchcrafts by said George Burroughs committed and done against the peace of our Sovereign Lord and Lady, the King and Queen, their crown and dignity, and against the form of the statute in that case made and provided.

TESTIMONY OF SAMUEL WEBBER

Samuel Webber, aged about 36 years, testifies and says that about seven or eight years ago, I lived at Casco Bay and George Burroughs was then minister there. And having heard much of the great strength of him, said Burroughs, he coming to our house, we were in discourse about the same, and he then told me that he had put his fingers into the bung of a barrel of molasses and lifted it up and carried it round him and set it down again.

Salem, August 2d, 1692.

                                                          Samuel Webber

TESTIMONY OF SIMON WILLARD

The deposition of Simon Willard, aged about forty two years, says, I being at the house of Mr. Robert Lawrence at Falmouth, in Casco Bay, in September 1689, said Mr. Lawrence was commenting [upon] Mr. George Borroughs's strength, saying that we, none of us, could do what he could do. For said Mr. Borroughs can hold out this gun with one hand. Mr. Borroughs, being there, said, I held my hand here behind the lock and took it up and held it out.

I, said deponent, saw Mr. Borroughs put his hand on the gun to show us how he held it and where he held his hand, and saying there he held his hand when he held said gun out. But I saw him not hold it out then. Said gun was about seven-foot barrel, and very heavy. I then tried to hold out said gun with both hands, but could not do it long enough to take sight.

Simon Willard

Simon Willard owned to the Jury of Inquest that the abovewritten evidence is the truth,
August 3, 1692

Capt. Wm. Wormall sworn to the above, and that he saw him raise it from the ground himself.

TESTIMONY OF THOMAS GREENSLIT

The deposition of Thomas Greenslit, aged about forty years, testifies that about the breaking out of this last Indian war, being at the house of Capt. Scottow's, at Black Point, he saw Mr. George Burroughs lift and hold out a gun of six foot barrel or thereabouts, putting the forefinger of his right hand into the muzzle of said gun, and so held it out at arm's end, only with that finger. And further this deponent testifies that at the same time he saw the said Burroughs take up a full barrel of molasses with but two fingers of one of his hands in the bung, and carry it from the stage head to the door at the end of the stage, without letting it down, and that Lieut. Richard Hunniwell and John Greenslit and some other persons that are since dead were then present.

Salem, September 15, 1692. Thomas Greenslit appeared before their Majesties' Justices of Oyer and Terminer in open court and made oath that the above mentioned particulars, and every part of them, were true.

attest   Step. Sewall, Clerk

ROBERT CALEF'S ACCOUNT OF
GEORGE BURROUGHS' EXECUTION

Mr. Burroughs was carried in a cart with the others, through the streets of Salem, to execution. When he was upon the ladder, he made a speech for the clearing of his innocency, with such solemn and serious expressions as were to the admiration of all present. His prayer (which he concluded by repeating the Lord's Prayer) was so well worded, and uttered with such composedness and such (at least seeming) fervency of spirit, as was very affecting, and drew tears from many, so that it seemed to some that the spectators would hinder the execution. The accusers said the black man stood and dictated to him. As soon as he was turned off, Mr. Cotton Mather, being mounted upon a horse, addressed himself to the people, partly to declare that he (Mr. Burroughs) was no ordained minister, and partly to possess the people of his guilt, saying that the Devil often had been transformed into an angel of light; and this somewhat appeased the people, and the executions went on. When he was cut down, he was dragged by a halter to a hole, or grave, between the rocks, about two feet deep; his shirt and breeches being pulled off, and an old pair of trousers of one executed put on his lower parts: he was so put in, together with Willard and Carrier, that one of his hands, and his chin, and a foot of one of them, was left uncovered.

10

Reconsidering the Verdict
Cotton Mather et al.

The witchcraft epidemic, so one interpretation has it, fed on local conflicts. In Salem, town and countryside were sharply diverging. Conservative back-country farmers struggled to cope with the demands of commerce. Sons coming of age—the potential marriage partners of the adolescent girls—needed land if they were to establish an independent family, but available reserves of land were shrinking. Puritan ministers lamented the "declension" from the piety of the colony's founders. Although ministers of every generation may be expected to denounce the decadence of their time, New England's preachers at the end of the seventeenth century had special reason to do so: The stern Puritanism of past generations was under real threat from a growth in luxury and secular manners. No wonder the people of Salem found it easy to believe the rantings of hysterical adolescents and think so ill of their neighbors.

Nor could the colony of which Salem was part provide the stability the beleaguered village needed. Massachusetts Bay as a whole was passing through a time of troubles. Its charter voided in 1684, Massachusetts had no stable legal base until it received a new and radically different charter from the king in 1691. People worried whether the old land claims would be valid under the new charter and whether voting would be restricted to church members. At the same time, the Devil in the form of Roman

Catholic France and heathen Indians was at their door. The Maine and New Hamp-shire frontiers had collapsed during King William's War (1689–1697), and the colony's counterattack had ended in disaster. Massachusetts Bay was bankrupt and in-creased taxes to unprecedented levels. The birthrate declined and refugees from the war were suddenly everywhere. Some of the bewitched teenagers were orphans of the war. During this time of political, religious, and social instability, how easy to believe that the Devil had launched his greatest assault on New England! In fact, for a time the larger the net of accusations grew and the more people confessed to witchcraft, the eas-ier it was to believe in the Devil's conspiracy against the colony.

Then the accusations went too far, extending to prominent members of Puritan so-ciety, including the governor's wife. The ministers' cautions concerning spectral evi-dence became more persuasive and the governor finally halted the trials. The public mood changed. To the regret of some but to the relief of many, the world of spirits again became invisible, and the witches fled New England, this time forever.

BEFORE YOU READ

1. Cotton Mather continued to defend the hanging of George Burroughs. What was his case against Burroughs? Does it depend on spectral evidence?

2. Why did Margaret Jacobs confess to being a witch? Do you consider her recan-tation sincere? Why or why not?

3. How did Governor Phips explain the witchcraft hysteria? Did he blame anyone for it?

4. Why did Samuel Sewall and Ann Putnam repent? What does it indicate about them?

COTTON MATHER EXPLAINS
THE DIFFICULTY
OF WITCHCRAFT TRIALS

Letter to John Foster,
One of the Salem Witchcraft Judges
(August 17, 1692)

Sir:

You would know whether I still retain my opinion about the horrible witch-crafts among us, and I acknowledge that I do.

I do still think that when there is no further evidence against a person but

George L. Burr, ed., *Narratives of the Witchcraft Cases, 1648–1706* (New York: Charles Scribner's Sons, 1914), pp. 215–22; Paul S. Boyer and Stephen Nissenbaum, *Salem-Village Witchcraft: A Documentary Record* (Belmont, CA: Wadsworth Pub. Co., 1972), pp. 118–22; Charles W. Upham, *Salem Witchcraft*, vol. 2 (New York: Ungar, 1969), p. 510; Harvey Wish, ed., *The Diary of Samuel Sewall* (New York: G.P. Putnam's Sons, 1967), pp. 80–81.

only this, that a specter in their shape does afflict a neighbor, that evidence is not enough to convict the [person] of witchcraft.

That the Devils have a natural power which makes them capable of exhibiting what shape they please I suppose nobody doubts, and I have no absolute promise of God that they shall not exhibit *mine*.

It is the opinion generally of all Protestant writers that the Devil may thus abuse the innocent; yea, 'tis the confession of some Popish ones. And our honorable judges are so eminent for their justice, wisdom, and goodness, that whatever their own particular sense may be, yet they will not proceed capitally against any upon a principle contested with great odds on the other side in the learned and Godly world.

Nevertheless, a very great use is to be made of the spectral impressions upon the sufferers. They justly introduce and determine an inquiry into the circumstances of the person accused, and they strengthen other presumptions.

When so much use is made of those things, I believe the use for which the great God intends them is made. And accordingly you see that the excellent judges have had such an encouraging presence of God with them as that scarce any, if at all any, have been tried before them against whom God has not strangely sent in other, and more human, and most convincing testimonies.

If any persons have been condemned about whom any of the judges are not easy in their minds that the evidence against them has been satisfactory, it would certainly be for the glory of the whole transaction to give that person a reprieve.

It would make all matters easier if at least bail were taken for people accused only by the invisible tormentors of the poor sufferers, and not blemished by any further grounds of suspicion against them.

The odd effects produced upon the sufferers by the look or touch of the accused are things wherein the Devils may as much impose upon some harmless people as by the representation of their shapes.

My notion of these matters is this. A suspected and unlawful communion with a familiar spirit is the thing inquired after. The communion on the Devil's part may be proved while, for aught I can say, the man may be innocent. The Devil may impudently impose his communion upon some that care not for his company. But if the communion on the man's part be proved, then the business is done.

I am suspicious lest the Devil may at some time or other serve us a trick by his constancy for a long while in one way of dealing. We may find the Devil using one constant course in nineteen several actions, and yet he be too hard for us at last, if we thence make a rule to form an infallible judgment of a twentieth. It is our singular happiness that we are blessed with judges who are aware of this danger. . . .

Our case is extraordinary. And so you and others will pardon the extraordinary liberty I take to address you on this occasion. But after all, I entreat you that whatever you do, you strengthen the hands of our honorable judges in the great work before them. They are persons for whom no man living has a greater veneration than

Sir,
Your servant
C. Mather

COTTON MATHER DEFENDS THE CONVICTION OF GEORGE BURROUGHS

This G.B. [George Burroughs] was indicted for witchcraft, and in the prosecution of the charge against him, he was accused by five or six of the bewitched, as the author of their miseries; he was accused by eight of the confessing witches as being a head actor at some of their hellish rendez-vouses and one who had the promise of being a king in Satan's kingdom, now going to be erected; he was accused by nine persons for extraordinary lifting, and such feats of strength, as could not be done without a diabolical assistance. And for other such things he was accused, until about thirty testimonies were brought in against him; nor were these judged the half of what might have been considered for his conviction: however, they were enough to fix the character of a witch upon him. . . .

And now upon his trial, one of the bewitched persons [Ann Putnam] testified that in her agonies a little black haired man came to her, saying his name was B. and bidding her set her hand unto a book which he showed her; and bragging that he was a conjurer, above the ordinary rank of witches. That he often persecuted her with the offer of that book, saying she should be well and need fear nobody if she would but sign it; but he inflicted cruel pains and hurts upon her because of her denying so to do. The testimonies of the other sufferers concurred with these, and it was remarkable, that whereas biting was one of the ways which the witches used for the vexing of the sufferers, when they cried out of G.B. biting them, the print of the teeth would be seen on the flesh of the complainers, and just such a set of teeth as G.B.'s would then appear upon them, which could be distinguished from those of some other men. . . .

It cost the court a wonderful deal of trouble to hear the testimonies of the sufferers, for when they were going to give in their depositions, they would for a long time be taken with fits that made them incapable of saying anything. The chief judge asked the prisoner who he thought hindered these witnesses from giving their testimonies and he answered, he supposed it was the Devil. That honorable person then replied, how comes the Devil, so loathe to have any testimony born against you? Which cast him into very great confusion.

It has been a frequent thing for the bewitched people to be entertained with apparitions of ghosts of murdered people, at the same time that the specters of the witches trouble them. Accordingly, several of the bewitched had given in their testimony that they had been troubled with the apparitions of two women, who said that they were G.B.'s two wives, and that he had been the death of them, and that the magistrates must be told of it before whom if B. upon his trial denied it, they did not know but that they should appear again in the Court. Now, G.B. had been infamous for the barbarous usage of his two successive wives, all the country over. . . .

[O]ne of the bewitched persons was cast into horror at the ghosts of B.'s two deceased wives then appearing before him, and crying for vengeance against him. Hereupon, several of the bewitched persons were successively called in, who all not knowing what the former had seen and said, concurred in their horror of the apparition, which they affirmed that he had before him. . . .

Judicious writers have assigned it a great place in the conviction of witches when persons are impeached by other notorious witches, to be as [evil] as themselves; especially if the persons have been much noted for neglecting the worship of God. Now, as there might have been testimonies enough of G.B.'s antipathy to prayer, and the other ordinances of God, though by his profession singularly obliged thereunto; so, there now came in against the prisoner the testimonies of several persons who confessed their own having been horrible witches, and ever since their confessions had been themselves terribly tortured by the devils and other witches, even like the other sufferers. . . .

These now testified that G.B. had been at witch meetings with them, and that he was the person who had seduced and compelled them into the snares of witchcraft. That he promised them fine clothes for doing it, that he brought dolls to them and thorns to stick into those dolls, for the afflicting of other people, and that he exhorted them with the rest of the crew to bewitch all Salem Village, but be sure to do it gradually, if they would prevail in what they did. . . .

A famous Divine recites this among the convictions of a witch, the testimony of the party bewitched, whether pining or dying, together with the joint oaths of sufficient persons that have seen certain prodigious pranks or feats wrought by the party accused. Now God had been pleased so to leave this G.B. that he had ensnared himself by several instances, which he had formerly given of a preternatural strength and which were now produced against him. He was a very puny man, yet he had often done things beyond the strength of a giant. A gun of about seven foot barrel and so heavy that strong men could not steadily hold it out with both hands, there were several testimonies given in by persons of credit and honor, that he made nothing of taking up such a gun behind the lock, with but one hand and holding it out like a pistol at arms' end. G.B. in his vindication was so foolish as to say, that an Indian was there, and held it out at the same time: whereas none of the spectators ever saw any such Indian, but they supposed the black man (as the witches call the devil, and they generally say he resembles an Indian) might give him that assistance. . . .

Faltering, faulty, inconsistent, and contrary answers upon judicial and deliberate examination are counted some unlucky symptoms of guilt in all crimes, especially in witchcraft. Now, there was never a prisoner more eminent for them then G.B. both at his examination and on his trial. His evasions, contradictions and falsehoods were very sensible, he had little to say, but that he had heard some things that he could not prove, reflecting upon the reputation of some of the witnesses. Only he gave in a paper to the jury, wherein although he had many times before granted not only that there are witches but also that the present sufferings of the country are the effect of horrible witchcrafts, yet he now goes to show that there neither are nor ever were witches that, having made a compact with the Devil, can send a devil to torment other people at a distance. . . .

The jury brought him in guilty. But when he came to die, he utterly denied the fact, whereof he had been thus convicted.

DECLARATION OF MARGARET JACOBS
TO THE SPECIAL WITCHCRAFT COURT
APPOINTED BY THE GOVERNOR

The humble declaration of Margaret Jacobs to the honoured court now sitting at Salem, showoi

That whereas your poor and humble declarant being closely confined here in Salem jail for the crime of witchcraft, which crime, thanks be to the Lord, I am altogether ignorant of, as will appear at the great day of judgment. May it please the honoured court, I was cried out upon by some of the possessed persons, as afflicting of them; whereupon I was brought to my examination, which persons at the sight of me fell down, which did very much startle and affright me. The Lord above knows I knew nothing, in the least measure, how or who afflicted them; they told me, without doubt I did, or else they would not fall down at me; they told me if I would not confess, I should be put down into the dungeon and would be hanged, but if I would confess I should have my life; the which did so affright me, with my own vile wicked heart, to save my life made me make the confession I did, which confession, may it please the honoured court, is altogether false and untrue. The very first night after I had made my confession, I was in such horror of conscience that I could not sleep, for fear the Devil should carry me away for telling such horrid lies. I was, may it please the honoured court, sworn to my confession, as I understand since, but then, at that time, was ignorant of it, not knowing what an oath did mean. The Lord, I hope, in whom I trust, out of the abundance of his mercy, will forgive me my false forswearing myself.

What I said was altogether false, against my grandfather, and Mr. Burroughs, which I did to save my life and to have my liberty; but the Lord, charging it to my conscience, made me in so much horror, that I could not contain myself before I had denied my confession, which I did, though I saw nothing but death before me, choosing rather death with a quiet conscience, than to live in such horror, which I could not suffer. . . .

GOVERNOR WILLIAM PHIPS
ENDS THE TRIALS

Letter to the Earl of Nottingham
(February 21, 1693)

Boston in New England Febry 21st, 1692–93

May it please your Lordship,

At my arrival here I found the prisons full of people committed upon suspicion of witchcraft, and that continual complaints were made to me that many persons were grievously tormented by witches, and that they cried out upon several persons by name, as the cause of their torments. The number of these complaints increasing every day, by advice of the Lieutenant Governor and the Council I gave a Commission of Oyer and Terminer to try the suspected witches and at that time the generality of the people represented the matter to me as real witchcraft and gave very strange instances of the same. The first in Commission was the Lieutenant Governor and the rest persons of the best prudence and figure that could then be pitched upon, and I depended upon the Court for a right method of proceeding in cases of witchcraft.

At that time I went to command the army at the eastern part of the Province, for the French and Indians had made an attack upon some of our frontier towns. I continued there for some time but when I returned I found people much dissatisfied at the proceedings of the Court, for about twenty persons were condemned and executed of which number some were thought by many persons to be innocent. The Court still proceeded in the same method of trying them, which was by the evidence of the afflicted persons who, when they were brought into the Court—as soon as the suspected witches looked upon them, instantly fell to the ground in strange agonies and grievous torments, but when touched by them upon the arm or some other part of their flesh they immediately revived and came to themselves, upon [which] they made oath that the prisoner at the bar did afflict them and that they saw their shape or specter come from their bodies which put them to such pains and torments. When I inquired into the matter I was informed by the Judges that they began with this, but had human testimony against such as were condemned and undoubted proof of their being witches. But at length I found that the Devil did take upon him the shape of Innocent persons and some were accused of whose innocency I was well assured and many considerable persons of unblameable life and conversation were cried out upon as witches and wizards.

The Deputy Governor, notwithstanding, persisted vigorously in the same method, to the great dissatisfaction and disturbance of the people, until I put an end to the Court and stopped the proceedings, which I did because I saw many innocent persons might otherwise perish. . . . When I put an end to the Court there were at least fifty persons in prison in great misery by reason of the extreme cold and their poverty, most of them having only specter evidence against them, and their *mittimusses* [warrants] being defective, I caused some of them to be let out upon bail and put the Judges upon considering of a way to relieve others and prevent them from perishing in prison, upon which some of them were convinced and acknowledged that their former proceedings were too violent and not grounded upon a right foundation but that if they might sit again, they would proceed after another method, and whereas Mr. Increase Mathew [Mather] and several other Divines did give it as their Judgment that the Devil might afflict in the shape of an innocent person and that the look and the touch of the suspected persons was not sufficient proof against them, these things had not the same stress laid upon them as before. And upon this consideration I permitted a special Superior Court to be held at Salem in the County of Essex on the third day of January, the Lieutenant Governor being Chief Judge. Their method of proceeding being altered, all that were brought to trial, to the number of fifty two, were cleared saving [except] three, and I was informed by the King's Attorney General that some of the cleared and the condemned were under the same circumstances or that there was the same reason to clear the three condemned as the rest according to his Judgment. The Deputy Governor signed a Warrant for their speedy execution and also of five others who were condemned at the former Court of Oyer and Terminer, but considering how the matter had been managed I sent a reprieve whereby the execution was stopped until their Majesties' pleasure be signified and declared. The Lieutenant Governor upon this occasion was enraged and filled with passionate anger and refused to sit upon the bench in a Superior Court then held at Charlestown, and indeed has from the beginning hurried on these matters with great precipitancy and by his warrant has caused the estates, goods and chattels of the executed to be seized and disposed of without my knowledge or consent.

The stop put to the first method of proceedings has dissipated the black cloud that threatened this Province with destruction; for whereas this delusion of the Devil did spread and its dismal effects touched the lives and estates of many of their Majesties' subjects and the reputation of some of the principal persons here, and indeed unhappily clogged and interrupted their Majesties' affairs which has been a great vexation to me, I have no new complaints but people's minds before divided and distracted by differing opinions concerning this matter are now well composed.

I am
Your Lordship's most faithful
humble Servant
William Phips

SAMUEL SEWALL'S CONFESSION (1697)

[January 1] On the 22ⁿᵈ of May I buried my abortive son; . . . The Lord pardon all my sins of omission and commission: and by his almighty power make me meet to be partaker of the inheritance with the Saints in Light. Second-day

January 11, 1697 God helped me to pray more than ordinarily, that He would make up our loss in the burial of our little daughter and other children, and that would give us a child to serve Him, pleading with Him as the institutor of marriage, and the author of every good work.

[January 15, 1697] Copy of the Bill I put up on the Fast day; giving it to Mr. Willard as he pass'd by, and standing up at the reading of it, and bowing when finished; in the Afternoon.

> Samuel Sewall, sensible of the reiterated strokes of God upon himself and family; and being sensible, that as to the Guilt contracted upon the opening of the late Commission of Oyer and Terminer at Salem [the special witchcraft court] (to which the order for this Day relates) he is, upon many accounts, more concerned than any that he knows of, desires to take the blame and shame of it, Asking pardon of men, And especially desiring prayers that God, who has an Unlimited Authority, would pardon that sin and all other his sins; personal and relative: And according to his infinite benignity, and sovereignty, not visit the sin of him, or of any other, upon himself or any of his, nor upon the land: But that He would powerfully defend him against all temptations to sin, for the future; and vouchsafe him the efficacious, saving conduct of his word and spirit.

ANN PUTNAM'S CONFESSION (1706)

I desire to be humbled before God for that sad and humbling providence that befell my father's family in the year about '92; that I, then being in my childhood, should, by such a providence of God, be made an instrument for the accusing of several persons of a grievous crime, whereby their lives were taken away from them, whom now I have just grounds and good reason to believe they were innocent persons; and that it was a great delusion of Satan that deceived me in that sad time, whereby I justly fear I have been instrumental, with others, though ignorantly and unwittingly, to bring upon myself and this land the guilt of innocent blood; though what was said or done by me against any person I can truly and uprightly say, before God and man, I did it not out of any anger, malice, or ill-will to any person, for I had no such thing against one of them; but what I did was ignorant, being deluded by Satan. And particularly, as I was a chief instrument of accusing of Goodwife Nurse and her two sisters, I desire to lie in the dust, and to be humbled for it, in that I was a cause, with others, of so sad a calamity to them and their families; for which cause I desire to lie in the dust, and earnestly beg forgiveness of God, and from all those unto whom I have given just cause of sorrow and offence, whose relations were taken away or accused.

[Signed]

This confession was read before the congregation, together with her relation, Aug. 25, 1706; and she acknowledged it.

J. GREEN, *Pastor*

FOR CRITICAL THINKING

1. Do you think trials are a good method for determining truth? In what ways did the Salem witchcraft trials obscure rather than clarify the truth about the witchcraft threat? Can you think of other trials in which the process of adjudication seems to have worked against revealing the truth? Can you think of trials where the public response of the time affected the ability of a court to arrive at justice?

2. Imagine Cotton Mather interviewing Margaret Jacobs. Would this interview have raised questions for him about George Burroughs's guilt? How might Mather have explained why Jacobs changed her story?

3. When Ann Putnam recanted her testimony, among her listeners were the sons and daughters of Rebecca Nurse, one of the people Ann Putnam had accused and who was subsequently hanged for witchcraft. If they had entered into conversation about it, what kind of dialogue might they have had regarding Putnam's confession?

11

Diary of a Puritan Girl
Hetty Shepard

*In the decades following the Pequot War, the English colonies had prospered greatly in
both wealth and population. By the middle of the seventeenth century they clearly
dominated the territory they uneasily shared with various Indian tribes. The Puritan
ministers continued to preach the strict religion and prophesied the coming wrath of
God on a new generation for its growing desire for silks and ribbons, merriment and
games. Then, in 1675, these ritual jeremiads turned into a temporary reality. King
Philip, sachem of the Wampanoags, hoping to forestall total subjugation to the English, assembled about half the Indians of New England against the Puritans and their
Indian allies. Alden Vaughan, speaking of both Indians and Puritans, has written: "A
higher percentage of the population suffered death or wounds in King Philip's War
than in any subsequent American conflict."*

*Hetty Shepard's diary accurately reflects this important transition period for the
Puritan experiment in New England. She made her first entries at age fifteen while
living with her parents in Rhode Island. Her family then sent her to Boston in 1677
to keep her away from the war. Her diary offers an engaging picture of the life of a
young Puritan woman and reflects the social, political, and religious strains of this dramatic era. Samuel Checkly, who according to her diary set her heart "fluttering,"
eventually became her husband.*

BEFORE YOU READ

1. Why did Shepard's Aunt Alice criticize her for dressing up for her birthday? And
why did Shepard take the criticism to heart?

2. How does Shepard's life reflect both Puritan religion and the changes that were
then taking place in New England society?

3. What was her reaction to King Philip's War?

4. What was her reaction to moving to Boston and what does this reaction say
about her?

December 5, 1675   I am fifteen years old today, and while sitting with my
stitchery in my hand, there came a man in all wet with the salt spray. He had
just landed by the boat from Sandwich, which had difficulty landing because
of the surf. I myself had been down to the shore and saw the great waves
breaking, and the high tide running up as far as the hillocks of dead grass. The
man, George, an Indian, brings word of much sickness in Boston, and great
trouble with the Quakers and Baptists; that many of the children throughout

Adeline E. H. Slicer, ed. "A Puritan Maiden's Diary," *The New England Magazine* 11 (1894–95),
pp. 20–25. Modernized by Elizabeth Marcus.

the country be not baptized, and without *that* religion comes to nothing. My mother has bid me this day put on a fresh kirtle and wimple, though it not be the Lord's day, and my Aunt Alice coming in did chide me and say that to pay attention to a birthday was putting myself with the world's people. It happens from this that my kirtle and wimple are no longer pleasing me, and what with this and the bad news from Boston my birthday has ended in sorrow.

December 25, 1675   My Cousin Jane, visiting today, has told me much of the merry ways of England on this day, of the yule log, and plum puddings, until I said that I would be glad to see those merry doings; but she told me it was far better to be in a state of grace and not given over to popish practices. But I thought she looked sad herself, and almost unhappy as she reminded of the coming of John Baily who is to preach tomorrow all day. If those things are so bad, why did she tell me of them?

January 1, 1676   Yesterday was a day indeed. The preaching began at ten in the morning, and held until twelve, when a strong prayer was made and I was, I hope, much built up. But when the sermon was preached in the afternoon I fell asleep, and lost much I fear of the discourse, and this weighed heavily on my conscience. When I went home and found that brother Stephen had received word that he was to be bound to Mr. Bates of Plymouth for five years I wept sore and felt to murmur greatly.

Yesterday our Indian, George, betrayed much uneasiness after father had read the account of the burning of Sodom and Gomorrah. He has learned to understand English, and sometimes I tremble lest he should betray us to the wandering Indians of the Narragansets, who sometimes are found prowling about. . . . Father has determined to join Uncle Benjamin's company. We hear that as many as two thousand men have been raised in Massachusetts to fight this terrible sachem Philip. Mother after much fearful anxiety has submitted to the will of the Lord, whose strong right arm has gotten us the victory in many sore straits in the past. Mother has counseled Father about many things, and when Father said that women knew naught about such matters she told him how Capt. Underhill's wife saved him in his expedition against the Block Islanders, in 1636, when our country had more straits to pass through than even now when Philip is breathing out threatenings and slaughter.

March 5, 1676   A very disgraceful thing has happened in our meeting, and much scandal has been caused. Hannah Smith is married with her husband's brother, and it is declared null by the court of assistants and she has been commanded not to entertain him further; and she did appear before the congregation on lecture day to make a full confession. A lesson this is to all young women, Mother says, not to act hastily or allow our minds to wander into forbidden ways.

March 12, 1676   Although it has been pointed out to me that in times of danger I ought not to be merry, I could not help laughing at the periwig of Elder

Jones, which had gone awry. The periwig has been greatly censured as encouraging worldly fashions, not suitable to the wearing of a minister of the gospel, and it has been preached about by Mr. Mather. Many think he is not severe enough in the matter, but rather finds excuse for it on account of health. . . .

March 20, 1676   This day had a private fast. Mr. Willard spoke about the second commandment. Mr. Elliot prayed. During a half-hour break, I saw Samuel Checkly and smiled; this was not the time to trifle, and I repented, especially as he looked at me so many times after that I found my mind wandering from the psalm. And afterwards when the biscuits, beer, cider and wine were distributed he whispered to me that he would rather serve me than the elders, which was a wicked thing to say, and I felt myself to blame.

April 5, 1676   There comes sad news from Plymouth. William Clark left his garrison house on Eel River with every man to attend Sunday morning service. They left the gate of the garrison open. Savages rushed in and killed Mistress Clark and ten other women and children. One boy was not quite dead, and the doctors have mended his skull with a piece of silver. All this happened on March 22nd, almost at the time that Mr. Southworth saw the Indians at Nunaquohqet Neck. Mother and Father are going to send me to Aunt Mehitable in Boston for safety. But surely I am none too good to share the fate of my dear mother, and my faith in God sustains me, as surely as does my dependence upon my Uncle Benjamin Church, who has great skill in Indian fighting and is a mighty warrior before the Lord.

June 1, 1676   Stephen has gotten a letter to us by the hand of a friendly Indian, in which he tells us of a burning of a part of Plymouth in May, but through the blessing of God none of the people were hurt. Uncle Benjamin has been made Captain, though they were so stingy with him it makes it hard to fight.

June 12, 1676   Not a day passes but something makes our heart faint within us. Yesterday, George, our faithful Indian, while laying a stone wall in the south pasture, saw two strange Indians skulking through the swamp.

June 19, 1676   My heart longs sorely for the ocean, and all day I am weary of staying in the house. The wind blows from the south. Last night I heard the surf rushing up on the shingle, and I can no longer wander among the rocks, for fear. No letter has come from Aunt Mehitable, and Boston may be already burned. Samuel Checkly has given his testimony, has witnessed a good confession, and become a Freeman; when I beg Stephen to unite with God's people, he always says that the great Miles Standish was not a member and cared not to go to meeting on the Lord's Day, and yet he subdued our enemies, laid out our roads, and everybody had respect for him. It is surely hard to understand these things.

August 24, 1676   Great and glorious news has come. The wily Philip has been killed. Jacob Cook missed him, but a Saconet Indian named Alderman shot him, so that he bounded into the air and fell with his face in the mire. Thus does the Lord deliver us from our enemies. Captain Church called him "a doleful dirty beast," so ill-favored and filthy was he, and yet, if it be not a sin, I can only feel pity for this miserable wretch who committed so many crimes. . . .

October 6, 1676   There is much talk about Philip's son, a boy of nine years old, who was taken prisoner with his mother. They do not know what to do with him. The ministers are bitter against him and would have him sold into slavery or even worse. How can so tender a child be accountable? But perhaps it is a sin to feel this.

November 1, 1676   Father has bought two Indians for farm labor and paid for them two fathoms of wampum.

January 2, 1676   The weather is bitter cold. Went to meeting this Lord's-Day morning, and listened to a discourse by Elder Increase Mather from Zephaniah, iii, 7: "I said, Surely you will fear me; you will receive correction: so her dwelling should not be cut off, according to that I have appointed concerning her: but they rose early and corrupted all their doings." I shed many bitter tears over my sins. I fear that I shall go to hell for all my corrupt doings. Aunt Mehitable told me to dry my eyes and fast all day tomorrow, saying the Lord would have mercy on me, for he would not allow the daughter of my good mother to be lost. Oh, what becomes of those girls who have not good mothers?

January 14, 1677 [Boston]   An inflammation of the throat was cured by taking the inside of a swallow's nest, stamped and applied to the throat externally.

January 30, 1677   I saw on the street today a man standing in the pillory, for counterfeiting a lease and making false bargains. I looked away.

February 3, 1677   Went to the meeting house, but could not sit with Uncle John because he had been voted to the first seat, while Aunt Mehitable was voted into the third. This seems unjust to me, but Aunt Mehitable told me to consider the judgment of the Elders and the tithing-man as above my own. The pews are larger than I ever saw, square, with balustrades around them. A chair in the center for the aged. One corner pew was lifted high above the stairs almost to the ceiling, and was sat in by the blacks.

March 4, 1677   Through all my life I have never seen such an array of fashion and splendor as I have seen here in Boston. Silken hoods, scarlet petticoats, with silver lace, white silk plaited gowns, bone lace and silken scarves. The men with periwigs, ruffles and ribbons. . . .

May 7, 1677   There has been a sad case. A woman and a man have been fined for playing cards. They lived very near the meeting house. The fine was five pounds, but Uncle John says it should be more for so grave a matter.

June 6, 1677   There is to be a training, and I am to go. I didn't sleep last night, thinking of it. This is a sin. I repented at morning prayers with many tears. Why am I so prone to sin? The devil goes around like a roaring lion, seeking those he can devour.

June 7, 1677   There were many men at the training. Foot and artillery. Elder Mather prayed at the beginning and at the end. The streets were full of people, and all seemed merry. . . .

November 16, 1677   A letter has come from Samuel Checkly by the hand of Eliphilet Tichmond, which has set my heart fluttering. Since good mistress Checkly has entered into her rest, poor Samuel has been very lonely.

12

The African Slave Trade
Olaudah Equiano

*The Life of Olaudah Equiano, or Gustavus Vassa, the African, Written by
Himself is one of the most important eyewitness accounts of the African slave trade.
While scholars have long agreed on the horrors of the trade and the accuracy of
Equiano's description, they have argued for more than a century over how many people were involved. Estimates range from about nine and a half million to nearly fifteen million Africans imported into the western hemisphere. And this does not include
those who were killed while resisting capture or who died during passage.*

*Equiano's book is also the pioneering African American narrative of the journey
from slavery to freedom, setting many of the conventions for the more than six thousand subsequent interviews, essays, and books by which ex-slaves told their dramatic
stories. And the book, a bestseller that has gone through many editions since it was first
published in London in 1789, is also a remarkable adventure story recounting
Equiano's travels in Africa, Europe, and America as well as his part in expeditions to
the Arctic and Turkey and his service in the Seven Years' War.*

*Equiano, an Ibo prince kidnapped into slavery when he was eleven years old, was
brought first to Barbados and then sent to Virginia. After service in the British navy,
he was at last sold to a Quaker merchant who allowed Equiano to purchase his freedom in 1766. In later years he worked to advance the Church of England, his adopted
religion, and to abolish the slave trade.*

BEFORE YOU READ

1. Describe the treatment of slaves in the slave trade.
2. What were Equiano's greatest fears during passage?
3. Equiano asks, "Learned you this from your God, who says unto you, Do unto all
men as you would men should do unto you?" How would a slave trader have answered
his question?

The first object which saluted my eyes when I arrived on the [Western Africa]
coast, was the sea, and a slave ship, which was then riding at anchor, and waiting for its cargo. These filled me with astonishment, which was soon converted into terror, when I was carried on board. I was immediately handled,
and tossed up to see if I were sound, by some of the crew; and I was now persuaded that I had gotten into a world of bad spirits, and that they were going
to kill me. Their complexions, too, differing so much from ours, their long

Olaudah Equiano, *The Life of Olaudah Equiano, or Gustavus Vassa, the African, Written by Himself*
(New York: Isaac Knapp, 1837), pp. 41–52.

hair, and the language they spoke, (which was very different from any I had ever heard) united to confirm me in this belief. Indeed, such were the horrors of my views and fears at the moment, that, if ten thousand worlds had been my own, I would have freely parted with them all to have exchanged my condition with that of the meanest slave in my own country. When I looked round the ship too, and saw a large furnace of copper boiling, and a multitude of black people of every description chained together, every one of their countenances expressing dejection and sorrow, I no longer doubted of my fate; and, quite overpowered with horror and anguish, I fell motionless on the deck and fainted. When I recovered a little, I found some black people about me, who I believed were some of those who had brought me on board, and had been receiving their pay; they talked to me in order to cheer me, but all in vain. I asked them if we were not to be eaten by those white men with horrible looks, red faces, and long hair. They told me I was not: and one of the crew brought me a small portion of spirituous liquor in a wine glass, but, being afraid of him, I would not take it out of his hand. One of the blacks, therefore, took it from him and gave it to me, and I took a little down my palate, which, instead of reviving me, as they thought it would, threw me into the greatest consternation at the strange feeling it produced, having never tasted any such liquor before. Soon after this, the blacks who brought me on board went off, and left me abandoned to despair.

I now saw myself deprived of all chance of returning to my native country, or even the least glimpse of hope of gaining the shore, which I now considered as friendly; and I even wished for my former slavery in preference to my present situation, which was filled with horrors of every kind, still heightened by my ignorance of what I was to undergo. I was not long suffered to indulge my grief; I was soon put down under the decks, and there I received such a salutation in my nostrils as I had never experienced in my life: so that, with the loathsomeness of the stench, and crying together, I became so sick and low that I was not able to eat, nor had I the least desire to taste any thing. I now wished for the last friend, death, to relieve me; but soon, to my grief, two of the white men offered me eatables; and, on my refusing to eat, one of them held me fast by the hands, and laid me across, I think the windlass, and tied my feet, while the other flogged me severely. I had never experienced any thing of this kind before, and although not being used to the water, I naturally feared that element the first time I saw it, yet, nevertheless, could I have got over the nettings, I would have jumped over the side, but I could not; and besides, the crew used to watch us very closely who were not chained down to the decks, lest we should leap into the water; and I have seen some of these poor African prisoners most severely cut, for attempting to do so, and hourly whipped for not eating. This indeed was often the case with myself. In a little time after, amongst the poor chained men, I found some of my own nation, which in a small degree gave ease to my mind. I inquired of these what was to be done with us? they gave me to understand, we were to be carried to these white people's country to work for them. I then was a little revived, and thought, if it were no worse than working, my situation was not so desperate; but still I feared I should be put to death, the white people looked and acted, as I thought, in so savage a manner; for I had never seen among any people such instances of brutal cruelty; and this not only shown towards us blacks, but also to some of the whites themselves. One white man in particular I saw, when we were permitted to be on deck, flogged so unmercifully with a large rope near the foremast, that he died in consequence of it; and they tossed him over the side as they would have done a brute. This made me fear these people the more; and I expected nothing less than to be treated in the same manner. I could not help expressing my fears and apprehensions to some of my coun- trymen; I asked them if these people had no country, but lived in this hollow place? (the ship) they told me they did not, but came from a distant one. "Then," said I, "how comes it in all our country we never heard of them?" They told me because they lived so very far off. I then asked where were their women? Had they any like themselves? I was told they had. "And why," said I, "do we not see them?" They answered, because they were left behind. I asked how the vessel could go? They told me they could not tell; but that there was cloth put upon the masts by the help of the ropes I saw, and then the vessel went on; and the white men had some spell or magic they put in the water when they liked, in order to stop the vessel. I was exceedingly amazed at this account, and really thought they were spirits. I therefore wished much to be from amongst them, for I expected they would sacrifice me; but my wishes were vain—for we were so quartered that it was impossible for any of us to make our escape.

While we stayed on the coast I was mostly on deck; and one day, to my great astonishment, I saw one of these vessels coming in with the sails up. As soon as the whites saw it, they gave a great shout, at which we were amazed; and the more so, as the vessel appeared larger by approaching nearer. At last, she came to an anchor in my sight, and when the anchor was let go, I and my country- men who saw it, were lost in astonishment to observe the vessel stop—and were now convinced it was done by magic. Soon after this the other ship got her boats out, and they came on board of us, and the people of both ships seemed very glad to see each other.—Several of the strangers also shook hands with us black people, and made motions with their hands, signifying I suppose, we were to go to their country, but we did not understand them.

At last, when the ship we were in, had got in all her cargo, they made ready with many fearful noises, and we were all put under deck, so that we could not see how they managed the vessel. But this disappointment was the least of my sorrow. The stench of the hold while we were on the coast was so intolerably loathsome, that it was dangerous to remain there for any time, and some of us had been permitted to stay on the deck for the fresh air; but now that the whole ship's cargo were confined together, it became absolutely pestilential. The closeness of the place, and the heat of the climate, added to the number in the ship, which was so crowded that each had scarcely room to turn himself, almost suffocated us. This produced copious perspirations, so that the air soon became unfit for respiration, from a variety of loathsome smells, and brought on a sickness among the slaves, of which many died—thus falling victims to the improvident avarice, as I may call it, of their purchasers. This wretched situation was again aggravated by the galling of the chains, now became insupportable; and the filth of the necessary tubs, into which the children often fell, and were almost suffocated. The shrieks of the women, and the groans of the dying, rendered the whole a scene of horror almost inconceivable. Happily perhaps, for myself, I was soon reduced so low here that it was thought necessary to keep me almost always on deck; and from my extreme youth I was not put in fetters. In this situation I expected every hour to share the fate of my companions, some of whom were almost daily brought upon deck at the point of death, which I began to hope would soon put an end to my miseries. Often did I think many of the inhabitants of the deep much more happy than myself. I envied them the freedom they enjoyed, and as often wished I could change my condition for theirs. Every circumstance I met with, served only to render my state more painful, and heightened my apprehensions, and my opinion of the cruelty of the whites.

One day they had taken a number of fishes; and when they had killed and satisfied themselves with as many as they thought fit, to our astonishment who were on deck, rather than give any of them to us to eat, as we expected, they tossed the remaining fish into the sea again, although we begged and prayed for some as well as we could, but in vain; and some of my countrymen, being pressed by hunger, took an opportunity, when they thought no one saw them, of trying to get a little privately; but they were discovered, and the attempt procured them some very severe floggings. One day, when we had a smooth sea and moderate wind, two of my wearied countrymen who were chained together, (I was near them at the time,) preferring death to such a life of misery, somehow made through the nettings and jumped into the sea: immediately, another quite dejected fellow, who, on account of his illness, was suffered to be out of irons, also followed their example; and I believe many more would very soon have done the same, if they had not been prevented by the ship's crew, who were instantly alarmed. Those of us that were the most active, were in a moment put down under the deck, and there was such a noise and confusion amongst the people of the ship as I never heard before, to stop her, and get the boat out to go after the slaves. However, two of the wretches were drowned, but they got the other, and afterward flogged him unmercifully, for thus attempting to prefer death to slavery. In this manner we continued to undergo more hardships than I can now relate, hardships which are inseparable from this accursed trade. Many a time we were near suffocation from the want of fresh air, which we were often without for whole days together. This, and the stench of the necessary tubs, carried off many.

During our passage, I first saw flying fishes, which surprised me very much; they used frequently to fly across the ship, and many of them fell on the deck. I also now first saw the use of the quadrant; I had often with astonishment seen the mariners make observations with it, and I could not think what it meant.

They at last took notice of my surprise; and one of them, willing to increase it, as well as to gratify my curiosity, made me one day look through it. The clouds appeared to me to be land, which disappeared as they passed along. This heightened my wonder; and I was now more persuaded than ever, that I was in another world, and that every thing about me was magic. At last, we came in sight of the island of Barbados, at which the whites on board gave a great shout, and made many signs of joy to us. We did not know what to think of this; but as the vessel drew nearer, we plainly saw the harbor, and other ships of different kinds and sizes, and we soon anchored amongst them, off Bridgetown. Many merchants and planters now came on board, though it was in the evening. They put us in separate parcels, and examined us attentively. They also made us jump, and pointed to the land, signifying we were to go there. We thought by this, we should be eaten by these ugly men, as they appeared to us; and, when soon after we were all put down under the deck again, there was much dread and trembling among us, and nothing but bitter cries to be heard all the night from these apprehensions, insomuch, that at last the white people got some old slaves from the land to pacify us. They told us we were not to be eaten, but to work, and were soon to go on land, where we should see many of our country people. This report eased us much. And sure enough, soon after we were landed, there came to us Africans of all languages.

We were conducted immediately to the merchant's yard, where we were all pent up together, like so many sheep in a fold, without regard to sex or age. As every object was new to me, every thing I saw filled me with surprise. What struck me first, was, that the houses were built with bricks and stories, and in every other respect different from those I had seen in Africa; but I was still more astonished on seeing people on horseback. I did not know what this could mean; and, indeed, I thought these people were full of nothing but magical arts. While I was in this astonishment, one of my fellow-prisoners spoke to a countryman of his, about the horses, who said they were the same kind they had in their country. I understood them, though they were from a distant part of Africa; and I thought it odd I had not seen any horses there; but afterwards, when I came to converse with different Africans, I found they had many horses amongst them, and much larger than those I then saw.

We were not many days in the merchant's custody before we were sold after their usual manner, which is this: — On a signal given, (as the beat of a drum,) the buyers rush at once into the yard where the slaves are confined, and make choice of that parcel they like best. The noise and clamor with which this is attended, and the eagerness visible in the countenances of the buyers, serve not a little to increase the apprehension of terrified Africans, who may well be supposed to consider them as the ministers of that destruction to which they think themselves devoted. In this manner, without scruple, are relations and friends separated, most of them never to see each other again. I remember, in the vessel in which I was brought over, in the men's apartment, there were several brothers, who, in the sale, were sold in different lots; and it was very moving on this occasion, to see and hear their cries at parting. O, ye nominal

Christians! might not an African ask you—Learned you this from your God, who says unto you, Do unto all men as you would men should do unto you? Is it not enough that we are torn from our country and friends, to toil for your luxury and lust of gain? Must every tender feeling be likewise sacrificed to your avarice? Are the dearest friends and relations, now rendered more dear by their separation from their kindred, still to be parted from each other, and thus prevented from cheering the gloom of slavery, with the small comfort of being together, and mingling their sufferings and sorrows? Why are parents to lose their children, brothers their sisters, or husbands their wives? Surely, this is a new refinement in cruelty, which, while it has no advantage to atone for it, thus aggravates distress, and adds fresh horrors even to the wretchedness of slavery.

13

On the Misfortune of Indentured Servants

Gottlieb Mittelberger

Indentured, or bonded, servants were an important source of labor in seventeenth- and eighteenth-century America. The term generally refers to immigrants who, in return for passage from Europe to America, bound themselves to work in America for a number of years, after which time they would become completely free. The practice was closely related to the tradition of apprenticeship, in which a youth was assigned to work for a master in a certain trade and in return was taught the skills of the trade. Convicts were another important source of colonial labor; thousands of English criminals were sentenced to labor in the colonies for a specified period, after which time they were freed.

Many indentured servants had valuable skills that they hoped to make better use of in the New World than they had been able to do at home. Some in fact did just that, while others, as Gottlieb Mittelberger describes, did not fare so well. Mittelberger came to Pennsylvania from Germany in 1750. His own fortunes were not so bleak as those of his shipmates. He served as a schoolmaster and organist in Philadelphia for three years, then returned to Germany in 1754.

Before You Read

1. Why do you think immigrants chose to endure the miseries of a transatlantic passage to come to the New World?

2. How did the treatment of indentured servants described by Mittelberger compare to the treatment of slaves in the slave trade described in the previous reading?

3. What happened to children whose parents died during the journey?

4. Why do you think Mittelberger returned to Germany?

Both in Rotterdam and in Amsterdam the people are packed densely, like herrings so to say, in the large sea-vessels. One person receives a place of scarcely 2 feet width and 6 feet length in the bedstead, while many a ship carries four to six hundred souls; not to mention the innumerable implements, tools, provisions, water-barrels and other things which likewise occupy much space.

On account of contrary winds it takes the ships sometimes 2, 3 and 4 weeks to make the trip from Holland to . . . England. But when the wind is good, they get there in 8 days or even sooner. Everything is examined there and the custom-duties paid, whence it comes that the ships ride there 8, 10 to 14 days and even longer at anchor, till they have taken in their full cargoes. During that

Gottlieb Mittelberger, *Journey to Pennsylvania in the Year 1750 and Return to Germany in the Year 1754*, trans. Carl Theo (Philadelphia: John Joseph McVey, 1898), pp. 19–29.

time every one is compelled to spend his last remaining money and to consume his little stock of provisions which had been reserved for the sea; so that most passengers, finding themselves on the ocean where they would be in greater need of them, must greatly suffer from hunger and want. Many suffer want already on the water between Holland and Old England.

When the ships have for the last time weighed their anchors near the city of Kaupp [Cowes] in Old England, the real misery begins with the long voyage. For from there the ships, unless they have good wind, must often sail 8, 9, 10 to 12 weeks before they reach Philadelphia. But even with the best wind the voyage lasts 7 weeks.

But during the voyage there is on board these ships terrible misery, stench, fumes, horror, vomiting, many kinds of sea-sickness, fever, dysentery, headache, heat, constipation, boils, scurvy, cancer, mouth-rot, and the like, all of which come from old and sharply salted food and meat, also from very bad and foul water, so that many die miserably.

Add to this want of provisions, hunger, thirst, frost, heat, dampness, anxiety, want, afflictions and lamentations, together with other trouble, as . . . the lice abound so frightfully, especially on sick people, that they can be scraped off the body. The misery reaches the climax when a gale rages for 2 or 3 nights and days, so that every one believes that the ship will go to the bottom with all human beings on board. In such a visitation the people cry and pray most piteously.

When in such a gale the sea rages and surges, so that the waves rise often like high mountains one above the other, and often tumble over the ship, so that one fears to go down with the ship; when the ship is constantly tossed from side to side by the storm and waves, so that no one can either walk, or sit, or lie, and the closely packed people in the berths are thereby tumbled over each other, both the sick and the well—it will be readily understood that many of these people, none of whom had been prepared for hardships, suffer so terribly from them that they do not survive it.

I myself had to pass through a severe illness at sea, and I best know how I felt at the time. These poor people often long for consolation, and I often entertained and comforted them with singing, praying and exhorting; and whenever it was possible and the winds and waves permitted it, I kept daily prayer-meetings with them on deck. Besides, I baptized five children in distress, because we had no ordained minister on board. I also held divine service every Sunday by reading sermons to the people; and when the dead were sunk in the water, I commended them and our souls to the mercy of God.

Among the healthy, impatience sometimes grows so great and cruel that one curses the other, or himself and the day of his birth, and sometimes come near killing each other. Misery and malice join each other, so that they cheat and rob one another. One always reproaches the other with having persuaded him to undertake the journey. Frequently children cry out against their parents, husbands against their wives and wives against their husbands, brothers and sisters, friends and acquaintances against each other. But most against the soul-traffickers.

Many sigh and cry: "Oh, that I were at home again, and if I had to lie in my pig-sty!" Or they say: "O God, if I only had a piece of good bread, or a good fresh drop of water." Many people whimper, sigh and cry piteously for their homes; most of them get home-sick. Many hundred people necessarily die and perish in such misery, and must be cast into the sea, which drives their relatives, or those who persuaded them to undertake the journey, to such despair that it is almost impossible to pacify and console them. . . .

No one can have an idea of the sufferings which women in confinement have to bear with their innocent children on board these ships. Few of this class escape with their lives; many a mother is cast into the water with her child as soon as she is dead. One day, just as we had a heavy gale, a woman in our ship, who was to give birth and could not give birth under the circumstances, was pushed through a loop-hole [port-hole] in the ship and dropped into the sea, because she was far in the rear of the ship and could not be brought forward.

Children from 1 to 7 years rarely survive the voyage. I witnessed . . . misery in no less than 32 children in our ship, all of whom were thrown into the sea. The parents grieve all the more since their children find no resting-place in the earth, but are devoured by the monsters of the sea.

That most of the people get sick is not surprising, because, in addition to all other trials and hardships, warm food is served only three times a week, the rations being very poor and very little. Such meals can hardly be eaten, on account of being so unclean. The water which is served out on the ships is often very black, thick and full of worms, so that one cannot drink it without loathing, even with the greatest thirst. Toward the end we were compelled to eat the ship's biscuit which had been spoiled long ago; though in a whole biscuit there was scarcely a piece the size of a dollar that had not been full of red worms and spiders' nests. . . .

At length, when, after a long and tedious voyage, the ships come in sight of land, so that the promontories can be seen, which the people were so eager and anxious to see, all creep from below on deck to see the land from afar, and they weep for joy, and pray and sing, thanking and praising God. The sight of the land makes the people on board the ship, especially the sick and the half dead, alive again, so that their hearts leap within them; they shout and rejoice, and are content to bear their misery in patience, in the hope that they may soon reach the land in safety. But alas!

When the ships have landed at Philadelphia after their long voyage, no one is permitted to leave them except those who pay for their passage or can give good security; the others, who cannot pay, must remain on board the ships till they are purchased, and are released from the ships by their purchasers. The sick always fare the worst, for the healthy are naturally preferred and purchased first; and so the sick and wretched must often remain on board in front of the city for 2 or 3 weeks, and frequently die, whereas many a one, if he could pay his debt and were permitted to leave the ship immediately, might recover and remain alive.

The sale of human beings in the market on board the ship is carried on thus: Every day Englishmen, Dutchmen, and High-German people come from the city of Philadelphia and other places, in part from a great distance, say 20, 30, or 40 hours away, and go on board the newly arrived ship that has brought and offers for sale passengers from Europe, and select among the healthy persons such as they deem suitable for their business, and bargain with them how long they will serve for their passage money, which most of them are still in debt for. When they have come to an agreement, it happens that adult persons bind themselves in writing to serve 3, 4, 5, or 6 years for the amount due by them, according to their age and strength. But very young people, from 10 to 15 years, must serve till they are 21 years old.

Many parents must sell and trade away their children like so many head of cattle; for if their children take the debt upon themselves, the parents can leave the ship free and unrestrained; but as the parents often do not know where and to what people their children are going, it often happens that such parents and children, after leaving the ship, do not see each other again for many years, perhaps no more in all their lives.

It often happens that whole families, husband, wife, and children, are separated by being sold to different purchasers, especially when they have not paid any part of their passage money.

When a husband or wife has died at sea, when the ship has made more than half of her trip, the survivor must pay or serve not only for himself or herself, but also for the deceased.

When both parents have died over half-way at sea, their children, especially when they are young and have nothing to pawn or to pay, must stand for their own and their parents' passage, and serve till they are 21 years old. When one has served his or her term, he or she is entitled to a new suit of clothes at parting; and if it has been so stipulated, a man gets in addition a horse, a woman, a cow.

When a serf has an opportunity to marry in this country, he or she must pay for each year which he or she would have yet to serve, 5 to 6 pounds. But many a one who has thus purchased and paid for his bride, has subsequently repented his bargain, so that he would gladly have returned his exorbitantly dear ware, and lost the money besides.

If some one in this country runs away from his master, who has treated him harshly, he cannot get far. Good provision has been made for such cases, so that a runaway is soon recovered. He who detains or returns a deserter receives a good reward.

If such a runaway has been away from his master one day, he must serve for it as a punishment a week, for a week a month, and for a month half a year.

14

A Man of the American Enlightenment
Benjamin Franklin

The new science of the Enlightenment, epitomized by Isaac Newton's Philosophiae Naturalis Principia Mathematica *(1687), profoundly influenced the outlook of educated people in eighteenth-century Europe and North America alike, including the leaders of the patriot cause in colonial America. Fundamental to the worldview of people like Benjamin Franklin was a belief in the power of human reason to understand the laws of nature, to improve human life, and to establish rational governments and a code of moral conduct.*

Franklin exemplified Enlightenment thinking in America. He was a scientist studying the natural laws of electricity; an inventor improving human life through such inventions as the lightning rod, the Franklin stove, and bifocals; a philanthropist organizing libraries and scientific societies to spread secular scientific knowledge, a journalist advancing popular learning; a reformer improving fire prevention and other civic amenities; and the author of an autobiography unlike anything that had preceded it in its didactic yet thoroughly secular account of his own remarkable moral development.

BEFORE YOU READ

1. What kind of character-building regime did Franklin devise for himself? Do you think he really expected to achieve moral perfection?

2. What did Franklin mean when he wrote that it might be better to be a "speckled ax" than a bright one? What does this tell you about his attitude toward his moral experiment?

3. Why did Franklin stop keeping his book?

It was about this time I conceived the bold and arduous project of arriving at moral perfection. I wished to live without committing any fault at any time; I would conquer all that either natural inclination, custom, or company might lead me into. As I knew, or thought I knew, what was right and wrong, I did not see why I might not always do the one and avoid the other. But I soon found I had undertaken a task of more difficulty than I had imagined. While my care was employed in guarding against one fault, I was often surprised by another; habit took the advantage of inattention; inclination was sometimes too strong for reason. I concluded, at length, that the mere speculative conviction that it was our interest to be completely virtuous was not sufficient to prevent our slipping, and that the contrary habits must be broken, and good ones acquired and established, before we can have any dependence on a steady,

The Autobiography of Benjamin Franklin (New York: The Century Co., 1901), pp. 141–53.

uniform rectitude of conduct. For this purpose I therefore contrived the following method.

In the various enumerations of the moral virtues I had met with in my reading, I found the catalogue more or less numerous, as different writers included more or fewer ideas under the same name. Temperance, for example, was by some confined to eating and drinking, while by others it was extended to mean the moderating every other pleasure, appetite, inclination, or passion, bodily or mental, even to our avarice and ambition. I proposed to myself, for the sake of clearness, to use rather more names, with fewer ideas annexed to each, than a few names with more ideas; and I included under thirteen names of virtues all that at that time occurred to me as necessary or desirable, and annexed to each a short precept, which fully expressed the extent I gave to its meaning.

These names of virtues, with their precepts, were:

1. Temperance

Eat not to dullness; drink not to elevation.

2. Silence

Speak not but what may benefit others or yourself; avoid trifling conversation.

3. Order

Let all your things have their places; let each part of your business have its time.

4. Resolution

Resolve to perform what you ought; perform without fail what you resolve.

5. Frugality

Make no expense but to do good to others or yourself, i.e., waste nothing.

6. Industry

Lose no time; be always employed in something useful; cut off all unnecessary actions.

7. Sincerity

Use no hurtful deceit; think innocently and justly, and, if you speak, speak accordingly.

8. Justice

Wrong none by doing injuries or omitting the benefits that are your duty.

9. Moderation

Avoid extremes; forbear resenting injuries so much as you think they deserve.

10. Cleanliness

Tolerate no uncleanliness in body, clothes, or habitation.

11. Tranquillity

Be not disturbed at trifles, or at accidents common or unavoidable.

12. Chastity

Rarely use venery but for health or offspring, never to dullness, weakness, or the injury of your own or another's peace or reputation.

13. Humility

Imitate Jesus and Socrates.

My intention being to acquire the *habitude* of all these virtues, I judged it would be well not to distract my attention by attempting the whole at once, but to fix it on one of them at a time, and, when I should be master of that, then to proceed to another, and so on, till I should have gone thro' the thirteen; and, as the previous acquisition of some might facilitate the acquisition of certain others, I arranged them with that view, as they stand above. Temperance first, as it tends to procure that coolness and clearness of head which is so necessary where constant vigilance was to be kept up, and guard maintained against the unremitting attraction of ancient habits and the force of perpetual temptations. This being acquired and established, Silence would be more easy; and my desire being to gain knowledge at the same time that I improved in virtue, and considering that in conversation it was obtained rather by the use of the ears than of the tongue, and therefore wishing to break a habit I was getting into of prattling, punning, and joking, which only made me acceptable to trifling company, I gave *Silence* the second place. This and the next, *Order*, I expected would allow me more time for attending to my project and my studies. *Resolution*, once become habitual, would keep me firm in my endeavors to obtain all the subsequent virtues; *Frugality* and Industry, freeing me from my remaining debt, and producing affluence and independence, would make more easy the practice of Sincerity and Justice, etc., etc. Conceiving, then, that, . . . daily examination would be necessary, I contrived the following method for conducting that examination.

I made a little book, in which I allotted a page for each of the virtues. I ruled each page with red ink, so as to have seven columns, one for each day of the week, marking each column with a letter for the day. I crossed these columns with thirteen red lines, marking the beginning of each line with the first letter of one of the virtues, on which line, and in its proper column, I might mark, by a little black spot, every fault I found upon examination to have been committed respecting that virtue upon that day.

I determined to give a week's strict attention to each of the virtues successively. Thus, in the first week, my great guard was to avoid every the least offense against *Temperance*, leaving the other virtues to their ordinary chance, only marking every evening the faults of the day. Thus, if in the first week I could keep my first line, marked T, clear of spots, I supposed the habit of that virtue so much strengthened, and its opposite weakened, that I might venture extending my attention to include the next, and for the following week keep both lines clear of spots. Proceeding thus to the last, I could go thro' a course complete in thirteen weeks, and four courses in a year. And like him who, having a garden to weed, does not attempt to eradicate all the bad herbs at once, which would exceed his reach and his strength, but works on one of the beds at a time, and, having accomplished the first, proceeds to a second, so I should have, I hoped, the encouraging pleasure of seeing on my pages the progress I made in virtue, by clearing successively my lines of their spots, till in the end, by a number of courses, I should be happy in viewing a clean book, after a thirteen weeks' daily examination.

The precept of *Order* requiring that *every part of my business should have its allotted time*, one page in my little book contained the following scheme of employment for the twenty-four hours of a natural day:

THE MORNING.		
Question. What good shall I do this day?	5	Rise, wash, and address *Powerful Goodness!* Contrive day's business, and take the resolution of the day; prosecute the present study, and breakfast.
	6	
	7	
	8	
	9	Work.
	10	
	11	
NOON.	12	Read, or overlook my accounts, and dine.
	1	
	2	
	3	Work.
	4	
	5	
EVENING. *Question.* What good have I done today?	6	Put things in their places. Supper. Music, or diversion, or conversation. Examination of the day.
	7	
	8	
	9	
NIGHT.	10	Sleep.
	11	
	12	
	1	
	2	
	3	
	4	

I entered upon the execution of this plan for self-examination, and continued it with occasional intermissions for some time. I was surprised to find myself so much fuller of faults than I had imagined; but I had the satisfaction of seeing them diminish. To avoid the trouble of renewing now and then my little book, which, by scraping out the marks on the paper of old faults to make room for new ones in a new course, became full of holes, I transferred my tables and precepts to the ivory leaves of a memorandum-book, on which the lines were drawn with red ink, that made a durable stain, and on those lines I marked my faults with a black-lead pencil, which marks I could easily wipe out with a wet sponge. After a while I went thro' one course only in a year, and afterward only one in several years, till at length I omitted them entirely, being employed in voyages and business abroad, with a multiplicity of affairs that interfered; but I always carried my little book with me.

My scheme of *Order* gave me the most trouble; and I found that, tho' it might be practicable where a man's business was such as to leave him the disposition of his time, that of a journeyman printer, for instance, it was not possible to be exactly observed by a master, who must mix with the world, and often receive people of business at their own hours. *Order,* too, with regard to places for things, papers, etc., I found extremely difficult to acquire. I had not been early accustomed to it, and, having an exceeding good memory, I was not so sensible of the inconvenience attending want of method. This article, therefore, cost me so much painful attention, and my faults in it vexed me so much, and I made so little progress in amendment, and had such frequent relapses, that I was almost ready to give up the attempt, and content myself with a faulty character in that respect like the man who, in buying an ax of a smith, my neighbor, desired to have the whole of its surface as bright as the edge. The smith consented to grind it bright for him if he would turn the wheel; he turned, while the smith pressed the broad face of the ax hard and heavily on the stone, which made the turning of it very fatiguing. The man came every now and then from the wheel to see how the work went on, and at length would take his ax as it was, without farther grinding. "No," said the smith; "turn on, turn on: we shall have it bright by and by; as yet, it is only speckled." "Yes," says the man, *"but I think I like a speckled ax best."* And I believe this may have been the case with many, who, having, for want of some such means as I employed, found the difficulty of obtaining good and breaking bad habits in other points of vice and virtue, have given up the struggle, and concluded that *"a speckled ax was best"*; for something, that pretended to be reason, was every now and then suggesting to me that such extreme nicety as I exacted of myself might be a kind of foppery in morals, which, if it were known, would make me ridiculous; that a perfect character might be attended with the inconvenience of being envied and hated; and that a benevolent man should allow a few faults in himself, to keep his friends in countenance.

In truth, I found myself incorrigible with respect to Order; and now I am grown old, and my memory bad, I feel very sensibly the want of it. But, on the whole, tho' I never arrived at the perfection I had been so ambitious of obtaining, but fell far short of it, yet I was, by the endeavor, a better and a happier man than I otherwise should have been if I had not attempted it. . . .

15

A Republican Woman
Eliza Pinckney

When George Washington at his own insistence served as a pallbearer at Eliza Pinckney's funeral in 1793, he was recognizing a daughter of the British Empire who had come to be considered one of the mothers of the American Republic. One of the most distinguished woman in the American colonies, she had over a long life been a successful planter and agricultural innovator, a staunch patriot who suffered greatly from the Revolutionary War, and the mother of two notable sons, Charles Cotesworth Pinckney and Thomas Pinckney, both generals in the war, then signers of the Constitution, and finally outstanding contributors to the new federal government.

Daughter of George Lucas, an imperial officer, Eliza Lucas was born in the West Indies in 1722 and educated in England. She moved to South Carolina in 1737. Two years later her father returned to Antigua to become governor, leaving Eliza in charge of three plantations, an invalid mother, and a younger sister. Overnight, the seventeen-year-old Eliza became a planter, proprietor, mistress of a great house, and, in effect, a parent as well.

Eliza Lucas was up to the challenge. With the counsel of her father's frequent letters, she managed house and family and met the obligations of social leadership while developing the plantations. She pioneered the cultivation of several new crops, most importantly indigo, a dyestuff that became a staple in the Carolinas for decades. In 1744 she married Charles Pinckney, a prominent lawyer and planter. When he became a colonial agent, she lived with him for six years in England, resuming childhood friendships and establishing her two sons in English schools. When her husband died in 1758, Eliza Pinckney oversaw even more extensive properties and mothered her sons from a distance by constant correspondence, much as her father had done for her. Holding them to her late husband's wishes, written into his will, that they never favor "wrong, oppression, or tyranny of any sort, public or private"—an injunction that apparently did not prohibit slaveholding—she had prepared them well for the revolutionary crises of the 1770s.

Eliza Pinckney and her sons shared with such contemporaries as Benjamin Franklin the confidence spawned by the Enlightenment that people could create a rational basis for a moral life. Her children would apply this faith in reason to political institutions as well, participating in writing constitutions for the state of South Carolina and for the national government.

BEFORE YOU READ

1. What examples do you find in Eliza Pinckney's writings of the use of reason to develop a moral code?

2. How practical are Eliza Pinckney's resolutions? Do they represent moderation of the sort that was cherished in the eighteenth century?

3. How do Eliza Pinckney's resolutions compare with Benjamin Franklin's scheme for moral perfection?

THE EIGHTEEN-YEAR-OLD ELIZA LUCAS DESCRIBES HER DAILY ROUTINE

To Miss Bartlett (1741)

In general then I rise at five o'Clock in the morning, read till seven — then take a walk in the garden or fields, see that the Servants are at their respective business, then to breakfast. The first hour after breakfast is spent in music, the next is constantly employed in recollecting something I have learned, least for want of practise it should be quite lost, such as French and short hand. After that, I devote the rest of the time till I dress for dinner, to our little Polly, and two black girls who I teach to read, and if I have my papa's approbation (my mama's I have got) I intend for school mistress's for the rest of the Negroe children. Another scheme you see, but to proceed, the first hour after dinner, as the first after breakfast, at music, the rest of the afternoon in needle work till candle light, and from that time to bed time read or write; 'tis the fashion here to carry our work abroad with us so that having company, without they are great strangers, is no interruption to your affair, but I have particular matters for particular days which is an interruption to mine. Mondays my music Master is here. Tuesday my friend Mrs. Chardon (about 3 miles distant) and I are constantly engaged to each other, she at our house one Tuesday I at hers the next, and this is one of the happiest days I spent at Wappoo. Thursday the whole day except what the necessary affairs of the family take up, is spent in writing, either on the business of the plantations or on letters to my friends. Every other Friday, if no company, we go a visiting, so that I go abroad once a week and no oftener.

ASSUMING ADULT RESPONSIBILITIES

To Miss Bartlett (between 1742 and 1744)

. . . I am engaged with the rudiments of the Law, to which I am yet but a stranger, and what adds to my mortification I soon discovered that Doctor Wood [a law book] wants the consideration of your good Uncle, who with a graceful ease and good nature peculiar to himself, is always ready to instruct the ignorant. But this rustic seems by no means to court my acquaintance for he often treats me with such cramp phrases, I am unable to understand him.

However I hope in a short time with the help of Dictionary's French and English, we shall be better friends; nor shall I grudge a little pains and application, if that will make me useful to any of my poor neighbours, we have some in this neighbourhood, who have a little land a few slaves and cattle to

Harriott Horry Ravenel, *Eliza Pinckney* (New York: Charles Scribner's Sons, 1896), pp. 30–31, 51–52, 100, 113, 115–18, 246, 313–14.

give their children, that never think of making a will 'till they come upon a sick bed, and find it too expensive to send to town for a lawyer.

If you will not laugh too immoderately at me I'll trust you with a secret. I have made two wills already! I know I have done no harm, for I learned my lesson very perfect, and know how to convey by will, Estates, Real and Personal, and never forget in its proper place, him and his heirs forever, nor that 'tis to be signed by three witnesses in presence of one another; but the most comfortable remembrance of all is that Doctor Wood says, the Law makes great allowance for Last Wills and Testaments, presuming the testator could not have council learned in the law. But after all what can I do if a poor creature lies a-dying, and their family takes it into their head that I can serve them. I can't refuse; but when they are well, and able to employ a lawyer, I always shall.

A widow hereabouts with a pretty little fortune, teased me intolerable to draw her a marriage settlement, but it was out of my depth and I absolutely refused it, so she got an abler hand to do it, indeed she could afford it, but I could not get off from being one of the Trustees to her Settlement, and an old gentleman the other.

I shall begin to think myself an old woman before I am well a young one, having these weighty affairs upon my hands.

RESPONDING TO ADVICE ABOUT HOW TO BEHAVE AS A WIFE

To Her Father (1742)

I am greatly obliged to you for your very good advice in my present happy relation. I think it entirely reasonable, and 'tis with great truth that I assure you 'tis not more my duty than my inclination to follow it; for making it the business of my life to please a man of Mr Pinckney's merit even in triffles, I esteem a pleasing task: and I am well assured the acting out of my proper province and invading his, would be an inexcusable breach of prudence; as his superiour understanding, (without any other consideration,) would point him to dictate, and leave me nothing but the easy task of obeying.

A REPUBLICAN MOTHER

To Mrs. Bartlett (May 20, 1745)

. . . Since Mr P's [Pinckney] last to Mr B. [Bartlett] Heaven has blest us with a son, and a fine boy it is. May he inherit all his father's virtues, his good Sense, his sincere and generous mind, with all his sweetness of disposition. Shall I give you the trouble my dear Madam to buy him the new toy (a discription of which I inclose) to teach him according to Mr Lock's [the philosopher John Locke] method (which I have carefully studied) to play himself into learning. Mr Pinckney himself has been contriving a set of toys to teach him his letters by the time he can speak, you perceive we begin by times for he is not yet four months old.

To Her Son Charles Cotesworth Pinckney
(about 1769)

I am alarmed my dear child at the account of your being extremely thin, it is said owing to intense study, and I apprehend your constitution may be hurt; which affects me very much, conscious as I am how much, and how often, I have urged you from your childhood to a close application to your studies; but how shortsighted are poor mortals! Should I by my over solicitude for your passing thro' life with every advantage, be a means of injuring your constitution, and depriving you of that invaluable blessing, health, how shall I answer to myself, the hurting a child so truly dear to me, and deservedly so; who has lived to near twenty-three years of age without once offending me.

ELIZA PINCKNEY'S RESOLUTIONS

I am resolved by the Grace of God assisting me to keep these resolutions which I have frequently made, and do now again renew.

I am resolved to believe in God; that he is, and is a rewarder of all that diligently seek him. To believe firmly and constantly in all his attributes etc. etc. I am resolved to believe in him, to fear him and love him with all the powers and faculties of my soul. To keep a steady eye to his commands, and to govern myself in every circumstance of life by the rules of the Gospel of Christ, whose disciple I profess myself, and as such will live and dye.

I am resolved by the Divine will, not to be anxious or doubtful, not to be fearful of any accident or misfortune that may happen to me or mine, not to regard the frowns of the world, but to keep a steady upright conduct before my God, and before man, doing my duty and contented to leave the event to God's Providence.

I am resolved by the same Grace to govern my passions, to endeavour constantly to subdue every vice and improve in every virtue, and in order to this I will not give way to any the least notions of pride, haughtiness, ambition, ostentation, or contempt of others. I will not give way to envy, ill will, evil speaking, ingratitude, or uncharitableness in word, in thought, or in deed, or to passion or peavishness, nor to sloth or idleness, but to endeavour after all the contrary virtues, humility, charity, etc, etc, and to be always usefully or innocently imploy'd.

I am resolved not to be luxurious or extravagant in the management of my table and family on the one hand, nor niggardly and covetous, or too anxiously concern'd about it on the other, but to endeavour after a due medium; to manage with hospitality and generosity as much as is in our power, to have always plenty with frugality and good economy.

To be decent but frugal in my own expences.

To be charitably disposed to all mankind.

I am resolved by the Divine Assistance to fill the several stations wherein Providence has placed me to the best advantage.

To make a good wife to my dear husband in all its several branches; to make all my actions correspond with that sincere love and duty I bear him. To pray for him, to contribute all in my power to the good of his Soul and to the peace and satisfaction of his mind, to be careful of his health, of his interests, of his children, and of his reputation; to do him all the good in my power; and next to my God, to make it my study to please him.

I am resolved to make a good child to my mother; to do all I am able to give her comfort and make her happy.

I am resolved to be a good mother to my children, to pray for them, to set them good examples, to give them good advice, to be careful both of their souls and bodys, to watch over their tender minds, to carefully root out the first appearing and buildings of vice, and to instill piety, virtue and true religion into them; to spair no pains or trouble to do them good; to correct their errors whatever uneasiness it may give myself; and never omit to encourage every virtue I may see dawning in them.

I am resolved to make a good sister both to my own and my husband's brothers and sisters, to do them all the good I can, to treat them with affection, kindness, and good-manners, to do them all the good I can etc, etc.

I am resolved to make a good mistress to my servants, to treat them with humanity and good nature; to give them sufficient and comfortable clothing and provisions, and all things necessary for them. To be careful and tender of them in their sickness, to reprove them for their faults, to encourage them when they do well, and pass over small faults; not to be tyrannical peavish or impatient towards them, but to make their lives as comfortable as I can.

I am resolved to be a sincere and faithful friend wherever I profess'd it, and as much as in me lies an agreeable and innocent companion, and a universal lover of all mankind.

All these resolutions by God's assistance I will keep to my life's end.

So help me O My God! AMEN.

Memorandum

Read over this dayly to assist my memory as to every particular contained in this paper. *Mem.* Before I leave my chamber recollect in General the business to be done that day.

ON OLD AGE

To Mr. Keate (April 2, 1786)

Outliving those we love is what gives the principal gloom to long protracted life. There was never anything very tremendous to me in the prospect of old age, the loss of friends excepted, but this loss I have keenly felt. This is all the terror that the Spectre with the Scythe and Hour-glass ever exhibited to my view, Nor since the arrival of this formidable period have I had anything else to deplore from it. I regret no pleasures that I can't enjoy, and I enjoy some that

I could not have had at an early season. I now see my children grown up, and, blessed be God! see them such as I hoped. What is there in youthful enjoyment preferable to this? What is there in youthful enjoyment preferable to passions subdued? What to the tranquility which the calm evening of life naturally produces? Sincere is my gratitude to Heaven for the advantages of this period of life, as well as for those that are passed.

The Bloody Massacre perpetrated in King — ¦ — Street BOSTON on March 5th 1770 by a party of the 29th REG

BUTCHER'S HALL

Engrav'd Printed & Sold by Paul Revere Boston

Unhappy Boston! see thy Sons deplore.
Thy hallow'd Walks besmear'd with guiltless Gore.
While faithless P——n and his savage Bands.
With murd'rous Rancour stretch their bloody Hands;
Like fierce Barbarians grinning o'er their Prey,
Approve the Carnage, and enjoy the Day.

If scalding drops from Rage from Anguish Wrung
If speechless Sorrows lab'ring for a Tongue,
Or if a weeping World can ought appease
The plaintive Ghosts of Victims such as these;
The Patriot's copious Tears for each are shed,
A glorious Tribute which embalms the Dead.

But know Fate summons to that awful Goal,
Where Justice strips the Murd'rer of his Soul
Should venal C——ts the scandal of the Land,
Snatch the relentless Villain from her Hand,
Keen Execrations on this Plate inscrib'd,
Shall reach a Judge who never can be brib'd

The unhappy Sufferers were Messrs. Saml. Gray, Saml. Maverick, Jams. Caldwell, Crispus Attucks & Patk. Carr

This most famous of all depictions of the Boston Massacre circulated widely both in England and the American colonies. Its title reads "The Fruits of Arbitrary Power; or THE BLOODY MASSACRE perpetrated in King Street, BOSTON, on March 5th, 1770, by a party of the 29TH REG. Engrav'd Printed & Sold by Paul Revere, *Boston*."

PART THREE

Resistance and Revolution

Struggling for Liberty

The generation that guided the colonies through the revolutionary era was welded together, despite the remarkable differences among colonies and their peoples, by a common commitment to American nationality. That nationality they defined partly by their placement in the new continent but in part also by their overwhelmingly British political heritage. Whatever their individual ancestry in the Old World, most Americans thought their practice of self-government to be staunchly and rightly British.

The colonists' adherence to what was perceived as the British past was a major ideological reason for the rupture with Great Britain. When, after 1763, the English enacted restrictive colonial policies to raise revenues for the administration of an enlarged empire that now included India and Canada, the colonists almost instantly perceived threats to their traditional liberties. Newspapers like the *Boston Gazette* and political leaders and pamphleteers like John Adams and Landon Carter directly challenged Great Britain's right to legislate for the colonies. So did many English critics of the mother country's governance of her North American colonies, as evidenced by the brisk market in England for Paul Revere's depiction of the Boston Massacre. Such leaders as Thomas Preston discovered how the rules of order had changed. Ordinary people like shoemaker George R. T. Hewes, who took part in both the Boston Massacre and the Boston Tea Party, and Joseph Plumb Martin, who fought throughout the long war, developed new visions of their position in society.

To other colonists, commitment to the British tradition meant adherence to Britain. At least one in six white Americans remained loyal to the king, often at great personal cost, as Philip and Catherine Van Cortlandt's experience illustrated.

For many blacks and native Americans, patriot success portended crushed expectations or even disaster. Landon Carter's slaves took desperate risks seeking freedom and suffered when their gamble failed. Others were more fortunate and secured freedom at the price of expatriation.

The American Revolution challenged long-held convictions that denied the capacity of human beings to use reason in creating a new form of government. Many Americans, like Abigail Adams and others who earnestly argued for and against ratification of the Constitution of the United States, possessed a vision of the American Revolution as one of the climactic events of human history: a demonstration that people of virtue and reason could deliberately establish order and justice.

Points of View:
The Boston Massacre (1770)

16

A British Officer's Description

Thomas Preston

Some historians in recent years have stressed the role of the "crowd" in the coming of the American Revolution. Anonymous colonists taking to the streets in the years after 1763 were an important part of the dynamic of revolution.

First-hand accounts of an event do not necessarily make it easy to determine precisely what occurred. In early 1770 British troops were quartered in Boston. Many townspeople resented their presence, and on March 5 a mob of about sixty attacked a small group of soldiers. In the ensuing disturbance, some soldiers, without orders, fired on the mob, killing five people and wounding eight. The incident was taken up by anti-British radicals—the "patriots"—in Boston, who called it the "Boston Massacre." This selection is the account of the British officer who was tried for murder along with several of his men. John Adams and Josiah Quincy, Jr., convinced that anyone accused of a crime should have legal counsel, defended the men. Two of the soldiers were convicted of manslaughter and the others, including Preston, were acquitted, but the "Massacre" served to inflame anti-British sentiment throughout the colonies.

BEFORE YOU READ

1. What was Captain Preston's view of the Boston crowd?
2. Do you think his soldiers were justified in using violence?
3. Do you think the outcome of the trial was fair?

CAPTAIN THOMAS PRESTON'S ACCOUNT
OF THE BOSTON MASSACRE
(MARCH 13, 1770)

It is [a] matter of too great notoriety to need any proofs that the arrival of his Majesty's troops in Boston was extremely obnoxious to its inhabitants. They have ever used all means in their power to weaken the regiments, and to bring them into contempt by promoting and aiding desertions, and with impunity, even where there has been the clearest evidence of the fact, and by grossly and falsely propagating untruths concerning them. On the arrival of the 64th and 65th their ardour seemingly began to abate; it being too expensive to buy off so many, and attempts of that kind rendered too dangerous from the numbers.

And [conflict in the streets of Boston] has ever since their departure been breaking out with greater violence after their embarkation. One of their justices, most thoroughly acquainted with the people and their intentions, on the trial of a man of the 14th Regiment, openly and publicly in the hearing of great numbers of people and from the seat of justice, declared "that the soldiers must now take care of themselves, *nor trust too much to their arms*, for they were but a handful; that the inhabitants carried weapons concealed under their clothes, and would destroy them in a moment, *if they pleased.*" This, considering the malicious temper of the people, was an alarming circumstance to the soldiery. Since which several disputes have happened between the townspeople and the soldiers of both regiments, the former being encouraged thereto by the countenance of even some of the magistrates, and by the protection of all the party against government. In general such disputes have been kept too secret from the officers. On the 2d instant two of the 29th going through one Gray's ropewalk, the rope-makers insultingly asked them if they would empty a vault. This unfortunately had the desired effect by provoking the soldiers, and from words they went to blows. Both parties suffered in this affray, and finally the soldiers retired to their quarters. The officers, on the first knowledge of this transaction, took every precaution in their power to prevent any ill consequence. Notwithstanding which, single quarrels could not be prevented, the inhabitants constantly provoking and abusing the soldiery. The insolence as well as utter hatred of the inhabitants to the troops increased daily, insomuch that Monday and Tuesday, the 5th and 6th instant, were privately agreed on for a general engagement, in consequence of which several of the militia came from the country armed to join their friends, menacing to destroy any who should oppose them. This plan has since been discovered.

On Monday night about 8 o'clock two soldiers were attacked and beat. But the party of the townspeople in order to carry matters to the utmost length, broke into two meeting houses and rang the alarm bells, which I supposed was for fire as usual, but was soon undeceived. About 9 some of the guard came to

Merrill Jensen, ed., *English Historical Documents*, vol. 9 (London, 1964), pp. 750–53.

and informed me the town inhabitants were assembling to attack the troops, and that the bells were ringing as the signal for that purpose and not for fire, and the beacon intended to be fired to bring in the distant people of the country. This, as I was captain of the day, occasioned my repairing immediately to the main guard. On my way there I saw the people in great commotion, and heard them use the most cruel and horrid threats against the troops. In a few minutes after I reached the guard, about 100 people passed it and went towards the custom house where the king's money is lodged. They immediately surrounded the sentry posted there, and with clubs and other weapons threatened to execute their vengeance on him. I was soon informed by a townsman their intention was to carry off the soldier from his post and probably murder him. On which I desired him to return for further intelligence, and he soon came back and assured me he heard the mob declare they would murder him. This I feared might be a prelude to their plundering the king's chest. I immediately sent a non-commissioned officer and 12 men to protect both the sentry and the king's money, and very soon followed myself to prevent, if possible, all disorder, fearing lest the officer and soldiers, by the insults and provocations of the rioters, should be thrown off their guard and commit some rash act. They soon rushed through the people, and by charging their bayonets in half-circles, kept them at a little distance. Nay, so far was I from intending the death of any person that I suffered the troops to go to the spot where the unhappy affair took place without any loading in their pieces; nor did I ever give orders for loading them. This remiss conduct in me perhaps merits censure; yet it is evidence, resulting from the nature of things, which is the best and surest that can be offered, that my intention was not to act offensively, but the contrary part, and that not without compulsion. The mob still increased and were more outrageous, striking their clubs or bludgeons one against another, and calling out, come on you rascals, you bloody backs, you lobster scoundrels, fire if you dare, G—d damn you, fire and be damned, we know you dare not, and much more such language was used. At this time I was between the soldiers and the mob, parleying with, and endeavouring all in my power to persuade them to retire peaceably, but to no purpose. They advanced to the points of the bayonets, struck some of them and even the muzzles of the pieces, and seemed to be endeavoring to close with the soldiers. On which some well behaved persons asked me if the guns were charged. I replied yes. They then asked me if I intended to order the men to fire. I answered no, by no means, observing to them that I was advanced before the muzzles of the men's pieces, and must fall a sacrifice if they fired; that the soldiers were upon the half cock and charged bayonets, and my giving the word fire under those circumstances would prove me to be no officer. While I was thus speaking, one of the soldiers having received a severe blow with a stick, stepped a little on one side and instantly fired, on which turning to and asking him why he fired without orders, I was struck with a club on my arm, which for some time deprived me of the use of it, which blow had it been placed on my head, most probably would have destroyed me. On this a general attack was made on the men by a great number of heavy clubs and snowballs being thrown at them, by which all our lives were in imminent danger, some persons at the same time from behind calling out, damn your bloods — why don't you fire. Instantly three or four of the soldiers fired, one after another, and directly after three more in the same confusion and hurry. The mob then ran away, except three unhappy men who instantly expired, in which number was Mr. Gray at whose rope-walk the prior quarrels took place; one more is since dead, three others are dangerously, and four slightly wounded. The whole of this melancholy affair was transacted in almost 20 minutes. On my asking the soldiers why they fired without orders, they said they heard the word fire and supposed it came from me. This might be the case as many of the mob called out fire, fire, but I assured the men that I gave no such order; that my words were, don't fire, stop your firing. In short, it was scarcely possible for the soldiers to know who said fire, or don't fire, or stop your firing. On the people's assembling again to take away the dead bodies, the soldiers supposing them coming to attack them, were making ready to fire again, which I prevented by striking up their firelocks with my hand. Immediately after a townsman came and told me that 4 or 5000 people were assembled in the next street, and had sworn to take my life with every man's with me. On which I judged it unsafe to remain there any longer, and therefore sent the party and sentry to the main guard, where the street is narrow and short, there telling them off into street firings, divided and planted them at each end of the street to secure their rear, momently expecting an attack, as there was a constant cry of the inhabitants to arms, to arms, turn out with your guns; and the town drums beating to arms, I ordered my drums to beat to arms, and being soon after joined by the different companies of the 29th regiment, I formed them as the guard into street firings. The 14th regiment also got under arms but remained at their barracks. I immediately sent a sergeant with a party to Colonel Dalrymple, the commanding officer, to acquaint him with every particular. Several officers going to join their regiment were knocked down by the mob, one very much wounded and his sword taken from him. The lieutenant-governor and Colonel Carr soon after met at the head of the 29th regiment and agreed that the regiment should retire to their barracks, and the people to their houses, but I kept the picket to strengthen the guard. It was with great difficulty that the lieutenant-governor prevailed on the people to be quiet and retire. At last they all went off, excepting about a hundred.

A Council was immediately called, on the breaking up of which three justices met and issued a warrant to apprehend me and eight soldiers. On hearing of this procedure I instantly went to the sheriff and surrendered myself, though for the space of 4 hours I had it in my power to have made my escape, which I most undoubtedly should have attempted and could have easily executed, had I been the least conscious of any guilt. On the examination before the justices, two witnesses swore that I gave the men orders to fire. The one testified he was within two feet of me; the other that I swore at the men for not firing at the first word. Others swore they heard me use the word "fire," but whether do or do not fire, they could not say; others that they heard the word fire, but could not say if it came from me. The next day they got 5 or 6 more to swear I gave the word to fire. So bitter and inveterate are many of the malcontents here that they are industriously using every method to fish out evidence to prove it was a concerted scheme to murder the inhabitants. Others are infusing the utmost malice and revenge into the minds of the people who are to be my jurors by false publications, votes of towns, and all other artifices. That so from a settled rancour against the officers and troops in general, the suddenness of my trial after the affair while the people's minds are all greatly inflamed, I am, though perfectly innocent, under most unhappy circumstances, having nothing in reason to expect but the loss of life in a very ignominious manner, without the interposition of his Majesty's royal goodness.

17

Colonial Accounts

George Robert Twelves Hewes and the *Boston Gazette and Country Journal*

George Robert Twelves Hewes (1742–1840) was in his nineties in 1833 when he told James Hawkes the story of his experiences in revolutionary Boston. Hewes claimed not to have read any published account of the happenings there and could "therefore only give the information which I derived from the event[s] of the day." Careful checking by the distinguished labor historian Alfred F. Young has authenticated much of Hewes's account. His story provides a rare opportunity to see an ordinary citizen taking a direct part in a great historical event. Hewes also participated in the Boston Tea Party of December 16, 1773, as one of the "Indians" pitching casks of tea into the harbor. These experiences had a profound personal effect on Hewes. In the 1760s he had been an awkward young cobbler nervously deferring to his aristocratic customers. A decade later, with these experiences behind him, he would risk his employment and perhaps even a beating for his refusal to take off his hat "for any man." For Hewes, the American Revolution meant that the poor and the ordinary no longer owed the rich and powerful what in the eighteenth century was called "deference."

The Boston Gazette and Country Journal *was one of several struggling journals published in Boston. Ever since being threatened with taxation under the Stamp Act of 1763, colonial newspapers, particularly those in Boston, had tended toward the patriot side. Journalism was not yet a profession, as most newspapers were produced by printers or postmasters, and the tradition of impartial reporting was still far in the future.*

BEFORE YOU READ

1. What according to Hewes sparked the Boston Massacre?
2. What was his role in the event and subsequent trial?

3. How does the account of the riot as reported in the *Boston Gazette and Country Journal* differ from Hewes's account?

4. What political points did the *Boston Gazette and Country Journal* make about the Boston Massacre?

ACCOUNT OF GEORGE ROBERT TWELVES HEWES

[W]hen I was at the age of twenty-six, I married the daughter of Benjamin Sumner, of Boston. At the time of our intermarriage, the age of my wife was seventeen. We lived together very happily seventy years. She died at the age of eighty-seven.

At the time when the British troops were first stationed at Boston, we had several children, the exact number I do not recollect. By our industry and mutual efforts we were improving our condition.

An account of the massacre of the citizens of Boston, in the year 1770, on the 5th of March, by some of the British troops, has been committed to the record of our history, as one of those interesting events which lead to the revolutionary contest that resulted in our Independence. . . . We have been informed by the historians of the revolution, that a series of provocations had excited strong prejudices, and inflamed the passion of the British soldiery against our citizens, previous to the commencement of open hostilities; and prepared their minds to burst out into acts of violence on the application of a single spark of additional excitement, and which finally resulted in the unfortunate massacre of a number of our citizens.

On my inquiring of Hewes what knowledge he had of that event, he replied, that he knew nothing from history, as he had never read any thing relating to it from any publication whatever, and can therefore only give the information which I derived from the event of the day upon which the catastrophe happened. On that day, one of the British officers applied to a barber, to be shaved and dressed; the master of the shop, whose name was Pemont, told his apprentice boy he might serve him, and receive the pay to himself, while Pemont left the shop. The boy accordingly served him, but the officer, for some reason unknown to me, went away from the shop without paying him for his service. After the officer had been gone some time, the boy went to the house where he was, with his account, to demand payment of his bill, but the sentinel, who was before the door, would not give him admittance, nor permit him to see the officer; and as some angry words were interchanged between the sentinel and the boy, a considerable number of the people from the vicinity, soon gathered at the place where they were, which was in King street, and I was soon on the ground among them. The violent agitation of the citizens, not only on account of the abuse offered to the boy, but other causes of excitement, then fresh in the recollection, was such that the sentinel began to be apprehensive of danger, and

James Hawkes [supposed author], *A Retrospect of the Boston Tea-Party, with a Memoir of George R. T. Hewes, a Survivor of the Little Band of Patriots who Drowned the Tea in Boston Harbour in 1773, by a Citizen of New York* (New York, 1834), pp. 27–33, 36–41.

knocked at the door of the house, where the officers were, and told the servant who came to the door, that he was afraid of his life, and would quit his post unless he was protected. The officers in the house then sent a messenger to the guard-house, to require Captain Preston to come with a sufficient number of his soldiers to defend them from the threatened violence of the people. On receiving the message, he came immediately with a small guard of grenadiers, and paraded them before the custom-house, where the British officers were shut up. Captain Preston then ordered the people to disperse, but they said they would not, they were in the king's highway, and had as good a right to be there as he had. The captain of the guard then said to them, if you do not disperse, I will fire upon you, and then gave orders to his men to make ready, and immediately after gave them orders to fire. Three of our citizens fell dead on the spot, and two, who were wounded, died the next day; and nine others were also wounded. The persons who were killed I well recollect, said Hewes; they were, Gray, a rope maker, Marverick, a young man, Colwell, who was the mate of Captain Colton, Attuck, a mulatto, and Carr, who was an Irishman. Captain Preston then immediately fled with his grenadiers back to the guard-house. The people who were assembled on that occasion, then immediately chose a committee to report to the governor the result of Captain Preston's conduct, and to demand of him satisfaction. The governor told the committee, that if the people would be quiet that night he would give them satisfaction, so far as was in his power; the next morning Captain Preston, and those of his guard who were concerned in the massacre, were, accordingly, by order of the governor, given up, and taken into custody the next morning, and committed to prison.

It is not recollected that the offence given to the barber's boy is mentioned by the historians of the revolution; yet there can be no doubt of its correctness. The account of this single one of the exciting causes of the massacre, related by Hewes, at this time, was in answer to the question of his personal knowledge of that event.

A knowledge of the spirit of those times will easily lead us to conceive, that the manner of the British officers application to the barber, was a little too strongly tinctured with the dictatorial hauteur, to conciliate the views of equality, which at that period were supremely predominant in the minds of those of the whig party, even in his humble occupation; and that the disrespectful notice of his loyal customer, in consigning him to the attention of his apprentice boy, and abruptly leaving his shop, was intended to be treated by the officer with contempt, by so underrating the services of his apprentice, as to deem any reward for them beneath his attention. The boy too, may be supposed to have imbibed so much of the spirit which distinguished that period of our history, that he was willing to improve any occasion to contribute his share to the public excitement; to add an additional spark to the fire of political dissention which was enkindling.

When Hewes arrived at the spot where the massacre happened, it appears his attention was principally engaged by the clamours of those who were disposed to aid the boy in avenging the insult offered to him by the British officer, and probably heard nothing, at that time, of any other of the many exciting causes which lead to that disastrous event, though it appeared from his general conversation, his knowledge of them was extensive and accurate.

But to pursue the destiny of Captain Preston, and the guard who fired on the citizens; in about a fortnight after, said Hewes, they were brought to trial and indicted for the crime of murder.

The soldiers were tried first, and acquitted, on the ground, that in firing upon the citizens of Boston, they only acted in proper obedience to the captain's orders. When Preston, their captain, was tried, I was called as one of the witnesses, on the part of the government, and testified, that I believed it was the same man, Captain Preston, that ordered his soldiers to make ready, who also ordered them to fire. Mr. John Adams, former president of the United States, was advocate for the prisoners, and denied the fact, that Captain Preston gave orders to his men to fire; and on his cross examination of me asked whether my position was such, that I could see the captain's lips in motion when the order to fire was given; to which I answered, that I could not. Although the evidence of Preston's having given orders to the soldiers to fire, was thought by the jury sufficient to acquit them, it was not thought to be of weight enough to convict him of a capital offence; he also was acquitted.

Although the excitement which had been occasioned by the wanton massacre of our citizens, had in some measure abated, it was never extinguished until open hostilities commenced, and we had declared our independence. The citizens of Boston continued inflexible in their demand, that every British soldier should be withdrawn from the town, and within four days after the massacre, the whole army decamped. But the measures of the British parliament, which led the American colonies to a separation from that government, were not abandoned.

ACCOUNT IN *BOSTON GAZETTE AND COUNTRY JOURNAL*

March 12, 1770

The town of Boston affords a recent and melancholy demonstration of the destructive consequences of quartering troops among citizens in a time of peace, under a pretence of supporting the laws and aiding civil authority; every considerate and unprejudiced person among us was deeply impressed with the apprehension of these consequences when it was known that a number of regiments were ordered to this town under such a pretext, but in reality to enforce oppressive measures; to awe and control the legislative as well as executive power of the province, and to quell a spirit of liberty, which however it may have been basely opposed and even ridiculed by some, would do honour to any age or country. A few persons amongst us had determined to use all their influence to procure so destructive a measure with a view to their securely en-

The Boston Gazette and Country Journal, March 12, 1770. Reprinted in Merrill Jensen, ed., *English Historical Documents*, vol. 9 (London: Eyre and Spottiswoode, 1955) pp. 745–49.

joying the profits of an American revenue, and unhappily both for Britain and this country they found means to effect it.

It is to Governor Bernard, the commissioners, their confidants and coadjutors, that we are indebted as the procuring cause of a military power in this capital. The Boston Journal of Occurrences, as printed in Mr. Holt's *New York Gazette*, from time to time, afforded many striking instances of the distresses brought upon the inhabitants by this measure; and since those Journals have been discontinued, our troubles from that quarter have been growing upon us. We have known a party of soldiers in the face of day fire off a loaden musket upon the inhabitants, others have been pricked with bayonets, and even our magistrates assaulted and put in danger of their lives, when offenders brought before them have been rescued; and why those and other bold and base criminals have as yet escaped the punishment due to their crimes may be soon matter of enquiry by the representative body of this people. It is natural to suppose that when the inhabitants of this town saw those laws which had been enacted for their security, and which they were ambitious of holding up to the soldiery, eluded, they should more commonly resent for themselves; and accordingly it has so happened. Many have been the squabbles between them and the soldiery; but it seems their being often worsted by our youth in those rencounters, has only served to irritate the former. What passed at Mr. Gray's rope-walk has already been given the public and may be said to have led the way to the late catastrophe. That the rope-walk lads, when attacked by superior numbers, should defend themselves with so much spirit and success in the club-way, was too mortifying, and perhaps it may hereafter appear that even some of their officers were unhappily affected with this circumstance. Divers stories were propagated among the soldiery that served to agitate their spirits; particularly on the Sabbath that one Chambers, a sergeant, represented as a sober man, had been missing the preceding day and must therefore have been murdered by the townsmen. An officer of distinction so far credited this report that he entered Mr. Gray's rope-walk that Sabbath; and when required of by that gentleman as soon as he could meet him, the occasion of his so doing, the officer replied that it was to look if the sergeant said to be murdered had not been hid there. This sober sergeant was found on the Monday unhurt in a house of pleasure. The evidences already collected show that many threatenings had been thrown out by the soldiery, but we do not pretend to say that there was any preconcerted plan. When the evidences are published, the world will judge. We may, however, venture to declare that it appears too probable from their conduct that some of the soldiery aimed to draw and provoke the townsmen into squabbles, and that they then intended to make use of other weapons than canes, clubs, or bludgeons.

On the evening of Monday, being the fifth current, several soldiers of the 29th Regiment were seen parading the streets with their drawn cutlasses and bayonets, abusing and wounding numbers of the inhabitants.

A few minutes after nine o'clock four youths, named Edward Archbald, William Merchant, Francis Archbald, and John Leech, jun., came down Cornhill together, and separating at Doctor Loring's corner, the two former were passing the narrow alley leading to Murray's barrack in which was a soldier brandishing a broad sword of an uncommon size against the walls, out of which he struck fire plentifully. A person of mean countenance armed with a large cudgel bore him company. Edward Archbald admonished Mr. Merchant to take care of the sword, on which the soldier turned round and struck Archbald on the arm, then pushed at Merchant and pierced through his clothes inside the arm close to the armpit and grazed the skin. Merchant then struck the soldier with a short stick he had; and the other person ran to the barrack and brought with him two soldiers, one armed with a pair of tongs, the other with a shovel. He with the tongs pursued Archbald back through the alley, collared and laid him over the head with the tongs. The noise brought people together; and John Hicks, a young lad, coming up, knocked the soldier down but let him get up again; and more lads gathering, drove them back to the barrack where the boys stood some time as it were to keep them in. In less than a minute ten or twelve of them came out with drawn cutlasses, clubs, and bayonets and set upon the unarmed boys and young folk who stood them a little while but, finding the inequality of their equipment, dispersed. On hearing the noise, one Samuel Atwood came up to see what was the matter; and entering the alley from dock square, heard the latter part of the combat; and when the boys had dispersed he met the ten or twelve soldiers aforesaid rushing down the alley towards the square and asked them if they intended to murder people? They answered Yes, by G—d, root and branch! With that one of them struck Mr. Atwood with a club which was repeated by another; and being unarmed, he turned to go off and received a wound on the left shoulder which reached the bone and gave him much pain. Retreating a few steps, Mr. Atwood met two officers and said, gentlemen, what is the matter? They answered, you'll see by and by. Immediately after, those heroes appeared in the square, asking where were the boogers? where were the cowards? But notwithstanding their fierceness to naked men, one of them advanced towards a youth who had a split of a raw stave in his hand and said, damn them, here is one of them. But the young man seeing a person near him with a drawn sword and good cane ready to support him, held up his stave in defiance; and they quietly passed by him up the little alley by Mr. Silsby's to King Street where they attacked single and unarmed persons till they raised much clamour, and then turned down Cornhill Street, insulting all they met in like manner and pursuing some to their very doors. Thirty or forty persons, mostly lads, being by this means gathered in King Street, Capt. Preston with a party of men with charged bayonets, came from the main guard to the commissioner's house, the soldiers pushing their bayonets, crying, make way! They took place by the custom house and, continuing to push to drive the people off, pricked some in several places, on which they were clamorous and, it is said, threw snow balls. On this, the Captain commanded them to fire; and more snow balls coming, he again said, damn you, fire, be the consequence what it will! One soldier then fired, and a townsman with a cudgel struck him over the hands with such force that he dropped his firelock; and, rushing forward, aimed a blow at the Captain's head which grazed his hat and fell pretty heavy upon his arm. However, the soldiers continued the fire successively till seven or eight or, as some say, eleven guns were discharged.

By this fatal maneuver three men were laid dead on the spot and two more struggling for life; but what showed a degree of cruelty unknown to British troops, at least since the house of Hanover has directed their operations, was an attempt to fire upon or push with their bayonets the persons who undertook to remove the slain and wounded!

Mr. Benjamin Leigh, now undertaker in the Delph manufactory, came up; and after some conversation with Capt. Preston relative to his conduct in this affair, advised him to draw off his men, with which he complied.

The dead are Mr. Samuel Gray, killed on the spot, the ball entering his head and beating off a large portion of his skull.

A mulatto man named Crispus Attucks, who was born in Framingham, but lately belonged to New-Providence and was here in order to go for North Carolina, also killed instantly, two balls entering his breast, one of them in special goring the right lobe of the lungs and a great part of the liver most horribly.

Mr. James Caldwell, mate of Capt. Morton's vessel, in like manner killed by two balls entering his back.

Mr. Samuel Maverick, a promising youth of seventeen years of age, son of the widow Maverick, and an apprentice to Mr. Greenwood, ivory-turner, mortally wounded; a ball went through his belly and was cut out at his back. He died the next morning.

A lad named Christopher Monk, about seventeen years of age, an apprentice to Mr. Walker, shipwright, wounded; a ball entered his back about four inches above the left kidney near the spine and was cut out of the breast on the same side. Apprehended he will die.

A lad named John Clark, about seventeen years of age, whose parents live at Medford, and an apprentice to Capt. Samuel Howard of this town, wounded; a ball entered just above his groin and came out at his hip on the opposite side. Apprehended he will die.

Mr. Edward Payne of this town, merchant, standing at his entry door received a ball in his arm which shattered some of the bones.

Mr. John Green, tailor, coming up Leverett's Lane, received a ball just under his hip and lodged in the under part of his thigh, which was extracted.

Mr. Robert Patterson, a seafaring man, who was the person that had his trousers shot through in Richardson's affair, wounded; a ball went through his right arm, and he suffered a great loss of blood.

Mr. Patrick Carr, about thirty years of age, who worked with Mr. Field, leather breeches-maker in Queen Street, wounded; a ball entered near his hip and went out at his side.

A lad named David Parker, an apprentice to Mr. Eddy, the wheelwright, wounded; a ball entered in his thigh.

The people were immediately alarmed with the report of this horrid massacre, the bells were set a-ringing, and great numbers soon assembled at the place where this tragical scene had been acted. Their feelings may be better conceived than expressed; and while some were taking care of the dead and wounded, the rest were in consultation what to do in those dreadful circumstances. But so little intimidated were they, notwithstanding their being within a few yards of the main guard and seeing the 29th Regiment under arms and drawn up in King Street, that they kept their station and appeared, as an officer of rank expressed it, ready to run upon the very muzzles of their muskets. The lieutenant-governor soon came into the town house and there met some of his Majesty's Council and a number of civil magistrates. A considerable body of the people immediately entered the council chamber and expressed themselves to his honour with a freedom and warmth becoming the occasion. He used his utmost endeavours to pacify them, requesting that they would let the matter subside for the night and promising to do all in his power that justice should be done and the law have its course. Men of influence and weight with the people were not wanting on their part to procure their compliance with his Honour's request by representing the horrible consequences of a promiscuous and rash engagement in the night, and assuring them that such measures should be entered upon in the morning as would be agreeable to their dignity and a more likely way of obtaining the best satisfaction for the blood of their fellow townsmen. The inhabitants attended to these suggestions; and the regiment under arms being ordered to their barracks, which was insisted upon by the people, they then separated and returned to their dwellings by one o'clock. At three o'clock Capt. Preston was committed, as were the soldiers who fired, a few hours after him.

Tuesday morning presented a most shocking scene, the blood of our fellow citizens running like water through King Street and the Merchants' Exchange, the principal spot of the military parade for about eighteen months past. Our blood might also be tracked up to the head of Long Lane, and through divers other streets and passages.

At eleven o'clock the inhabitants met at Faneuil Hall; and after some animated speeches becoming the occasion, they chose a committee of fifteen respectable gentlemen to wait upon the lieutenant-governor in Council to request of him to issue his orders for the immediate removal of the troops.

FOR CRITICAL THINKING

1. Look closely at Paul Revere's widely circulated cartoon "The Fruits of Arbitrary Power; or the Bloody Massacre, Perpetuated in King-street, Boston, by a Party of the 29th Regt" (p. 94). Compare the scene Revere depicts with each of the two written accounts of the Boston Massacre. How accurate is Revere's cartoon? With which account does it best agree?

2. If you were John Adams, determined to prove that British officers and soldiers could receive a fair trial in Boston, how would you defend Captain Preston?

3. Compare the Boston Massacre with later urban riots in American history described in your textbook. What similarities and differences do you find?

18

Secret Correspondence of a Loyalist Wife
Catherine Van Cortlandt

The Revolution was also a civil war. While most white Americans favored the patriot cause, loyalists were strong in many areas and among many groups. The areas surrounding New York City and along the Hudson River were predominately Tory, as were the eastern shore of Maryland and much of what was then the western frontier, particularly in the Carolinas and Georgia. Old loyalties died hard. While Eliza Pinckney stood with her sons in the patriot cause, Benjamin Franklin's son William, as governor of New Jersey, was a prominent loyalist. George Washington, already commanding the Continental Army, still drank to the king's health daily until January 1776, when Thomas Paine's Common Sense *convinced him that the day of monarchy had passed.*

Philip Van Cortlandt of Hanover, New Jersey, retaining his allegiance to the king, escaped arrest by a patriot party in December 1776 and entered military service on the British side, receiving his commission from William Franklin. In letters sent to him by secret messenger from the patriot stronghold in which they were living, his wife described the family's plight. Finally, George Washington took pity on the family and gave them a pass to join Van Cortlandt in New York. The Van Cortlandts never returned to New Jersey. Like many loyalists, they migrated first to Nova Scotia and then to England.

BEFORE YOU READ

1. Do you think that Revolutionary soldiers had the right to seize Catherine Van Cortlandt's provisions and destroy her property?

2. Why do you think George Washington gave the family a pass to rejoin Van Cortlandt in New York?

December 15, 1776, Hanover, New Jersey

My dearest love,

You had not left us ten minutes last Sunday when a party of Light Horsemen, headed by Joseph Morris, came to our once peaceful mansion all armed, who said they had positive orders to take you, my dear Philly, prisoner to Easton, and your favourite horse Sampson to be carried to Morristown for the use of General Lee from whom these cruel mandates were issued. What were my emotions on seeing these wretches alight and without ceremony enter the doors you can only conceive, you who know their base characters and how their present errand must be received by your beloved family. When these bloody-minded men came into the dining room our little flock gathered

H. O. H. Vernon-Jackson, ed., "A Loyalist's Wife: Letters of Mrs. Philip Van Cortlandt, December 1776–February 1777," *History Today* 14 (1964): 574–80.

around me and with anxious eyes watched my looks, whilst I was answering questions. . . . One of them (flourishing his sword) swore bitterly that, if you was to be found alive on earth, he would take you or have your heart's blood. This was too much. They fled into their nursery, bursting into tears; screams out, "Oh my dear Pappa, they will kill him, they will kill him." One of the in-human men seemed touched and endeavoured an excuse by saying they were sent by their General and therefore were obliged to do their duty, even though against a person they formerly much esteemed, but had been represented to General Lee as one too dangerous to be permitted to stay in the country. Finding you was certainly gone . . . they went off and left me in a situation . . . scarce to be described. My first care was the nursery to comfort those innocent pledges of our mutual love. . . . Their sobbing and crying had almost overcome them; and they would not be persuaded from a belief that the wretches were gone to murder their dear Pappa. . . .

. . . The house is surrounded by eighteen or twenty armed men every night in expectation of intercepting you, as they observed that you was too much at-tached to your family to be long absent. Our dear children are again taken from school in consequence of the cruel insults they daily receive for the principles of their parents

I now write in fear and trembling and venture this by an honest Dutch farmer who says he will deliver it into your hands.

January 20, 1777, Hanover, New Jersey

My beloved Philly,

. . . The arrival of the Rebel Troops in this neighbourhood has been severely felt by us. Parties continually passing this way were always directed by officious people to stop at our house to breakfast, dine, or stay the night; the horses from the teams were put into our barns to feed, without even the ceremony of ask-ing liberty. During the stay of the officers of the hospital we had some pro-tection. But immediately on their removal, several field officers from the New England line and a company of privates took possession. . . . They were the most disorderly of their species and their officers were from the dregs of the people. Indeed, two lieutenants messed and slept in the kitchen altogether, and would not be prevailed upon to leave their quarters. . . . A French general has also come on the hill at Dashwood, and daily draws his supply for his numer-ous cavalry from our granary and barrack.

Many of our female neighbours have been here, but I find their visits are only to gratify curiosity and to add insult to our unremitted distress. One of them who lives across the river, whose family we took so much pleasure in re-lieving when friendless . . . said that formerly she always respected you and loved the ground over which you walked, but now could with pleasure see your blood run down the road. . . . The pious, devout and Reverend Mr. Green is very industrious in promoting your ruin by declaring you an enemy to their cause. The farmers are forbid to sell me provisions, and the millers to grind our grain. Our woods are cut down for the use of their army, and that which you bought and left corded near the river my servants are forbid to touch, though we are in the greatest distress for the want of it. . . . Our dear children have been six weeks without any other covering to their tender feet but woollen rags sewed round them to keep them from freezing.

A few days ago, the colonel and other officers quartered here told me they expected some of their brother officers to dine and spend the evening with them. This I understood as a hint to provide accordingly, which I was determined to do to the utmost of my powers, *though from necessity.* . . . After removal of the cloth, I took the earliest opportunity . . . to absent myself; and then they set in for a drinking match, every few minutes calling aloud upon the *landlady* to replenish the decanters which were kept continually going. . . . At length, one of them [the children] observed that the Gentlemen who used to dine with Papa never did so; and if these were not his friends, why did Mamma treat them so well. . . .

A Servant came down and said the Gentlemen desired my company, as they were going to dance. This confounded me. . . . Though I was much distressed, my resolution supported me whilst I told him that the present situation of myself and children would sufficiently apologize for my refusing to partake of any scenes of mirth where my husband could not attend me. . . . Near ten o'clock . . . he returned and entreated me to honour the Company for a few minutes as a Spectator. . . . The Officers were dancing Reels with some tawdry dressed females I had never seen. . . .

February 12, 1777, Hanover, New Jersey

. . . The narrow escape of your last was something remarkable. I was sitting about the dusk of evening in my room, very disconsolate with our dear children around me, reflecting on our deplorable situation and the gloomy prospects before me, when I heard a sudden rap at the street door. . . . I went myself to see who it was, and lucky I did. A tall, thin man presented himself, and on my stooping to unbolt the door whispered, he had a letter for me. My heart fluttered. The sentry was walking before the door, and two of the Officers were coming towards me. I recollected myself and *"desired the good man to walk into my room until I could give him a little wine for the sick woman."* He took the hint, and as soon as he came to my fireside gave me a letter, the outside of which I just looked at and threw it under the head of my bed and immediately set about getting him some wine for his wife to prevent suspicion. . . . The honest man after taking a dram went away, being followed out of doors and questioned by the Officers, who had been venting, cursing, and swearing against the sentry for permitting anyone to approach the house or speak to me without their first being acquainted with it. . . . The frequent frolics of the Officers in the house, the Soldiers in the Nursery, and Cattle constantly fed here has reduced our late Stock of plenty to a miserable pittance. The other day was almost too much for me. We had been several days without bread and were subsisting upon a half bushel of Indian meal which had been given me by a Dutch farmer I did not know, who said he had heard of our situation and would take no pay. . . . Our stock of meal had been expended five days and the Soldiers not being about, our little Sally immediately went into the Nursery, and picking up a piece of dirty bread which had been trod under their feet came running up to me, wiping it with her frock, and with joy sparkling in her eyes presented it to me crying out, "Do eat it, Mamma. 'Tis good. 'Tis charming good bread. Indeed it is. I have tasted it." This was too much.

The next day Doctor Bond . . . came to the house, and passing me suddenly went into the back room and taking from under his coat a loaf of bread he gave it to the children and before I could thank him he ran past me with his handkerchief and hat before his face. . . .

A few days after, Doctor Bond came here and with a faltering voice told me he was sent by General Washington to inform me that it was his positive orders that our house should be taken as an Hospital to innoculate his Army with the smallpox, and if I chose he would innoculate my family at the same time. . . . He . . . promised to use his influence with the General to obtain the only favour I had now to ask of him; which was, to go to my husband with my children, servants, and such effects as I could take with me. . . .

February 19, 1777, Hoboken Ferry

My beloved husband,

Doctor Bond succeeded and with orders for my removal brought me General Washington's pass which I now enclose.

To describe the scene at parting with our few though sincere friends, the destruction of our property, the insulting looks and behaviour of those who had been accessory to our ruin . . . is more than I dare attempt. At four in the afternoon, a cold, disagreeable day, we bid adieu to our home to make room for the sick of General Washington's Army and, after an unpleasant and fatiguing journey, arrived at twelve o'clock at night at the Fork of the Rivers Rockaway, Pompton and Haakinsack. A Young Woman, whose father and brother were both in the Rebel service, was much affected with my situation and endeavoured to remove me into another room. The next evening, after a most distressing ride through snow and rain . . . we arrived at Campbell's Tavern at Haakinsack, the mistress of which refused me admittance when she was informed whose family it was, alleging as an excuse that she expected a number of Officers. . . .

The town was filled with Soldiers and the night advancing . . . a person came up to me, looked me in the face, and asked me to accompany him to his Uncle's house with my whole family. On entering a room with a large fire, it had an effect on the children, whose stomachs had been empty the greatest part of the day, that caused instant puking, and was near proving fatal to them.

The next morning early, we again set off in a most uncomfortable sleet and snow. . . . Our youngest children could not pass a farm yard where they were milking cows without wishing for some. My little Willing was almost in agonies, springing in my Arms and calling for milk. I therefore rode up and requested the good man to let me have some from one of his pails. . . . The man stopped, asked who we were, and . . . swore bitterly he would not give a drop to any Tory Bitch. I offered him money, my children screamed; and, as I could not prevail, I drove on.

. . . the servants . . . had been obliged to leave me soon after setting off from Haakinsack, on account of the baggage and the badness of the roads. About two hours ago, they came in and inform me that, crossing the river on the ice at the ferry, they were stopped and fired upon by a party of armed Rebels, nearly killing several of them. . . . Upon being shewn a copy of General Washington's pass, . . . they damned the General "for giving the mistress a pass" and said they were sorry they had not come a little sooner as they would have stopped the whole . . . and immediately fell to plundering chests, trunks, boxes, etc., throwing the heavy Articles into a hole in the ice, and breaking a barrel of old fashioned China into a thousand pieces. . . .

. . . be not surprised, my dear Pappa, if you see your Kitty altered. Indeed, I am much altered. But I know your heart, you will not love me less, but heal with redoubled affection and tenderness the wounds received in your behalf for those principles of loyalty which alone induced you to leave to the mercy of Rebels nine innocent children and your fond and ever affectionate Wife,

C.V.C.

19

War in the South
Landon Carter

Late in 1775, with British and colonial armies already clashing, Lord Dunmore, the governor of Virginia, offered freedom to slaves who joined the British army. About eight hundred slaves risked the many dangers of answering his call. Many died from disease or in battle and most of the rest suffered the fate of Moses, Joe, Billy, Postillion John, Mulatto Peter, Tom, Panticove, Manuel, and Lancaster Sam, the runaway slaves of Landon Carter.

Other slaves were more successful in gaining freedom during the Revolutionary War. Southern slaves generally realized that defecting to the British offered the best chance of emancipation. About 10 percent of slaves in the colonies took the dangerous gamble. While some were treated as property and resold and others abandoned or recaptured to face their owners' anger, most of those who made it safely behind British lines eventually achieved their freedom in England or in British colonies — including one established for ex-slaves in Sierra Leone in West Africa.

A son of one of the wealthiest men in the colonies, Landon Carter was born in 1710. Educated in England and then briefly at the College of William and Mary, he followed his father in becoming a successful planter, an active leader in public life, and a writer of considerable reputation who, early on, consistently and strongly supported the American cause in speeches, letters, and essays. Carter began keeping a diary in 1752 and continued writing entries almost to the day of his death in December 1778.

BEFORE YOU READ

1. What kind of master was Landon Carter? How did he treat his slaves?
2. What was the significance of Carter's dream?
3. What was Carter's reaction to his slaves' flight? How did he explain their actions?

26. *Wednesday.* [June 1776]

Last night after going to bed, Moses, my son's man, Joe, Billy, Postillion John, Mulatto Peter, Tom, Panticove, Manuel and Lancaster Sam, ran away, to be sure, to Ld. Dunmore, for they got privately into Beale's room before dark and took out my son's gun and one I had there, took out of his drawer in my passage all his ammunition furniture, Landon's bag of bullets and all the Powder, and went off in my Petty Auger new trimmed, and it is supposed that Mr. Robinson's People are gone with them, for a skow they came down in is, it seems, at my Landing. These accursed villains have stolen Landon's silver

Jack P. Greene, ed., *The Diary of Colonel Landon Carter of Sabine Hall, 1752–1778*, vol. 1 (Charlottesville: University Press of Virginia, 1965), pp. 1051–52, 1054–56, 1064, 1084–95, 1109–10.

buckles, George's shirts, Tom Parker's new waistcoat and breeches; and yet have not touched one thing of mine, though my door was open, my line filled with stockings and my buckles in my shoes at the door. [Col. Carter attributed this to his keeping the slaves in their places. This fellow Moses, who belonged to his son, was the occasion of Col. Carter's receiving once an affront from his son (Robert Wormeley Carter) who because Col. Carter reproved him for cutting off victuals at table to give Moses, called Col. Carter] an inhuman creature to his slaves. [Col. Carter had retorted with much indignation at the time, because he had never used an angry word to Moses or the deluded fellow slaves] these 6 or 7 years.

29. *Saturday.*

[Col. Carter tells of the fugitive slaves.] At 7 in the morning after their departure some minute men at Mousquito Point saw the Petty Auger with ten stout men in her going very fast on the Middlesex shore. They pursued and fired at them, whereupon the negroes left the boat and took to the shore where they were followed by the minute men. By their firing they alarmed 100 King and Queen minute men who were waiting for the *Roebuck's* men, should any of them come ashore there. It is supposed that Moses and many of the negroes were killed.

5. *Friday.* [July 1776]

Hearing so many contradictory stories about Moses and his gang, I sent Beale off this morning to get fully informed either in Lancaster, Middlesex, or Gloster. I gave him 10s to bear his expenses. The Gent. made a demur about his breeches being dirty. I told him dirty breeches are as certainly good to ride in as to stay at home in. He is to bring an account of Mr. J. Beale about Bluff Point and also from Norris and carry letters to both.

6. *Saturday.*

Much is said of the slavery of negroes, but how will servants be provided in these times? Those few servants that we have don't do as much as the poorest slaves we have. If you free the slaves, you must send them out of the country or they must steal for their support.

9. *Tuesday.*

Beale returned but brought no account of Moses and his gang. He went to the King and Queen camp on the point between Rappahannock and Pianketank and talked with the commander. They had catched other people's negroes but not mine. Beale reported that the men who followed my people in the Petty Auger when they were driven ashore was the Towles Point guard in a boat of Burgess Ball. [Col. Carter thinks they could readily have overtaken the Petty Auger if they tried.]

Another report from Guthrie, who I have a long time known to be an egregious liar, that some runaways told him that they saw some slaves who had run away from Dunmore, who told him that they saw Moses on the Island; who swore to them if he could get back he would return to his master; for Dunmore had deceived all the Poor Slaves and he never met so barbarous or so vile a fellow in all his life.

Beale owns the Captain of that guard told him the slaves were returning daily, most miserably and barbecued, and did aver the whole gang of slaves must leave the Island as soon as they could get off.

25. Thursday [July, 1777].

A strange dream this day about these runaway people. One of them I dreamt awakened me; and appeared most wretchedly meager and wan. He told me of their great sorrow, that all of them had been wounded by the minutemen, had hid themselves in a cave they had dug and had lived ever since on what roots they could grabble and he had come to ask if I would endeavor to get them pardoned, should they come in, for they knew they should be hanged for what they had done. I replied a good deal. He acknowledged Moses persuaded them off and Johnny, his wife's father, had helped them to the milk they had, to wit, 4 bottles. He was to have gone with [them] but somehow was not in the way; declared I had not a greater villian belonging to me. I can't conceive how this dream came into my brain sleeping, and I don't remember to have collected so much of a dream as I have done of this these many years. It seems my daughter Judy dreamt much of them too last night. I am just weak enough to fancy we shall soon hear about them.

24. Monday [February 1777].

There is a Story also brought down by a certain Rig Graham about Moses, my son's waiting man. At first Graham asked my son if he had not got him; for Colo. Robt Lawson in the army told him that he knew Moses very well and saw him in Philadelphia. After this Graham told others that Moses was taken coming home to his Master who he had run away from; but they imprisoned him in Philadelphia. All this is said after many other stories, some of his waiting on Capt. Squires, who was with Dunmore at Gwins Island where he ran away. Some that he died there of the Smallpox or in Maryland at St. George's Island of the Contagious fever. As to this Mr. Graham, his character is that of an Original something of [torn] and I'll be swore Colo. Lawson never said anything about Moses. Addison of Maryland told me Graham was truely an Original, whom nobody believed, for everybody knew him almost never to be without a Story to tell.

9. *Wednesday* [July 1777].

Natan Sullivan brought up old Will, Ben, and Molly, my runaways, in Irons. I had them seperately secured and confined. They shall be till I can sell them.

10. *Thursday.*

I am glad when I reflect on my own conduct to Moses and his gang of runaways that I have no kind of Severity in the least to accuse myself of to one of them; but on the contrary a behaviour should have taught them gratitude if there ever was a virtue of the sort in such creatures. 1s[t], Mr. Moses, before I lent him to my son, was so very subject to worms as to be at times almost in the Jaws of death, And yet by God's blessing my care constantly saved him. 2d, Mr. Manuel I really obliged by bringing Suky, his wife; he then took a fancy from a distant quarter And at last [I] purchased the rascal's life condemned by the law and at the expence of £ 16, it being the smallpox time. 3d, Mr. Pentie run a tobacco Stick at his calf almost into his body and he, to the astonishment of Dr. Jones, I saved by God's Permission. 4, Mr. Peter was so accustomed to bleed at the nose that though often given over by the Docters I entirely cured, by the favour of heaven. 5th, Mr. Joe to appearance struck dead with lightning for some days, and yet by God's grace I alone saved and restored him. 6th, Mr. Sam, a Sheep stealer under a process below which never reached him. I endeavoured to protect him. 7, Mr. Tom I ever used with the greatest respect and 8, Mr. Billy a fellow too honest, and mild in temper who could not have gone away but to please his father Manuel who ever was a Villain and his brother Will confined the same cursed breed. He sent off two of his sons below and was contriving to get off more but after 3 months trial I have catched him and to Carolina he shall go if I give him away.

13. *Sunday.*

. . . Yesterday I ordered to whip Nassau naked. He it seems only gave him a stroke or two over his cloaths. I told him I would be obeyed and he was to go. He said he had all along intended it. Joy go with him. An ungrateful fellow.

20

Letters of a Republican Wife and Mother
Abigail Adams

Abigail Adams (1744–1818), whose vast correspondence has made her an important figure in American literature and history, was born Abigail Smith in Weymouth, Massachusetts. Like most young women of the era, she did not attend school. Her parents and other relatives educated her at home, providing a structure for her own interest in books. John Adams, a serious young lawyer, began courting her in 1761 and three years later they wed. It was an extraordinary marriage. As a recent biographer has written, "John and Abigail . . . achieved in this marriage the fullest equality permitted by their society, a remarkable tribute to her understanding of the possibilities as well as the limits of her place as a woman in a man's world."

Abigail Adams's letters to her husband and her son John Quincy Adams illustrate the power of her personality and the sense of authority — different from the authority accorded eighteenth-century men but equal to it — that she created from the role of wife and mother. Never forgetting the sharp distinction that society then made between male and female tasks, she nonetheless assumed her right to take a clear stand on the moral and political issues of her day and to mold her son into a man of virtue and patriotism according to her own definitions of those traits.

BEFORE YOU READ

1. What standards did Abigail Adams set for her son?
2. What did she expect her son to learn from the American Revolution?
3. Compare the tone of her letters to her son with that of the letter to her husband. What does this famous letter ask of John Adams?

LETTERS TO JOHN QUINCY ADAMS

June, 1778.

My Dear Son,

'Tis almost four months since you left your native land, and embarked upon the mighty waters, in quest of a foreign country. Although I have not particularly written to you since, yet you may be assured you have constantly been upon my heart and mind.

It is a very difficult task, my dear son, for a tender parent to bring her mind to part with a child of your years going to a distant land; nor could I have acquiesced in such a separation under any other care than that of the most

Charles Francis Adams, ed., *Letters of Mrs. Adams, the Wife of John Adams* (Boston: Wilkins, Carter and Co., 1848), pp. 94–96, 112–16, 152–55; Charles Francis Adams, ed., *Familiar Letters of John Adams and his Wife Abigail Adams, During the Revolution* (Boston: Houghton, Mifflin and Company, 1875), pp. 148–50.

excellent parent and guardian who accompanied you. You have arrived at years capable of improving under the advantages you will be likely to have, if you do but properly attend to them. They are talents put into your hands, of which an account will be required of you hereafter; and being possessed of one, two, or four, see to it that you double your numbers.

The most amiable and most useful disposition in a young mind is diffidence of itself; and this should lead you to seek advice and instruction from him, who is your natural guardian, and will always counsel and direct you in the best manner, both for your present and future happiness. You are in possession of a natural good understanding, and of spirits unbroken by adversity and untamed with care. Improve your understanding by acquiring useful knowledge and virtue, such as will render you an ornament to society, an honor to your country, and a blessing to your parents. Great learning and superior abilities, should you ever possess them, will be of little value and small estimation, unless virtue, honor, truth, and integrity are added to them. Adhere to those religious sentiments and principles which were early instilled into your mind, and remember that you are accountable to your Maker for all your words and actions.

You have entered early in life upon the great theatre of the world, which is full of temptations and vice of every kind. You are not wholly unacquainted with history, in which you have read of crimes which your inexperienced mind could scarcely believe credible. You have been taught to think of them with horror, and to view vice as

> a monster of so frightful mien,
> That, to be hated, needs but to be seen.

Yet you must keep a strict guard upon yourself, or the odious monster will soon lose its terror by becoming familiar to you. The modern history of our own times, furnishes as black a list of crimes, as can be paralleled in ancient times, even if we go back to Nero, Caligula, or Cæsar Borgia. Young as you are, the cruel war, into which we have been compelled by the haughty tyrant of Britain and the bloody emissaries of his vengeance, may stamp upon your mind this certain truth, that the welfare and prosperity of all countries, communities, and, I may add, individuals, depend upon their morals. That nation to which we were once united, as it has departed from justice, eluded and subverted the wise laws which formerly governed it, and suffered the worst of crimes to go unpunished, has lost its valor, wisdom and humanity, and, from being the dread and terror of Europe, has sunk into derision and infamy.

Be assured I am most affectionately yours,

————.

12 January, 1780.

My Dear Son,

. . . These are times in which a genius would wish to live. It is not in the still calm of life, or the repose of a pacific station, that great characters are formed. Would Cicero have shone so distinguished an orator if he had not been roused, kindled, and inflamed by the tyranny of Catiline, Verres, and Mark Anthony? The habits of a vigorous mind are formed in contending with difficulties. All history will convince you of this, and that wisdom and penetration are the fruit of experience, not the lessons of retirement and leisure. Great necessities call out great virtues. When a mind is raised and animated by scenes that engage the heart, then those qualities, which would otherwise lie dormant, wake into life and form the character of the hero and the statesman. War, tyranny, and desolation are the scourges of the Almighty, and ought no doubt to be deprecated. Yet it is your lot, my son, to be an eyewitness of these calamities in your own native land, and, at the same time, to owe your existence among a people who have made a glorious defence of their invaded liberties, and who, aided by a generous and powerful ally, with the blessing of Heaven, will transmit this inheritance to ages yet unborn.

Nor ought it to be one of the least of your incitements towards exerting every power and faculty of your mind, that you have a parent who has taken so large and active a share in this contest, and discharged the trust reposed in him with so much satisfaction as to be honored with the important embassy which at present calls him abroad.

The strict and inviolable regard you have ever paid to truth, gives me pleasing hopes that you will not swerve from her dictates, but add justice, fortitude, and every manly virtue which can adorn a good citizen, do honor to your country, and render your parents supremely happy, particularly your ever affectionate mother,

A. A.

20 March, 1780.

My Dear Son,

Your letter . . . relieved me from much anxiety. . . . I feared you were sick, unable to write, and your papa, unwilling to give me uneasiness, had concealed it from me. . . .

Your father's letters came to Salem, yours to Newburyport, and soon gave ease to my anxiety, at the same time that it excited gratitude and thankfulness to Heaven, for the preservation you all experienced in the imminent dangers which threatened you. You express in both your letters a degree of thankfulness. I hope it amounts to more than words, and that you will never be insensible to the particular preservation you have experienced in both your voyages. You have seen how inadequate the aid of man would have been, if the winds and the seas had not been under the particular government of that Being, who "stretched out the heavens as a span," who "holdeth the ocean in the hollow of his hand," and "rideth upon the wings of the wind."

If you have a due sense of your preservation, your next consideration will be, for what purpose you are continued in life. It is not to rove from clime to clime, to gratify an idle curiosity; but every new mercy you receive is a new debt upon you, a new obligation to a diligent discharge of the various relations in which you stand connected; in the first place, to your great Preserver; in the next, to society in general; in particular, to your country, to your parents, and to yourself.

The only sure and permanent foundation of virtue is religion. Let this important truth be engraven upon your heart. And also, that the foundation of religion is the belief of the one only God, and a just sense of his attributes, as a being infinitely wise, just, and good, to whom you owe the highest reverence, gratitude, and adoration; who superintends and governs all nature, even to clothing the lilies of the field, and hearing the young ravens when they cry; but more particularly regards man, whom he created after his own image, and breathed into him an immortal spirit, capable of a happiness beyond the grave; for the attainment of which he is bound to the performance of certain duties, which all tend to the happiness and welfare of society, and are comprised in one short sentence, expressive of universal benevolence, "Thou shalt love thy neighbor as thyself." . . .

Thus has the Supreme Being made the good will of man towards his fellow-creatures an evidence of his regard to Him, and for this purpose has constituted him a dependent being and made his happiness to consist in society. Man early discovered this propensity of his nature, and found

Eden was tasteless till an Eve was there.

Justice, humanity, and benevolence are the duties you owe to society in general. To your country the same duties are incumbent upon you, with the additional obligation of sacrificing ease, pleasure, wealth, and life itself for its defence and security. To your parents you owe love, reverence, and obedience to all just and equitable commands. To yourself, — here, indeed, is a wide field to expatiate upon. To become what you ought to be, and what a fond mother wishes to see you, attend to some precepts and instructions from the pen of one, who can have no motive but your welfare and happiness, and who wishes in this way to supply to you the personal watchfulness and care, which a separation from you deprived you of at a period of life, when habits are easiest acquired and fixed; and though the advice may not be new, yet suffer it to obtain a place in your memory, for occasions may offer, and perhaps some concurring circumstances unite, to give it weight and force.

Suffer me to recommend to you one of the most useful lessons of life, the knowledge and study of yourself. There you run the greatest hazard of being deceived. Self-love and partiality cast a mist before the eyes, and there is no knowledge so hard to be acquired, nor of more benefit when once thoroughly understood. . . .

You, my dear son, are formed with a constitution feelingly alive; your passions are strong and impetuous; and, though I have sometimes seen them hurry you into excesses, yet with pleasure I have observed a frankness and generosity accompany your efforts to govern and subdue them. Few persons are so subject to passion, but that they can command themselves, when they have a motive sufficiently strong; and those who are most apt to transgress will restrain themselves through respect and reverence to superiors, and even, where they wish to recommend themselves, to their equals. The due government of the passions, has been considered in all ages as a most valuable acquisition. Hence an inspired writer observes, "He that is slow to anger, is better than the mighty; and he that ruleth his spirit, than he that taketh a city." This passion, coöperating with power, and unrestrained by reason, has produced the subversion of cities, the desolation of countries, the massacre of nations, and filled the world with injustice and oppression. Behold your own country, your native land, suffering from the effects of lawless power and malignant passions, and learn betimes, from your own observation and experience, to govern and control yourself. Having once obtained this self-government, you will find a foundation laid for happiness to yourself and usefulness to mankind. "Virtue alone is happiness below;" and consists in cultivating and improving every good inclination, and in checking and subduing every propensity to evil. I have been particular upon the passion of anger, as it is generally the most predominant passion at your age, the soonest excited, and the least pains are taken to subdue it;

—"what composes man, can man destroy."

I do not mean, however, to have you insensible to real injuries. He who will not turn when he is trodden upon is deficient in point of spirit; yet, if you can preserve good breeding and decency of manners, you will have an advantage over the aggressor, and will maintain a dignity of character, which will always insure you respect, even from the offender.

I will not overburden your mind at this time. I mean to pursue the subject of self-knowledge in some future letter, and give you my sentiments upon your future conduct in life, when I feel disposed to resume my pen.

In the mean time, be assured, no one is more sincerely interested in your happiness, than your ever affectionate mother,

A. A.

Braintree, 26 December, 1783.

My Dear Son,

The early age at which you went abroad gave you not an opportunity of becoming acquainted with your own country. Yet the revolution, in which we were engaged, held it up in so striking and important a light, that you could not avoid being in some measure irradiated with the view. The characters with which you were connected, and the conversation you continually heard, must have impressed your mind with a sense of the laws, the liberties, and the glorious privileges, which distinguish the free, sovereign, independent States of America.

Let your observations and comparisons produce in your mind an abhorrence of domination and power, the parent of slavery, ignorance, and barbarism, which places man upon a level with his fellow tenants of the woods;

> A day, an hour, of virtuous liberty
> Is worth a whole eternity of bondage.

You have seen power in its various forms, — a benign deity, when exercised in the suppression of fraud, injustice, and tyranny, but a demon, when united with unbounded ambition, — a wide-wasting fury, who has destroyed her thousands. Not an age of the world but has produced characters, to which whole human hecatombs[1] have been sacrificed.

What is the history of mighty kingdoms and nations, but a detail of the ravages and cruelties of the powerful over the weak? Yet it is instructive to trace the various causes, which produced the strength of one nation, and the decline and weakness of another; to learn by what arts one man has been able to subjugate millions of his fellow creatures, the motives which have put him upon action, and the causes of his success; — sometimes driven by ambition and a lust of power; at other times, swallowed up by religious enthusiasm, blind bigotry, and ignorant zeal; sometimes enervated with luxury and debauched by pleasure, until the most powerful nations have become a prey and been subdued by these Sirens, when neither the number of their enemies, nor the prowess of their arms, could conquer them. . . .

The history of your own country and the late revolution are striking and recent instances of the mighty things achieved by a brave, enlightened, and hardy people, determined to be free; the very yeomanry[2] of which, in many instances, have shown themselves superior to corruption, as Britain well knows, on more occasions than the loss of her André. Glory, my son, in a country which has given birth to characters, both in the civil and military departments, which may vie with the wisdom and valor of antiquity. As an immediate descendant of one of those characters, may you be led to an imitation of that disinterested patriotism and that noble love of your country, which will teach you to despise wealth, titles, pomp, and equipage, as mere external advantages, which cannot add to the internal excellence of your mind, or compensate for the want of integrity and virtue.

May your mind be thoroughly impressed with the absolute necessity of universal virtue and goodness, as the only sure road to happiness, and may you

1. **hecatombs:** ancient Greek and Roman sacrifice of one hundred oxen or cows.
2. **yeomanry:** independent farmers.

walk therein with undeviating steps, — is the sincere and most affectionate wish of

Your mother,
A. Adams.

LETTER TO JOHN ADAMS

Braintree, 31 March, 1776.

I wish you would ever write me a letter half as long as I write you, and tell me, if you may, where your fleet are gone; what sort of defense Virginia can make against our common enemy; whether it is so situated as to make an able defense. Are not the gentry lords, and the common people vassals? Are they not like the uncivilized vassals Britain represents us to be? I hope their riflemen, who have shown themselves very savage and even blood-thirsty, are not a specimen of the generality of the people. I am willing to allow the colony great merit for having produced a Washington; but they have been shamefully duped by a Dunmore [British commander].

I have sometimes been ready to think that the passion for liberty cannot be equally strong in the breasts of those who have been accustomed to deprive their fellow-creatures of theirs. Of this I am certain, that it is not founded upon that generous and Christian principle of doing to others as we would that others should do unto us.

I long to hear that you have declared an independency. And, by the way, in the new code of laws which I suppose it will be necessary for you to make, I desire you would remember the ladies and be more generous and favorable to them than your ancestors. Do not put such unlimited power into the hands of the husbands. Remember, all men would be tyrants if they could. If particular care and attention is not paid to the ladies, we are determined to foment a rebellion, and will not hold ourselves bound by any laws in which we have no voice or representation.

That your sex are naturally tyrannical is a truth so thoroughly established as to admit of no dispute; but such of you as wish to be happy willingly give up the harsh title of master for the more tender and endearing one of friend. Why, then, not put it out of the power of the vicious and the lawless to use us with cruelty and indignity with impunity? Men of sense in all ages abhor those customs which treat us only as the vassals of your sex; regard us then as beings placed by Providence under your protection, and in imitation of the Supreme Being make use of that power only for our happiness.

21

A Soldier's View of Victory at Yorktown
Joseph Plumb Martin

Joseph Plumb Martin was born in western Massachusetts in 1760 and became a soldier in the Revolution before his sixteenth birthday. After serving with Connecticut state troops in 1776, he enlisted as a regular in the Continental army in April 1777 and persevered until the army was demobilized in 1783. During this period he fought with the Light Infantry as well as in the Corps of Sappers and Miners, who built fortifications and dug trenches. Martin was at Yorktown in the fall of 1781 when British general Charles Cornwallis made his fatal miscalculation. Counting on protection and supplies from the seemingly invincible Royal Navy, Cornwallis moved his army onto a narrow peninsula between the York and James Rivers. Soon the French navy was at his back and a combined force of nine thousand Americans and seventy-eight hundred French besieged him by land. Hopelessly trapped, he surrendered his whole army on October 19, 1781.

One of the liveliest and most engaging of soldier memoirs, Martin's A Narrative of Some of the Adventures, Dangers and Sufferings of a Revolutionary Soldier, *published in Maine in 1830, is a good-humored, unvarnished picture of a common soldier, whose major concern often is his next meal or keeping warm through a cold night.*

BEFORE YOU READ

1. What was the French and American strategy for defeating the British at Yorktown?

2. How would you characterize Martin's experience in the Continental army?

3. According to Martin, how well did the people support the soldiers of the Continental army?

The first of August, I think it was the 1st day of that month, we all of a sudden marched from this ground and directed our course toward King's Ferry near the Highlands, crossed the Hudson, and lay there a few days till the baggage, artillery, &c. had crossed, and then proceeded into New Jersey. We went down to Chatham, where were ovens built for the accommodation of the French troops. We then expected we were to attack New York in that quarter, but after staying here a day or two we again moved off and arrived at Trenton by rapid marches.

It was about sunset when we arrived here and instead of encamping for the night, as we expected, we were ordered immediately on board vessels then lying at the landing place, and a little after sunrise found ourselves at Philadelphia. We, that is the Sappers and Miners, stayed here some days, proving and packing off shells, shot, and other military stores. While we stayed here we

Joseph Plumb Martin, *Ordinary Courage: The Revolutionary War Adventures of Joseph Plumb Martin,* ed. James Kirby Martin (New York: Brandywine Press, 1993), pp. 130–41.

drew a few articles of clothing, consisting of a few tow shirts, some overalls and a few pairs of silk-and-oakum stockings. And here or soon after, we each of us received a MONTH'S PAY in specie, borrowed as I was informed by our French officers from the officers in the French army. This was the first that could be called money, which we had received as wages since the year '76, or that we ever did receive till the close of the war, or indeed ever after as wages.

When we had finished our business at Philadelphia, we (the Miners) left the city. A part of our men with myself went down the Delaware in a schooner which had her hold nearly full of gunpowder. We passed Mud Island, where I had experienced such hardships in Nov. '77. It had quite a different appearance to what it had then, much like a fine, fair, warm, and sunny day succeeding a cold, dark, stormy night. Just after passing Mud Island in the afternoon, we had a smart thundershower; I did not feel very agreeably, I confess, during its continuance, with such a quantity of powder under my feet. I was not quite sure that a stroke of the electric fluid might not compel me to leave the vessel sooner than I wished; but no accident happened, and we proceeded down the river to the mouth of Christiana [Christina] Creek, up which we were bound.

We were compelled to anchor here on account of wind and tide. Here we passed an uneasy night from fear of British cruisers, several of which were in the bay. In the morning we got under weigh [way], the wind serving, and proceeded up the creek 14 miles, the creek passing the most of its course through a marsh as crooked as a snake in motion. . . . We went on till the vessel grounded for lack of water. We then lightened her by taking out a part of her cargo, and when the tide came in we got up to the wharves and left her at the disposal of the artillerists.

We then crossed over land to the head of the Elk, or the head, or rather bottom, of Chesapeake Bay. Here we found a *large* fleet of *small* vessels waiting to convey us and other troops, stores, &c. down the bay. We soon embarked, that is such of us as went by water, the greater part of the army having gone on by land. I was in a small schooner called the *Birmingham*. . . .

We passed down the bay making a grand appearance with our mosquito fleet to Annapolis (which I had left about five months before for West Point). Here we stopped, fearing to proceed any further at present, not knowing exactly how matters were going on down the bay. A French cutter was dispatched to procure intelligence. She returned in the course of three or four days, bringing word that the passage was clear; we then proceeded and soon arrived at the mouth of the James River, where were a number of armed French vessels and two or three 50-gun ships. We passed in sight of the French fleet, then lying in Lynnhaven Bay; they resembled a swamp of dry pine trees. We had passed several of their men-of-war higher up the bay.

We were obliged to stay here a day or two on account of a severe northeast rainstorm. . . . After the storm had ceased, we proceeded up the [James] river to a place called Burwell's Ferry, where the fleet all anchored. . . . Soon after landing we marched to Williamsburg, where we joined General Lafayette, and very soon after, our whole army arriving, we prepared to move down and pay our old acquaintance, the British at Yorktown, a visit. I doubt not but their wish was not to have so many of us come at once, as their accommodations were rather scanty. They thought, "The fewer the better cheer." We thought, "The more the merrier." We had come a long way to see them and were unwilling to be put off with excuses; we thought the present time quite as convenient (at least for us) as any future time could be, and we accordingly persisted, hoping that, as they pretended to be a very courtly people, they would have the politeness to come out and meet us, which would greatly shorten the time to be spent in the visit, and save themselves and us much labor and trouble; but they were too impolite at this time to do so.

We marched from Williamsburg the last of September. It was a warm day; when we had proceeded about halfway to Yorktown we halted and rested two or three hours. . . .

Here, or about this time, we had orders from the Commander in Chief that, in case the enemy should come out to meet us, we should exchange but one round with them and then decide the conflict with the bayonet, as they valued themselves at that instrument. The French forces could play their part at it, and the Americans were never backward at trying its virtue. The British, however, did not think fit at that time to give us an opportunity to soil our bayonets in their carcasses, but why they did not we could never conjecture; we as much expected it as we expected to find them there.

We went on and soon arrived and encamped in their neighborhood, without . . . molestation. Our Miners lay about a mile and a half from their works in open view of them. Here again we encountered our old associate, hunger. Affairs, as they respected provisions, &c. were not yet regulated. No eatable stores had arrived, nor could we expect they should until we knew what reception the enemy would give us. We were, therefore, compelled to try our hands at foraging again. We, that is, our corps of Miners, were encamped near a large wood. There was a plenty of shoats [young hogs] all about this wood, fat and plump, weighing generally from 50 to 100 pounds apiece. We soon found some of them, and as no owner appeared to be at hand and the hogs not understanding our inquiries (if we made any) sufficiently to inform us to whom they belonged, we made free with some of them to satisfy the calls of nature till we could be better supplied, if better we could be. Our officers countenanced us and that was all the permission we wanted; and many of us did not want even that.

We now began to make preparations for laying close siege to the enemy. We had holed him, and nothing remained but to dig him out. Accordingly, after taking every precaution to prevent his escape, [we] settled our guards, provided fascines[1] and gabions,[2] made platforms for the batteries to be laid down when needed, brought on our battering pieces, ammunition, &c; on the 5th of October we began to put our plans into execution.

One-third part of all the troops were put in requisition to be employed in opening the trenches. A third part of our Sappers and Miners were ordered out

1. **fascines:** long, cylindrical bunch of sticks bound together for use in fortifications.
2. **gabions:** hollow cylinders filled with earth used in fortifications.

this night to assist the engineers in laying out the works. It was a very dark and rainy night. However, we repaired to the place and began by following the engineers and laying laths [narrow strips] of pine wood end-to-end upon the line marked out by the officers for the trenches. We had not proceeded far in the business before the engineers ordered us to desist and remain where we were, and be sure not to straggle a foot from the spot while they were absent from us. In a few minutes after their departure, there came a man alone to us having on a surtout [long overcoat], as we conjectured (it being exceeding dark), and inquired for the engineers. We now began to be a little jealous for our safety, being alone and without arms, and within 40 rods of the British trenches. The stranger inquired what troops we were, talked familiarly with us a few minutes, when being informed which way the officers had gone, he went off in the same direction, after strictly charging us, in case we should be taken prisoners, not to discover to the enemy what troops we were. We were obliged to him for his kind advice, but we considered ourselves as standing in no great need of it; for we knew as well as he did that Sappers and Miners were allowed no quarters, at least are entitled to none by the laws of warfare, and of course should take care, if taken and the enemy did not find us out, not to betray our own secret.

In a short time the engineers returned and the afore-mentioned stranger with them. They discoursed together some time when, by the officers often calling him "Your Excellency," we discovered that it was General Washington. Had we dared, we might have cautioned him for exposing himself too carelessly to danger at such a time, and doubtless he would have taken it in good part if we had. But nothing ill happened to either him or ourselves.

It coming on to rain hard, we were ordered back to our tents, and nothing more was done that night. The next night, which was the 6th of October, the same men were ordered to the lines that had been there the night before. We this night completed laying out the works. The troops of the line were there ready with entrenching tools and began to entrench after General Washington had struck a few blows with a pickax, a mere ceremony that it might be said "General Washington with his own hands first broke ground at the siege of Yorktown." The ground was sandy and soft, and the men employed that night ate no "idle bread" (and I question if they ate any other), so that by daylight they had covered themselves from danger from the enemy's shot, who it appeared never mistrusted that we were so near them the whole night, their attention being directed to another quarter. There was upon the right of their works a marsh; our people had sent to the western side of this marsh a detachment to make a number of fires, by which, and our men often passing before the fires, the British were led to imagine that we were about some secret mischief there, and consequently directed their whole fire to that quarter, while we were entrenching literally under their noses.

As soon as it was day they perceived their mistake and began to fire where they ought to have done sooner. They brought out a fieldpiece or two without their trenches, and discharged several shots at the men who were at work erecting a bomb battery; but their shot had no effect, and they soon gave it over. . . .

I do not remember exactly the number of days we were employed before we got our batteries in readiness to open upon the enemy, but think it was not more than two or three. The French, who were upon our left, had completed their batteries a few hours before us, but were not allowed to discharge their pieces till the American batteries were ready. Our commanding battery was on the near bank of the [York] river and contained 10 heavy guns; the next was a bomb battery of three large mortars; and so on through the whole line. The whole number, American and French, was 92 cannon, mortars and howitzers. Our flagstaff was in the 10-gun battery upon the right of the whole. I was in the trenches the day that the batteries were to be opened. All were upon the tiptoe of expectation and impatience to see the signal given to open the whole line of batteries, which was to be the hoisting of the American flag in the 10-gun battery.

About noon the much-wished-for signal went up. I confess I felt a secret pride swell my heart when I saw the "star-spangled banner" waving majestically in the very faces of our implacable adversaries; it appeared like an omen of success to our enterprise, and so it proved in reality. A simultaneous discharge of all the guns in the line followed, the French troops accompanying it with "Huzza for the Americans!" It was said that the first shell sent from our batteries entered an elegant house formerly owned or occupied by the Secretary of State under the British government, and burned directly over a table surrounded by a large party of British officers at dinner, killing and wounding a number of them. This was a warm day to the British.

The siege was carried on warmly for several days, when most of the guns in the enemy's works were silenced. We now began our second parallel, about halfway between our works and theirs. There were two strong redoubts held by the British on their left. It was necessary for us to possess those redoubts before we could complete our trenches. One afternoon, I, with the rest of our corps that had been on duty in the trenches the night but one before, were ordered to the lines. I mistrusted something extraordinary, serious, or comical was going forward, but what I could not easily conjecture.

We arrived at the trenches a little before sunset. I saw several officers fixing bayonets on long staves. I then concluded we were about to make a general assault upon the enemy's works, but before dark I was informed of the whole plan, which was to storm the redoubts, the one by the Americans and the other by the French. The Sappers and Miners were furnished with axes and were to proceed in front and cut a passage for the troops through the abatis, which are composed of the tops of trees, the small branches cut off with a slanting stroke which renders them as sharp as spikes. These trees are then laid at a small distance from the trench or ditch, pointing outwards, and the butts fastened to the ground in such a manner that they cannot be removed by those on the outside of them; it is almost impossible to get through them. Through these we were to cut a passage before we or the other assailants could enter.

At dark the detachment was formed and advanced beyond the trenches and lay down on the ground to await the signal for advancing to the attack, which was to be three shells from a certain battery near where we were lying. All the batteries in our line were silent, and we lay anxiously waiting for the signal. The two brilliant planets, Jupiter and Venus, were in close contact in the western hemisphere (the same direction that the signal was to be made in). When I happened to cast my eyes to that quarter, which was often, and I caught a glance of them, I was ready to spring on my feet, thinking they were the signal for starting. Our watchword was "Rochambeau," the commander of the French forces' name, a good watchword, for being pronounced *Ro-sham-bow*, it sounded, when pronounced quick, like *rush-on-boys*.

We had not lain here long before the expected signal was given, for us and the French, who were to storm the other redoubt, by the three shells with their fiery trains mounting the air in quick succession. The word up, up, was then re-iterated through the detachment. We immediately moved silently on toward the redoubt we were to attack with unloaded muskets. Just as we arrived at the abatis, the enemy discovered us and directly opened a sharp fire upon us. We were now at a place where many of our large shells had burst in the ground, making holes sufficient to bury an ox in; the men having their eyes fixed upon what was transacting before them, were every now and then falling into these holes. I thought the British were killing us off at a great rate. At length one of the holes happening to pick me up, I found out the mystery of the huge slaughter.

As soon as the firing began, our people began to cry, "The fort's our own!" and it was "Rush on boys." The Sappers and Miners soon cleared a passage for the infantry, who entered it rapidly. Our Miners were ordered not to enter the fort, but there was no stopping them. "We will go," said they. "Then go to the d---l," said the commanding officer of our corps, "if you will." I could not pass at the entrance we had made, it was so crowded; I therefore forced a passage at a place where I saw our shot had cut away some of the abatis. Several others entered at the same place.

While passing, a man at my side received a ball in his head and fell under my feet, crying out bitterly. While crossing the trench, the enemy threw hand grenades (small shells) into it; they were so thick that I at first thought them cartridge papers on fire, but was soon undeceived by their cracking. As I mounted the breastwork, I met an old associate hitching himself down into the trench. I knew him by the light of the enemy's musketry, it was so vivid. The fort was taken and all quiet in a very short time. Immediately after the firing ceased, I went out to see what had become of my wounded friend and the other that fell in the passage; they were both dead. In the heat of the action I saw a British soldier jump over the walls of the fort next the river and go down the bank, which was almost perpendicular and 20 or 30 feet high. When he came to the beach he made off for the town, and if he did not make good use of his legs I never saw a man that did.

All that were in the action of storming the redoubt were exempted from further duty that night. We laid down upon the ground and rested the remainder of the night as well as a constant discharge of grape and canister shot would permit us to do, while those who were on duty for the day completed the second parallel by including the captured redoubts within it. We returned to camp early in the morning, all safe and sound, except one of our lieutenants, who had received a slight wound on the top of the shoulder by a musket shot. Seven or eight men belonging to the infantry were killed, and a number wounded. . . .

We were on duty in the trenches 24 hours, and 48 hours in camp. The invalids did the camp duty, and we had nothing else to do but to attend morning and evening roll calls and recreate ourselves as we pleased the rest of the time, till we were called upon to take our turns on duty in the trenches again. The greatest inconvenience we felt was the want of good water, there being none near our camp but nasty frog ponds where all the horses in the neighborhood were watered, and we were forced to wade through the water in the skirts of the ponds, thick with mud and filth, to get at water in any wise fit for use, and that full of frogs. All the springs about the country, although they looked well, tasted like copperas water or like water that had been standing in iron or copper vessels. . . .

After we had finished our second line of trenches there was but little firing on either side. After Lord Cornwallis had failed to get off, upon the 17th day of October (a rather unlucky day for the British) he requested a cessation of hostilities for, I think, 24 hours when commissioners from both armies met at a house between the lines to agree upon articles of capitulation. We waited with anxiety the termination of the armistice, and as the time drew nearer our anxiety increased. The time at length arrived; it passed, and all remained quiet. And now we concluded that we had obtained what we had taken so much pains for—for which we had encountered so many dangers and had so anxiously wished. Before night we were informed that the British had surrendered and that the siege was ended.

The next day we were ordered to put ourselves in as good order as our circumstances would admit, to see (what was the completion of our present wishes) the British army march out and stack their arms. The trenches, where they crossed the road leading to the town, were leveled and all things put in order for this grand exhibition. After breakfast on the 19th, we were marched onto the ground and paraded on the right-hand side of the road, and the French forces on the left. We waited two or three hours before the British made their appearance; they were not always so dilatory, but they were compelled at last by necessity to appear all armed, with bayonets fixed, drums beating, and faces lengthening.

They were led by General O'Hara, with the American General Lincoln on his right, the Americans and French beating a march as they passed out between them. It was a noble sight to us, and the more so, as it seemed to promise a speedy conclusion to the contest. The British did not make so good an appearance as the German forces; but there was certainly some allowance to be made in their favor. The English felt their honor wounded; the Germans did not greatly care whose hands they were in. The British paid the Americans, seemingly, but little attention as they passed them, but they eyed the French with considerable malice depicted in their countenances. They marched to the place appointed and stacked their arms; they then returned to the town in the same manner they had marched out, except being divested of their arms. After the prisoners were marched off into the country our army separated, the French remaining where they then were and the Americans marching for the Hudson.

22

Ratifying the Constitution
Mr. Parsons et al.

During the 1780s, political conflict splintered much of the country. Small farmers were pitted against merchants, urban artisans, former army officers, larger commercial farmers, and southern planters. For relief from the economic hardships that followed the war, farmers looked to local and state government for laws and courts that favored debtors over creditors. Their more cosmopolitan neighbors wanted strong government that would ensure sound money, promote trade, pay the public debt, and keep order. Nowhere was the battle more fierce than in Massachusetts, where Shays's Rebellion in the winter of 1786–87 turned political dispute into armed confrontation.

Against this background, the battle in Massachusetts over ratifying the Constitution was fierce. Historians generally agree that the outcome demonstrated the truth of the political proverb that a disciplined minority will defeat an unorganized majority. Over the course of a convention that lasted nearly a month, amid spying, delays, outbursts of temper, and charges of corruption, the richer, better educated, and more smoothly organized Federalists wore down their less-experienced and unprepared rivals, finally achieving ratification by the close vote of 187 to 168. "Bad measures in a good cause" was the judgment of the Convention's secretary.

Yet for all the bad feeling of the lengthy meeting in Massachusetts, many good arguments had been aired and probably some Anti-Federalist fears regarding the new Constitution had been dispelled. Federalists offered assurances that the states would retain considerable powers, met objections to union with southern slaveholders, and responded to fears that political control would rest exclusively with lawyers and other educated men. Anti-Federalists offered classic arguments for the superiority of local government and—as occurred in several other states—persuaded Federalists to support a Bill of Rights once the Constitution should take effect. The Anti-Federalists promptly indicated, moreover, that despite their misgivings they would give the new government a chance to prove its worth.

BEFORE YOU READ

1. The Revolutionary generation greatly feared abuse of power. Why did Anti-Federalists fear that the Constitution would lead to abuse and how did the Federalists answer them?

2. How did Shays's Rebellion enter into the arguments between Federalists and Anti-Federalists in Massachusetts?

3. How did the Federalists answer objections to the recognition of slavery in the Constitution?

DEBATE ON THE CONSTITUTION

Mr. Parsons
of Newburyport (Federalist)

It has been objected, that we have not so good security against the abuse of power under the new constitution as the confederation gives us. It is my deliberate opinion that we have a better security. Under the confederation the whole power, executive and legislative, is vested in one body, in which the people have no representation, and where the states, the great and the small states, are equally represented; and all the checks the states have is a power to remove and disgrace an unfaithful servant, after the mischief is perpetrated. Under this constitution, an equal representation, immediately from the people, is introduced, who by their negative, and the exclusive right of originating money bills, have the power to control the senate, where the sovereignty of the states are represented. But it has been objected, that in the old confederation the states could at any time recall their delegates, and there was a rotation. No essential benefit could be derived to the people from these provisions, but great inconveniencies will result from them. It has been observed by a gentleman who has argued against the constitution, that a representative ought to have an intimate acquaintance with the circumstances of his constituents, and after comparing them with the situation of every part of the union, so conduct as to promote the common good. The sentiment is an excellent one, and ought to be engraved on the hearts of every representative. But what is the effect of the power of recalling? Your representative, with an operating revocation over his head, will lose all ideas of the general good, and will dwindle to a servile agent, attempting to serve local and partial benefits by cabal and intrigue. There are great and insuperable objections to a rotation. It is an abridgement of the rights of the people, and it may deprive them at critical seasons of the services of the most important characters in the nation. It deprives a man of honorable ambition, whose highest duty is the applause of his fellow citizens, of an efficient motive to great and patriotic exertions. The people individually have no method of testifying their esteem, but by a reelection: and shall they be deprived of the honest satisfaction of wreathing for their friend and patriot a crown of laurel more durable than monarchy can bestow?

It has been objected, that the senate are made too independent upon the state legislatures. No business under the constitution of the federal convention could have been more embarrassing, than the constructing the senate; as that body must conduct our foreign negotiations, and establish and preserve a system of national politics, an uniform adherence to which can alone induce other nations to negotiate with and confide in us. It is certain the change of the men who compose it should not be too frequent, and should be gradual. At the same

Jonathan Elliot, ed., *The Debates . . . on the Adoption of the Federal Constitution*, vol. 1, *Massachusetts and New York* (Philadelphia: J. B. Lippincott, 1863), pp. 33–34, 38–39, 42, 103–05, 107, 112, 117.

time, suitable checks should be provided to prevent an abuse of power, and to continue their dependence on their constituents.—I think the convention have most happily extricated themselves from the embarrassment. Although the senators are elected for six years, yet the senate, as a body composed of the same men, can exist only for two years, without the consent of the states. If the states think proper, one third of that body may, at the end of every second year, be new men. When the senate acts as legislators they are controllable at all times by the representatives; and in their executive capacity, in making treaties and conducting the national negotiations, the consent of two thirds is necessary, who must be united, to a man, (which is hardly possible) or the new men biennially sent to the senate, if the states choose it, can control them; and at all times there will also be one third of the senate, who, at the expiration of two years must obtain a re-election, or return to the mass of the people. And the change of men in the senate will be so gradual as not to destroy or disturb any national system of politics.

It is objected, that it is dangerous to allow the senate a right of proposing alterations or amendments in money bills; that the senate may by this power increase the supplies, and establish profuse salaries, that for these reasons the lords in the British parliament have not this power, which is a great security to the liberties of Englishmen. I was much surprised at hearing this objection, and the grounds upon which it was supported. The reason why the lords have not this power, is founded on a principle in the English constitution, that the commons alone represent the whole property of the nation; and as a money-bill is a grant to the king, none can make the grant but those who represent the property of the nation; and the negative of the lords is introduced to check the profusion of the commons, and to guard their own property. The manner of passing a money-bill is conclusive evidence of these principles; for, after the assent of the lords, it does not remain with the clerk of the parliament, but is returned to the commons, who, by their speaker, present it to the king as the gift of the commons. But every supposed control the senate, by this power may have over money-bills, they can have without it: for, by private communications with the representatives, they may as well insist upon the increase of the supplies, or salaries, as by official communications. But had not the senate this power, the representatives might take any foreign matter to a money-bill, and compel the senate to concur, or lose the supplies. This might be done in critical seasons, when the senate might give way to the encroachments of the representatives, rather than sustain the odium of embarrassing the affairs of the nation—the balance between the two branches of the legislature, would, in this way, be endangered, if not destroyed, and the constitution materially injured. This subject was fully considered by the convention for forming the constitution of Massachusetts, and the provision made by that body after mature deliberation is introduced into the federal constitution.

It was objected that by giving congress a power of direct taxation, we give them power to destroy the state governments, by prohibiting them from raising any moneys: but this objection is not founded in the constitution. Congress have only a concurrent right with each state, in laying direct taxes, not an exclusive right: and the right of each state to direct taxation is equally extensive and perfect as the right of congress—any law, therefore, of the United States for securing to congress more than a concurrent right with each state, is usurpation and void. . . .

DEBATE ON TAXATION

Mr. Singletary (Anti-Federalist)

Mr. President—I should not have troubled the convention again, if some gentlemen had not called on them that were on the stage in the beginning of our troubles, in the year 1775. I was one of them. I have had the honor to be a member of the court all the time, Mr President, and I say, that if any body had proposed such a constitution as this, in that day, it would have been thrown away at once. It would not have been looked at. We contended with Great Britain—some said for a three-penny duty on tea; but it was not that—it was because they claimed a right to tax us and bind us in all cases whatever. And does not this constitution do the same? does it not take away all we have—all our property? does it not lay *all* taxes, duties, imposts[1] and excises? and what more have we to give? They tell us congress won't lay dry taxes upon us, but collect all the money they want by impost. I say there has always been a difficulty about impost. Whenever the general court was a going to lay an impost, they would tell us it was more than trade could bear, that it hurt the fair trader, and encouraged smuggling; and there will always be the same objection; they won't be able to raise money enough by impost, and then they will lay it on the land and take all we have got. These lawyers and men of learning, and moneyed men, that talk so finely and gloss over matters so smoothly, to make us, poor illiterate people, swallow down the pill, expect to get into congress themselves; they expect to be the managers of this constitution, and get all the power and all the money into their own hands, and then they will swallow up all us little folks, like the great *Leviathan*,[2] . . .

Mr. Smith (Federalist)

Mr President, I am a plain man, and get my living by the plough. I am not used to speaking in public, but I beg your leave to say a few words to my brother plough-joggers in this house. I have lived in a part of the country where I have known the worth of good government by the want of it. There was a black cloud that rose in the east last winter, and spread over the west. [Here Mr Widgery interrupted.—Mr President, I wish to know what the gentleman means by the east.] I mean, sir, the county of Bristol; the cloud rose there and burst upon us, and produced a dreadful effect. It brought on a state of *anarchy*, and that lead to *tyranny*. I say, it brought anarchy. People that used to live peaceably, and were before good neighbors, got distracted, and took up arms

1. **imposts:** a tax.
2. *Leviathan:* a whale; also a powerful state.

against government. [Here Mr Kinsley called to order, and asked, what had the history of last winter to do with the constitution? Several gentlemen, and among the rest the hon. Mr Adams, said the gentleman was in order—let him go on in his own way.] I am a going, Mr President, to shew you, my brother farmers, what were the effects of anarchy, that you may see the reasons, why I wish for good government. People, I say, took up arms, and then, if you went to speak to them, you had the *musket of death*, presented to your breast. They would rob you of your property, threaten to burn your houses; oblige you to be on your guard night and day; alarms spread from town to town; families were broke up; the tender mother would cry, O, my son is among them! What shall I do for my child! Some were taken captive, children taken out of their schools and carried away. Then we should hear of an *action*, and the poor prisoners were *set in the front*, to be killed by their own friends. How dreadful, how distressing was this! Our distress was so great that we should have been glad to snatch at any thing that looked like a government for protection. Had any person, that was able to protect us, come and set up his standard, we should all have flocked to it, even if it had been a *monarch*, and that monarch might have proved a tyrant; so that you see that anarchy leads to tyranny, and better have *one* tyrant than so many at once.

Now, Mr President, when I saw this constitution, I found that it was a cure for these disorders. It was just such a thing as we wanted. I got a copy of it and read it over and over. I had been a member of the convention to form our own state constitution, and had learnt something of the checks and balances of power, and I found them all here. I did not go to any lawyer, to ask his opinion: we have no lawyer in our town, and we do well enough without. I formed my own opinion, and was pleased with this constitution. My honorable old daddy there (pointing to Mr Singletary,) won't think that I expect to be a congress-man, and swallow up the liberties of the people. I never had any post, nor do I want one, and before I am done you will think that I don't deserve one. But I don't think the worse of the constitution because lawyers, and men of learning, and monied men, are fond of it. I don't suspect that they want to get into congress and abuse their power. I am not of such a jealous make. They that are honest men themselves are not apt to suspect other people. I don't know why our constituents have not as good a right to be jealous of us, as we seem to be of the congress; and I think those gentlemen who are so very suspicious, that as soon as a man gets into power he turns rogue, had better look *at home*.

We are by this constitution allowed to send *ten* members to congress. Have we not more than that number fit to go? I dare say if we pick out ten, we shall have another ten left, and I hope ten times ten; and will not these be a check upon those that go? Will they go to congress and abuse their power and do mischief, when they know that they must return and look the other ten in the face, and be called to account for their conduct? Some gentlemen think that our liberty and property is not safe in the hands of monied men, and men of learning. I am not of that mind.

Brother farmers, let us suppose a case now: Suppose you had a farm of fifty acres, and your title was disputed, and there was a farm of 5,000 acres joined to you that belonged to a man of learning, and his title was involved in the same difficulty; would you not be glad to have him for your friend, rather than to stand alone in the dispute? Well, the case is the same, these lawyers, these monied men, these men of learning, are all embarked in the same cause with us and we must all swim or sink together; and shall we throw the constitution overboard, because it does not please us alike? Suppose two or three of you had been at the pains to break up a piece of rough land, and sow it with wheat — would you let it lay waste, because you could not agree what *sort* of a fence to make? would it not be better to put up a fence that did not please every one's fancy, rather than not fence it at all, or keep disputing about it, until the wild beast came in and devoured it? Some gentlemen say, don't be in a hurry — take time to consider, and don't take a leap in the dark. I say, take things in time — gather fruit when it is ripe. There is a time to sow and a time to reap; we sowed our seed when we sent men to the federal convention, now is the harvest, now is the time to reap. . . .

DEBATE ON SLAVERY

Mr. Neal (from Kittery) [an Anti-Federalist] went over the ground of objection to this section on the idea that slave trade was allowed to be continued for 20 years. His profession, he said, obliged him to bear witness against any thing that should favor the making merchandize of the bodies of men, and unless his objection was removed, he could not put his hand to the constitution. Other gentlemen said, in addition to this idea, that there was not even a proposition that the negroes ever shall be free: and Gen. Thompson exclaimed —

> Mr. President, shall it be said, that after we have established our own independence and freedom, we make slaves of others? Oh! Washington, what a name has he had! How he has immortalized himself! but he holds those in slavery who have a good right to be free as he has — he is still for self; and, in my opinion, his character has sunk 50 per cent.

On the other side, gentlemen said, that the step taken in this article, towards the abolition of slavery, was one of the beauties of the constitution. They observed, that in the confederation there was no provision whatever for its ever being abolished; but this constitution provides, that congress may, after 20 years, totally annihilate the slave trade; and that, as all the states, except two, have passed laws to this effect, it might reasonably be expected, that it would then be done. In the interim, all the states were at liberty to prohibit it.

Mr. Heath (Federalist)

. . . I apprehend that it is not in our power to do any thing for or against those who are in slavery in the southern states. No gentleman within these walls detests every idea of slavery more than I do: it is generally detested by the people of this commonwealth, and I ardently hope that the time will soon come, when our brethren in the southern states will view it as we do, and put a stop to it; but to this we have no right to compel them. Two questions naturally arise: if we ratify the Constitution, shall we do any thing by our act to hold the blacks in slavery—or shall we become the partakers of other men's sins? I think neither of them: Each state is sovereign and independent to a certain degree, and they have a right, and will regulate their own internal affairs, as to themselves appear proper; and shall we refuse to eat, or to drink, or to be united, with those who do not think, or act, just as we do? surely not. We are not in this case partakers of other men's sins, for in nothing do we voluntarily encourage the slavery of our fellow men, a restriction is laid on the federal government, which could not be avoided, and a union take place: The federal convention went as far as they could: the migration or importation, &c. is confined to the states, now *existing only*, new states cannot claim it. Congress, by their ordinance for erecting new states, some time since, declared that the new states shall be republican, and that there shall be no slavery in them. But whether those in slavery in the southern states, will be emancipated after the year 1808, I do not pretend to determine: I rather doubt it.

Davy Crockett as imagined by an anonymous artist in a spurious autobiography written within days of Crockett's death. The artist's caption reads "Colonel Crockett stood in an angle of the fort, his shattered rifle in his right hand, and in his left his huge bowie-knife, dripping blood."

PART FOUR

The New and Expanding Nation

Competition for the West

For almost two hundred years American society had grown in the corridor between the Atlantic Ocean and the Appalachian range. Mountains, Indians, and conflict among European powers discouraged Americans from pushing into the West. Then, after about 1795, with the Revolution won, the Indian tribes dispersed, and the price of good eastern land rising, a vast folk migration began. The return of peace on the frontier after the War of 1812, along with rising prices worldwide for agricultural products and a revolution in transportation, quickened the migration. In time, turnpikes replaced stump-filled rutted paths; steamboats overtook sailing ships and river rafts; canals offered the first economical means of moving eastward the bulky products of western farms; finally, railroads spread westward in the 1840s and 1850s, overshadowing all other forms of long-distance transportation. The land seemed permanently to have tilted, shaking its human burden westward in a long, rough tumble toward the Pacific. In the span of a person's life, the United States became a vast continental republic.

These new Westerners were not entering empty territory. Meriwether Lewis and William Clark and other early explorers became diplomats among the Indians who were thinly spread across the lands they explored. Even native Americans forced westward, such as the Cherokee led by John Ross, faced competition from other tribes in the West. And the Spanish and then their heirs, the Mexicans, owned much of these territories. Conflicts with Mexico, of which the battle of the Alamo is a central incident, determined the future of nearly a million square miles of what is now Texas, New Mexico, Arizona, Nevada, California, Utah, and parts of Colorado, Wyoming, Kansas, and Oklahoma. The discovery of gold in California in 1848 and the rush of miners, guided by books like that by Edward Gould Buffum, accelerated the evolution of the West, forcing decisions about its future that rapidly led to the Civil War.

For only a moment—repeated at each westward edge of migration—did the frontier seem to be just what legend said it was, a land where a man (in the legend, it was always a man) could boast, as Davy Crockett supposedly did, that he was "half alligator, a little touched with the snapping turtle; can wade the Mississippi, leap the Ohio, ride upon a streak of lightning." The institutions of eastern society tamed the wildness of the West more rapidly than we usually assume. Peter Cartwright and other circuit riders brought the values of Protestantism to the rawest frontiers. Migrants like Priscilla Merriman Evans carried with them not just a few goods in the handcarts they pulled across the plains but dreams of an orderly Zion in the desert. And settlers such as Frithjof Meidell understood that the railroads that had brought them west carried as well the prospect of towns, commerce, and settled prosperity that would quickly transform the frontier into a society that approximated the world the settlers had left behind.

Points of View:
Battle of the Alamo (1836)

23

A Mexican Account
José Enrique de la Peña

In the early nineteenth century, no place had a larger reputation for wild living than Texas. Men tired of society could move to the frontier; if the frontier offered too little excitement, room, danger, and opportunity, they could go to Texas.

For nearly three centuries Texas had belonged to Spain, but hundreds of miles of desert and mountains separated it from other Spanish territories. The land, which Mexico inherited with its independence from Spain, had long been ungoverned. Mexico first made Texas part of its state of Coahuila, with the promise that when its population was large enough, it would become a separate Mexican state. The newly established Mexican government developed Texas by encouraging settlers from the United States, provided they became at least nominal Catholics and Mexican citizens.

The plan, however, worked too well. By 1831, twenty thousand settlers had poured into Texas, most of them from the United States. And although slavery was illegal under Mexican law, many settlers brought slaves with them. The Mexicans soon feared the loss of this potentially rich province. So they banned further immigration, raised tariffs, restricted trade, and reinforced their military presence. Unstable Mexican politics further complicated the situation. Antonio Lopez de Santa Anna, a Mexican general, was challenging his own government. The Texans, led by Stephen F.

Austin, petitioned for separate statehood. Then in 1834 Santa Anna proclaimed him-
self president of Mexico forever and sent its Congress home. Said Austin: "War is our
only resource."

Santa Anna moved to garrison his northern province and the Texans prepared to
fight. In late 1835 Santa Anna's Texas campaign began. On February 23, 1836, his
army of about four thousand began its siege of the mission at Béjar—the Alamo—in
present-day San Antonio.

José Enrique de la Peña, the author of this eyewitness account of the battle of the
Alamo, was born in 1807. He trained as a mining engineer and was a lieutenant
colonel in Santa Anna's army. His military file described him as "a young man of good
breeding, strong, of medium height, intelligent, of outstanding nobility of character,
observant, tireless, and eager to hold important positions and to enrich his already wide
and profound knowledge." His criticisms of Santa Anna and other leaders apparently
led to the destruction of all the military records of his participation in the war with
Texas. After his death in 1842, his manuscript lay unread for over a century until its
first publication in 1955.

BEFORE YOU READ

1. Why did Santa Anna attack the Alamo when he did?
2. What was Santa Anna's strategy? According to Peña, what mistakes did he make?
3. Upon reflecting on the outcome of the battle, what questions did Peña ask? How
would you answer them?

Information given by General Cos, by wounded officers he had left at Béjar,
and by some townspeople of this locality . . . made clear to us the limited
strength of the garrison at the Alamo and the shortage of supplies and munitions at their disposal. They had walled themselves in so quickly that they had
not had time to supply themselves with very much.

Travis's resistance was on the verge of being overcome; for several days his
followers had been urging him to surrender, giving the lack of food and the
scarcity of munitions as reasons, but he had quieted their restlessness with the
hope of quick relief, something not difficult for them to believe since they
had seen some reinforcements arrive. Nevertheless, they had pressed him so
hard that on the 5th he promised them that if no help arrived on that day they
would surrender the next day or would try to escape under cover of darkness;
these facts were given to us by a lady from Béjar, a Negro who was the only
male who escaped, and several women who were found inside and were rescued
by Colonels Morales and Miñón. The enemy was in communication with
some of the Béjar townspeople who were their sympathizers, and it was said as
a fact during those days that the president-general had known of Travis's decision, and that it was for this reason that he precipitated the assault, because

José Enrique de la Peña, trans. and ed. Carmen Perry, *With Santa Anna in Texas: A Personal Nar-*
rative of the Revolution (College Station: Texas A&M Press, 1975), pp. 44–56.

he wanted to cause a sensation and would have regretted taking the Alamo without clamor and without bloodshed, for some believed that without these there is no glory.

Once the order was issued, even those opposing it were ready to carry it out; no one doubted that we would triumph, but it was anticipated that the struggle would be bloody, as indeed it was. . . .

The Alamo was an irregular fortification without flank fires which a wise general would have taken with insignificant losses, but we lost more than three hundred brave men.

Four columns were chosen for the attack. The first, under command of General Cos and made up of a battalion from Aldama and three companies from the San Luis contingent, was to move against the western front, which faced the city. The second, under Colonel Duque and made up of the battalion under his command and three other companies from San Luis, was entrusted with a like mission against the front facing the north, which had two mounted batteries at each end of its walls. These two columns had a total strength of seven hundred men. The third, under command of Colonel Romero and made up of two companies of fusiliers[1] from the Matamoros and Jiménez battalions, had less strength, for it only came up to three hundred or more men; it was to attack the east front, which was the strongest, perhaps because of its height or perhaps because of the number of cannon that were defending it, three of them situated in a battery over the church ruins, which appeared as a sort of high fortress. The fourth column, under command of Colonel Morales and made up of over a hundred chasseurs,[2] was entrusted with taking the entrance to the fort and the entrenchments defending it.

The Sapper Battalion and five grenadier[3] companies made up the reserve of four hundred men. The commander in chief headed this column. . . .

Our commander made much of Travis's courage, for it saved him from the insulting intimation that the critical circumstances surrounding Travis would have sufficed to spare the army a great sacrifice.

Beginning at one o'clock in the morning of the 6th, the columns were set in motion, and at three they silently advanced toward the river, which they crossed marching two abreast over some narrow wooden bridges. A few minor obstacles were explored in order to reach the enemy without being noticed, to a point personally designated by the commander in chief, where they stationed themselves, resting with weapons in hand. Silence was again ordered and smoking was prohibited. The moon was up, but the density of the clouds that covered it allowed only an opaque light in our direction, seeming thus to contribute to our designs. . . . Light began to appear on the horizon, the beautiful dawn would soon let herself be seen behind her golden curtain; a bugle call

1. **fusiliers:** soldiers armed with fusils—light, flintlock muskets.
2. **chasseurs:** light cavalry or infantry trained for rapid maneuvering.
3. **grenadier:** a member of a special regiment or corps.

to attention was the agreed signal and we soon heard that terrible bugle call of death, which stirred our hearts, altered our expressions, and aroused us all suddenly from our painful meditations. . . . Seconds later the horror of this sound fled from among us, honor and glory replacing it.

The columns advanced with as much speed as possible; shortly after beginning the march they were ordered to open fire while they were still out of range, but there were some officers who wisely disregarded the signal. Alerted to our attack by the given signal, which all columns answered, the enemy vigorously returned our fire, which had not even touched him but had retarded our advance. Travis, to compensate for the reduced number of the defenders, had placed three or four rifles by the side of each man, so that the initial fire was very rapid and deadly. Our columns left along their path a wide trail of blood, of wounded, and of dead. The bands from all the corps, gathered around our commander, sounded the charge; with a most vivid ardor and enthusiasm, we answered that call which electrifies the heart, elevates the soul, and makes others tremble. The second column, seized by this spirit, burst out in acclamations for the Republic and for the president-general. The officers were unable to repress this act of folly, which was paid for dearly. His attention drawn by this act, the enemy seized the opportunity, at the moment that light was beginning to make objects discernible around us, to redouble the fire on this column, making it suffer the greatest blows. . . .

The columns, bravely storming the fort in the midst of a terrible shower of bullets and cannon-fire, had reached the base of the walls, with the exception of the third, which had been sorely punished on its left flank by a battery of three cannon on a barbette that cut a serious breach in its ranks; since it was being attacked frontally at the same time from the height of a position, it was forced to seek a less bloody entrance, and thus changed its course toward the right angle of the north front. The few poor ladders that we were bringing had not arrived, because their bearers had either perished on the way or had escaped. Only one was seen of all those that were planned. General Cos, looking for a starting point from which to climb, had advanced frontally with his column to where the second and third were. All united at one point, mixing and forming a confused mass. Fortunately the wall reinforcement on this front was of lumber, its excavation was hardly begun, and the height of the parapet was eight or nine feet; there was therefore a starting point, and it could be climbed, though with some difficulty. But disorder had already begun; officers of all ranks shouted but were hardly heard. The most daring of our veterans tried to be the first to climb, which they accomplished, yelling wildly so that room could be made for them, at times climbing over their own comrades. Others, jammed together, made useless efforts, obstructing each other, getting in the way of the more agile ones and pushing down those who were about to carry out their courageous effort. A lively rifle fire coming from the roof of the barracks and other points caused painful havoc, increasing the confusion of our disorderly mass. The first to climb were thrown down by bayonets already waiting for them behind the parapet, or by pistol fire, but the courage of our soldiers was not diminished as they saw their comrades falling dead or wounded, and they hurried to occupy their places and to avenge them, climbing over their bleeding bodies. The sharp reports of the rifles, the whistling of bullets, the groans of the wounded, the cursing of the men, the sighs and anguished cries of the dying, the arrogant harangues of the officers, the noise of the instruments of war, and the inordinate shouts of the attackers, who climbed vigorously, bewildered all and made of this moment a tremendous and critical one. The shouting of those being attacked was no less loud and from the beginning had pierced our ears with desperate, terrible cries of alarm in a language we did not understand.

From his point of observation, General Santa Anna viewed with concern this horrible scene and, misled by the difficulties encountered in the climbing of the walls and by the maneuver executed by the third column, believed we were being repulsed; he therefore ordered Colonel Amat to move in with the rest of the reserves; the Sapper Battalion, already ordered to move their column of attack, arrived and began to climb at the same time. He then also ordered into battle his general staff and everyone at his side. This gallant reserve merely added to the noise and the victims, the more regrettable since there was no necessity for them to engage in the combat. Before the Sapper Battalion, advancing through a shower of bullets and volley of shrapnel, had a chance to reach the foot of the walls, half their officers had been wounded. Another one of these officers, young Torres, died within the fort at the very moment of taking a flag. He died at one blow without uttering a word, covered with glory and lamented by his comrades. . . .

A quarter of an hour had elapsed, during which our soldiers remained in a terrible situation, wearing themselves out as they climbed in quest of a less obscure death than that visited on them, crowded in a single mass; later and after much effort, they were able in sufficient numbers to reach the parapet, without distinction of ranks. The terrified defenders withdrew at once into quarters placed to the right and the left of the small area that constituted their second line of defense. They had bolted and reinforced the doors, but in order to form trenches they had excavated some places inside that were now a hindrance to them. Not all of them took refuge, for some remained in the open, looking at us before firing, as if dumbfounded at our daring. Travis was seen to hesitate, but not about the death that he would choose. He would take a few steps and stop, turning his proud face toward us to discharge his shots; he fought like a true soldier. Finally he died, but he died after having traded his life very dearly. None of his men died with greater heroism, and they all died. Travis behaved as a hero; one must do him justice, for with a handful of men without discipline, he resolved to face men used to war and much superior in numbers, without supplies, with scarce munitions, and against the will of his subordinates. He was a handsome blond, with a physique as robust as his spirit was strong.

Our soldiers, some stimulated by courage and others by fury, burst into the quarters where the enemy had entrenched themselves, from which issued an infernal fire. Behind these came others, who, nearing the doors and blind with fury and smoke, fired their shots against friends and enemies alike, and in this way our losses were most grievous. On the other hand, they turned the enemy's own cannon to bring down the doors to the rooms or the rooms themselves; a horrible carnage took place, and some were trampled to death. The tumult was great, the disorder frightful; it seemed as if the furies had descended upon us; different groups of soldiers were firing in all directions, on their comrades and on their officers, so that one was as likely to die by a friendly hand as by an enemy's. In the midst of this thundering din, there was such confusion that orders could not be understood, although those in command would raise their voices when the opportunity occurred. Some may believe that this narrative is exaggerated, but those who were witnesses will confess that this is exact, and in truth, any moderation in relating it would fall short.

It was thus time to end the confusion that was increasing the number of our victims, and on my advice and at my insistence General Cos ordered the fire silenced; but the bugler Tamayo of the sappers blew his instrument in vain, for the fire did not cease until there was no one left to kill and around fifty thousand cartridges had been used up. Whoever doubts this, let him estimate for himself, as I have done, with data that I have given.

Among the defenders there were thirty or more colonists; the rest were pirates, used to defying danger and to disdaining death, and who for that reason fought courageously; their courage, to my way of thinking, merited them the mercy for which, toward the last, some of them pleaded; others, not knowing the language, were unable to do so. In fact, when these men noted the loss of their leader and saw that they were being attacked by superior forces, they faltered. Some, with an accent hardly intelligible, desperately cried, *Mercy, valiant Mexicans;* others poked the points of their bayonets through a hole or a door with a white cloth, the symbol of cease-fire, and some even used their socks. Our trusting soldiers, seeing these demonstrations, would confidently enter their quarters, but those among the enemy who had not pleaded for mercy, who had no thought of surrendering, and who relied on no other recourse than selling their lives dearly, would meet them with pistol shots and bayonets. Thus betrayed, our men rekindled their anger and at every moment fresh skirmishes broke out with renewed fury. The order had been given to spare no one but the women and this was carried out, but such carnage was useless and had we prevented it, we would have saved much blood on our part. Those of the enemy who tried to escape fell victims to the sabers of the cavalry, which had been drawn up for this purpose, but even as they fled they defended themselves. An unfortunate father with a young son in his arms was seen to hurl himself from a considerable height, both perishing at the same blow.

This scene of extermination went on for an hour before the curtain of death covered and ended it: shortly after six in the morning it was all finished; the corps were beginning to reassemble and to identify themselves, their sorrowful countenances revealing the losses in the thinned ranks of their officers and comrades, when the commander in chief appeared. He could see for himself the desolation among his battalions and that devastated area littered with corpses, with scattered limbs and bullets, with weapons and torn uniforms. Some of these were burning together with the corpses, which produced an unbearable and nauseating odor. The bodies, with their blackened and bloody faces disfigured by a desperate death, their hair and uniforms burning at once, presented a dreadful and truly hellish sight. What trophies—those of the battlefield! Quite soon some of the bodies were left naked by fire, others by disgraceful rapacity, especially among our men. The enemy could be identified by their whiteness, by their robust and bulky shapes. What a sad spectacle, that of the dead and dying! What a horror, to inspect the area and find the remains of friends—! With what anxiety did some seek others and with what ecstasy did they embrace each other! Questions followed one after the other, even while the bullets were still whistling around, in the midst of the groans of the wounded and the last breaths of the dying.

The general then addressed his crippled battalions, lauding their courage and thanking them in the name of their country. . . .

Shortly before Santa Anna's speech, an unpleasant episode had taken place, which, since it occurred after the end of the skirmish, was looked upon as base murder and which contributed greatly to the coolness that was noted. Some seven men had survived the general carnage and, under the protection of General Castrillón, they were brought before Santa Anna. Among them was one of great stature, well proportioned, with regular features, in whose face there was the imprint of adversity, but in whom one also noticed a degree of resignation and nobility that did him honor. He was the naturalist David Crockett, well known in North America for his unusual adventures, who had undertaken to explore the country and who, finding himself in Béjar at the very moment of surprise, had taken refuge in the Alamo, fearing that his status as a foreigner might not be respected. Santa Anna answered Castrillón's intervention in Crockett's behalf with a gesture of indignation and, addressing himself to the sappers, the troops closest to him, ordered his execution. The commanders and officers were outraged at this action and did not support the order, hoping that once the fury of the moment had blown over these men would be spared; but several officers who were around the president and who, perhaps, had not been present during the moment of danger, became noteworthy by an infamous deed, surpassing the soldiers in cruelty. They thrust themselves forward, in order to flatter their commander, and with swords in hand, fell upon these unfortunate, defenseless men just as a tiger leaps upon his prey. Though tortured before they were killed, these unfortunates died without complaining and without humiliating themselves before their torturers. . . . I confess that the very memory of it makes me tremble and that my ear can still hear the penetrating, doleful sound of the victims.

To whom was this sacrifice useful and what advantage was derived by increasing the number of victims? It was paid for dearly, though it could have been otherwise had these men been required to walk across the floor carpeted with the bodies over which we stepped, had they been rehabilitated generously and required to communicate to their comrades the fate that awaited them if they did not desist from their unjust cause. They could have informed their comrades of the force and resources that the enemy had. According to documents found among these men and to subsequent information, the force within the Alamo consisted of 182 men; but according to the number counted by us it was 253. Doubtless the total did not exceed either of these two, and in any case the number is less than that referred to by the commander in chief in his communiqúe, which contends that in the excavations and the trenches alone more than 600 bodies had been buried. What was the object of this misrepresentation? Some believe that it was done to give greater importance to the episode, others, that it was done to excuse our losses and to make it less painful.

Death united in one place both friends and enemies; within a few hours a funeral pyre rendered into ashes those men who moments before had been so brave that in a blind fury they had unselfishly offered their lives and had met their ends in combat. The greater part of our dead were buried by their comrades, but the enemy, who seems to have some respect for the dead, attributed the great pyre of their dead to our hatred. I, for one, wishing to count the bodies for myself, arrived at the moment the flames were reddening, ready to consume them.

The reflections after the assault, even a few days after it had taken place, were generally well founded; for instance, it was questioned why a breach had not been opened? What had been the use of bringing up the artillery if it were not to be used when necessity required, and why should we have been forced to leap over a fortified place as if we were flying birds? Why, before agreeing on the sacrifice, which was great indeed, had no one borne in mind that we had no means at our disposal to save our wounded? Why were our lives uselessly sacrificed in a deserted and totally hostile country if our losses could not be replaced? These thoughts were followed by others more or less well based, for the taking of the Alamo was not considered a happy event, but rather a defeat that saddened us all. In Béjar one heard nothing but laments; each officer who died aroused compassion and renewed reproaches. Those who arrived later added their criticism to ours, and some of these, one must say, regretted not having been present, because those who obeyed against their own judgment nonetheless attained eternal glory.

All military authors agree that battles should be undertaken only in extreme situations, and I will take full advantage of these opinions; they affirm that as a general rule, so long as there is a way to weaken and overcome the enemy without combat, it should be adopted and combat avoided. Civilization has humanized man and thanks to its good effects the more barbarous methods that were prevalent before, to kill the greatest number of men in the least possible time, have been abandoned; murderous maneuvers to destroy a whole army at a single blow have been discarded. It has been established as an axiom that a general entrusted with the command of an army should devote as much zeal to sparing the blood of his army as to the enemy. The opinion of the military sages, together with that of the moralists, states that the general who is frugal with the blood of his soldiers is the savior of his country, whereas he who squanders and sacrifices it foolishly is the murderer of his compatriots.

24

View from the American Side

William Barret Travis and the San Felipe *Telegraph*

Facing Santa Anna's army, the Texans sought to defend the Alamo. Jim Bowie, a figure of the rugged southwest frontier, having recently returned from land speculation, slave trading, and brawling with the aid of his famous eight-and-a-half-inch-long knife, is said to have declared: "We will rather die in these ditches than give up [the Alamo] to the enemy." The Alamo desperately needed reinforcements. And it got a few, powerful in legend. William Barret Travis, a frontier lawyer, politician, and soldier who had come to Texas on his "big black hoss" after murdering a man and leaving behind a wife and family in Alabama, arrived with thirty soldiers from the ragtag Texas army to join Bowie's volunteers. When Bowie fell ill with pneumonia, Travis took command of the beleaguered fort. Davy Crockett arrived from Tennessee with twelve men and his long rifle. Then as now he was the epitome of the American frontiersman, the teller and subject of tall tales. Following his legend right into the West, by some instinct he wound up at the place that would transform his essentially comic career into real and towering heroism. Eventually thirty-two more volunteers arrived from the nearby town of Gonzales, bringing the garrison's defenders to 187 men. Travis's calls for Texas army troops were never answered: Colonel Fannin, the commander nearest the Alamo, feared abandoning the position he held.

Published all over the country, Travis's letters made the battle of the Alamo famous. His prediction that "the victory will cost the enemy so dear, that it will be worse for him than a defeat" proved true. When the siege ended on March 6, 1836, with all the Alamo's defender's dead, Santa Anna's army had already suffered a fatal blow. He had lost sixteen hundred of his best troops, with many more wounded. He had sacrificed not only the weeks it took to besiege the fortress, but the weeks his army needed afterward to recover. When the two sides again met at San Jacinto near Galveston Bay on April 21, the Texans, shouting as their battle cry "Remember the Alamo!," destroyed the Mexican army in an afternoon. Until 1845, when it was admitted to the Union as the twenty-eighth state, Texas was an independent nation, the Lone Star Republic.

BEFORE YOU READ

1. Why did Travis write his letters? What did he hope to gain from them?
2. What was Travis's attitude toward the Mexican inhabitants of Béjar?
3. How did the newspaper account characterize the battle? How reliable do you think the account is?

LETTERS FROM THE ALAMO

To the People in Texas, and All Americans in the World.

Commandancy of the Alamo, Béjar, Feb. 24, 1836.

Fellow-citizens and compatriots,—

I am besieged by a thousand or more of the Mexicans, under Santa Anna. I have sustained a continual bombardment and cannonade for twenty-four hours, and have not lost a man. The enemy have demanded a surrender at discretion, otherwise the garrison is to be put to the sword, if the fort is taken. I have answered the summons with a cannon-shot, and our flag still waves proudly from the walls. *I shall never surrender or retreat:* then I call on you, in the name of Liberty, of Patriotism, and of every thing dear to the American character, to come to our aid with all despatch. The enemy are receiving reinforcements daily, and will no doubt increase to three or four thousand in four or five days. Though this call may be neglected, I am determined to sustain myself as long as possible, and die like a soldier, who never forgets what is due to his own honour and that of his country. *Victory or Death!*

W. BARRET TRAVIS,
Lieutenant-Colonel, Commanding.

P. S. The Lord is on our side. When the enemy appeared in sight, we had not three bushels of corn. We have since found, in deserted houses, eighty or ninety bushels, and got into the walls twenty or thirty head of beeves.

T.

To the President of the Convention.

Commandancy of the Alamo, Béjar, March 3, 1836.

Sir,—In the present confusion of the political authorities of the country, and in the absence of the commander-in-chief, I beg leave to communicate to you the situation of this garrison. You have doubtless already seen my official report of the action of the 25th ult., made on that day to General Sam. Houston, together with the various communications heretofore sent by express. I shall, therefore, confine myself to what has transpired since that date.

From the 25th to the present date, the enemy have kept up a bombardment from two howitzers, (one a five and a half inch, and the other an eight inch,) and a heavy cannonade from two long nine-pounders, mounted on a battery on the opposite side of the river, at the distance of four hundred yards from our walls. During this period, the enemy have been busily employed in encircling us with intrenched encampments on all sides, at the following distances, to wit,—in Bexar, four hundred yards west; in Lavilleta, three hundred yards south; at the powder-house, one thousand yards east by south; on the ditch,

Henry Stuart Foote, *Texas and the Texans; or, Advance of the Anglo-Americans to the South-West*, vol. 2, (Philadelphia: Thomas, Cowperthwait and Co., 1841), pp. 218–24.

eight hundred yards north-east; and at the old mill, eight hundred yards north. Notwithstanding all this, a company of thirty-two men from Gonzales, made their way into us on the morning of the 1st inst. at three o'clock, and Col. J. B. Bonham (a courier from Gonzales) got in this morning at eleven o'clock, without molestation. I have so fortified this place, that the walls are generally proof against cannon-balls; and I still continue to intrench on the inside, and strengthen the walls by throwing up the dirt. At least two hundred shells have fallen inside of our works without having injured a single man; indeed, we have been so fortunate as not to lose a man from any cause, and we have killed many of the enemy. The spirits of my men are still high, although they have had much to depress them. We have contended for ten days against an enemy whose numbers are variously estimated at from fifteen hundred to six thousand men, with Gen. Ramirez Sezma and Col. Bartres, the aid-de-camp of Santa Anna, at their head. A report was circulated that Santa Anna himself was with the enemy, but I think it was false. A reinforcement of about one thousand men is now entering Bexar from the west, and I think it more than probable that Santa Anna is now in town, from the rejoicing we hear. Col. Fannin is said to be on the march to this place with reinforcements; but I fear it is not true, as I have repeatedly sent to him for aid without receiving any. Col. Bonham, my special messenger, arrived at Labahia fourteen days ago, with a request for aid; and on the arrival of the enemy in Bexar ten days ago, I sent an express to Col. F., which arrived at Goliad on the next day, urging him to send us rein-forcements—*none have yet arrived.* I look to the *colonies alone* for aid; unless it arrives soon, I shall have to fight the enemy on his own terms. I will, however, do the best I can under the circumstances, and I feel confident that the deter-mined valour and desperate courage, heretofore evinced by my men, will not fail them in the last struggle, and although they may be sacrificed to the vengeance of a Gothic enemy, the victory will cost the enemy so dear, that it will be worse for him than a defeat. I hope your honourable body will hasten on reinforcements, ammunition, and provisions to our aid, as soon as possible. We have provisions for twenty days for the men we have; our supply of am-munition is limited. At least five hundred pounds of cannon powder, and two hundred rounds of six, nine, twelve, and eighteen pound balls—ten kegs of rifle powder, and a supply of lead, should be sent to this place without delay, under a sufficient guard.

If these things are promptly sent, and large reinforcements are hastened to this frontier, this neighbourhood will be the great and decisive battle ground. The power of Santa Anna is to be met here or in the colonies; we had better meet them here, than to suffer a war of desolation to rage in our settlements. A blood-red banner waves from the church of Bexar, and in the camp above us, in token that the war is one of vengeance against rebels; they have declared us as such, and demanded that we should surrender at discretion, or that this garrison should be put to the sword. Their threats have had no influence on me or my men, but to make all fight with desperation, and that high-souled courage which characterizes the patriot, who is willing to die in defence of his country's liberty and his own honour.

The citizens of this municipality are all our enemies except those who have joined us heretofore; we have but three Mexicans now in the fort; those who have not joined us in this extremity, should be declared public enemies, and their property should aid in paying the expenses of the war.

The bearer of this will give your honourable body, a statement more in detail, should he escape through the enemy's lines. *God and Texas!—Victory or Death!!*

Your obedient ser't.
W. BARRET TRAVIS, *Lieut. Col. Comm.*

P. S. The enemy's troops are still arriving, and the reinforcement will probably amount to two or three thousand.

T.

SAN FELIPE *Telegraph*, MARCH 24, 1836

At day-break of the 6th inst. the enemy surrounded the fort with their infantry, with the cavalry forming a circle outside to prevent escape on the part of the garrison; the number consisted of at least 4000 against 140! General Santa Anna commanded in person, assisted by four Generals and a formidable train of artillery. Our men had been previously much fatigued and harassed by nightwatching and incessant toils, having experienced for some days past, a heavy bombardment and several real and feigned attacks. But, American valour and American love of Liberty displayed themselves to the last; they were never more conspicuous: twice did the enemy apply to the walls their scaling ladders, and, twice did they receive a check; for our men were determined to verify the words of the immortal Travis, "to make the victory worse to the enemy than a defeat." A pause ensued after the second attack, which was renewed on the third time, owing to the exertions of Santa Anna and his officers; they then poured in over the walls, "like sheep;" the struggle, however, did not even there cease—unable from the crowd and for want of time to load their guns and rifles, our men made use of the but-ends of the latter, and continued to fight and to resist, until life ebbed out through their numberless wounds, and the enemy had conquered the fort, but not its brave, its matchless defenders: they perished, but they yielded not: only one (Warner) remained to ask for quarter, which was denied by the unrelenting enemy—total extermination succeeded, and the darkness of death occupied the memorable Alamo, but recently so teeming with gallant spirits and filled with deeds of never-failing remembrance. We envy not the feelings of the victors, for they must have been bitter and galling; not proud ones. Who would not be rather one of the Alamo heroes, than of the living of its merciless victors? Spirits of the mighty, though fallen! honours and rest are with ye; the spark of immortality which animated your forms, shall brighten into a flame, and Texas, the whole world, shall hail ye like demi-gods of old, as founders of new actions, and as patterns for imitation!

From the commencement to its close, the storming lasted less than an hour. Major Evans, master of ordnance, was killed when in the act of setting fire to the powder magazine, agreeably to the previous orders from Travis. The end of David Crocket of Tennessee, the great hunter of the West, was as glorious as his career through life had been useful. He and his companions were found surrounded by piles of assailants, whom they had immolated on the altar of Texas liberties. The countenance of Crocket was unchanged: he had in death that freshness of hue, which his exercise of pursuing the beasts of the forest and the prairie had imparted to him. Texas places him, exultingly, amongst the martyrs in her cause. Col. Travis stood on the walls cheering his men, exclaiming "Hurra, my boys!" till he received a second shot, and fell; it is stated that a Mexican general (Mora) then rushed upon him, and lifted his sword to destroy his victim, who, collecting all his last expiring energies, directed a thrust at the former, which changed their relative positions; for the victim became the victor, and the remains of both descended to eternal sleep; but not alike to everlasting fame.

Travis's negro was spared, because, as the enemy said, "his master had behaved like a brave man;" words which of themselves form an epitaph: they are already engraved on the hearts of Texans, and should be inscribed on his tomb. Col. James Bowie, who had for several days been sick, was murdered in his bed; his remains were mutilated. Humanity shudders at describing these scenes; and the pen, as if a living thing, stops to gain fresh force, that sensibility may give way to duty.

Mrs. Dickinson and her child, and a negro of Bowie's, and, as before said, Travis's, were spared.

Our dead were denied the right of Christian burial; being stripped and thrown into a pile, and burned. Would that we could gather up their ashes and place them in urns!

It is stated that about fifteen hundred of the enemy were killed and wounded in the last and previous attacks.

FOR CRITICAL THINKING

1. The battle of the Alamo is one of the legendary events of the history of the United States. What aspects of the battle explain why it became legend? Do you think the writers of this time were aware of their part in creating the legend, the heroic story of the Alamo?

2. Of the accounts of the battle of the Alamo you have read, which seems the fairest and most accurate? Why? What makes one account more or less convincing than another?

25

Crossing the Great Divide
Meriwether Lewis and William Clark

The most famous expedition in American history was the brainchild of Thomas Jefferson. For years Jefferson had dreamed that a party of explorers could search out a passage to the Pacific, win the Indians to the new republic, and study the geography, plants, and minerals of a vast and unknown territory.

Meriwether Lewis and William Clark were two young men willing to follow Jefferson's dream. Their expedition from St. Louis to the mouth of the Columbia River and back is one of the great adventure stories of our history. The journals and notebooks that members of the party kept have been invaluable to historians, geographers, anthropologists, botanists, and zoologists.

The selections here present the expedition crossing the Great Divide—the peak of the Rocky Mountains where the rivers flow either to the east or the west— in one of the most difficult parts of their journey. The reader can see their careful search for information about the best way west, and their close observation of native American ways. Here also is the most famous single dramatic episode of the expedition: the extraordinary moment when Sacajawea, wife of one of their interpreters, meets a party of Shoshone, her native nation, headed by a chief who is the brother she has not seen since she was a small child. The first excerpt was written by Nicholas Biddle, who was later head of the Bank of the United States. Biddle's descriptions are taken from the notes of various participants in the expedition. They have sometimes been published— incorrectly—as part of the actual journals of Lewis and Clark.

BEFORE YOU READ

1. How did Lewis characterize the Indians and Indian life? What about them did he find fascinating, hard to understand, or admirable?
2. What did he offer Chief Cameahwait in return for his help and horses?
3. Why was crossing the Rocky Mountains so difficult?

SATURDAY, AUGUST 17TH 1805.

[Biddle]

Captain Lewis rose very early and despatched Drewyer and the Indian down the river in quest of the boats. Sheilds was sent out at the same time to hunt,

Bernard DeVoto, *The Journals of Lewis and Clark* (Boston: Houghton Mifflin Co., 1953), pp. 202–06, 207–11, 213–14.

while M'Neal prepared a breakfast out of the remainder of the meat. Drewyer had been gone about two hours, and the Indians were all anxiously waiting for some news, when an Indian who had straggled a short distance down the river, returned with a report that he had seen the white men, who were only a short distance below, and were coming on. The Indians were all transported with joy, and the chief in the warmth of his satisfaction renewed his embrace to Capt. Lewis. . . .

On setting out at seven o'clock, Captain Clarke with Chaboneau and his wife walked on shore, but they had not gone more than a mile before Clarke saw Sacajawea, who was with her husband 100 yards ahead, began to dance and show every mark of the most extravagant joy, turning round him and pointing to several Indians, whom he now saw advancing on horseback, sucking her fingers at the same time to indicate that they were of her native tribe. As they advanced, Captain Clarke discovered among them Drewyer dressed like an Indian, from whom he learnt the situation of the party. While the boats were performing the circuit, he went towards the forks with the Indians, who as they went along, sang aloud with the greatest appearance of delight.

We soon drew near to the camp, and just as we approached it a woman made her way through the crowd towards Sacajawea, and recognising each other, they embraced with the most tender affection. The meeting of these two young women had in it something peculiarly touching, not only in the ardent manner in which their feelings were expressed, but from the real interest of their situation. They had been companions in childhood, in the war with the Minetarees they had both been taken prisoners in the same battle, they had shared and softened the rigours of their captivity, till one of them had escaped from the Minetarees, with scarce a hope of ever seeing her friend relieved from the hands of her enemies. While Sacajawea was renewing among the women the friendships of former days, Captain Clarke went on, and was received by Captain Lewis and the chief, who after the first embraces and salutations were over, conducted him to a sort of circular tent or shade of willows. Here he was seated on a white robe; and the chief immediately tied in his hair six small shells resembling pearls, an ornament highly valued by these people, who procure them in the course of trade from the sea-coast. The moccasins of the whole party were then taken off, and after much ceremony the smoking began. After this the conference was to be opened, and glad of an opportunity of being able to converse more intelligibly, Sacajawea was sent for; she came into the tent, sat down, and was beginning to interpret, when in the person of Cameahwait she recognised her brother: She instantly jumped up, and ran and embraced him, throwing over him her blanket and weeping profusely: The chief was himself moved, though not in the same degree. After some conversation between them she resumed her seat, and attempted to interpret for us, but her new situation seemed to overpower her, and she was frequently interrupted by her tears. After the council was finished the unfortunate woman learnt that all her family were dead except two brothers, one of whom was absent, and a son of her eldest sister, a small boy, who was immediately adopted by her.

[Lewis]

SATURDAY AUGUST 17TH 1805.

we made them [the Indians] sensible of their dependance on the will of our government for every species of merchandize as well for their defence & comfort; and apprized them of the strength of our government and it's friendly dispositions towards them. we also gave them as a reason why we wished to pe[ne]trate the country as far as the ocean to the west of them was to examine and find out a more direct way to bring merchandize to them. that as no trade could by carryed on with them before our return to our homes that it was mutually advantageous to them as well as to ourselves that they should render us such aids as they had in their power to furnish in order to haisten our voyage and of course our return home. that such were their horses to transport our baggage without which we could not subsist, and that a pilot to conduct us through the mountains was also necessary if we could not decend the river by water. but that we did not ask either their horses or their services without giving a satisfactory compensation in return. that at present we wished them to collect as many horses as were necessary to transport our baggage to their village on the Columbia where we would then trade with them at our leasure for such horses as they could spare us.

the chief thanked us for friendship towards himself and nation & declared his wish to serve us in every rispect. that he was sorry to find that it must yet be some time before they could be furnished with firearms but said they could live as they had done heretofore until we brought them as we had promised. he said they had not horses enough with them at present to remove our baggage to their village over the mountain, but that he would return tomorrow and encourage his people to come over with their horses and that he would bring his own and assist us. this was complying with all we wished at present.

we next enquired who were chiefs among them. Cameahwait pointed out two others whom he said were Chiefs. we gave him a medal of the small size with the likeness of Mr. Jefferson the President of the U' States in releif on one side and clasp hands with a pipe and tomahawk in the other, to the other Chiefs we gave each a small medal which were struck in the Presidency of George Washing[ton] Esqr. we also gave small medals of the last discription two young men whom the 1st Chief informed us were good young men and much rispected among them. we gave the 1st Chief an uniform coat shirt a pair of scarlet legings a carrot of tobacco and some small articles to each of the others we gave a shi[r]t leging[s] handkerchief a knife some tobacco and a few small articles we also distributed a good quantity paint mockerson awles knives beads looking-glasses &c among the other Indians and gave them a plentifull meal of lyed corn which was the first they had ever eaten in their lives. they were much pleased with it. every article about us appeared to excite astonishment in there minds; the appearance of the men, their arms, the canoes, our manner of working them, the b[l]ack man york and the sagacity of my dog were equally objects of admiration. I also shot my air-gun which was so perfectly incomprehensible that they immediately denominated it the great medicine.

Capt. Clark and myself now concerted measures for our future operations, and it was mutually agreed that he should set out tomorrow morning with eleven men furnished with axes and other necessary tools for making canoes, their arms accoutrements and as much of their baggage as they could carry. also to take the indians, C[h]arbono and the indian woman with him; that on his arrival at the Shoshone camp he was to leave Charbono and the Indian woman to haisten the return of the Indians with their horses to this place, and to proceede himself with the eleven men down the Columbia in order to examine the river and if he found it navigable and could obtain timber to set about making canoes immediately. In the mean time I was to bring the party and baggage to the Shoshone Camp, calculating that by the time I should reach that place that he would have sufficiently informed himself with rispect to the state of the river &c. as to determine us whether to prosicute our journey from thence by land or water. in the former case we should want all the horses which we could perchase, and in the latter only to hire the Indians to transport our baggage to the place at which we made the canoes.

SUNDAY AUGUST 18TH 1805.

This morning while Capt. Clark was busily engaged in preparing for his rout, I exposed some articles to barter with the Indians for horses as I wished a few at this moment to releive the men who were going with Capt Clark from the labour of carrying their baggage, and also one to keep here in order to pack the meat to camp which the hunters might kill. I soon obtained three very good horses. for which I gave an uniform coat, a pair of legings, a few handkerchiefs, three knives and some other small articles the whole of which did not cost more than about 20$ in the U' States. the Indians seemed quite as well pleased with their bargin as I was. the men also purchased one for an old checked shirt a pair of old legings and a knife. two of those I purchased Capt. C. took on with him. at 10 A.M. Capt. Clark departed with his detachment and all the Indians except 2 men and 2 women who remained with us.

after there departure this morning I had all the stores and baggage of every discription opened and aired. and began the operation of forming the packages in proper parsels for the purpose of transporting them on horseback. the rain in the evening compelled me to desist from my operations. I had the raw hides put in the water in order to cut them in throngs proper for lashing the packages and forming the necessary geer for pack horses, a business which I fortunately had not to learn on this occasion. I had the net arranged and set this evening to catch some trout which we could see in great abundance at the bottom of the river.

MONDAY AUGUST 19TH 1805.

The Shoshonees may be estimated at about 100 warriors, and about three times that number of women and children[1] they have more children among them than I expected to have seen among a people who procure subsistence with such difficulty. there are but few very old persons, nor did they appear to treat those with much tenderness or rispect. The man is the sole propryetor of his wives and daughters, and can barter or dispose of either as he thinks proper. a plurality of wives is common among them, but these are not generally sisters as with the Minnitares & Mandans but are purchased of different fathers. The father frequently disposes of his infant daughters in marriage to men who are grown or to men who have sons for whom they think proper to provide wives. the compensation given in such cases usually consists of horses or mules which the father receives at the time of contract and converts to his own uce. the girl remains with her parents untill she is conceived to have obtained the age of puberty which with them is considered to be about the age of 13 or 14 years. the female at this age is surrendered to her soveriegn lord and husband agreeably to contract, and with her is frequently restored by the father quite as much as he received in the first instance in payment for his daughter; but this is discretionary with the father. Sah-car-gar-we-ah had been thus disposed of before she was taken by the Minnetares, or had arrived to the years of puberty. the husband was yet living with this band. he was more than double her age and had two other wives. he claimed her as his wife but said that as she had had a child by another man, who was Charbono, that he did not want her.

They seldom correct their children particularly the boys who soon become masters of their own acts. they give as a reason that it cows and breaks the sperit of the boy to whip him, and that he never recovers his independence of mind after he is grown. They treat their women but with little rispect, and compel them to perform every species of drudgery. they collect the wild fruits and roots, attend to the horses or assist in that duty, cook, dress the skins and make all their apparel, collect wood and make their fires, arrange and form their lodges, and when they travel pack the horses and take charge of all the baggage; in short the man dose little else except attend his horses hunt and fish. the man considers himself degraded if he is compelled to walk any distance; and if he is so unfortunately poor as only to possess two horses he rides the best himself and leavs the woman or women if he has more than one, to transport their baggage and children on the other, and to walk if the horse is unable to carry the additional weight of their persons. the chastity of their women is not held in high estimation, and the husband will for a trifle barter the companion of his bead for a night or longer if he conceives the reward adiquate; tho' they are not so importunate that we should caress their women as the siouxs were. and some of their women appear to be held more sacred than in any nation we have seen. I have requested the men to give them no cause of jealousy

---

1. Lewis's figures refer to this band only.

by having connection with their women without their knowledge, which with them, strange as it may seem is considered as disgracefull to the husband as clandestine connections of a similar kind are among civilized nations. to prevent this mutual exchange of good officies altogether I know it impossible to effect, particularly on the part of our young men whom some months abstanence have made very polite to those tawney damsels. no evil has yet resulted and I hope will not from these connections.

notwithstanding the late loss of horses which this people sustained by the Minnetares the stock of the band may be very safely estimated at seven hundred of which they are perhaps about 40 coalts and half that number of mules. their arms offensive and defensive consist in the bow and arrows shield, some, lances, and a weapon called by the Cippeways who formerly used it, the poggar'-mag-gon' [war club]. in fishing they employ wairs, gigs, and fishing hooks. the salmon is the principal object of their pursuit. they snair wolves and foxes.

I was anxious to learn whether these people had the venerial, and made the enquiry through the interpreter and his wife; the information was that they sometimes had it but I could not learn their remedy; they most usually die with it's effects. this seems a strong proof that these disorders bothe ganaraehah and Louis Venerae[2] are native disorders of America. tho' these people have suffered much by the small pox which is known to be imported and perhaps those other disorders might have been contracted from other indian tribes who by a round of communications might have obtained from the Europeans since it was introduced into that quarter of the globe. but so much detached on the other ha[n]d from all communication with the whites that I think it most probable that those disorders are original with them.

from the middle of May to the first of September these people reside on the waters of the Columbia where they consider themselves in perfect security from their enimies as they have not as yet ever found their way to this retreat; during this season the salmon furnish the principal part of their subsistence and as this fish either perishes or returns about the 1st of September they are compelled at this season in surch of subsistence to resort to the Missouri, in the vallies of which, there is more game even [than] within the mountains. here they move slowly down the river in order to collect and join other bands either of their own nation or the Flatheads, and having become sufficiently strong as they conceive venture on the Eastern side of the Rocky mountains into the plains, where the buffaloe abound. but they never leave the interior of the mountains while they can obtain a scanty subsistence, and always return as soon as they have acquired a good stock of dryed meat in the plains; when this stock is consumed they venture again into the plains; thus alternately obtaining their food at the risk of their lives and retiring to the mountains, while they consume it. These people are now on the eve of their departure for the Missouri, and inform us that they expect to be joined at or about the three forks by several bands of their own nation, and a band of the Flatheads.

2. **ganaraehah and Louis Venerae:** Gonorrhea and syphilis.

[Lewis]

TUESDAY AUGUST 20TH 1805.

I walked down the river about 3/4 of a mile and selected a place near the river bank unperceived by the Indians for a cash [cache], which I set three men to make, and directed the centinel to discharge his gun if he perceived any of the Indians going down in that direction which was to be the signal for the men at work on the cash to desist and seperate, least these people should discover our deposit and rob us of the baggage we intend leaving here. by evening the cash was completed unperceived by the Indians, and all our packages made up. the Pack-saddles and harness is not yet complete. in this operation we find ourselves at a loss for nails and boards; for the first we substitute throngs of raw hide which answer verry well, and for the last [had] to cut off the blades of our oars and use the plank of some boxes which have heretofore held other articles and put those articles into sacks of raw hide which I have had made for the purpose. by this means I have obtained as many boards as will make 20 saddles which I suppose will be sufficient for our present exegencies. I made up a small assortment of medicines, together with the specemines of plants, minerals, seeds &c, which, I have collected between this place and the falls of the Missouri which I shall deposit here.

I now prevailed on the Chief to instruct me with rispect to the geography of his country. this he undertook very cheerfully, by delineating the rivers on the ground. but I soon found that his information fell far short of my expectation or wishes. he drew the river on which we now are [the Lemhi] to which he placed two branches just above us, which he shewed me from the openings of the mountains were in view; he next made it discharge itself into a large river which flowed from the S.W. about ten miles below us [the Salmon], then continued this joint stream in the same direction of this valley or N.W. for one days march and then enclined it to the West for 2 more days march. here we placed a number of heaps of sand on each side which he informed me represented the vast mountains of rock eternally covered with snow through which the river passed. that the perpendicular and even juting rocks so closely hemned in the river that there was no possibil[it]y of passing along the shore; that the bed of the river was obstructed by sharp pointed rocks and the rapidity of the stream such that the whole surface of the river was beat into perfect foam as far as the eye could reach. that the mountains were also inaccessible to man or horse. he said that this being the state of the country in that direction that himself nor none of his nation had ever been further down the river than these mountains.

in this manner I spend the day smoking with them and acquiring what information I could with respect to their country. they informed me that they could pass to the Spaniards by the way of the yellowstone river in 10 days. I can discover that these people are by no means friendly to the Spaniards. their complaint is, that the Spaniards will not let them have fire arms and ammunition, that they put them off by telling them that if they suffer them to have guns they will kill each other, thus leaving them defenceless and an easy prey to their bloodthirsty neighbours to the East of them, who being in possession of fire arms hunt them up and murder them without rispect to sex or age and plunder them of their horses on all occasions. they told me that to avoid their enemies who were eternally harrassing them that they were obliged to remain in the interior of these mountains at least two thirds of the year where the[y] suffered as we then saw great heardships for the want of food sometimes living for weeks without meat and only a little fish roots and berries. but this added Câmeahwait, with his ferce eyes and lank jaws grown meager for the want of food, would not be the case if we had guns, we could then live in the country of buffaloe and eat as our enimies do and not be compelled to hide ourselves in these mountains and live on roots and berries as the bear do. we do not fear our enimies when placed on an equal footing with them. I told them that the Minnetares Mandans . . . had promised us to desist from making war on them & that we would indevour to find the means of making the Minnetares of fort d[e] Prarie or as they call them Pahkees desist from waging war against them also. that after our finally returning to our homes towards the rising sun whitemen would come to them with an abundance of guns and every other article necessary to their defence and comfort, and that they would be enabled to supply themselves with these articles on reasonable terms in exchange for the skins of the beaver Otter and Ermin so abundant in their country. they expressed great pleasure at this information and said they had been long anxious to see the whitemen that traded guns; and that we might rest assured of their friendship and that they would do whatever we wished them.

26

Autobiography of a Circuit Rider
Peter Cartwright

Peter Cartwright was a pioneer minister who contributed greatly to the work of the Methodists in bringing evangelical Protestantism to new settlements in the West. Born in Virginia in 1785 and raised in Kentucky, Cartwright as an itinerant preacher of enthusiastic religion rode circuit through parts of Kentucky, Tennessee, Indiana, and Ohio. In 1824, his hatred of slavery brought the transfer of his circuit to Illinois. Evidently, he was more persuasive as a revivalist than as a politician; in 1846 Cartwright lost an election for the United States House of Representatives. The winner was Abraham Lincoln.

The circuit riders preached a highly emotional form of religion, yet one that emphasized personal morality, civic virtue, and the importance of education. Their contribution to the characteristic culture of the American Middle West quickly came to distinguish much of American life. Cartwright's experience of conversion and his subsequent career are highly representative of circuit riders. He wrote his autobiography in 1857.

BEFORE YOU READ

1. What spurred Cartwright's conversion?
2. How did circuit riders recruit and convert people? Why do you think enthusiastic religion was so popular on the frontier?
3. What were the *jerks?* How do you explain them?
4. What were the main problems Cartwright faced in his mission?

CONVERSION

In 1801, when I was in my sixteenth year, my father, my eldest half brother, and myself, attended a wedding about five miles from home, where there was a great deal of drinking and dancing, which was very common at marriages in those days. I drank little or nothing; my delight was in dancing. After a late hour in the night, we mounted our horses and started for home. I was riding my racehorse.

A few minutes after we had put up the horses, and were sitting by the fire, I began to reflect on the manner in which I had spent the day and evening. I felt guilty and condemned. I rose and walked the floor. My mother was in bed. It seemed to me, all of a sudden, my blood rushed to my head, my heart

W. P. Strickland, ed., *Autobiography of Peter Cartwright, The Backwoods Preacher* (New York: Phillips and Hunt, 1856), pp. 34–38, 40–46, 48–53.

palpitated, in a few minutes I turned blind; an awful impression rested on my mind that death had come and I was unprepared to die. I fell on my knees and began to ask God to have mercy on me.

My mother sprang from her bed, and was soon on her knees by my side, praying for me, and exhorting me to look to Christ for mercy, and then and there I promised the Lord that if he would spare me, I would seek and serve him; and I never fully broke that promise. My mother prayed for me a long time. At length we lay down, but there was little sleep for me. Next morning I rose, feeling wretched beyond expression. I tried to read in the Testament, and retired many times to secret prayer through the day, but found no relief. I gave up my racehorse to my father, and requested him to sell him. I went and brought my pack of cards, and gave them to mother, who threw them into the fire, and they were consumed. I fasted, watched, and prayed, and engaged in regular reading of the Testament. I was so distressed and miserable, that I was incapable of any regular business.

My father was greatly distressed on my account, thinking I must die, and he would lose his only son. He bade me retire altogether from business, and take care of myself.

Soon it was noised abroad that I was distracted, and many of my associates in wickedness came to see me, to try and divert my mind from those gloomy thoughts of my wretchedness; but all in vain. I exhorted them to desist from the course of wickedness which we had been guilty of together. The class-leader and local preacher were sent for. They tried to point me to the bleeding Lamb, they prayed for me most fervently. Still I found no comfort, and although I had never believed in the doctrine of unconditional election and reprobation, I was sorely tempted to believe I was a reprobate, and doomed, and lost eternally, without any chance of salvation.

At length one day I retired to the horse-lot, and was walking and wringing my hands in great anguish, trying to pray, on the borders of utter despair. It appeared to me that I heard a voice from heaven, saying "Peter, look at me." A feeling of relief flashed over me as quick as an electric shock. It gave me hopeful feelings, and some encouragement to seek mercy, but still my load of guilt remained. I repaired to the house, and told my mother what had happened to me in the horse-lot. Instantly she seemed to understand it, and told me the Lord had done this to encourage me to hope for mercy, and exhorted me to take encouragement, and seek on, and God would bless me with the pardon of my sins at another time.

Some days after this, I retired to a cave on my father's farm to pray in secret. My soul was in an agony; I wept, I prayed, and said, "Now, Lord, if there is mercy for me, let me find it," and it really seemed to me that I could almost lay hold of the Saviour, and realize a reconciled God. All of a sudden, such a fear of the devil fell upon me that it really appeared to me that he was surely personally there, to seize and drag me down to hell, soul and body, and such a horror fell on me that I sprang to my feet and ran to my mother at the house.

My mother told me that this was a device of Satan to prevent me from finding the blessing then. Three months rolled away, and still I did not find the blessing of the pardon of my sins.

This year, 1801, the Western Conference [of preachers] existed, and I think there was but one presiding elder's district in it, called the Kentucky District. William M'Kendree (afterward bishop) was appointed to the Kentucky District. Cumberland Circuit, which, perhaps, was six hundred miles round, and lying partly in Kentucky and partly in Tennessee, was one of the circuits of this district. John Page and Thomas Wilkerson were appointed to this circuit.

In the spring of this year, Mr. M'Grady, a minister of the Presbyterian Church, who had a congregation and meeting-house, as we then called them, about three miles north of my father's house, appointed a sacramental meeting in this congregation, and invited the Methodist preachers to attend with them, and especially John Page, who was a powerful Gospel minister, and was very popular among the Presbyterians. Accordingly he came, and preached with great power and success.

There were no camp-meetings in regular form at this time, but as there was a great waking up among the Churches, from the revival that had broken out at Cane Ridge, before mentioned, many flocked to those sacramental meetings. The church would not hold the tenth part of the congregation. Accordingly, the officers of the Church erected a stand in a contiguous shady grove, and prepared seats for a large congregation.

The people crowded to this meeting from far and near. They came in their large wagons, with victuals mostly prepared. The women slept in the wagons, and the men under them. Many stayed on the ground night and day for a number of nights and days together. Others were provided for among the neighbors around. The power of God was wonderfully displayed; scores of sinners fell under the preaching, like men slain in mighty battle; Christians shouted aloud for joy.

To this meeting I repaired, a guilty, wretched sinner. On the Saturday evening of said meeting, I went, with weeping multitudes, and bowed before the stand, and earnestly prayed for mercy. In the midst of a solemn struggle of soul, an impression was made on my mind, as though a voice said to me, "Thy sins are all forgiven thee." Divine light flashed all round me, unspeakable joy sprung up in my soul. I rose to my feet, opened my eyes, and it really seemed as if I was in heaven; the trees, the leaves on them, and everything seemed, and I really thought were, praising God. My mother raised the shout, my Christian friends crowded around me and joined me in praising God; and though I have been since then, in many instances, unfaithful, yet I have never, for one moment, doubted that the Lord did, then and there, forgive my sins and give me religion.

Our meeting lasted without intermission all night, and it was believed by those who had a very good right to know, that over eighty souls were converted to God during its continuance. I went on my way rejoicing for many days.

There were in the congregation a very wicked Dutchman and his wife, both of whom were profoundly ignorant of the Scriptures and the plan of salvation. His wife was a notorious scold, and so much was she given to this practice, that she made her husband unhappy, and kept him almost always in a perfect fret, so that he led a most miserable and uncomfortable life. It pleased God that day to cause the preaching of Mr. Lee to reach their guilty souls and break up the great deep of their hearts. They wept aloud, seeing their lost condition, and they, then and there, resolved to do better, and from that time forward to take up the cross and bear it, be it what it might.

The congregation were generally deeply affected. Mr. Lee exhorted them and prayed for them as long as he consistently could, and, having another appointment some distance off that evening, he dismissed the congregation, got a little refreshment, saddled his horse, mounted, and started for his evening appointment. After riding some distance, he saw, a little ahead of him, a man trudging along, carrying a woman on his back. This greatly surprised Mr. Lee. He very naturally supposed that the woman was a cripple, or had hurt herself in some way, so that she could not walk. The traveller was a small man, and the woman large and heavy.

Before he overtook them Mr. Lee began to cast about in his mind how he could render them assistance. When he came up to them, lo and behold, who should it be but the Dutchman and his wife that had been so affected under his sermon at meeting. Mr. Lee rode up and spoke to them, and inquired of the man what had happened, or what was the matter, that he was carrying his wife.

The Dutchman turned to Mr. Lee and said, "Be sure you did tell us in your sarmon dat we must take up de cross and follow de Saviour, or dat we could not be saved to go to heaven, and I does desire to go to heaven so much as any pody; and dish vife is so pad, she scold and scold all de time, and dish woman is de createst cross I have in de whole world, and I does take her up and pare her, for I must save my soul."

You may be sure Mr. Lee was posed for once, but after a few moments' reflection he told the Dutchman to put his wife down, and he dismounted from his horse. He directed them to sit down on a log by the road side. He held the reins of his horse's bridle and sat down by them, took out his Bible, read to them several passages of Scripture, and explained and expounded to them the way of the Lord more perfectly. He opened to them the nature of the cross of Christ, what it is, how it is to be taken up, and how they were to bear that cross; and after teaching and advising them some time, he prayed for them by the road side, left them deeply affected, mounted his horse, and rode on to his evening appointment.

Long before Mr. Lee came around his circuit to his next appointment the Dutchman and his scolding wife were both powerfully converted to God, and when he came round he took them into the Church. The Dutchman's wife was cured of her scolding. Of course he got clear of this cross. They lived together long and happily, adorning their profession, and giving ample evidence that re-

ligion could cure a scolding wife, and that God could and did convert poor ignorant Dutch people.

This Dutchman often told his experience in love-feasts, with thrilling effect,
and hardly ever failed to melt the whole congregation into a flood of tears; and
on one particular occasion which is vividly printed on my recollection, I believe
the whole congregation in the love-feast, which lasted beyond the time allotted for such meetings, broke out into a loud shout.

Thus Brother Lee was the honored instrument in the hand of God of planting Methodism, amid clouds of ignorance and opposition, among the early settlers of the far West. Brother Lee witnessed a good confession to the end. At
an early period of his ministry he fell from the walls of Zion with the trump of
God in his hand, and has gone to his reward in heaven. Peace to his memory.

THE GREAT REVIVAL

From 1801 for years a blessed revival of religion spread through almost the entire inhabited parts of the West, Kentucky, Tennessee, the Carolinas, and many
other parts, especially through the Cumberland country, which was so called
from the Cumberland River, which headed and mouthed in Kentucky, but in
its great bend circled south through Tennessee, near Nashville. The Presbyterians and Methodists in a great measure united in this work, met together,
prayed together, and preached together.

In this revival originated our camp-meetings, and in both these denominations they were held every year, and, indeed, have been ever since, more or less.
They would erect their camps with logs or frame them, and cover them with
clapboards or shingles. They would also erect a shed, sufficiently large to protect five thousand people from wind and rain, and cover it with boards or shingles; build a large stand, seat the shed, and here they would collect together
from forty to fifty miles around, sometimes further than that. Ten, twenty,
and sometimes thirty ministers, of different denominations, would come together and preach night and day, four or five days together; and, indeed, I
have known these camp-meetings to last three or four weeks, and great good
resulted from them. I have seen more than a hundred sinners fall like dead men
under one powerful sermon, and I have seen and heard more than five hundred
Christians all shouting aloud the high praises of God at once; and I will venture to assert that many happy thousands were awakened and converted to God
at these camp-meetings. Some sinners mocked, some of the old dry professors
opposed, some of the old starched Presbyterian preachers preached against
these exercises, but still the work went on and spread almost in every direction,
gathering additional force, until our country seemed all coming home to God.

[A] new exercise broke out among us, called the *jerks*, which was overwhelming in its effects upon the bodies and minds of the people. No matter whether
they were saints or sinners, they would be taken under a warm song or sermon,

and seized with a convulsive jerking all over, which they could not by any possibility avoid, and the more they resisted the more they jerked. If they would not strive against it and pray in good earnest, the jerking would usually abate. I have seen more than five hundred persons jerking at one time in my large congregations. Most usually persons taken with the jerks, to obtain relief, as they said, would rise up and dance. Some would run, but could not get away. Some would resist; on such the jerks were generally very severe.

To see those proud young gentlemen and young ladies, dressed in their silks, jewelry, and prunella, from top to toe, take the jerks would often excite my risibilities. The first jerk or so, you would see their fine bonnets, caps, and combs fly; and so sudden would be the jerking of the head that their long loose hair would crack almost as loud as a wagoners whip.

At one of my appointments in 1804 there was a very large congregation turned out to hear the Kentucky boy, as they called me. Among the rest there were two very finely-dressed, fashionable young ladies, attended by two brothers with loaded horsewhips. Although the house was large, it was crowded. The two young ladies, coming in late, took their seats near where I stood, and their two brothers stood in the door. I was a little unwell, and I had a phial of peppermint in my pocket. Before I commenced preaching I took out my phial and swallowed a little of the peppermint. While I was preaching, the congregation was melted into tears. The two young gentlemen moved off to the yard fence, and both the young ladies took the jerks, and they were greatly mortified about it. There was a great stir in the congregation. Some wept, some shouted, and before our meeting closed several were converted.

As I dismissed the assembly a man stepped up to me, and warned me to be on my guard, for he had heard the two brothers swear they would horsewhip me when meeting was out, for giving their sisters the jerks. "Well," said I, "I'll see to that."

I went out and said to the young men that I understood they intended to horsewhip me for giving their sisters the jerks. One replied that he did. I undertook to expostulate with him on the absurdity of the charge against me, but he swore I need not deny it; for he had seen me take out a phial, in which I carried some truck that gave his sisters the jerks. As quick as thought it came into my mind how I would get clear of my whipping, and, jerking out the peppermint phial, said I, "Yes; if I gave your sisters the jerks I'll give them to you." In a moment I saw he was scared. I moved towards him, he backed, I advanced, and he wheeled and ran, warning me not to come near him, or he would kill me. It raised the laugh on him, and I escaped my whipping. I had the pleasure, before the year was out, of seeing all four soundly converted to God, and I took them into the Church.

I always looked upon the jerks as a judgment sent from God, first, to bring sinners to repentance; and, secondly to show professors that God could work with or without means, and that he could work over and above means, and do whatsoever seemeth him good, to the glory of his grace and the salvation of the world.

There is no doubt in my mind that, with weak-minded, ignorant, and superstitious persons, there was a great deal of sympathetic feeling with many that claimed to be under the influence of this jerking exercise; and yet, with many, it was perfectly involuntary. It was, on all occasions, my practice to recommend fervent prayer as a remedy, and it almost universally proved an effectual antidote.

There were many other strange and wild exercises into which the subjects of this revival fell; such, for instance, as what was called the running, jumping, barking exercise. The Methodist preachers generally preached against this extravagant wildness. I did it uniformly in my little ministrations, and sometimes gave great offense; but I feared no consequences when I felt my awful responsibilities to God. From these wild exercises, another great evil arose from the heated and wild imaginations of some. They professed to fall into trances and see visions; they would fall at meetings and sometimes at home, and lay apparently powerless and motionless for days, sometimes for a week at a time, without food or drink; and when they came to, they professed to have seen heaven and hell, to have seen God, angels, the devil and the damned; they would prophesy, and, under the pretense of Divine inspiration, predict the time of the end of the world, and the ushering in of the great millennium.

This was the most troublesome delusion of all; it made such an appeal to the ignorance, superstition, and credulity of the people, even saint as well as sinner. I watched this matter with a vigilant eye. If I opposed it, I would have to meet the clamor of the multitude; and if any one opposed it, these very visionists would single him out, and denounce the dreadful judgments of God against him. They would even set the very day that God was to burn the world. . . . They would prophesy, that if any one did oppose them, God would send fire down from heaven and consume him, like the blasphemous Shakers. They would proclaim that they could heal all manner of diseases, and raise the dead. . . . They professed to have converse with spirits of the dead in heaven and hell, like the modern spirit rappers. Such a state of things I never saw before, and I hope in God I shall never see again.

I pondered well the whole matter in view of my responsibilities, searched the Bible for the true fulfillment of promise and prophecy, prayed to God for light and Divine aid, and proclaimed open war against these delusions. In the midst of them along came the Shakers, and Mr. Rankin, one of the Presbyterian revival preachers, joined them; Mr. G. Wall, a visionary local preacher among the Methodists, joined them; all the country was in commotion.

I made public appointments and drew multitudes together, and openly showed from the Scriptures that these delusions were false. Some of these visionary men and women prophesied that God would kill me. The Shakers soon pretended to seal my damnation. But nothing daunted, for I knew Him in whom I had believed, I threw my appointments in the midst of them, and proclaimed to listening thousands the more sure word of prophecy. This mode of attack threw a damper on these visionary, self-deluded, false prophets, sobered some, reclaimed others, and stayed the fearful tide of delusion that was sweeping over the country.

27

The Trail of Tears

John Ross

John Ross, of mixed Cherokee and white ancestry, was exactly the phenomenon that led Georgians and their great ally, Andrew Jackson, to insist on the removal of the so-called civilized tribes. Ross epitomized the "civilized," literate, prosperous, politically astute native American who successfully competed with whites. He had fought as an officer under Jackson against the Creek Indians at Horseshoe Bend. In the years after the War of 1812, he became a leader of the Cherokee as well as the successful owner of a three hundred-acre plantation run with the labor of more than twenty slaves. As leader of the fight against the removal, Ross was the chief author of the Cherokee nation's Memorial and Petition *against Jackson's policy and took the bitter responsibility for managing his people's journey west (in which his wife, Quatie, was one of the many casualties) after all his efforts to prevent it had failed.*

Ross never ceased his service to the Cherokee, remaining as principal chief of the nation in Indian territory until his death in 1866. He also developed a new cotton plantation in the West, again using numerous slaves.

BEFORE YOU READ

1. How did John Ross argue the case against the removal of the Cherokees in the *Memorial and Petition* submitted to the Senate and House of Representatives? What are the chief points he made? How persuasive do you think his argument is?

2. What were the main problems facing Ross in carrying out the removal of his people to the West?

TO THE SENATE AND
HOUSE OF REPRESENTATIVES

Washington City February 22ed 1837

The memorial and petition of the undersigned, a delegation appointed by the Cherokee nation in full council respectfully showeth:

That the Cherokee Nation deeply sensible of the evils under which they are now laboring and the still more frightful miseries which they have too much reason to apprehend, have in the most formal and solemn manner known to them, assembled in General Council to deliberate upon their existing relations with the Government of the United States, and to lay their case with respectful deference before your honorable bodies.

Gary E. Moulten, ed., *The Papers of Chief John Ross: Volume I, 1807–1839* (Tulsa: University of Oklahoma Press, 1985).

Invested with full powers to conclude an arrangement upon all the matters which interest them we have arrived at the seat of Government, and, in accordance with our usual forms of proceeding have notified the Honorable the Secretary of War [Benjamin F. Butler] that we had reached this place and, through him, solicited an interview with the Executive [Andrew Jackson]. This request has not yet been granted, nor has it to this day received an official answer, but we have reason to apprehend from circumstances which have reached us that we shall be denied this application, and are thus compelled in the discharge of our duty to our constituents, to submit to your Honorable bodies the memorial of which we are the bearers.

On former occasions we have in much detail laid before you the prominent facts of our case. We have reminded you of our long and intimate connexion with the United States, of the scenes of peril and difficulty which we have shared in common; of the friendship which had so long been generously proffered and affectionately and gratefully accepted; of the aids which were supplied us in promoting our advancement in the arts of civilized life, of the political principles which we had imbibed, of the religious faith we have been taught.

We have called your attention to the progress which under your auspices we have made, of the improvements which have marked our social and individual states; our lands brought into cultivation, our natural resources developed, our farms, workshops and factories, approximating in character and value to those of our brethren whose example we had diligently imitated.

A smooth and beautiful prospect of future advancement was opened before us. Our people had abandoned the pursuits, the habits and the tastes of the savage, and had put on the vestments of civilization, of intelligence and of a pure religion. The progress we had made furnished us with the most assured hopes of continued improvement, and we indulged in the anticipation that the time was not far distant when we should be recognised, on the footing of equality by the brethren from whom we had received all which we were now taught to prize.

This promise of golden sunshine is now overspread. Clouds and darkness have obscured its brilliancy. The winds are beginning to mutter their awful forebodings, the tempest is gathering thick and heavy over our heads, and threatens to burst upon us with terrific energy and overwhelming ruin.

In this season of calamity, where can we turn with hope or confidence? On all former occasions of peril or of doubt the Government of the United States spread over us its broad and paternal shield. It invited us to seek an asylum and a protection under its mighty arm. It assisted us with its encouragement and advice, it soothed us with its consoling assurances, it inspired us with hope and gave us a feeling of confidence and security.

But alas! this our long-cherished friend seems now to be alienated from us: this our father has raised his arm to inflict the hostile blow; this strength so long our protection is now exerted against us, and on the wide scene of existence no human aid is left us. Unless you avert your arm we are destroyed. Unless your feelings of affection and compassion are once more awakened towards your destitute and despairing children our annihilation is complete.

It is a natural inquiry among all who commiserate our situation what are the causes which have led to this disastrous revolution, to this entire change of relations? By what agency have such results been accomplished?

We have asked, and we reiterate the question how have we offended? Show us in what manner we have, however unwittingly, inflicted upon you a wrong, you shall yourselves be the judges of the extent and manner of compensation. Show us the offence which has awakened your feelings of justice against us and we will submit to that measure of punishment which you shall tell us we have merited. We cannot bring to our recollections anything we have done or anything we have omitted calculated to awaken your resentment against us.

But we are told a treaty has been made and all that is required at our hands is to comply with its stipulations. Will the faithful historian, who shall hereafter record our lamentable fate, say—the Cherokee Nation executed a treaty by which they freely and absolutely ceded the country in which they were born and educated, the property they had been industriously accumulating and improving, and, abandoning the high road to which they had been advancing from savagism had precipitated themselves into worse than their pristine degradation, will not the reader of such a narrative require the most ample proof before he will credit such a story? Will he not inquire where was the kind and parental guardian who had heretofore aided the weak, assisted the forlorn, instructed the ignorant and elevated the depressed? Where was the Government of the United States with its vigilant care over the Indian when such a bargain was made? How will he be surprised at hearing that the United States was a party to the transaction—that the authority of that Government, and the representatives of that people, which had for years been employed in leading the Cherokees from ignorance to light, from barbarism to civilization, from paganism to christianity, who had taught them new habits and new hopes was the very party which was about to appropriate to itself the fruits of the Indian's industry, the birth places of his children and the graves of his ancestors.

If such a recital could command credence must it not be on the ground that experience had shown the utter failure of all the efforts and the disappointment of all the hopes of the philanthropist and the Christian? That the natives of this favored spot of God's creation were incapable of improvement and unsusceptible of education and that they in wilful blindness, spurning the blessings which had been proffered and urged upon them would pertinaciously prefer the degradation from which it had been attempted to lead them and the barbarism from which it had been sought to elevate them?

How will his astonishment be augmented when he learns that the Cherokee people almost to a man denied the existence and the obligation of the alleged compact—that they proclaimed it to have been based in fraud and concocted in perfidy—that no authority was ever given to those who undertook in their names and on their behalf to negotiate it; that it was repudiated with unexampled unanimity when it was brought to their knowledge; that they denied that it conferred any rights or imposed any obligations.

Yet such must be the story which the faithful historian must record. In the name of the whole Cherokee people we protest against this unhallowed and unauthorized and unacknowledged compact. We deny its binding force. We recognise none of its stipulations. If contrary to every principle of justice it is to be enforced upon us, we shall at least be free from the disgrace of self humiliation. We hold the solemn disavowal of its provisions by eighteen thousand of our people.

We, the regularly commissioned delegation of the Cherokee Nation in the face of Heaven and appealing to the Searcher of all hearts for the truth of our statements ask you to listen to our remonstrances. We implore you to examine into the truth of our allegations. We refer you to your own records, to your own agents, to men deservedly enjoying your esteem and confidence as our witnesses, and we proffer ourselves ready if you will direct the inquiry to establish the truth of what we aver. If we fail to substantiate our statements overwhelm us with ignominy and disgrace. Cast us off from you forever. If however on the other hand every allegation we make shall be sustained by the most convincing and abundant proof, need we make further or stronger appeals than the simple facts of the case will themselves furnish, to secure your friendship, your sympathy and your justice.

We will not and we cannot believe after the long connexion that has subsisted between us, after all that has been done and all that has been promised that our whole nation will be forcibly ejected from their native land and from their social hearths without the pretence of crime, without charge, without evidence, without trial: that we shall be exiled from all that we hold dear and venerable and sacred, and driven into a remote, a strange and a sterile region, without even the imputation of guilt. We will not believe that this will be done by our ancient allies, our friends, our brethren. Yet between this and the abrogation to the pretended treaty there is no medium. Such an instrument so obtained, so contaminated cannot cover the real nature of the acts which it is invoked to sanction. If power is to be exerted let it come unveiled. We shall but submit and die.

Jno Ross

TO WINFIELD SCOTT[1]

Cherokee Agency East October 6th 1838

Sir

I had the honor to receive your communication of the 3rd inst. on the subject of my requisition of the 2ed and the state of the emigration generally. In reply, I beg leave to say, that although those detachments, only, which are in the greatest state of forwardness, are formally announced in my estimates and requisition; it ought to be borne in mind that, our efforts are directed, to carrying on the emigration with so much dispatch that, simultaneous preparations must be going on for the whole number of detachments by land, and even for

1. **Winfield Scott:** Major General Scott was in overall charge of the Cherokee removal.

the final clearing out of the sick, the infirm, the aged &c by water, who are unable to bear the fatigues of the journey by land. And that these preparations, may be made, with the least possible delay, I deemed it indispensable to have the necessary funds in readiness.

With regard to the number in some of the detachments, I would respectfully observe that the number one thousand, was understood by the Cherokees to be merely a common measure, assumed as the basis of the pecuniary calculations; and not as a precise, stipulated number which must absolutely be filled by each detachment; yet, their intention was, that each detachment should approximate that number as nearly as might be convenient. And it was expected that some would exceed and some come short of it.

In regard to Capt. [Hair] Conrad's detachment, I am sorry to say that it has been greatly diminished by causes beyond human control. That detachment was not, at first, expected to be large, and the amount of sickness with which it has been visited has greatly reduced its numbers, and even deprived it of the original conductor. I am happy to find, however, that a considerable number who have recovered are now on their way to join their friends in that detachment

Mr. [George] Hick's detachment was expected to number one thousand or more, but the same afflictive causes have operated extensively among them also, and a considerable number were unavoidably left behind. In addition to this it may not be improper to say that Mr. Hicks and some of the other conductors have had to contend with extraneous, counteracting influences which were used to frustrate their arrangements in particular, and to embarrass and retard the progress of the general arrangements, between yourself and the authorities of the nation. And here, Sir, permit me to say, that having secured your confidence in our good faith and integrity, on which we place the highest estimate; we should be extremely sorry that you should find the authority or the moral influence of the Nation inadequate to the prompt and faithful, discharge of its duties. I trust there does exist, in the Nation, a sufficient amount of energy, moral and official, for the performance of all its engagements. And here it may be proper to call your attention to the fact that certain individual Cherokees namely [John A.] Bell, [William] Boling & their associates under the assumed protection of the United States prompted and sustained, as I am assured, by individuals in official stations, of whose conduct I have more than once verbally complained; have been practising a course of interference, tending to retard the progress and disturb the arrangements of the detachments preparing for the road. We have refrained from exercising, the National Authority over those persons, from the feeling of uncertainty, whether, they were to be considered under the jurisdiction of the United States or that of the Cherokee Nation. If they are under the control of the Nation it would be desirable to have the fact known; but if they are under the control of the U. States we would respectfully call upon you to apply the corrective. In this connexion, it may not be out of place to add, that the continuing to issue rations, by the Govt. Agents at places from which the detachments have removed or after the regular organization of the detachments preparatory to their journey, as well as issuing, at the Agency, to little secluded parties, some of them many miles distant; is calculated to produce delay, in their being embodied with the detachments to which they properly belong, and more especially so, when this practice is connected with a systematic propagation of falsehoods and misrepresentations by the individuals alluded to and their emissaries.

The counteracting of these malign influences by prudent and gentle means, has, it is true, occasioned a little undesirable delay; but I have the pleasure to say, that our movements are now in a state of activity, which I trust will preclude all cause of complaint, with the assurance that our best efforts will be exerted to carry out our arrangements, with all reasonable dispatch. I remain with high respect, Sir, your obt. Servt.

Jno Ross

TO MATTHEW ARBUCKLE[2]

Illinois [Cherokee Nation] Apl 23rd 1839

Sir

From the many complaints which are daily made to me by Cherokees who have been recently removed into this country, of their sufferings, from the want of being properly subsisted with provisions, I am constrained to address you this hasty letter. It is reported that, apart from the scantiness of the ration allowed under the contract made on the part of the United States Government with [James] Glasgow & [James] Harrison, many inconveniences have been experienced by the Cherokee people, from the irregularity of proceedings on the part of those employed for carrying out the contract.

It has also been stated that the contractors were only required to furnish "one pound of fresh beef, three half pints of corn & four qts. of salt to every 100 lbs. of beef—or, if they (the contractors) choose they might furnish in lieu of the beef, 3/4 lb. salt pork or bacon provided the Indians will receive it." The beef being poor & not considered wholesome this season of the year, the Cherokees have generally objected to and refused receiving it and have insisted on being furnished with Salt Pork or Bacon in lieu of the beef, but it seems that the contractors do not choose and have refused to comply with the demand; saying that they were only bound to furnish Beef rations. Yet they would commute the ration by paying in money one dollar pr. month for the same. Thus the Cherokees are placed in a situation by compulsion to accept of either the beef or the money offered or to go unsupplied altogether. Here I must beg leave to remark, that previous to the removal of the Cherokees from the East to the West, the subject of providing subsistence for them after their arrival in this country was fully discussed with Major Genl. [Winfield] Scott who communicated with the War Deptmt. in reference to it. And we were afterwards informed by that distinguished officer that the Hon. Secry. of War [Joel R. Poinsett] had decided that the Cherokees should at least for a time be subsisted with provisions in kind, until

2. **Matthew Arbuckle:** Brigadier General Arbuckle was area commander in the Indian Territory.

they could provide for themselves, and then such an arrangement as would be most satisfactory to them should be made with them through Capt. Collins. Now Sir, it is evident from the exorbitant prices of meat and bread stuffs in this country that the Cherokees who have thus been forced to receive commutation in money from the contractors at the rate stated will soon be found in a starving condition—instead of being provided with subsistence as was anticipated and promised them. If the articles of agreement entered into with the contractors are to be construed so as to leave it wholly optional with them whether to furnish Salt Pork or Bacon in lieu of Beef, then it is obvious that there were no practical advantage for the interest of the Cherokees to have inserted any clause in that instrument in regard to Salt Pork or Bacon—for its effect has only been and will continue to be to mislead the mind of the people. And how it can be reconciled with the obligations imposed by the contract for the contractors to adopt the mode of commuting the subsistence rations they have engaged to furnish the Cherokees with and that too by a rate fixed by themselves, is a mystery which the Cherokees cannot understand—for it is not pretended that such a right or discretion has ever been given to them by the contract with the agents or the U.S. Govt. for subsisting the Cherokees. Nor can the sacred principle of justice sanction such a course under existing circumstances. Confiding however in the fair intentions of the Government towards them on this subject, the Cherokees still believe that the Hon. Secry. of War will when deemed expedient commute their rations at a rate at least equal to any sum fully ample to purchase provisions with for their comfortable subsistence—and that no sum less will be offered than what others would engage to supply the same for. I beg leave herewith to lay before you copies of sundry letters which I have just received from several leading men on behalf of the Cherokees on this very unpleasant subject. And in conclusion will further remark, that the health and existence of the whole Cherokee people who have recently been removed to this distant country demands a speedy remedy for the inconveniences and evils complained of, & unless a change of the quantity and the kind of rations as well as of the mode of issuing the same, be made from that which has heretofore been granted and observed, the Cherokees must inevitably suffer. Therefore to avoid hunger & starvation they are reduced to the necessity of calling upon you and other officers as the proper representatives of the U.S. Govt. in this matter, to take immediate steps as will ensure the immediate subsistence of the Cherokees who have recently been removed here, with ample and wholesome provisions, until such other arrangements, as may be most satisfactory to them, can be made for subsisting themselves &c. When every thing in reference to the late removal of the Cherokee nation from the East to the West is considered, and seen that it has been consummated through the military authority of the U.S. Govt. I trust you will pardon me for addressing this communication to you, especially when you are assured that the Cherokee people have been taught to expect that justice and protection would be extended to them through the Commanding General in this Hemisphere.

Jno Ross

28

Six Months in the Gold Mines
Edward Gould Buffum

On January 24, 1848, while erecting a sawmill on a branch of the American River in the lower Sacramento Valley, about forty miles from present-day Sacramento, workers found tiny nuggets of gold in the riverbed. Although the story at first was greeted with skepticism, word spread quickly once President James K. Polk confirmed the discovery in his annual message to Congress that December. Then, lured by dreams of the fortunes to be made there, adventurers from all over the world flocked to California by the thousands.

When news of the gold strikes first spread, Edward Gould Buffum was an army lieutenant in California. As soon as he mustered out in September 1848, Buffum headed for the gold fields. His Six Months in the Gold Mines, *hurriedly published in 1850 "in consequence of the public interest in all that pertains to California," is one of the most important accounts of the California gold rush. Many ambitious easterners, relying on his detailed accounts of mining procedures, used the book as a combined atlas and instruction manual as they headed west in search of riches. Buffum's vivid and exciting account of life on the mining frontier still attracts students of the American West.*

BEFORE YOU READ

1. California has long been seen as the land of the American Dream. Does Buffum's account contribute to that image? If so, how?
2. What social and economic effects of the gold rush did Buffum depict?
3. What kinds of books today are like Buffum's?

Next morning early, in better spirits than we had enjoyed for a week previously, we started for Yuba River [north of Sacramento]. About a mile from the camping-place we struck into the mountains, the same range at whose base we had been before travelling, and which are a portion of the Sierra Nevada. The hills here were steep and rugged, but covered with a magnificent growth of oak and red-wood. As we reached the summit of a lofty hill, the Yuba River broke upon our view, winding like a silver thread beneath us, its banks dotted with white tents, and fringed with trees and shrubbery.

We had at last reached the "mines," although a very different portion of them than that for which we started. We turned out our tired horses, and immediately set forth on an exploring expedition. As my clothing was all dirty and wet, I concluded to indulge in the luxury of a new shirt, and going down to the river found a shrewd Yankee in a tent surrounded by a party of naked

Edward Gould Buffum, *Six Months in the Gold Mines* (Ann Arbor: University Microfilms Inc., 1966), pp. 50–58, 60–65, 110 11.

Indians, and exposing for sale jerked beef at a dollar a pound, flour at a dollar and a half do., and for a coarse striped shirt which I picked up with the intention of purchasing, he coolly asked me the moderate price of sixteen dollars! I looked at my dirty shirt, then at the clean new one I held in my hand,
and finally at my little gold bag, not yet replenished by digging, and concluded
to postpone my purchase until I had struck my pick and crowbar into the
bowels of the earth, and extracted therefrom at least a sufficiency to purchase
a shirt. The diggings on Yuba River had at that time been discovered only
about three months, and were confined entirely to the "bars," as they are
called, extending nearly a mile each way from where the road strikes the river,
on both its banks. The principal diggings were then called the "upper" and the
"lower diggings," each about half a mile above and below the road. We started
for the upper diggings to "see the elephant," and winding through the hills,
for it was impossible to travel all the way on the river's bank, struck the principal bar then wrought on the river. This has since been called Foster's Bar,
after an American who was then keeping a store there, and who had a claim
on a large portion of the bar.

Upon reaching the bar, a curious scene presented itself. About one hundred
men, in miner's costume, were at work, performing the various portions of the
labour necessary in digging the earth and working a rocking machine. The ap-
paratus then used upon the Yuba River, and which has always been the
favourite assistant of the gold-digger, was the common rocker or cradle, con-
structed in the simplest manner. It consists of nothing more than wooden box
or hollowed log, two sides and one end of which are closed, while the other end
is left open. At the end which is closed and called the "mouth" of the machine,
a sieve, usually made of a plate of sheet iron, or a piece of raw hide, perforated
with holes about half an inch in diameter, is rested upon the sides. A number
of "bars" or "rifflers," which are little pieces of board from one to two inches
in height, are nailed to the bottom, and extend laterally across it. Of these,
there are three or four in the machine, and one at the "tail," as it is called, i.e.
the end where the dirt is washed out. This, with a pair of rockers like those of
a child's cradle, and a handle to rock it with, complete the description of the
machine, which being placed with the rockers upon two logs, and the "mouth"
elevated at a slight angle above the tail, is ready for operation. Modified and
improved as this may be, and as in fact it already has been, so long as manual
labour is employed for washing gold, the "cradle" is the best agent to use for
that purpose.

The manner of procuring and washing the golden earth was this. The loose
stones and surface earth being removed from any portion of the bar, a hole
from four to six feet square was opened, and the dirt extracted therefrom was
thrown upon a raw hide placed at the side of the machine. One man shovelled
the dirt into the sieve, another dipped up water and threw it on, and a third
rocked the "cradle." The earth, thrown upon the sieve, is washed through
with the water, while the stones and gravel are retained and thrown off. The
continued motion of the machine, and the constant stream of water pouring

through it, washes the earth over the various bars or rifflers to the "tail," where it runs out, while the gold, being of greater specific gravity, sinks to the bottom, and is prevented from escaping by the rifflers. When a certain amount of earth has been thus washed (usually about sixty pans full are called "a washing"), the gold, mixed with a heavy black sand, which is always found mingled with gold in California, is taken out and washed in a tin pan, until nearly all the sand is washed away. It is then put into a cup or pan, and when the day's labour is over is dried before the fire, and the sand remaining carefully blown out. This is a simple explanation of the process of gold-washing in the placers of California. At present, however, instead of dipping and pouring on water by hand, it is usually led on by a hose or forced by a pump, thereby giving a better and more constant stream, and saving the labour of one man. The excavation is continued until the solid rock is struck, or the water rushing in renders it impossible to obtain any more earth, when a new place is opened. We found the gold on the Yuba in exceedingly fine particles, and it has always been considered of a very superior quality. We inquired of the washers as to their success, and they, seeing we were "green horns," and thinking we might possibly interfere with them, gave us either evasive answers, or in some cases told us direct lies. We understood from them that they were making about twenty dollars per day, while I afterwards learned, from the most positive testimony of two men who were at work there at the time, that one hundred dollars a man was not below the average estimate of a day's labour.

On this visit to Foster's Bar I made my first essay in gold-digging. I scraped up with my hand my tin cup full of earth, and washed it in the river. How eagerly I strained my eyes as the earth was washing out, and the bottom of the cup was coming in view! and how delighted, when, on reaching the bottom, I discerned about twenty little golden particles sparkling in the sun's rays, and worth probably about fifty cents. I wrapped them carefully in a piece of paper, and preserved them for a long time, — but, like much more gold in larger quantities, which it has since been my lot to possess, it has escaped my grasp, and where it now is Heaven only knows.

The labour on Yuba River appeared very severe, the excavations being sometimes made to a depth of twelve feet before the soil containing the gold, which was a gravelly clay, was reached. We had not brought our tools with us, intending, if our expedition in the mountains had succeeded, that one of our party should return for our remaining stock of provisions and tools. We had no facilities for constructing a machine, and no money to buy one (two hundred dollars being the price for which a mere hollowed pine log was offered us), and besides, all the bars upon which men were then engaged in labour were "claimed," a claim at that time being considered good when the claimant had cleared off the top soil from any portion of the bar. We returned to our camp, and talked over our prospects, in a quandary what to do. Little did we then dream that, in less than six months, the Yuba River, then only explored some three miles above where we were, would be successfully wrought for forty miles above us, and that thousands would find their fortunes upon it.

We concluded to return to the *Embarcadero*, and take a new start. Accordingly, next morning we packed up and set off, leaving at work upon the river about two hundred men. Having retraced our steps, we arrived at Sutter's Fort in safety on the evening of November 30th, just in time to find the member of our party whom we had left behind, packing all our remaining provisions and tools into a cart, ready to start for the "dry diggings" on the following morning.

The history of John A. Sutter, and his remarkable settlement on the banks of the Sacramento, has been one of interest since California first began to attract attention. Captain Sutter is by birth a Swiss, and was formerly an officer in the French army. He emigrated to the United States, became a naturalized citizen, and resided in Missouri several years. In the year 1839 he emigrated to the then wilderness of California, where he obtained a large grant of land, to the extent of about eleven leagues, bordering on the Sacramento River, and made a settlement directly in the heart of an Indian country, among tribes of hostile savages. For a long time he suffered continual attacks and depredations from the Indians, but finally succeeded, by kind treatment and good offices, in reducing them to subjection, and persuading them to come into his settlement, which he called New Helvetia. With their labour he built a large fort of *adobes* or sunburnt bricks, brought a party of his Indians under military discipline, and established a regular garrison. His wheat-fields were very extensive, and his cattle soon numbered five thousand, the whole labour being performed by Indians. These he paid with a species of money made of tin, which was stamped with dots, indicating the number of days' labour for which each one was given; and they were returned to him in exchange for cotton cloth, at a dollar a yard, and trinkets and sweetmeats at corresponding prices. The discovery of the gold mines of California has, however, added more to Sutter's fame than did his bold settlement in the wilderness. This has introduced him to the world almost as a man of gold, and connected his name for ever with the most prized metal upon earth. He is quite "a gentleman of the old school," his manners being very cordial and prepossessing. . . .

With all our worldly gear packed in an ox-wagon, we left Sutter's Fort on the morning of the 1st of December, and travelling about seven miles on the road, encamped in a beautiful grove of evergreen oak, to give the cattle an opportunity to lay in a sufficient supply of grass and acorns, preparatory to a long march. As we were to remain here during the day, we improved the opportunity by taking our dirty clothing, of which by that time we had accumulated a considerable quantity, down to the banks of the American Fork, distant about one mile from camp, for the purpose of washing. While we were employed in this laborious but useful occupation, Higgins called my attention to the salmon which were working up the river over a little rapid opposite us. Some sport suggested itself; and more anxious for this than labour, we dropped our half-washed shirts, and started back to camp for our rifles, which we soon procured, and brought down to the river. In making their way over the bar, the backs of the salmon were exposed some two inches above water; and the instant one appeared, a well-directed rifle-ball perforated his spine. The result was, that before dark Higgins and myself carried into camp thirty-five splendid salmon, procured by this novel mode of sport. We luxuriated on them, and gave what we could not eat for supper and breakfast to some lazy Indians, who had been employed the whole day in spearing some half dozen each. There is every probability that the salmon fishery will yet prove a highly lucrative business in California.

Next morning we packed up and made a fresh start. That night we encamped at the "Green Springs," about twenty-five miles distant from Sutter's Fort. These springs are directly upon the road, and bubble up from a muddy black loam, while around them is the greenest verdure, — the surrounding plain being dotted with beautiful groves and magnificent flowers. Their waters are delicious.

As the ox-team was a slow traveller, and quarters were to be looked for in our new winter home, on the next morning Higgins and myself were appointed a deputation to mount two horses we had brought with us and proceed post-haste to the "dry diggings." We started at 10 A.M., and travelled through some beautiful valleys and over lofty hills. As we reached the summit of a high ridge, we paused by common consent to gaze upon the landscape and breathe the delicious air. The broad and fertile valleys of the Sacramento and San Joaquin lay stretched at our feet like a highly coloured map. The noble rivers which lend their names to these rich valleys were plainly visible, winding like silver threads through dark lines of timber fringing their banks; now plunging amid dense forests, and now coming in view sparkling and bright as the riches they contain; the intermediate plains, here parched and browned with the sun's fierce rays; there brilliant with all the hues of the rainbow, and dotted with the autumnal flowers and open groves of evergreen oak. Herds of elk, black-tailed deer, and antelope browsed near the mountain sides, on the summit of which the eagle builds his eyry. The surrounding atmosphere, fragrant with delightful odours, was so pure and transparent as to render objects visible at a great distance, and so elastic and bracing as to create a perceptible effect on our feelings. Far in the distance the massive peak of Shaste reared its snow-capped head, from amid a dense forest, fourteen thousand feet into the sky. We arrived at what was then called Weaver's Creek, about dusk. . . .

The "dry diggings" of Weaver's Creek being a fair specimen of dry diggings in all parts of the mining region, a description of them will give the reader a general idea of the various diggings of the same kind in California. They are called "dry" in contradistinction to the "wet" diggings, or those lying directly on the banks of streams, and where all the gold is procured by washing. As I before said, the stream coursed between lofty tree-clad hills, broken on both sides of the river into little ravines or gorges. In these ravines most of the gold was found. The loose stones and top earth being thrown off, the gravelly clay that followed it was usually laid aside for washing, and the digging continued until the bottom rock of the ravine was reached, commonly at a depth of from one to six feet. The surface of this rock was carefully cleared off, and usually found to contain little crevices and holes, the latter in miner's parlance called

"pockets," and in which the gold was found concealed, sparkling like the treasures in the cave of Monte Cristo. A careful examination of the rock being
made, and every little crevice and pocket being searched with a sharp pointed-
knife, gold in greater or less quantities invariably made its appearance. I shall
never forget the delight with which I first struck and worked out a crevice. It
was the second day after our installation in our little log hut; the first having
been employed in what is called "prospecting," or searching for the most
favourable place at which to commence operations. I had slung pick, shovel,
and bar upon my shoulder, and trudged merrily away to a ravine about a mile
from our house. Pick, shovel, and bar did their duty, and I soon had a large rock
in view. Getting down into the excavation I had made, and seating myself upon
the rock, I commenced a careful search for a crevice, and at last found one extending longitudinally along the rock. It appeared to be filled with a hard,
bluish clay and gravel, which I took out with my knife, and there at the bottom, strewn along the whole length of the rock, was bright, yellow gold, in little pieces about the size and shape of a grain of barley. Eureka! Oh how my
heart beat! I sat still and looked at it some minutes before I touched it, greed-
ily drinking in the pleasure of gazing upon gold that was in my very grasp, and
feeling a sort of independent bravado in allowing it to remain there. When my
eyes were sufficiently feasted, I scooped it out with the point of my knife and
an iron spoon, and placing it in my pan, ran home with it very much delighted.
I weighed it, and found that my first day's labour in the mines had made me
thirty-one dollars richer than I was in the morning.

The gold, which, by some great volcanic eruption, has been scattered upon
the soil over an extensive territory, by the continual rains of the winter season
has been sunk into the hills, until it has reached either a hard clay which it cannot penetrate, or a rock on which it rests. The gold in the hills, by the continual
rains, has been washing lower and lower, until it has reached the ravines. It has
washed down the ravines until it has there reached the rock, and thence, it has
washed along the bed of the ravines until it has found some little crevice in
which it rests, where the water can carry it no farther. Here it gathers, and thus
are formed the "pockets" and "nests" of gold, one of which presents such a
glowing golden sight to the eye of the miner, and such a field for his imagination to revel in. How often, when I have struck one of these, have I fondly
wished that it might reach to the centre of the earth, and be filled as it was at
its mouth with pure, bright, yellow gold.

Our party's first day's labour produced one hundred and fifty dollars, I having been the most successful of all. But we were satisfied, although our experience had not fulfilled the golden stories we had heard previous to our reaching the *placers*. Finding the average amount of gold dug on Weaver's Creek at
that time to be about an ounce per day to a man, we were content so long as
we could keep pace with our neighbours. There is a spirit of emulation among
miners which prevents them from being ever satisfied with success whilst others around them are more successful. We continued our labours for a week,
and found, at the end of that time, our whole party had dug out more than a

thousand dollars; and after paying for our house, and settling between ourselves our little private expenses, we were again on a clear track, unencumbered
by debt, and in the heart of a region where treasures of unknown wealth were
lying hidden in the earth on which we daily trod.

About this time, the most extravagant reports reached us from the Middle
Fork, distant in a northerly direction about thirty miles from Weaver's Creek.
Parties who had been there described the river as being lined with gold of the
finest quality. One and two hundred dollars was not considered a great day's
labour, and now was the time to take advantage of it, while in its pristine rich-
ness. The news was too blooming for me to withstand. I threw down my pick-
axe, and leaving a half-wrought crevice for some other digger to work out, I
packed up and held myself in readiness to proceed by the earliest opportunity,
and with the first party ready to go for the Middle Fork. . . .

Passing to the northward of the Dry Diggings, we encamped at dusk in a little oak grove about three miles from Sutter's Mill, killed a deer, ate a hearty
supper, spread our blankets on the ground, and slept quietly and peacefully beneath a star-studded and cloudless heaven. Next morning we went into Cu-
loma, the Indian name for the territory around Sutter's Mill, and here we were
to purchase our provisions previous to going to the river. Three stores only, at
that time, disputed the trade at what is now the great centre of the northern
mining region; and where now are busy streets, and long rows of tents and
houses, was a beautiful hollow, which, in our romantic version, we named as
we were entering it, "The Devil's Punch-Bowl." Surrounded on all sides by
lofty mountains, its ingress and egress guarded by an ascent and descent
through narrow passes, it seemed like a huge bowl which some lofty spirit
might seize, and placing it to his lips, quaff the waters of the golden stream that
circled through it. Here it was that gold was first discovered in California; this
was the locality where was commenced a new era, and where a new page was
opened in the history of mankind.

The city of Sacramento had assumed a very different aspect at the time I
reached it on my return from the northern mines, from that which it exhibited
when I previously left it. Where the old store-ship used to be, on the banks of
the Sacramento, tall-masted ships were moored, and the extensive plain on
which I pitched my tent was dotted with houses. Around the fort itself, which
is nearly two miles from the bank of the river, houses had begun to spring up.
Building-lots which, four months previously, had sold at from fifty to two hundred dollars, were now held by their owners at from one to three thousand. I
looked on with astonishment at the remarkable progress, and then little
thought that the ensuing six months would develope a growth, both in size and
prices, which would entirely outstrip what I then witnessed.

Getting on board a launch, I spent a weary five days in sailing down the
Sacramento, and arrived at San Francisco in the early part of May. What a
change had occurred in six months! San Francisco, when I saw it before, was
almost entircly deserted, everybody having gone to the mines. Now it was

being daily recruited by the arrival of travellers across the plains, by vessels around Cape Horn, by Sandwich Islanders, Chinese, French, English, and Mexicans. The age of speculation had commenced. The building-lots which, when I landed in San Francisco, were granted by the alcaldes for the sum of fifteen dollars, and in the autumn before were worth but five hundred, had now risen in value to from three to five thousand. Hundreds and thousands of men with capital were arriving, who readily seized upon the opportunities for speculating. Houses were going up on the vacant lots, and the town beginning to assume an air of business. Goods of all kinds had fallen in price, owing to the arrival of fleets of loaded ships from all parts of the world, and in some cases from wilful neglect on the part of consignees. Large hotels had been erected, and life began to be rendered comfortable. Gambling in all its forms was carried on to an enormous extent, and money, as before, was almost as plentiful as the sea-sands.

29

Pulling a Handcart to the Mormon Zion
Priscilla Merriman Evans

Many of the men and women who settled the Far West often endured extraordinary physical hardships and dangers to reach their destinations. The Mormon pioneers who walked from Iowa City, Iowa, to Salt Lake City, Utah, pulling handcarts made of hickory, were driven by both economic and religious motives. The handcart immigrants were poor: If they could have afforded to migrate any other way they would have. They spoke one or more of several languages — German, Welsh, Danish, Swedish — as well as English. And they did not all have so successful a journey as the pregnant Mrs. Evans. With her one-legged husband, she walked the 1,000 miles in five months, arriving in Salt Lake City in October 1856, comfortably ahead of the winter weather. In two parties later that year, hundreds died in winter blizzards.

Nine more handcart companies reached the Mormon Zion in the five years after the Evanses' journey. All received rich welcomes with prayers and hymns. Priscilla Merriman Evans concluded her narrative by saying that she always "thanked the Lord for a contented mind, a home and something to eat."

BEFORE YOU READ

1. Why do you think Priscilla Merriman Evans became a Mormon and chose to emigrate?
2. What were the principal difficulties of the trip to Utah?
3. What rewards did Evans find in "Zion"?

I, Priscilla Merriman Evans, born May 4, 1835 at Mounton New Marbeth, Pembrokeshire, Wales, am the daughter of Joseph and Ann James Merriman. About 1839, father moved his family from Mounton up to Tenby, about ten miles distant. Our family consisted of father, mother, Sarah, aged six, and myself, aged four. Tenby was a beautiful place, as are all those Celtic Islands, with remains of old castles, vine-and moss-covered walls, gone to ruin since the time of the Conqueror. . . .

Besides reading, writing, spelling, and arithmetic, we were taught sewing and sampler making. The sampler work was done in cross stitch, worked in bright colors, on canvas made for that purpose. . . . We were also taught the Bible. I was greatly interested in school, but was taken out at eleven years of age, owing to the illness in our family. I was a natural student, and greatly desired to continue my studies, but mother's health was very poor, so I was taken

Kate B. Carter, ed., *Hearts of the West*, vol. 9 (Salt Lake City: International Society Daughters of Utah Pioneers), pp. 8–13.

out to help with the work. My sister, Sarah, continued school, as she did not
like housework and wished to learn a trade. She went to Mrs. Hentin and
learned the millinery trade. Mother's health continued [to be] poor, and she
died at the birth of her eighth child, Emma, when I was sixteen. I had many
duties for a girl so young, caring for my sisters and brothers. While Sarah was
learning millinery, she would sometimes wake me in the night to try on a
hat—one she was practicing on. She learned the millinery business and then
went up to London, opened a shop of her own and was very successful. She
married a gentleman . . . who was devoted to her, and followed her to London.
She died at the birth of her fourth child.

[When] Mother died on the eighth of November 1851 . . . the responsibility of the family rested on my young shoulders. . . . After the death of my
mother we were very lonely, and one evening I accompanied my father to the
house of a friend. When we reached there, we learned that they were holding
a cottage meeting. Two Mormon Elders were the speakers, and I was very
much interested in the principles they advocated. I could see that my father was
very worried, and would have taken me away, had he known how. When he became aware that I believed in the Gospel as taught by the Elders, I asked him
if he had ever heard of the restored Gospel. He replied, "Oh, yes, I have heard
of Old Joe Smith, and his Golden Bible." When my father argued against the
principles taught by the Elders, I said, "If the Bible is true, then Mormonism
is true."

My father was very much opposed to my joining the Church . . . as he
thought the Saints were too slow to associate with. . . . But I had found the
truth and was baptized into the Church of Jesus Christ of Latter-day Saints in
Tenby, February 26, 1852. My sister Sarah took turns with me going out every
Sunday. She would go where she pleased on Sunday, while I would walk seven
miles to Stepaside and attend the Mormon meeting. My father was very much
displeased with me going out every Sunday. He forbade me to read the Church
literature, and threatened to burn all I brought home. At the time I had a
Book of Mormon borrowed from a friend, and when Father found out I had
it, he began looking for it. It was in plain sight, among other books in the book
case. I saw him handling it with the other books, and I sent up a silent prayer
that he might not notice it, which he did not, although it was before him in
plain sight. I do not think my father was as bitter against the principles of the
Gospel as he seemed to be, for many times when the Elders were persecuted,
he defended them, and gave them food and shelter. But he could not bear the
idea of my joining them and leaving home.

About this time, Thomas D. Evans, a young Mormon Elder, was sent up
from Merthyr Tydfil, Wales, as a missionary to Pembrokeshire. He was a fine
speaker, and had a fine tenor voice, and I used to like to go around with the
missionaries and help with the singing. Elder Evans and I seemed to be con-
genial from our first meeting, and we were soon engaged. He was traveling and
preaching the restored Gospel without purse or script. Perhaps his mission will
be better understood if I give a little account: [his father had died] and left his

mother a widow with eight children, Thomas D. being four years old and the youngest. He was placed in a large forge of two-thousand men at the age of seven years to learn the profession of Iron Roller. At nine years of age, he had the misfortune to lose his left leg at the knee. He went through the courses and graduated as an Iron Roller. When I think of [when they met in 1852] it seems that we had put the world aside, and were not thinking of our worldly pleasures, and what our next dress would be. We had no dancing in those days, but we were happy in the enjoyment of the spirit of the Gospel. . . .

I was familiar with the Bible doctrine, and when I heard the Elders explain it, it seemed as though I had always known it, and it sounded like music in my ears. We had the spirit of gathering and were busy making preparations to emigrate.

About that time the Principle of Plurality of Wives was preached to the world, and it caused quite a commotion in our branch. One of the girls came to me with tears in her eyes and said, "Is it true that Brigham Young has nine wives? I can't stand that, Oh, I can't stand it!" I asked her how long it had been since I had heard her testify that she knew the Church was true, and I said if it was then, it is true now. I told her I did not see anything for her to cry about. After I talked to her awhile, she dried her eyes and completed her arrangements to get married and emigrate. She came with us. My promised husband and I went to Merthyr to visit his Mother, brothers, sisters, and friends, preparatory to emigrating. His family did all in their power to persuade him to remain with them. They were all well off, and his brothers said they would send him to school, support his wife, and pay all of his expenses but all to no avail. He bade them all goodbye, and returned to Tenby.

I think I would have had a harder time getting away, had it not been that my father was going to be married again, and I do not suppose the lady cared to have in the home, the grown daughter who had taken the place of the mother for so many years.

Elder Thomas D. Evans, my promised husband, and I walked the ten miles from Tenby to Pembroke, where we got our license and were married, and walked back to Tenby. We were married on the third of April, 1856. On our return from Pembroke we found a few of our friends awaiting us with supper ready. We visited our friends and relatives and made our preparations to emigrate to Zion. We took a tug from Pembroke to Liverpool, where we set sail on the 17th of April, 1856, on the sailing vessel S.S. Curling. Captain Curling said he would prefer to take a load of Saints than others, as he always felt safe with Saints on board. We learned that the next trip across the water that he was loaded with gentiles and his vessel sank with all on board. We were on the sea five weeks; we lived on the ship's rations. I was sick all the way. [Priscilla was then pregnant with their first child.]

We landed in Boston on May 23rd, then travelled in cattle cars . . . to Iowa City. We remained in Iowa City three weeks, waiting for our carts to be made. We were offered many inducements to stay there. My husband was offered ten dollars a day to work at his trade of Iron Roller, but money was no inducement to us, for we were anxious to get to Zion. We learned afterwards that many who stayed there apostatized or died of cholera.

When the carts were ready we started on a three-hundred-mile walk to Winterquarters on the Missouri River. There were a great many who made fun of us as we walked, pulling our carts, but the weather was fine and the roads were excellent and although I was sick and we were tired out at night, we still thought, "This is a glorious way to come to Zion."

We began our journey of one thousand miles on foot with a handcart for each family, some families consisting of man and wife, and some had quite large families. There were five mule teams to haul the tents and surplus flour. Each handcart had one hundred pounds of flour, that was to be divided and [more got] from the wagons as required. At first we had a little coffee and bacon, but that was soon gone and we had no use for any cooking utensils but a frying pan. The flour was self-raising and we took water and baked a little cake; that was all we had to eat.

After months of travelling we were put on half rations and at one time, before help came, we were out of flour for two days. We washed out the flour sacks to make a little gravy.

There were in our tent my husband with one leg, two blind men . . . a man with one arm, and a widow with five children. The widow, her children, and myself were the only ones who could not talk Welsh. My husband was commissary for our tent, and he cut his own rations short many times to help little children who had to walk and did not have enough to eat to keep up their strength.

The tent was our covering, and the overcoat spread on the bare ground with the shawl over us was our bed. My feather bed, and bedding, pillows, all our good clothing, my husband's church books, which he had collected through six years of missionary work, with some genealogy he had collected, all had to be left in a storehouse. We were promised that they would come to us with the next emigration in the spring, but we never did receive them. It was reported that the storehouse burned down, so that was a dreadful loss to us.

Edward Bunker was the Captain of our Company. His orders of the day were, "If any are sick among you, and are not able to walk, you must help them along, or pull them on your carts." No one rode in the wagons. Strong men would help the weaker ones, until they themselves were worn out, and some died from the struggle and want of food, and were buried along the wayside. It was heart rending for parents to move on and leave their loved ones to such a fate, as they were so helpless, and had no material for coffins. Children and young folks, too, had to move on and leave father or mother or both.

Sometimes a bunch of buffaloes would come and the carts would stop until they passed. Had we been prepared with guns and ammunition, like people who came in wagons, we might have had meat, and would not have come to near starving. President Young ordered extra cattle sent along to be killed to help the sick and weak, but they were never used for that purpose. One incident happened which came near being serious. Some Indians came to our camp and my husband told an Indian who admired me that he could have me for a pony. He was always getting off jokes. He thought no more about it, but in a day or two, here came the Indian with the pony, and wanted his pretty little squaw. It was no joke with him. I never was so frightened in all my life. There was no place to hide, and we did not know what to do. The Captain was called, and they had some difficulty in settling with the Indian without trouble.

In crossing rivers, the weak women and the children were carried over the deep places, and they waded the others. We were much more fortunate than those who came later, as they had snow and freezing weather. Many lost limbs, and many froze to death. President Young advised them to start earlier, but they got started too late. My husband, in walking from twenty to twenty-five miles per day [had pain] where the knee rested on the pad: the friction caused it to gather and break and was most painful. But he had to endure it, or remain behind, as he was never asked to ride in a wagon.

We reached Salt Lake City on October 2, 1856, tired, weary, with bleeding feet, our clothing worn out and so weak we were nearly starved, but thankful to our Heavenly Father for bringing us to Zion. William R. Jones met us on the Public Square in Salt Lake City and brought us to his home in Spanish Fork. I think we were over three days coming from Salt Lake City to Spanish Fork by ox team, but what a change to ride in a wagon after walking 1330 miles from Iowa City to Salt Lake City!

We stayed in the home of an ex-bishop, Stephen Markham. His home was a dugout. It was a very large room built half underground. His family consisted of three wives, and seven children. . . . There was a large fireplace in one end with bars, hooks, frying pans, and bake ovens, where they did the cooking for the large family, and boiled, fried, baked, and heated their water for washing.

There was a long table in one corner, and pole bedsteads fastened to the walls in the three other corners. They were laced back and forth with rawhide cut in strips, and made a nice springy bed. There were three trundle beds, made like shallow boxes, with wooden wheels, which rolled under the mother's bed in the daytime to utilize space. There was a dirt roof, and the dirt floor was kept hard and smooth by sprinkling and sweeping. The bed ticks were filled with straw. . . .

Aunt Mary [Markham] put her two children . . . in the foot of her bed and gave us the trundle bed. . . . How delightful to sleep on a bed again, after sleeping on the ground for so many months with our clothes on. We had not slept in a bed since we left the ship *Sam Curling*.

On the 31st of December, 1856, our first daughter was born. . . . My baby's wardrobe was rather meager: I made one night gown from her father's white shirt, another out of a factory lining of an oilcloth sack. Mrs. Markham gave me a square of homemade linsey for a shoulder blanket, and a neighbor gave me some old underwear, that I worked up into little things. They told me I could have an old pair of jean pants left at the adobe yard. I washed them and made them into petticoats. I walked down to the Indian farm and traded a gold pen for four yards of calico that made her two dresses.

One day my husband went down in the field to cut some willows to burn. The ax slipped and cut his good knee cap. It was with difficulty that he crawled to the house. He was very weak from the loss of blood. My baby was but a few days old, and the three of us had to occupy the trundle bed for awhile.

Wood and timber were about thirty miles up in the canyon, and when the men went after timber to burn, they went in crowds, armed, for they never knew when they would be attacked by Indians. Adobe houses were cheaper than log or frame, as timber was so far away. Many of the people who had lived in the dugouts after coming from Palmyra got into houses before the next winter. They exchanged work with each other, and in that way got along fine. Mr. Markham had an upright saw, run by water. The next spring they got timber from the canyon, and my husband helped Mr. Markham put up a three-roomed house and worked at farming.

He worked for William Markham a year, for which he received two acres of land. I helped in the house, for which, besides the land, we got our board and keep. The next Spring we went to work for ourselves. We saved our two acres of wheat, and made adobes for a two-roomed house, and paid a man in adobes for laying it up. It had a dirt roof. He got timber from Mr. Markham to finish the doors, windows, floors, shelves, and to make furniture. My husband made me a good big bedstead and laced it with rawhides. There were benches and the frames of chairs with the rawhide seat, with the hair left on; a table, shelves in the wall on either side of the fireplace, which was fitted with iron bars and hooks to hang kettles on to boil, frying pans and bake oven. A tick for a bed had to be pieced out of all kinds of scraps, as there were no stores, and everything was on a trade basis.

If one neighbor had something they could get along without, they would exchange it for something they could use. We were lucky to get factory, or sheeting to put up to the windows instead of glass. We raised a good crop of wheat that fall, for which we traded one bushel for two bushels of potatoes. We also exchanged for molasses and vegetables. We had no tea, coffee, meat, or grease of any kind for seasoning. No sugar, milk, or butter. In 1855–1856 the grasshoppers and crickets took the crops and the cattle nearly all died. They were dragged down in the field west [and left to die].

We bought a lot on Main Street, and my husband gave his parents our first little home with five acres of land. They had a good ox team, two cows, a new wagon, and they soon got pigs, chickens and a few sheep. It wasn't long before they were well off. . . .

It was indeed comfortable to be in a good house with a shingled roof and good floors. He set out an orchard of all kinds of fruit; also currents and gooseberries, planted lucern . . . in a patch by itself for cows and pigs. We had a nice garden spot, and we soon had butter, milk, eggs, and meat. We raised our bread, potatoes, and vegetables. While our fruit trees were growing is when the saleratus helped. When I had the babies all about the same size, I could not get out to gather saleratus as others did; so we went with team and wagon, pans, buckets, old brooms, and sacks down on the alkali land, between Spanish Fork and Springville. The smallest children were put under the wagon on a quilt, and the rest of us swept and filled the sacks, and the happiest time was when we were headed for home. The canyon wind seemed always to blow and our faces, hands and eyes were sore for some time after. We took our saleratus over to Provo, where they had some kind of refining machinery where it was made into soda for bread. It was also used extensively in soap making. We got our pay in merchandise.

Most people who had land kept a few sheep which furnished them meat, light and clothing. We had no sheep, but I, and my oldest daughter, learned to spin and we did spinning on shares to get our yarn for stockings and socks, which we knitted for the family. Before this time my sister, Sarah, had sent me a black silk dress pattern, with other things, which I sold [and] I bought a cow and a pair of blankets. Before the building of the Provo factory, the people had wool-picking bees. The wool was greased and the trash picked out of it; then it was carded into rolls. We made our own cloth, which was mostly gray in color, for dresses, by mixing the black and white wool. If a light gray was wanted, more white than black was put in, and dark was added if a darker gray was wanted. The dresses for grown people were three widths, and for younger women two widths, one yard wide. There was a row of bright colors—red, blue, green—about half way up the skirt, which was hemmed and pleated onto a plain waist with coat sleeves. When our dresses wore thin in front, they could be turned back to front and upside down, and have a new lease on life. With madder, Indigo, logwood, copperas, and other roots, I have colored beautiful fast colors. We were kept busy in those days carding, spinning, knitting, and doing all of our own sewing by hand.

After getting settled in our new home, my husband went over to Camp Floyd, where he worked quite a bit. He found a friend who was selling out prior to leaving for California. He bought quite a number of articles, which greatly helped us. One thing was a door knob and lock. He also bought me a stepstove. Stoves were very scarce at that time in Spanish Fork. I had never cooked on a stove in my life, and I burned my first batch of bread. Where I came from people mixed their dough and had it baked in the public oven, and at home we had a gate with an oven at the side. When the soldier camp broke up, they left many useful things which helped the people.

. . . My husband had poor luck farming. His farm was in the low land, near the river where the sugar factory now stands. Sometimes it would be high water, sometimes grasshoppers or crickets would take his crop; so he got discouraged with farming, sold his farm and put up a store. We had just got well started in the business and had got a bill of goods, when in the spring of 1875 my husband was called on another mission to England.

Before starting on his mission he sold his team and all available property, also mortgaged our home, for although he was called to travel without purse or scrip, he had to raise enough money to pay his passage and his expenses to his field of labor in Europe. He had too tender a heart for a merchant; he simply could not say no when people came to him with pitiful stories of sickness and privation. He would give them credit, and the consequence was that when he was suddenly called on a mission, the goods were gone and there were hundreds of dollars coming to us from the people, some of which we never got. Everything was left in my hands.

On the 24th of October 1875, after my husband's departure, our daughter Ada was born. . . . I nursed her, along with my little granddaughter Maud, as twins, kept all the books and accounts . . . and was sustained as President and Secretary of the Relief Society Teachers, which office I held through many re-organizations.

During my husband's absence, we had considerable sickness. My little daughter, Mary, came near dying with scarlet fever. To help out, our eldest daughter, Emma, got a position as clerk in the Co-op store. I appreciated that action of the Board very much, as before that time they had not been employing lady clerks and she was the first girl to work in the store. . . .

In 1877, my twelfth child was born. . . . I have had seven daughters and five sons. . . .

My husband's health was not good after his return from his mission. He had pneumonia twice. We sold our home on Main Street, paid off the mortgage and put up a little house on the five acres of land we had given his parents. They had left it to us when they died. We have some of our children as near neighbors and are quite comfortable in our new home.

30

A Railroad Town
Frithjof Meidell

By the 1850s railroads were becoming the sinews of the American economy. Construction of a few small tramways had begun during the 1820s, and in 1828 the first major railroad, the Baltimore and Ohio, was chartered. Many of the early railroads ran only short distances, being designed to serve mainly as feeders into nearby rivers and canals, but major eastern cities like Boston and Baltimore, which lacked adequate water connections to the West, promoted longer lines. The rapid technical improvement of locomotives and roadbeds speeded the development of railroads. By 1840 the nation's total railway mileage equaled that of canals, and many lines were competing successfully with canal companies for business. The nearly nine thousand miles of track laid in the 1840s and the twenty-two thousand more in the next decade made railroads the dominant form of long-distance transportation in the country.

With railroads came new towns. Sometimes the towns actually were built first in anticipation of a rail line's construction along a particular route. Railroads sold acreage they owned along the right-of-way and actively advertised for settlers from Europe and the eastern United States. Frithjof Meidell, a Norwegian immigrant writing to his family from Springfield, Illinois on August 7, 1855, describes the way the railroad and enterprising settlers created prosperous towns in the West.

BEFORE YOU READ

1. What did Meidell think of railroads? Of speculators? Of taverns? Why was he so optimistic? Did he overlook any of the problems that townspeople later encountered in midwestern towns?

2. What was Meidell's opinion of Irish workers? Why did he portray them as so different from the others who came to populate his imaginary new town?

Dear Mother:

I received Hansine's letter a couple of days ago, and I was indeed glad to hear that all of you are getting along so well. . . .

How pleased I should be if I could only secure copies of *Aftenbladet* [Norwegian newspaper] from time to time. Could not this be arranged? In the Norwegian paper *Emigranten*, which is published in Wisconsin, I find many articles from *Aftenbladet*. In the same paper I also see that you now have both railroad and telegraph. Hurrah for old Norway!

How is the railroad getting along? Here in America it is the railroads that build up the whole country. Because of them the farmers get wider markets and higher prices for their products. They seem to put new life into everything.

Norwegian-American Studies and Records, vol. 9 (1936): 48–53.

Even the old apple woman sets off at a dogtrot when she hears that whistle to sell her apples to the passengers. Every ten miles along the railways there are stations, which soon grow up into towns. "Soon," did I say? I should have said "immediately," because it is really remarkable how rapidly the stations are transformed into little towns. I can but compare it with the building of Aladdin's castle by means of his wonderful lamp, only that things move still faster here, where it is not necessary to sit and rub a rusty old oil lantern. Here you can buy houses all ready to be placed on the freight car, and in half a day's time they can be nailed together.

Since I have nothing else to write about this time, I shall attempt to describe how these towns spring up. First—that is, after the two old log houses that stand one on each side of the tracks—first, I say, the railroad company builds a depot. Next, a speculator buys the surrounding 100 acres and lays it out in lots, streets, and a marketplace. Then he graces the prospective town with the name of an early President or a famous general—or his own name—holds an auction, and realizes many hundred percent on his investment.

A young wagonmaker who has just completed his apprenticeship hears about the station, that it is beautifully located in a rich farming country, is blessed with good water, and, most important of all, that it has no wagonmaker. Making a hasty decision, he buys the barest necessities for setting up in his profession, hurries off to the place, rents one of the old log houses, and is soon at work. One absolute necessity he still lacks, however: a sign, of course, which is the most important part of a man's equipment here in America. The next day he hears that there is a tramp painter aboard the train; he gets him off, puts him to work, and the very next day the farmers are surprised to see a monstrous sign straddling the roof of the old log house.

The sign is an immediate success, for the farmers rush to the shop and order wagons, wheels, and the like. The poor man is overwhelmed with more work than he can handle for ever so long. He is about to regret that sign notion of his, but suddenly he has another idea. He accepts every order, and no sooner are the customers away than he seizes his pen and writes to the editors of three different newspapers that three good apprentices can secure steady work with high wages in the "flourishing town of L." Within two days he has help enough, and the work goes "like a song."

The train stops again, and off steps a blacksmith who went broke in one of the larger towns. He saunters over to the wagonmaker's shop as unconcerned as if he only wished to light his cigar. In a casual way he inquires about the neighborhood and wonders what its prospects are, without indicating that he intends to settle there—by no means! But the wagoner, with his keen Yankee nose, soon smells a rat and starts boosting the place with all his might. This inspires the smith with ecstasy; he starts jumping around and making sledge-hammer motions with his arms. Off he goes and rents the other log house and nails a horseshoe over the door as a sign. The horseshoe, to be sure, cannot be seen any great distance, but the smith has a remedy for this, and he starts to hammer and pound away at his anvil so that the farmers for miles around can hear the echoes. They immediately flock to his door, and there is work enough for the blacksmith.

Within a short week, a carpenter, a tailor, and a shoemaker also arrive in town. The wagoner orders a house from the carpenter and rents the second story to the tailor and the shoemaker. Soon the blacksmith also builds a house, and things progress with giant strides toward the bigger and better.

Again the train stops. This time two young fellows jump off, look around, and go over to have a chat with the blacksmith. One of them is a doctor, the other a lawyer. Both of them rent rooms from the blacksmith and start business.

Once more the locomotive stops. But—what's this getting off? Be patient! Just let it come closer. It is nothing more nor less than a mustachioed, velvet-frocked German with an old, overworked hurdy-gurdy strapped to his back. On the hurdy-gurdy perches a measly little monkey dressed in red. The German goes over to the blacksmith shop and begins to crank his music box while the monkey smokes tobacco, dances a polka, and grinds coffee. But the German receives no encouragement for his art, nor does the monkey—except some rusty nails which the smith tosses to him. The artist realizes that his audience is very unappreciative, and the poor man's face is overcast with sorrow.

Then he looks about inquiringly as if searching for something and steps up to the doctor to ask if there is a restaurant in town. On receiving a negative reply, his face brightens again; and, after a short conversation with the doctor and lawyer, he steams off with the next train and jumps off at the first big town, where he sells his hurdy-gurdy and monkey and buys a barrel of whiskey, another barrel of biscuits, two large cheeses, tobacco, cigars, and sausages—miles of them. Thereupon he engages a painter to make an appropriate sign, and in three days he is back again in the new town. Now he rents the blacksmith's old log house and rigs it up as a shop. Soon the sign swings over the door, the whiskey barrel is half empty, and the sausages are dispatched by the yard.

But how could it be otherwise? Our clever German calls them *egyptische Bratwürste*, an irresistible name, *nicht wahr?* And what of the sign? *Polz tausend noch einmal.* In the center rests a large barrel adorned with the magic word *Lagerbier.* On one side of the barrel is a large cheese and on the other a necklace of sausages. Between these German Valhalla delicacies we read in large yellow letters, *Wirtschafthaus zur deutschen Republik* [Restaurant of the German Republic] *bei Carl Klor.* Fortune smiles upon the German innkeeper.

His best customers are the railroad workers, most of whom are Irishmen. They discovered the shop one Sunday afternoon while it was closed. But, fortunately, two Germans in the crowd were attracted by the sign and interpreted its mysteries to the Irishmen, who at once burst into frenzies of joy and started to dance about to the accompaniment of war whoops. Then they stuck their thumbs into their mouths and pulled them out with popping sounds like the uncorking of bottles, after which they hammered at the door. The German immediately opened both his mouth and his door and began murdering the English language and tapping whiskey. He is now well on his way to becoming a capitalist, because these fellows have tremendous capacities and swallow a quart of firewater without batting an eye.

I believe I must have mentioned them before. They consist mostly of the worst riffraff of Europe, to whom America is a promised land where you earn a dollar a day and are not hanged for stealing. When these roughnecks get together it is a pretty dull party unless there are a couple of fights and someone gets a good hiding. As you go along a railway under construction, it is easy to detect the places where they have had their frolics by the torn-up sod, the tufts of hair, the broken bottles, pipes, pants buttons, blood, and so forth, which they have left behind them. I imagine that if the most brutish hog in the world could express himself he would do it something like these fellows.

But to get back to my town again. The German, the blacksmith, and the tailor do a rushing business. The train stops again, and this time it is a printer who makes his appearance. He gets in touch with the doctor and lawyer; an old printing press is for sale in the next town; they buy it, and with this new event we can really say that the town has "arrived." Some little trouble there is, to be sure, concerning the political affiliations of the paper, because it develops that the lawyer is a Democrat, the doctor an Abolitionist, and the printer a Whig. But a compromise is soon reached and the paper announces itself as "independent." The lawyer volunteers to write the editorials, while the doctor promises a wealth of death announcements, and the German and the blacksmith undertake to fill the rest of the paper with advertisements.

Within a few years the town is very large. The wagonmaker owns practically half of it. The German deals only in wholesale. The lawyer is mayor of the town, and the blacksmith does nothing but smoke cigars, for he is now a man of affluence.

Nat Turner as portrayed in contemporary newspapers. Whether this likeness by an unknown artist was drawn from life or merely from descriptions of Turner is unknown.

PART FIVE

An Age of Reform

Rearranging Social Patterns

During the second quarter of the nineteenth century, new social forces broke in upon the American villages, farms, and regions that had once existed in near isolation, their denizens practicing slow, traditional ways of work and life. The transportation revolution overcame barriers of distance, linking and transforming established communities and existing markets. Farmers and craftsmen, inventors and factory owners, were pressing form and efficiency upon the physical world. Enterprises like the Lowell Mills introduced new methods of work as well as new forms of social organization that changed the lives of workers like Harriet Hanson Robinson. The growing public school system worked to inculcate common ideals and goals in American minds; evangelical Protestantism labored to purify souls. Amidst these efforts, numerous reform movements of the time represented a determination among many to perfect the republic envisioned by the founders and, if possible, the lands beyond the nation's borders.

A few reformers questioned the foundations of capitalism. Some turned to religious or social experiments designed to reshape society. Most aimed at correcting specific problems. More than a million Americans crusaded against the excessive use of alcohol. Many of them read Timothy Shay Arthur's *Ten Nights in a Bar-Room* or saw it performed as a play. Reformers disagreed on goals and methods. But they were responding to either or both of two contradictory moods: frustration at disorder in society, apprehension about loss of community, and fear that morality was declining; or an optimistic faith in the ultimate perfectibility of the world in general and American society in particular.

As the nation slid toward Civil War, the crusade against slavery came to dominate American reform. Slaves themselves generated much of the heat that ignited the fierce controversy. Nat Turner's rebellion in 1831 did much to usher in an angrier era. Charles Ball, Josiah Henson, Francis Henderson, Harriet Jacobs, and Jacob Stroyer were among those former slaves who, after running away or purchasing their freedom, wrote accounts of their lives under slavery. Such writings provided the growing abolition movement with texts and examples to argue against the peculiar institution. White reformers like William Lloyd Garrison, whose newspaper *The Liberator* began publication in the same year as Nat Turner's rebellion, made southern leaders fearful by insisting upon immediate abolition. And most of the early leaders of the women's rights movement got their first taste of organizing, petitioning, and public speaking in the antislavery movement. From this beginning, Elizabeth Cady Stanton, Susan B. Anthony, and others pioneered a women's rights movement that over many years would powerfully effect the lives of American women.

Points of View:
Nat Turner's Rebellion (1831)

31

A Slave Insurrection

Nat Turner

Slaveowners, especially those in areas with large slave populations, lived in dread of slave uprisings. Rebellions in 1739 in South Carolina, in 1800 in Virginia, in 1811 in Louisiana, and in 1822 in South Carolina kept such fears alive. Nat Turner, a slave in Southampton County, Virginia, led the most sensational rebellion in 1831. Beginning on August 21, Turner's rebellion lasted only five days, but it claimed the lives of fifty-one whites and terrified white southerners. The uprising resulted in increased restrictions on slaves' education, marriage, and the right to assemble. The rebellion also dealt a serious blow to any chance of the South's voluntarily emancipating its slaves.

The Confessions of Nat Turner was published in 1832 by Thomas R. Gray, who interviewed Turner shortly before he was tried and executed. How much of the language of these confessions is Turner's and how much is Gray's is impossible to determine. Gray's account was widely read throughout the South.

BEFORE YOU READ

1. What was Nat Turner's revelation? What purpose did he consider himself destined to fulfill?

2. How well planned was the rebellion?

3. What do you think Turner and his compatriots expected to achieve by their rebellion?

Agreeable to his own appointment, on the evening he was committed to prison, with permission of the jailer, I visited Nat on Tuesday the first of November, when, without being questioned at all, he commenced his narrative in the following words:

Sir,

You have asked me to give a history of the motives which induced me to undertake the late insurrection, as you call it. To do so I must go back to the days of my infancy, and even before I was born. I was thirty-one years of age the second of October last, and born the property of Benjamin Turner, of this county. In my childhood a circumstance occurred which made an indelible impression on my mind, and laid the groundwork of that enthusiasm which has terminated so fatally to many both white and black, and for which I am about to atone at the gallows. It is here necessary to relate this circumstance — trifling as it may seem, it was the commencement of that belief which has grown with time, and even now, sir, in this dungeon, helpless and forsaken as I am, I cannot divest myself of. Being at play with other children, when three or four years old, I was telling them something, which my mother overhearing, said it had happened before I was born. I stuck to my story, however, and related some things which went in her opinion to confirm it. Others being called on were greatly astonished, knowing that these things had happened, and caused them to say in my hearing, I surely would be a prophet, as the Lord had shown me things that had happened before my birth. And my father and mother strengthened me in this my first impression, saying in my presence, I was intended for some great purpose, which they had always thought from certain marks on my head and breast.

My grandmother, who was very religious, and to whom I was much attached — my master, who belonged to the church, and other religious persons who visited the house, and whom I often saw at prayers, noticing the singularity of my manners, I suppose, and my uncommon intelligence for a child, remarked I had too much sense to be raised — and if I was, I would never be of any service to any one — as a slave. The manner in which I learned to read and write, not only had great influence on my own mind, as I acquired it with the most perfect ease, so much so that I have no recollection whatever of learning the alphabet — but to the astonishment of the family, one day, when a book was shown me to keep me from crying, I began spelling the names of different objects — this was a source of wonder to all in the neighborhood, particularly the blacks — and this learning was constantly improved at all opportuni-

The Confessions of Nat Turner, Leader of the Late Insurrection in Southampton, Virginia, as Fully and Voluntarily Made to Thomas C. Gray. (1832; New York, 1964) pp. 5–17.

ties. When I got large enough to go to work, while employed, I was reflecting on many things that would present themselves to my imagination. I was not addicted to stealing in my youth, nor have never been. Yet such was the confidence of the Negroes in the neighborhood, even at this early period of my life, in my superior judgment, that they would often carry me with them when they were going on any roguery, to plan for them. Growing up among them, with this confidence in my superior judgment, and when this, in their opinions, was perfected by divine inspiration, from the circumstances already alluded to in my infancy, and which belief was ever afterward zealously inculcated by the austerity of my life and manners, which became the subject of remark by white and black. By this time, having arrived to man's estate, and hearing the Scriptures commented on at meetings, I was struck with that particular passage which says: "Seek ye the kingdom of Heaven and all things shall be added unto you." I reflected much on this passage, and prayed daily for light on this subject. As I was praying one day at my plough, the spirit spoke to me, saying "Seek ye the kingdom of Heaven and all things shall be added unto you." *Question*—What do you mean by the Spirit. *Answer*—The Spirit that spoke to the prophets in former days—and I was greatly astonished, and for two years prayed continually, whenever my duty would permit—and then again I had the same revelation, which fully confirmed me in the impression that I was ordained for some great purpose in the hands of the Almighty. Several years rolled round, in which many events occurred to strengthen me in this my belief. At this time I reverted in my mind to the remarks made of me in my childhood, and the things that had been shown me. And as it had been said of me in my childhood by those whom I had been taught to pray, both white and black, and in whom I had the greatest confidence, that I had too much sense to be raised, and if I was I would never be of any use to anyone as a slave. Now finding I had arrived to man's estate, and was a slave, and these revelations being made known to me, I began to direct my attention to this great object, to fulfill the purpose for which, by this time, I felt assured I was intended. Knowing the influence I had obtained over the minds of my fellow servants, (not by the means of conjuring and such like tricks—for to them I always spoke of such things with contempt) but by the communion of the Spirit whose revelations I often communicated to them, and they believed and said my wisdom came from God.

And on the twelfth of May 1828, I heard a loud noise in the heavens, and the Spirit instantly appeared to me and said the Serpent was loosened, and Christ had laid down the yoke he had borne for the sins of men, and that I should take it on and fight against the Serpent, for the time was fast approaching, when the first should be last and the last should be first. *Question*— Do you not find yourself mistaken now? *Answer*—Was not Christ crucified? And by signs in the heavens that it would make known to me when I should commence the great work—and until the first sign appeared, I should conceal it from the knowledge of men—and on the appearance of the sign (the eclipse of the sun last February), I should arise and prepare myself, and slay my enemies with their own weapons. And immediately on the sign appearing in the heavens, the seal was removed from my lips, and I communicated the great work laid out for me to do, to four in whom I had the greatest confidence (Henry, Hark, Nelson, and Sam). It was intended by us to have begun the work of death on the fourth of July last. Many were the plans formed and rejected by us, and it affected my mind to such a degree that I fell sick, and the time passed without our coming to any determination how to commence — still forming new schemes and rejecting them when the sign appeared again, which determined me not to wait longer.

Since the commencement of 1830, I had been living with Mr. Joseph Travis, who was to me a kind master, and placed the greatest confidence in me; in fact, I had no cause to complain of his treatment to me. On Saturday evening, the twentieth of August, it was agreed between Henry, Hark, and myself to prepare a dinner the next day for the men we expected, and then to concert a plan, as we had not yet determined on any. Hark on the following morning brought a pig, and Henry brandy, and being joined by Sam, Nelson, Will, and Jack, they prepared in the woods a dinner, where, about three o'clock, I joined them. . . .

I saluted them on coming up, and asked Will how came he there; he answered his life was worth no more than others, and his liberty as dear to him. I asked him if he thought to obtain it? He said he would or lose his life. This was enough to put him in full confidence. Jack, I knew, was only a tool in the hands of Hark. It was quickly agreed we should commence at home (Mr. J. Travis') on that night, and until we had armed and equipped ourselves, and gathered sufficient force, neither age nor sex was to be spared (which was invariably adhered to). We remained at the feast until about two hours in the night, when we went to the house and found Austin; they all went to the cider press and drank, except myself. On returning to the house, Hark went to the door with an ax, for the purpose of breaking it open, as we knew we were strong enough to murder the family, if they were awakened by the noise; but reflecting that it might create an alarm in the neighborhood, we determined to enter the house secretly, and murder them while sleeping. Hark got a ladder and set it against the chimney, on which I ascended, and hoisting a window, entered and came down stairs, unbarred the door, and removed the guns from their places. It was then observed that I must spill the first blood. On which armed with a hatchet, and accompanied by Will, I entered my master's chamber; it being dark, I could not give a death blow, the hatchet glanced from his head, he sprang from the bed and called his wife, it was his last word. Will laid him dead, with a blow of his ax, and Mrs. Travis shared the same fate, as she lay in bed. The murder of this family, five in number, was the work of a moment, not one of them awoke; there was a little infant sleeping in a cradle, that was forgotten, until we had left the house and gone some distance, when Henry and Will returned and killed it. We got here four guns that would shoot, and several old muskets, with a pound or two of powder. We remained some time at the barn, where we paraded; I formed them in a line as soldiers, and after carrying them through all the maneuvers I was master of, marched them off to Mr. Salathul Francis', about six hundred yards distant. Sam and Will went to the door and knocked. Mr. Francis asked who was there, Sam replied it was him, and he had a letter for him, on which he got up and came to the door; they immediately seized him, and dragging him out a little from the door, he was dispatched by repeated blows on the head; there was no other white person in the family. We started from there for Mrs. Reese's, maintaining the most perfect silence on our march, where finding the door unlocked, we entered, and murdered Mrs. Reese in her bed, while sleeping; her son awoke, but it was only to sleep the sleep of death, he had only time to say who is that, and he was no more. From Mrs. Reese's we went to Mrs. Turner's, a mile distant, which we reached about sunrise on Monday morning. Henry, Austin, and Sam went to the still, where, finding Mr. Pebbles, Austin shot him, and the rest of us went to the house; as we approached, the family discovered us, and shut the door. Vain hope! Will, with one stroke of his ax, opened it, and we entered and found Mrs. Turner and Mrs. Newsome in the middle of a room almost frightened to death. Will immediately killed Mrs. Turner, with one blow of his ax. I took Mrs. Newsome by the hand, and with the sword I had when I was apprehended, I struck her several blows over the head, but not being able to kill her, as the sword was dull. Will turning around and discovering it, dispatched her also. A general destruction of property and search for money and ammunition always succeeded the murders. By this time my company amounted to fifteen, and nine men mounted, who started for Mrs. Whitehead's (the other six were to go through a byway to Mr. Bryant's and rejoin us at Mrs. Whitehead's). . . . As we pushed on to the house, I discovered someone running round the garden, and thinking it was some of the white family, I pursued them, but finding it was a servant girl belonging to the house, I returned to commence the work of death, but they whom I left had not been idle; all the family were already murdered, but Mrs. Whitehead and her daughter Margaret. As I came round to the door I saw Will pulling Mrs. Whitehead out of the house, and at the step he nearly severed her head from her body, with his broad ax. Miss Margaret, when I discovered her had concealed herself in the corner, formed by the projection of the cellar cap from the house; on my approach she fled, but was soon overtaken, and after repeated blows with a sword, I killed her by a blow on the head with a fence rail. By this time, the six who had gone by Mr. Bryant's rejoined us, and informed me they had done the work of death assigned them. We again divided, part going to Mr. Richard Porter's and from thence to Nathaniel Francis', the others to Mr. Howell Harris', and Mr. T. Doyle's. On my reaching Mr. Porter's, he had escaped with his family. I understood there that the alarm had already spread.

I proceeded to Mr. Levi Waller's, two or three miles distant. I took my station in the rear, and as it was my object to carry terror and devastation wherever we went, I placed fifteen or twenty of the best armed and most to be relied on in front, who generally approached the houses as fast as their horses could run; this was for two purposes, to prevent their escape and strike terror to the inhabitants—on this account I never got to the houses, after leaving Mrs. Whitehead's, until the murders were committed, except in one case. I sometimes got in sight in time to see the work of death completed, viewed the mangled bodies as they lay, in silent satisfaction, and immediately started in quest of other victims. Having murdered Mrs. Waller and ten children, we started for Mr. William Williams'—having killed him and two little boys that were there; while engaged in this, Mrs. Williams fled and got some distance from the house, but she was pursued, overtaken, and compelled to get up behind one of the company, who brought her back, and after showing her the mangled body of her lifeless husband, she was told to get down and lay by his side, where she was shot dead. I then started for Mr. Jacob Williams', where the family were murdered. Here we found a young man named Drury, who had come on business with Mr. Williams. He was pursued, overtaken, and shot. Mrs. Vaughan's was the next place we visited—and after murdering the family here, I determined on starting for Jerusalem. Our number amounted now to fifty or sixty, all mounted and armed with guns, axes, swords, and clubs. On reaching Mr. James W. Parker's gate, immediately on the road leading to Jerusalem, and about three miles distant, it was proposed to me to call there, but I objected, as I knew he was gone to Jerusalem, and my object was to reach there as soon as possible; but some of the men having relations at Mr. Parker's it was agreed that they might call and get his people. I remained at the gate on the road, with seven or eight; the others going across the field to the house, about half a mile off. After waiting some time for them, I became impatient, and started to the house for them, and on our return we were met by a party of white men, who had pursued our blood-stained track and who had fired on those at the gate and dispersed them, which I knew nothing of, not having been at that time rejoined by any of them. Immediately on discovering the whites, I order my men to halt and form, as they appeared to be alarmed. The white men, eighteen in number, approached us in about one hundred yards, when one of them fired.

I then ordered my men to fire and rush on them; the few remaining stood their ground until we approached within fifty yards, when they fired and retreated. We pursued and overtook some of them who we thought we left dead; after pursuing them about two hundred yards, and rising a little hill, I discovered they were met by another party, and had halted, and were reloading their guns, thinking that those who retreated first, and the party who fired on us at fifty or sixty yards distant, had all only fallen back to meet others with ammunition. As I saw them reloading their guns, and more coming up than I saw at first, and several of my bravest men being wounded, the others became panic struck and squandered over the field; the white men pursued and fired on us several times. Hark had his horse shot under him, and I caught another for him as it was running by me; five or six of my men were wounded, but none left on the field; finding myself defeated here I instantly determined to go through a private way, and cross the Nottoway River at the Cypress Bridge, three miles below Jerusalem, and attack that place in the rear, as I expected they would look for me on the other road, and I had a great desire to get there to procure arms and ammunition. After going a short distance in this private way, accompanied by about twenty men, I overtook two or three who told me the others were dispersed in every direction. After trying in vain to collect a sufficient force to proceed to Jerusalem, I determined to return, as I was sure they would make back to their old neighborhood, where they would rejoin me, make new recruits, and come down again. On my way back, I called at Mrs. Thomas's, Mrs. Spencer's, and several other places. The white families having fled, we found no more victims to gratify our thirst for blood, we stopped at Major Ridley's quarter for the night, and being joined by four of his men, with the recruits made since my defeat, we mustered now about forty strong. After placing out sentinels, I laid down to sleep, but was quickly roused by a great racket. Starting up, I found some mounted, and others in great confusion; one of the sentinels having given the alarm that we were about to be attacked, I ordered some to ride round and reconnoiter, and on their return the others being more alarmed, not knowing who they were, fled in different ways, so that I was reduced to about twenty again; with this I determined to attempt to recruit, and proceed on to rally in the neighborhood I had left. Dr. Blunt's was the nearest house, which we reached just before day; on riding up the yard, Hark fired a gun. We expected Dr. Blunt and his family were at Major Ridley's, as I knew there was a company of men there; the gun was fired to ascertain if any of they family were at home; we were immediately fired upon and retreated leaving several of my men. I do not know what became of them, as I never saw them afterward. Pursuing our course back, and coming in sight of Captain Harris's, where we had been the day before, we discovered a party of white men at the house, on which all deserted me but two (Jacob and Nat), we concealed ourselves in the woods until near night, when I sent them in search of Henry, Sam, Nelson, and Hark, and directed them to rally all they could at the place we had had our dinner the Sunday before, where they would find me, and I accordingly returned there as soon as it was dark, and remained until Wednesday evening, when discovering white men riding around the place as though they were looking for someone, and none of my men joining me, I concluded Jacob and Nat had been taken, and compelled to betray me. On this I gave up all hope for the present; and on Thursday night, after having supplied myself with provisions from Mr. Travis's, I scratched a hole under a pile of fence rails in a field, where I concealed myself for six weeks, never leaving my hiding place but for a few minutes in the dead of night to get water, which was very near; thinking by this time I could venture out, I began to go about in the night and eavesdrop the houses in the neighborhood; pursuing this course for about a fortnight and gathering little or no intelligence, afraid of speaking to any human being, and returning every morning to my cave before the dawn of day. I know not how long I might have led this life, if accident had not betrayed me, a dog in the neighborhood passing by my hiding place one night while I was out was attracted by some meat I had in my cave, and crawled in and stole it, and was coming out just as I returned. A few nights after, two Negroes having started to go hunting with the same dog, and passed that way, the dog came again to the place, and having just gone out to walk about, discovered me and barked, on which, thinking myself discovered, I spoke to them to beg concealment. On making myself known, they fled from me. Knowing then they would betray me, I immediately left my hiding place, and was pursued almost incessantly until I was taken a fortnight afterward by Mr. Benjamin Phipps, in a little hole I had dug out with my sword, for the purpose of concealment, under the top of a fallen tree. On Mr. Phipps discovering the place of my concealment, he cocked his gun and aimed at me. I requested him not to shoot, and I would give up, upon which he demanded my sword. I delivered it to him, and he brought me to prison. During the time I was pursued, I had many hair breadth escapes, which your time will not permit you to relate. I am here loaded with chains, and willing to suffer the fate that awaits me.

[Gray:] I here proceeded to make some inquiries of him, after assuring him of the certain death that awaited him, and that concealment would only bring destruction of the innocent as well as guilty, of his own color, if he knew of any extensive or concerted plan. His answer was, I do not. When I questioned him as to the insurrection in North Carolina happening about the same time, he denied any knowledge of it.

32

Who Is to Blame?

William Lloyd Garrison
et al.

Nat Turner's rebellion occurred just when slavery was under attack from other quarters. In 1829, a free black named David Walker published his incendiary Walker's Appeal in Four Articles, Together with a Preamble to the Colored Citizens of the World, But in Particular and Very Expressly to Those of the United States of America, *which quoted the Declaration of Independence in justification of a slave insurrection. Then William Lloyd Garrison, who would also cite the Declaration of Independence, broke with the tradition among white abolitionists of calling for gradual emancipation. From the first issue of* The Liberator, *published in Boston on January 1, 1831, Garrison demanded the immediate and unconditional abolition of slavery.*

The southern states reacted viscerally to Nat Turner's rebellion. In the immediate hysteria, slaves and free blacks were gunned down. The ongoing debate in Virginia over gradual emancipation ended. Instead, the southern states moved toward strengthening the slave system by restricting the rights of free blacks as well as the right of owners to free slaves, augmenting the patrols that constricted the mobility of the slave population, setting limits on black religious meetings, and ensuring that marriage did not restrict the slave trade. And they moved on many fronts to close the South to antislavery propaganda, even touching off a national debate by forbidding the federal post office to deliver such antislavery writings as Garrison's Liberator *in southern states.*

BEFORE YOU READ

1. Did William Lloyd Garrison approve of Nat Turner's rebellion?
2. How did he explain its occurrence?
3. Did John Hampden Pleasants, editor of the Richmond *Constitutional Whig*, approve of the treatment of blacks in the wake of the rebellion?
4. How did he explain its occurrence?
5. How did Virginia Governor John Floyd explain the rebellion?
6. What did he propose to avoid further uprisings?

WILLIAM LLOYD GARRISON

The Liberator, September 3, 1831

What we have so long predicted,—at the peril of being stigmatized as an alarmist and declaimer,—has commenced its fulfilment. The first step of the earthquake, which is ultimately to shake down the fabric of oppression, leaving not one stone upon another, has been made. The first drops of blood, which are but the prelude to a deluge from the gathering clouds, have fallen. The first flash of the lightning, which is to smite and consume, has been felt. The first wailings of a bereavement, which is to clothe the earth in sackcloth, have broken upon our ears.

In the first number of the *Liberator*, we alluded to the hour of vengeance in the following lines:

> Wo if it come with storm, and blood, and fire,
> When midnight darkness veils the earth and sky!
> *Wo to the innocent babe*—the guilty sire—
> *Mother and daughter*—friends of kindred tie!
> *Stranger and citizen alike shall die!*
> Red-handed Slaughter his revenge shall feed,
> And Havoc yell his ominous death-cry,
> And wild Despair in vain for mercy plead—
> While hell itself shall shrink and sicken at the deed!

Read the account of the insurrection in Virginia, and say whether our prophecy be not fulfilled. What was poetry—imagination—in January, is now a bloody reality. "Wo to the innocent babe—to mother and daughter!" Is it not true? Turn again to the record of slaughter! Whole families have been cut off—not a mother, not a daughter, not a babe left. Dreadful retaliation! "The

Cain, William E., ed., *William Lloyd Garrison and the Fight against Slavery* (Boston: Bedford Books of St. Martin's Press, 1995), p. 80.

dead bodies of white and black lying just as they were slain, unburied"—the oppressor and the oppressed equal at last in death—what a spectacle!

True, the rebellion is quelled. Those of the slaves who were not killed in combat, have been secured, and the prison is crowded with victims destined for the gallows!

> Yet laugh not in your carnival of crime
> Too proudly, ye oppressors!

You have seen, it is to be feared, but the beginning of sorrows. All the blood which has been shed will be required at your hands. At your hands alone? No—but at the hands of the people of New-England and of all the free states. The crime of oppression is national. The south is only the agent in this guilty traffic. But, remember! the same causes are at work which must inevitably produce the same effects; and when the contest shall have again begun, it must be again a war of extermination. In the present instance, no quarters have been asked or given.

But we have killed and routed them now—we can do it again and again—we are invincible! A dastardly triumph, well becoming a nation of oppressors. Detestable complacency, that can think, without emotion, of the extermination of the blacks! We have the power to kill *all*—let us, therefore, continue to apply the whip and forge new fetters!

In his fury against the revolters, who will remember their wrongs? What will it avail them, though the catalogue of their sufferings, dripping with warm blood fresh from their lacerated bodies, be held up to extenuate their conduct? It is enough that the victims were black—that circumstance makes them less precious than the dogs which have been slain in our streets! They were black—brutes, pretending to be men—legions of curses upon their memories! They were black—God made them to serve us!

Ye patriotic hypocrites! ye panegyrists[1] of Frenchmen, Greeks, and Poles! ye fustian[2] declaimers for liberty! ye valiant sticklers for equal rights among yourselves! ye haters of aristocracy! ye assailants of monarchies! ye republican nullifiers! ye treasonable disunionists! be dumb! Cast no reproach upon the conduct of the slaves, but let your lips and cheeks wear the blisters of condemnation!

Ye accuse the pacific friends of emancipation of instigating the slaves to revolt. Take back the charge as a foul slander. The slaves need no incentives at our hands. They will find them in their stripes—in their emaciated bodies—in their ceaseless toil—in their ignorant minds—in every field, in every valley, on every hill-top and mountain, wherever you and your fathers have fought for liberty—in your speeches, your conversations, your celebrations, your pamphlets, your newspapers—voices in the air, sounds from across the ocean,

---

1. **panegyrists:** people who celebrate a person, group, or deed.
2. **fustian:** pretentious writing or speech.

invitations to resistance above, below, around them! What more do they need? Surrounded by such influences, and smarting under their newly made wounds, is it wonderful that they should rise to contend—as other "heroes" have contended—for their lost rights? It is *not* wonderful.

In all that we have written, is there aught to justify the excesses of the slaves? No. Nevertheless, they deserve no more censure than the Greeks in destroying the Turks, or the Poles in exterminating the Russians, or our fathers in slaughtering the British. Dreadful, indeed, is the standard erected by worldly patriotism!

For ourselves, we are horror-struck at the late tidings. We have exerted our utmost efforts to avert the calamity. We have warned our countrymen of the danger of persisting in their unrighteous conduct. We have preached to the slaves the pacific precepts of Jesus Christ. We have appealed to christians, philanthropists and patriots, for their assistance to accomplish the great work of national redemption through the agency of moral power—of public opinion—of individual duty. How have we been received? We have been threatened, proscribed, vilified and imprisoned—a laughing-stock and a reproach. Do we falter, in view of these things? Let time answer. If we have been hitherto urgent, and bold, and denunciatory in our efforts,—hereafter we shall grow vehement and active with the increase of danger. We shall cry, in trumpet tones, night and day,—Wo to this guilty land, unless she speedily repent of her evil doings! The blood of millions of her sons cries aloud for redress! IMMEDIATE EMANCIPATION can alone save her from the vengeance of Heaven, and cancel the debt of ages!

JOHN HAMPDEN PLEASANTS

Constitutional Whig, September 3, 1831

We have been astonished since our return from Southampton (whither we went with Capt. Harrison's Troop of Horse) in reading over the mass of exchange papers accumulated in our absence, to see the number of false, absurd, and idle rumors, circulated by the Press, touching the insurrection in that county. Editors seem to have applied themselves to the task of alarming the public mind as much as possible by persuading the slaves to entertain a high opinion of their strength and consequences. While truth is always the best policy, and best remedy, the exaggerations to which we have alluded are calculated to give the slaves false conceptions of their numbers and capacity, by exhibiting the terror and confusion of the whites, and to induce them to think that practicable, which they see is so much feared by their superiors.

We have little to say of the Southampton Tragedy beyond what is already known. The origin of the conspiracy, the prime agents, its extent and ultimate direction, is matter of conjecture.—The universal opinion in that part of the country is that Nat, a slave, a preacher, and a pretended prophet was the first [blurred word], the actual leader, and the most remorseless of the executioners. According to the evidence of a negro boy whom they carried along to hold their horses, Nat commenced the scene of murder at the first house (Travis') with his own hand. Having called upon two others to make good their valiant boasting, so often repeated, of what they would do, and these shrinking from the requisition, Nat proceeded to dispatch one of the family with his own hand. Animated by the example and exhortations of their leader, having a taste of blood and convinced that they had now gone too far to recede, his followers dismissed their doubts and became as ferocious as their leader wished them. To follow the [blurred word] capture of Travis' house early that day, to their dispersion at Parker's cornfield early in the afternoon, when they had traversed near 20 miles, murdered 63 whites, and approached within 3 or 4 miles of the Village of Jerusalem; the immediate object of their movement— to describe the scenes at each house, the circumstances of the murders, the hair breadth escapes of the few who were lucky enough to escape—would prove as interesting as heart rending. Many of the details have reached us but not in so authentic a shape as to justify their publication, nor have we the time or space. Let a few suffice. Of the event at Dr. Blount's we had a narrative from the gallant old gentleman himself, and his son, a lad about 15, distinguished for his gallantry and modesty, and whom we take leave to recommend to Gen. Jackson, for a warrant in the Navy or at West Point. The Doctor had received information of the insurrection, and that his house would be attacked a short time before the attack was made. Crippled with the gout, and indisposed to leave, he decided to defend his home. His force was his son, overseer and three other white men. Luckily there were six guns, and plenty of powder and shot in the house. These were barely loaded, his force posted, and the instructions given, when the negroes from 15 to 30 strong, rode up about day break. The Doctor's orders were that each man should be particular in his aim and should fire one at a time; he himself reserved one gun, resolved if the house was forced to sell his life as dearly as he could. The remaining five fired in succession upon the assailants, at the distance of fifteen or twenty steps. The blacks, upon the fifth fire, retreated, leaving one killed (we believe) and one wounded (a fellow named Hark,) and were pursued by the Doctor's negroes with shouts and execrations. Had the shot been larger, more execution doubtless would have been done.

Mrs. Vaughan's was among the last houses attacked. A venerable negro woman described the scene which she had witnessed with great emphasis: it was near noon and her mistress was making some preparations in the porch for dinner, when happening to look towards the road she discerned a dust and wondered what it could mean. In a second, the negroes mounted and armed, rushed into view, and making an exclamation indicative of her horror and agony, Mrs. Vaughan ran into the house.—The negroes dismounted and ran around the house, pointing their guns at the doors and windows. Mrs. Vaughan appeared at a window, and begged for her life, inviting them to take everything she had. The prayer was answered by one of them firing at her, which was followed by another, and a fatal, shot. In the meantime, Miss Vaughan, who was upstairs, and unap-praised of the terrible advent until she heard the noise of the attack, rushed down, and begging for her life, was shot as she ran a few steps from the door. A son of Mrs. Vaughan, about 15, was at the still house, when hearing a gun and conjecturing, it is supposed, that his brother had come from Jerusalem, ap-proached the house and was shot as he got over the fence. It is difficult for the imagination to conceive a situation so truly and horribly awful, as that in which these unfortunate ladies were placed. Alone, unprotected, and unconscious of danger, to find themselves without a moment's notice for escape or defence, in the power of a band of ruffians, from whom instant death was the least they could expect! In a most lively and picturesque manner, did the old negress describe the horrors of the scene; the blacks riding up with imprecations, the looks of her mis-tress, white as a sheet, her prayers for her life, and the actions of the scoundrels environing the house and pointing their guns at the doors and windows, ready to fire as occasion offered. When the work was done they called for drink, and food, and becoming nice, damned the brandy as vile stuff.

The scene at Vaughan's may suffice to give an idea of what was done at the other houses. A bloodier and more accursed tragedy was never acted, even by the agency of the tomahawk and scalping knife. Interesting details will no doubt be evolved in the progress of the trials and made known to the public.

It is with pain we speak of another feature of the Southampton Rebellion; for we have been most unwilling to have our sympathies for the sufferers di-minished or affected by their misconduct. We allude to the slaughter of many blacks, without trial, and under circumstances of great barbarity. How many have thus been put into death (generally by decapitation or shooting) reports vary; probably however some five and twenty and from that to 40; possibly a yet larger number. To the great honor of General Eppes, he used every pre-caution in his power, and we hope and believe with success, to put a stop to the disgraceful procedure.—We met with one individual of intelligence, who stated that he himself had killed between 10 and 15. He justified himself on the grounds of the barbarities committed on the whites; and that he thought him-self right is certain from the fact that he narrowly escaped losing his own life in an attempt to save a negro woman whom he thought innocent but who was shot by the multitude in despite of his exertions. We (the Richmond Troop) witnessed with surprise the sanguinary temper of the population who evinced a strong disposition to inflict immediate death on every prisoner. Not having witnessed the horrors committed by the blacks, or seen the unburried and dis-figured remains of their wives and children, we were unprepared to understand their feelings, and could not at first admit of their extenuation, which a closer observation of the atrocities of the insurgents suggested. Now, however, we feel individually compelled to offer an apology for the people of Southampton, while we deeply deplore that human nature urged them to such extremities. Let the fact not be doubted by those whom it most concerns, that another such insurrection will be the signal for the extirmination of the whole black popu-lation in the quarter of the state where it occurs.

The numbers engaged in the insurrection are variously reported. They probably did not exceed 40 or 50, and were fluctuating from desertions and new recruits. About fifty are in Southampton jail, some of them on suspicion only. — We trust and believe that the intelligent magistracy of the county, will have the firmness to oppose the popular passions, should it be disposed to involve the innocent with the guilty, and to take suspicion for proof.

The presence of the troops from Norfolk and Richmond alone prevented retaliation from being carried much farther.

At the date of Capt. Harrison's departure from Jerusalem, Gen. Nat had not been taken. On that morning, however, Dred, another insurgent chief, was brought prisoner to Jerusalem, having surrendered himself to his master, in the apprehension, no doubt, of starving in the swamps or being shot by the numerous parties of local militia, who were in pursuit. Nat had not certainly been heard from since the skirmish in Parker's cornfield, which was in fact, the termination of the insurrection; the negroes after that dispersing themselves, and making no further attempt. He is represented as a shrewd fellow, reads, writes, and preaches; and by various artifices had acquired great influence over the minds of the wretched beings whom he has led into destruction. It is supposed that he induced them to believe that there were only 80,000 whites in the country, who, being exterminated, the blacks might take possession. Various of his tricks to acquire and preserve influence had been mentioned, but they are not worth repeating. If there was any ulterior purpose, he probably alone knows it. For our own part, we still believe there was none; and if he be the intelligent man represented, we are incapable of conceiving the arguments by which he persuaded his own mind of the feasibility of his attempt, or how it could possibly end but in certain destruction. We therefore incline to the belief that he acted upon no higher principle that the impulse of revenge against the whites, as the enslavers of himself and his race; that, being a fanatic, he possibly persuaded himself that Heaven would interfere; and that he may have convinced himself, as he certainly did his deluded followers to some extent, that the appearance of the sun some weeks ago, prognosticated something favorable to their cause. We are inclined to think that the solar phenomenon exercised considerable influence in promoting the insurrection; calculated as it was to impress the imaginations of the ignorant.

A more important inquiry remains — whether the conspiracy was circumscribed to the neighborhood in which it broke out, or had its ramifications through other counties. We, at first, adopted the first opinion; but there are several circumstances which favor the latter. We understand that the confessions of all the prisoners go to show that the insurrection broke out too soon, as it is supposed, in consequence of the last day of July being a Sunday, and not, as the negroes in Southampton believed, the Saturday before. The report is that the rising was fixed for the fourth Sunday in August, and that they supposing Sunday, the 31st of July to be the first Sunday in August, they were betrayed into considering the 3d Sunday as the 4th. This is the popular impression founded upon confessions, upon the indications of an intention of the

negroes in Nansemond and other places to unite, and upon the allegation that
Gen. Nat extended his preaching excursions to Petersburg and this city; allegations which we, however, disbelieve. It is more than probable, nevertheless,
that the mischief was concerted and concocted under the cloak of religion. The
trials which are now proceeding in Southampton, Sussex, and elsewhere, will
develop all the truth. We suspect the truth will turn out to be that the conspiracy was confined to Southampton, and that the idea of its extensiveness
originated in the panic which seized upon the South East of Virginia.

GOVERNOR JOHN FLOYD OF VIRGINIA

Letter to Governor James Hamilton, Jr., of South Carolina

Richmond
November 19, 1831

Sir:

I received your letter yesterday and with great pleasure will give you my impressions freely—

I will notice this affair in my annual message, but here only give a very
careless history of it, as it appeared to the public—

I am fully persuaded, the spirit of insubordination which has, and still man-
ifests itself in Virginia, had its origin among, and eminated from, the Yankee
population, upon their *first* arrival amongst us, but mostly especially the Yankee pedlers and traders.

The course has been by no means a direct one—they began first, by making them religious—their conversations were of that character—telling the
blacks, God was no respecter of persons—the black man was as good as the
white—that all men were born free and equal—that they cannot serve two
masters—that the white people rebelled against England to obtain freedom,
so have the blacks a right to do.

In the mean time, I am sure without any purpose of this kind, the preachers, principally Northern—were very assidious in operating upon our population, day and night, they were at work—and religion became, and is, the
fashion of the times—finally our females and of the most respectable were persuaded that it was piety to teach negroes to read and write, to the end that they
might read the *Scriptures*—many of them became tutoresses in Sunday schools
and, pious distributors of tracts, from the New York Tract Society.

At this point, more active operations commenced—our magistrates and
laws became more inactive—large assemblages of negroes were suffered to
take place for religious purposes—Then commenced the efforts of the black
preachers, often from the pulpits these pamphlets and papers were read—followed by the incendiary publications of Walker,[3] Garrison and Knapp[4] of

3. **Walker:** free black whose published writing justified slave insurrection.
4. **Knapp:** abolitionist editor and associate of William Lloyd Garrison.

Boston, these too with songs and hymns of a similar character were circulated, read and commented upon—We resting in apathetic security until the Southampton affair.

From all that has come to my knowledge during and since this affair—I am fully convinced that every black preacher in the whole country east of the Blue Ridge was in the secret, that the plans as published by those Northern presses were adopted and acted upon by them—that their congregations, as they were called knew nothing of this intended rebellion, except a few leading and intelligent men, who may have been head men in the Church—*the mass* were prepared by making them aspire to an equal station by such conversations as I have related as the first step.

I am informed that they had settled the form of government to be that of white people, whom they intended to cut off to a man—with the difference that the preachers were to be their Governors, Generals and Judges. I feel fully justified to myself, in believing the Northern incendiaries, tracts, Sunday Schools, religion and reading and writing has accomplished this end.

I shall in my annual message recommend that laws be passed—To confine the Slaves to the estates of their masters—prohibit negroes from preaching—absolutely to drive from this State all free negroes—and to substitute the surplus revenue in our Treasury annually for slaves, to work for a time upon our Rail Roads etc etc and these sent out of the country, preparatory, or rather as the first step to emancipation—This last point will of course be tenderly and cautiously managed and will be urged or delayed as your State and Georgia may be disposed to co-operate.

In relation to the extent of this insurrection I think it greater than will ever appear—the facts will as now considered, appear to be these—It commenced with Nat and nine others on Sunday night—two o'clock, we date it, Monday morning before day and ceased by the dispersion of the negroes on Tuesday morning at ten o'clock—During this time the negroes had murdered sixty one persons, and traversed a distance of twenty miles, and increased to about seventy slave men—they spared but one family and that one was so wretched as to be in all respects upon a par with them—all died bravely indicating no reluctance to loose [sic] their lives in such a cause.

I am Sir,
with consideration and respect
Your obt Sevnt
John Floyd

His Excy
James Hamilton, Jr.
Governor of South Carolina

FOR CRITICAL THINKING

1. Examine the language of *The Confessions of Nat Turner*. Can you pick out parts that seem to be the language expected of a Virginia lawyer like Thomas Gray and parts that you might imagine to be Nat Turner's own words? Compose a defense of his actions as you think Nat Turner might have presented it.

2. Why do you think that so many people identified Turner's rebellion with the writings of William Lloyd Garrison? What does that say about their view of the slaves? What was Garrison's response to this allegation?

3. Compose a possible reply from South Carolina Governor James Hamilton, Jr., to Governor Floyd's letter.

33

Life of a Female Slave
Harriet Jacobs

Harriet Jacobs's Incidents in the Life of a Slave Girl *is only now emerging as the classic narrative of a woman slave, a work to rank with the several autobiographies of Frederick Douglass. Published under a pseudonym in 1861, edited by a white abolitionist, and borrowing form and rhetoric from sentimental novels such as Harriet Beecher Stowe's* Uncle Tom's Cabin, *the authenticity of the work remained suspect for 120 years. Only in 1981, when Jean Fagan Yellin published documentary evidence for Jacobs's authorship (*American Literature, *November 1981: 479–86), did recognition come that this is a major work of African American literature, as well as an essential document for the history of antebellum slavery.*

Jacobs (1813–1897), writing under the pseudonym of Linda Brent, emerges as a remarkably determined woman. To prevent the permanent enslavement of her children, she hid for seven years in the attic of her grandmother's house, a tiny space only three feet high, while deceiving her master into thinking she had escaped to the North by smuggling out letters to be mailed from New York City and Boston. Finally she and then her children escaped from slave territory to discover the ambiguities of freedom in the so-called free states.

Before You Read

1. What did Harriet Jacobs's account of her experience add to our picture of slavery?

2. Did she picture herself as a victim? What did she emphasize about her reaction to the position her master placed her in?

3. How do you think readers of the time reacted to her picture of the experiences of young female slaves?

THE TRIALS OF GIRLHOOD

During the first years of my service in Dr. Flint's family, I was accustomed to share some indulgences with the children of my mistress. Though this seemed to me no more than right, I was grateful for it, and tried to merit the kindness by the faithful discharge of my duties. But I now entered on my fifteenth year—a sad epoch in the life of a slave girl. My master began to whisper foul words in my ear. Young as I was, I could not remain ignorant of their import. I tried to treat them with indifference or contempt. The master's age, my extreme youth, and the fear that his conduct would be reported to my grandmother, made me bear this treatment for many months. He was a crafty man, and resorted to many means to accomplish his purposes. Sometimes he had stormy, terrific ways, that made his victims tremble; sometimes he assumed a

Harriet Jacobs, *Incidents in the Life of a Slave Girl* (Boston, 1861), pp. 44–49, 51–55, 57–67, 82–89.

gentleness that he thought must surely subdue. Of the two, I preferred his stormy moods, although they left me trembling. He tried his utmost to corrupt the pure principles my grandmother had instilled. He peopled my young mind with unclean images, such as only a vile monster could think of. I turned from him with disgust and hatred. But he was my master. I was compelled to live under the same roof with him—where I saw a man forty years my senior daily violating the most sacred commandments of nature. He told me I was his property; that I must be subject to his will in all things. My soul revolted against the mean tyranny. But where could I turn for protection? No matter whether the slave girl be as black as ebony or as fair as her mistress. In either case, there is no shadow of law to protect her from insult, from violence, or even from death; all these are inflicted by fiends who bear the shape of men. The mistress, who ought to protect the helpless victim, has no other feelings towards her but those of jealousy and rage. The degradation, the wrongs, the vices, that grow out of slavery, are more than I can describe. They are greater than you would willingly believe. Surely, if you credited one half the truths that are told you concerning the helpless millions suffering in this cruel bondage, you at the north would not help to tighten the yoke. You surely would refuse to do for the master, on your own soil, the mean and cruel work which trained bloodhounds and the lowest class of whites do for him at the south.

Every where the years bring to all enough of sin and sorrow; but in slavery the very dawn of life is darkened by these shadows. Even the little child, who is accustomed to wait on her mistress and her children, will learn, before she is twelve years old, why it is that her mistress hates such and such a one among the slaves. Perhaps the child's own mother is among those hated ones. She listens to violent outbreaks of jealous passion, and cannot help understanding what is the cause. She will become prematurely knowing in evil things. Soon she will learn to tremble when she hears her master's footfall. She will be compelled to realize that she is no longer a child. If God has bestowed beauty upon her; it will prove her greatest curse. That which commands admiration in the white woman only hastens the degradation of the female slave. I know that some are too much brutalized by slavery to feel the humiliation of their position; but many slaves feel it most acutely, and shrink from the memory of it. I cannot tell how much I suffered in the presence of these wrongs, nor how I am still pained by the retrospect. My master met me at every turn, reminding me that I belonged to him, and swearing by heaven and earth that he would compel me to submit to him. If I went out for a breath of fresh air, after a day of unwearied toil, his footsteps dogged me. If I knelt by my mother's grave, his dark shadow fell on me even there. The light heart which nature had given me became heavy with sad forebodings. The other slaves in my master's house noticed the change. Many of them pitied me; but none dared to ask the cause. They had no need to inquire. They knew too well the guilty practices under that roof; and they were aware that to speak of them was an offence that never went unpunished.

I longed for some one to confide in. I would have given the world to have laid my head on my grandmother's faithful bosom, and told her all my troubles. But Dr. Flint swore he would kill me, if I was not as silent as the grave. Then, although my grandmother was all in all to me, I feared her as well as loved her. I had been accustomed to look up to her with a respect bordering upon awe. I was very young, and felt shamefaced about telling her such impure things, especially as I knew her to be very strict on such subjects. Moreover, she was a woman of a high spirit. She was usually very quiet in her demeanor; but if her indignation was once roused, it was not very easily quelled. I had been told that she once chased a white gentleman with a loaded pistol, because he insulted one of her daughters. I dreaded the consequences of a violent outbreak; and both pride and fear kept me silent. But though I did not confide in my grandmother, and even evaded her vigilant watchfulness and inquiry, her presence in the neighborhood was some protection to me. Though she had been a slave, Dr. Flint was afraid of her. He dreaded her scorching rebukes. Moreover, she was known and patronized by many people; and he did not wish to have his villany made public. It was lucky for me that I did not live on a distant plantation, but in a town not so large that the inhabitants were ignorant of each other's affairs. Bad as are the laws and customs in a slaveholding community, the doctor, as a professional man, deemed it prudent to keep up some outward show of decency. . . .

I once saw two beautiful children playing together. One was a fair white child; the other was her slave; and also her sister. When I saw them embracing each other, and heard their joyous laughter, I turned sadly away from the lovely sight. I foresaw the inevitable blight that would fall on the little slave's heart. I knew how soon her laughter would be changed to sighs. The fair child grew up to be a still fairer woman. From childhood to womanhood her pathway was blooming with flowers, and overarched by a sunny sky. Scarcely one day of her life had been clouded when the sun rose on her happy bridal morning.

How had those years dealt with her slave sister, the little playmate of her childhood? She, also, was very beautiful; but the flowers and sunshine of love were not for her. She drank the cup of sin, and shame, and misery, whereof her persecuted race are compelled to drink.

In view of these things, why are ye silent, ye free men and women of the north? Why do your tongues falter in maintenance of the right? Would that I had more ability! But my heart is so full, and my pen is so weak! There are noble men and women who plead for us, striving to help those who cannot help themselves. God bless them! God give them strength and courage to go on! God bless those, every where, who are laboring to advance the cause of humanity!

THE JEALOUS MISTRESS

I would ten thousand times rather that my children should be the half-starved paupers of Ireland than to be the most pampered among the slaves of America. I would rather drudge out my life on a cotton plantation, till the grave opened to give me rest, than to live with an unprincipled master and a jealous mistress. The felon's home in a penitentiary is preferable. He may repent, and turn from the error of his ways, and so find peace; but it is not so with a favorite slave. She is not allowed to have any pride of character. It is deemed a crime in her to wish to be virtuous. . . .

I had entered my sixteenth year, and every day it became more apparent that my presence was intolerable to Mrs. Flint. Angry words frequently passed between her and her husband. He had never punished me himself, and he would not allow any body else to punish me. In that respect, she was never satisfied; but, in her angry moods, no terms were too vile for her to bestow upon me. Yet I, whom she detested so bitterly, had far more pity for her than he had, whose duty it was to make her life happy. I never wronged her, or wished to wrong her; and one word of kindness from her would have brought me to her feet.

After repeated quarrels between the doctor and his wife, he announced his intention to take his youngest daughter, then four years old, to sleep in his apartment. It was necessary that a servant should sleep in the same room, to be on hand if the child stirred. I was selected for that office, and informed for what purpose that arrangement had been made. By managing to keep within sight of people, as much as possible, during the daytime, I had hitherto succeeded in eluding my master, though a razor was often held to my throat to force me to change this line of policy. At night I slept by the side of my great aunt, where I felt safe. He was too prudent to come into her room. She was an old woman, and had been in the family many years. Moreover, as a married man, and a professional man, he deemed it necessary to save appearances in some degree. But he resolved to remove the obstacle in the way of his scheme; and he thought he had planned it so that he should evade suspicion. He was well aware how much I prized my refuge by the side of my old aunt, and he determined to dispossess me of it. The first night the doctor had the little child in his room alone. The next morning, I was ordered to take my station as nurse the following night. A kind Providence interposed in my favor. During the day Mrs. Flint heard of this new arrangement, and a storm followed. I rejoiced to hear it rage. . . .

The secrets of slavery are concealed like those of the Inquisition. My master was, to my knowledge, the father of eleven slaves. But did the mothers dare to tell who was the father of their children? Did the other slaves dare to allude to it, except in whispers among themselves? No, indeed! They knew too well the terrible consequences. . . .

Southern women often marry a man knowing that he is the father of many little slaves. They do not trouble themselves about it. They regard such children as property, as marketable as the pigs on the plantation; and it is seldom that they do not make them aware of this by passing them into the slave-trader's hands as soon as possible, and thus getting them out of their sight. I am glad to say there are some honorable exceptions.

I have myself known two southern wives who exhorted their husbands to free those slaves towards whom they stood in a "parental relation;" and their request was granted. These husbands blushed before the superior nobleness of their wives' natures. Though they had only counselled them to do that which it was their duty to do, it commanded their respect, and rendered their conduct more exemplary. Concealment was at an end, and confidence took the place of distrust.

Though this bad institution deadens the moral sense, even in white women, to a fearful extent, it is not altogether extinct. I have heard southern ladies say of Mr. Such a one, "He not only thinks it no disgrace to be the father of those little niggers, but he is not ashamed to call himself their master. I declare, such things ought not to be tolerated in any decent society!"

A PERILOUS PASSAGE
IN THE SLAVE GIRL'S LIFE

Dr. Flint contrived a new plan. He seemed to have an idea that my fear of my mistress was his greatest obstacle. In the blandest tones, he told me that he was going to build a small house for me, in a secluded place, four miles away from the town. I shuddered; but I was constrained to listen, while he talked of his intention to give me a home of my own, and to make a lady of me. Hitherto, I had escaped my dreaded fate, by being in the midst of people. My grandmother had already had high words with my master about me. She had told him pretty plainly what she thought of his character, and there was considerable gossip in the neighborhood about our affairs, to which the open-mouthed jealousy of Mrs. Flint contributed not a little. When my master said he was going to build a house for me, and that he could do it with little trouble and expense, I was in hopes something would happen to frustrate his scheme; but I soon heard that the house was actually begun. I vowed before my Maker that I would never enter it. I had rather toil on the plantation from dawn till dark; I had rather live and die in jail, than drag on, from day to day, through such a living death. I was determined that the master, whom I so hated and loathed, who had blighted the prospects of my youth, and made my life a desert, should not, after my long struggle with him, succeed at last in trampling his victim under his feet. I would do any thing, every thing, for the sake of defeating him. What *could* I do? I thought and thought, till I became desperate, and made a plunge into the abyss.

And now, reader, I come to a period in my unhappy life, which I would gladly forget if I could. The remembrance fills me with sorrow and shame. It pains me to tell you of it; but I have promised to tell you the truth, and I will do it honestly, let it cost me what it may. I will not try to screen myself behind the plea of compulsion from a master; for it was not so. Neither can I plead ignorance or thoughtlessness. For years, my master had done his utmost to pollute my mind with foul images, and to destroy the pure principles inculcated by my grandmother, and the good mistress of my childhood. The influences of slavery had had the same effect on me that they had on other young girls; they had made me prematurely knowing, concerning the evil ways of the world. I knew what I did, and I did it with deliberate calculation.

But, O, ye happy women, whose purity has been sheltered from childhood, who have been free to choose the objects of your affection, whose homes are protected by law, do not judge the poor desolate slave girl too severely! If slavery had been abolished, I, also, could have married the man of my choice; I could have had a home shielded by the laws; and I should have been spared the painful task of confessing what I am now about to relate; but all my prospects had been blighted by slavery. I wanted to keep myself pure; and, under the most adverse circumstances, I tried hard to preserve my self-respect; but I was struggling alone in the powerful grasp of the demon Slavery; and the monster proved too strong for me. I felt as if I was forsaken by God and man; as if all my efforts must be frustrated; and I became reckless in my despair.

I have told you that Dr. Flint's persecutions and his wife's jealousy had given rise to some gossip in the neighborhood. Among others, it chanced that a white unmarried gentleman had obtained some knowledge of the circumstances in which I was placed. He knew my grandmother, and often spoke to me in the street. He became interested for me, and asked questions about my master, which I answered in part. He expressed a great deal of sympathy, and a wish to aid me. He constantly sought opportunities to see me, and wrote to me frequently. I was a poor slave girl, only fifteen years old.

So much attention from a superior person was, of course, flattering; for human nature is the same in all. I also felt grateful for his sympathy, and encouraged by his kind words. It seemed to me a great thing to have such a friend. By degrees, a more tender feeling crept into my heart. He was an educated and eloquent gentleman; too eloquent, alas, for the poor slave girl who trusted in him. Of course I saw whither all this was tending. I knew the impassable gulf between us; but to be an object of interest to a man who is not married, and who is not her master, is agreeable to the pride and feelings of a slave, if her miserable situation has left her any pride or sentiment. It seems less degrading to give one's self, than to submit to compulsion. There is something akin to freedom in having a lover who has no control over you, except that which he gains by kindness and attachment. A master may treat you as rudely as he pleases, and you dare not speak; moreover, the wrong does not seem so great with an unmarried man, as with one who has a wife to be made unhappy. There may be sophistry in all this; but the condition of a slave confuses all principles of morality, and, in fact, renders the practice of them impossible.

When I found that my master had actually begun to build the lonely cottage, other feelings mixed with those I have described. Revenge, and calculations of interest, were added to flattered vanity and sincere gratitude for kindness. I knew nothing would enrage Dr. Flint so much as to know that I favored another; and it was something to triumph over my tyrant even in that small way. I thought he would revenge himself by selling me, and I was sure my friend, Mr. Sands, would buy me. He was a man of more generosity and feeling than my master, and I thought my freedom could be easily obtained from him. The crisis of my fate now came so near that I was desperate. I shuddered to think of being the mother of children that should be owned by my old tyrant. I knew that as soon as a new fancy took him, his victims were sold far off to get rid of them; especially if they had children. I had seen several women sold, with his babies at the breast. He never allowed his offspring by slaves to remain long in sight of himself and his wife. Of a man who was not my master I could ask to have my children well supported; and in this case, I felt confident I should obtain the boon. I also felt quite sure that they would be made free. With all these thoughts revolving in my mind, and seeing no other way of escaping the doom I so much dreaded, I made a headlong plunge. Pity me, and pardon me, O virtuous reader! You never knew what it is to be a slave; to be entirely unprotected by law or custom; to have the laws reduce you to the condition of a chattel, entirely subject to the will of another. You never exhausted your ingenuity in avoiding the snares, and eluding the power of a hated tyrant; you never shuddered at the sound of his footsteps, and trembled within hearing of his voice. I know I did wrong. No one can feel it more sensibly than I do. The painful and humiliating memory will haunt me to my dying day. Still, in looking back, calmly, on the events of my life, I feel that the slave woman ought not to be judged by the same standard of others.

The months passed on. I had many unhappy hours. I secretly mourned over the sorrow I was bringing on my grandmother, who had so tried to shield me from harm. I knew that I was the greatest comfort of her old age, and that it was a source of pride to her that I had not degraded myself, like most of the slaves. I wanted to confess to her that I was no longer worthy of her love; but I could not utter the dreaded words.

As for Dr. Flint, I had a feeling of satisfaction and triumph in the thought of telling *him*. From time to time he told me of his intended arrangements, and I was silent. At last, he came and told me the cottage was completed, and ordered me to go to it. I told him I would never enter it. He said, "I have heard enough of such talk as that. You shall go, if you are carried by force; and you shall remain there."

I replied, "I will never go there. In a few months I shall be a mother."

He stood and looked at me in dumb amazement, and left the house without a word. I thought I should be happy in my triumph over him. But now that the truth was out, and my relatives would hear of it, I felt wretched. Humble as were their circumstances, they had pride in my good character. Now, how could I look them in the face? My self-respect was gone! I had resolved that I would be virtuous, though I was a slave. I had said, "Let the storm beat! I will brave it till I die." And now, how humiliated I felt!

I went to my grandmother. My lips moved to make confession, but the words stuck in my throat. I sat down in the shade of a tree at her door and began to sew. I think she saw something unusual was the matter with me. The mother of slaves is very watchful. She knows there is no security for her children. After they have entered their teens she lives in daily expectation of trouble. This leads to many questions. If the girl is of a sensitive nature, timidity keeps her from answering truthfully, and this well-meant course has a tendency to drive her from maternal counsels. Presently, in came my mistress, like a mad woman, and accused me concerning her husband. My grandmother, whose suspicions had been previously awakened, believed what she said. She exclaimed, "O Linda! has it come to this? I had rather see you dead than to see you as you now are. You are a disgrace to your dead mother." She tore from my fingers my mother's wedding ring and her silver thimble. "Go away!" she exclaimed, "and never come to my house, again." Her reproaches fell so hot and heavy, that they left me no chance to answer. Bitter tears, such as the eyes never shed but once, were my only answer. I rose from my seat, but fell back again, sobbing. She did not speak to me; but the tears were running down her furrowed cheeks, and they scorched me like fire. She had always been so kind to me! *So* kind! How I longed to throw myself at her feet, and tell her all the truth! But she had ordered me to go, and never to come there again. After a few minutes, I mustered strength, and started to obey her. With what feelings did I now close that little gate, which I used to open with such an eager hand in my childhood! It closed upon me with a sound I never heard before.

Where could I go? I was afraid to return to my master's. I walked on recklessly, not caring where I went, or what would become of me. When I had gone four or five miles, fatigue compelled me to stop. I sat down on the stump of an old tree. The stars were shining through the boughs above me. How they mocked me, with their bright, calm light! The hours passed by, and as I sat there alone a chilliness and deadly sickness came over me. I sank on the ground. My mind was full of horrid thoughts. I prayed to die; but the prayer was not answered. At last, with great effort I roused myself, and walked some distance further, to the house of a woman who had been a friend of my mother. When I told her why I was there, she spoke soothingly to me; but I could not be comforted. I thought I could bear my shame if I could only be reconciled to my grandmother. I longed to open my heart to her. I thought if she could know the real state of the case, and all I had been bearing for years, she would perhaps judge me less harshly. My friend advised me to send for her. I did so; but days of agonizing suspense passed before she came. Had she utterly forsaken me? No. She came at last. I knelt before her, and told her the things that had poisoned my life; how long I had been persecuted; that I saw no way of escape; and in an hour of extremity I had become desperate. She listened in silence. I told her I would bear any thing and do any thing, if in time I had hopes of obtaining her forgiveness. I begged of her to pity me, for my dead mother's sake. And she did pity me. She did not say, "I forgive you;" but she looked at me lovingly, with her eyes full of tears. She laid her old hand gently on my head, and murmured, "Poor child! Poor child!"

34

The Lowell Textile Workers

Harriet Hanson Robinson

The transportation revolution, making the movement of goods easier and cheaper, greatly expanded the potential market for manufactured products, particularly textiles. Moreover, incorporation permitted manufacturing concerns and transportation projects to grow large. But where would the workers come from?

One early answer was the Waltham system, the brainchild of New England industrialist and reformer Francis Cabot Lowell. To recruit respectable young women from New England farms to work in his mills, he developed a highly organized paternal system. Lowell offered reasonable wages and working conditions as well as carefully chaperoned boarding houses. He even sponsored literary journals to create a genteel atmosphere. But within a few years, under the pressure of business competition, working and living conditions worsened and eventually the farm girls were replaced by desperately poor Irish immigrant workers.

As a young girl in the 1830s, Harriet Hanson Robinson worked in the Lowell mills. She became deeply troubled by the deteriorating conditions under which many young women labored. This led her into reform movements, including the women's suffrage movement. In 1898, more than sixty years after she worked in the mills, she published Loom and Spindle, *telling of her experience.*

BEFORE YOU READ

1. Why did Harriet Hanson Robinson go to work in the mills?
2. What did she like about life at the mills?
3. How did she think working at the mills affected the status of women?
4. Why did the young women go on strike?

CHAPTER II.
CHILD-LIFE IN THE LOWELL COTTON-MILLS

In 1831, under the shadow of a great sorrow, which had made her four children fatherless, — the oldest but seven years of age, — my mother was left to struggle alone; and, although she tried to earn bread enough to fill our hungry mouths, she could not do it, even with the help of kind friends. And so it happened that one of her more wealthy neighbors, who had looked with longing eyes on the one little daughter of the family, offered to adopt me. But my mother, who had had a hard experience in her youth in living amongst strangers, said, "No; while I have one meal of victuals a day, I will not part with

Harriet Hanson Robinson, *Loom and Spindle or Life among the Early Mill Girls* (New York: T. Y. Crowell, 1898), pp. 16–22, 37–43, 51–53.

my children." I always remembered this speech because of the word "vict-uals," and I wondered for a long time what this good old Bible word meant.

That was a hard, cold winter; and for warmth's sake my mother and her four children all slept in one bed, two at the foot and three at the head, — but her richer neighbor could not get the little daughter; and, contrary to all the mod-ern notions about hygiene, we were a healthful and a robust brood.

Shortly after this my mother's widowed sister, Mrs. Angeline Cudworth, who kept a factory boarding-house in Lowell, advised her to come to that city.

I had been to school constantly until I was about ten years of age, when my mother, feeling obliged to have help in her work besides what I could give, and also needing the money which I could earn, allowed me, at my urgent request (for I wanted to earn *money* like the other little girls), to go to work in the mill. I worked first in the spinning-room as a "doffer." The doffers were the very youngest girls, whose work was to doff, or take off, the full bobbins, and re-place them with the empty ones.

Some of us learned to embroider in crewels,[1] and I still have a lamb worked on cloth, a relic of those early days, when I was first taught to improve my time in the good old New England fashion. When not doffing, we were often al-lowed to go home, for a time, and thus we were able to help our mothers in their housework. We were paid two dollars a week; and how proud I was when my turn came to stand up on the bobbin-box, and write my name in the pay-master's book, and how indignant I was when he asked me if I could "write." "Of course I can," said I, and he smiled as he looked down on me.

The working-hours of all the girls extended from five o'clock in the morn-ing until seven in the evening, with one-half hour for breakfast and for dinner. Even the doffers were forced to be on duty nearly fourteen hours a day, and this was the greatest hardship in the lives of these children. For it was not until 1842 that the hours of labor for children under twelve years of age were limited to ten per day; but the "ten-hour law" itself was not passed until long after some of these little doffers were old enough to appear before the legisla-tive committee on the subject, and plead, by their presence, for a reduction of the hours of labor.

I do not recall any particular hardship connected with this life, except get-ting up so early in the morning, and to this habit, I never was, and never shall be, reconciled, for it has taken nearly a lifetime for me to make up the sleep lost at that early age. But in every other respect it was a pleasant life. We were not hurried any more than was for our good, and no more work was required of us than we were able easily to do.

1. **crewels:** embroidery or embroidery yarn.

Most of us children lived at home, and we were well fed, drinking both tea and coffee, and eating substantial meals (besides luncheons) three times a day. We had very happy hours with the older girls, many of whom treated us like babies, or talked in a motherly way, and so had a good influence over us. And in the long winter evenings, when we could not run home between the doffings, we gathered in groups and told each other stories, and sung the old-time songs our mothers had sung, such as "Barbara Allen," "Lord Lovell," "Captain Kid," "Hull's Victory," and sometimes a hymn.

Among the ghost stories I remember some that would delight the hearts of the "Society for Psychical Research." The more imaginative ones told of what they had read in fairy books, or related tales of old castles and distressed maidens; and the scene of their adventures was sometimes laid among the foundation stones of the new mill, just building.

And we told each other of our little hopes and desires, and what we meant to do when we grew up. For we had our aspirations; and one of us, who danced the "shawl dance," as she called it, in the spinning-room alley, for the amusement of her admiring companions, discussed seriously with another little girl the scheme of their running away together, and joining the circus.

I cannot tell how it happened that some of us knew about the English factory children, who, it was said, were treated so badly, and were even whipped by their cruel overseers. But we did know of it, and used to sing, to a doleful little tune, some verses called, "The Factory Girl's Last Day." I do not remember it well enough to quote it as written, but have refreshed my memory by reading it lately in Robert Dale Owen's writings: —

The Factory Girl's Last Day

'Twas on a winter morning,
    The weather wet and wild,
Two hours before the dawning
    The father roused his child,
Her daily morsel bringing,
    The darksome room he paced,
And cried, 'The bell is ringing —
    My hapless darling, haste!'

The overlooker met her
    As to her frame she crept;
And with this thong he beat her,
    And cursed her when she wept.
It seemed as she grew weaker,
    The threads the oftener broke,
The rapid wheels ran quicker,
    And heavier fell the stroke.

The song goes on to tell the sad story of her death while her "pitying comrades" were carrying her home to die, and ends:—

> That night a chariot passed her,
>   While on the ground she lay;
> The daughters of her master,
>   An evening visit pay.
> Their tender hearts were sighing,
>   As negroes' wrongs were told,
> While the white slave was dying
>   Who gained her father's gold.

In contrast with this sad picture, we thought of ourselves as well off, in our cosey corner of the mill, enjoying ourselves in our own way, with our good mothers and our warm suppers awaiting us when the going-out bell should ring.

CHAPTER IV. THE CHARACTERISTICS OF THE EARLY FACTORY GIRLS

When I look back into the factory life of fifty or sixty years ago, I do not see what is called "a class" of young men and women going to and from their daily work, like so many ants that cannot be distinguished one from another; I see them as individuals, with personalities of their own. This one has about her the atmosphere of her early home. That one is impelled by a strong and noble purpose. The other,—what she is, has been an influence for good to me and to all womankind.

Yet they were a class of factory operatives, and were spoken of (as the same class is spoken of now) as a set of persons who earned their daily bread, whose condition was fixed, and who must continue to spin and to weave to the end of their natural existence. Nothing but this was expected of them, and they were not supposed to be capable of social or mental improvement. That they could be educated and developed into something more than mere workpeople, was an idea that had not yet entered the public mind. So little does one class of persons really know about the thoughts and aspirations of another! It was the good fortune of these early mill-girls to teach the people of that time that this sort of labor is not degrading; that the operative is not only "capable of virtue," but also capable of self-cultivation.

At the time the Lowell cotton-mills were started, the factory girl was the lowest among women. In England, and in France particularly, great injustice had been done to her real character; she was represented as subjected to influences that could not fail to destroy her purity and self-respect. In the eyes of her overseer she was but a brute, a slave, to be beaten, pinched, and pushed about. It was to overcome this prejudice that such high wages had been offered to women that they might be induced to become mill-girls, in spite of the opprobrium that still clung to this "degrading occupation." At first only a few came; for, though tempted by the high wages to be regularly paid in "cash," there were many who still preferred to go on working at some more *genteel* employment at seventy-five cents a week and their board.

But in a short time the prejudice against factory labor wore away, and the Lowell mills became filled with blooming and energetic New England women.

In 1831 Lowell was little more than a factory village. Several corporations were started, and the cotton-mills belonging to them were building. Help was in great demand; and stories were told all over the country of the new factory town, and the high wages that were offered to all classes of work-people, — stories that reached the ears of mechanics' and farmers' sons, and gave new life to lonely and dependent women in distant towns and farmhouses. Into this Yankee El Dorado, these needy people began to pour by the various modes of travel known to those slow old days. The stage-coach and the canal-boat came every day, always filled with new recruits for this army of useful people. The mechanic and machinist came, each with his homemade chest of tools, and often-times his wife and little ones. The widow came with her little flock and her scanty housekeeping goods to open a boarding-house or variety store, and so provided a home for her fatherless children. Many farmers' daughters came to earn money to complete their wedding outfit, or buy the bride's share of housekeeping articles.

Women with past histories came, to hide their griefs and their identity, and to earn an honest living in the "sweat of their brow." Single young men came, full of hope and life, to get money for an education, or to lift the mortgage from the home-farm. Troops of young girls came by stages and baggage-wagons, men often being employed to go to other States and to Canada, to collect them at so much a head, and deliver them at the factories.

[The] country girls had queer names, which added to the singularity of their appearance. Samantha, Triphena, Plumy, Kezia, Aseneth, Elgardy, Leafy, Ruhamah, Lovey, Almaretta, Sarepta, and Florilla were among them.

Their dialect was also very peculiar. On the broken English and Scotch of their ancestors was ingrafted the nasal Yankee twang; so that many of them, when they had just come *daown*, spoke a language almost unintelligible. But the severe discipline and ridicule which met them was as good as a school education, and they were soon taught the "city way of speaking."

Their dress was also peculiar, and was of the plainest of homespun, cut in such an old-fashioned style that each young girl looked as if she had borrowed her grandmother's gown. Their only head-covering was a shawl, which was pinned under the chin; but after the first payday, a "shaker" (or "scooter") sunbonnet usually replaced this primitive headgear of their rural life.

But the early factory girls were not all country girls. There were others also, who had been taught that "work is no disgrace." There were some who came to Lowell solely on account of the social or literary advantages to be found there. They lived in secluded parts of New England, where books were scarce, and there was no cultivated society. They had comfortable homes, and did not perhaps need the *money* they would earn; but they longed to see this new "City of Spindles." . . .

The laws relating to women were such, that a husband could claim his wife wherever he found her, and also the children she was trying to shield from his influence; and I have seen more than one poor woman skulk behind her loom or her frame when visitors were approaching the end of the aisle where she worked. Some of these were known under assumed names, to prevent their husbands from trusteeing their wages. It was a very common thing for a male person of a certain kind to do this, thus depriving his wife of *all* her wages, perhaps, month after month. The wages of minor children could be trusteed, unless the children (being fourteen years of age) were given their time. Women's wages were also trusteed for the debts of their husbands, and children's for the debts of their parents.

It must be remembered that at this date woman had no property rights. A widow could be left without her share of her husband's (or the family) property, a legal "incumbrance" to his estate. A father could make his will without reference to his daughter's share of the inheritance. He usually left her a home on the farm as long as she remained single. A woman was not supposed to be capable of spending her own or of using other people's money. In Massachusetts, before 1840, a woman could not legally be treasurer of her own sewing-society, unless some man were responsible for her.

The law took no cognizance of woman as a money-spender. She was a ward, an appendage, a relict. Thus it happened, that if a woman did not choose to marry, or, when left a widow, to re-marry, she had no choice but to enter one of the few employments open to her, or to become a burden on the charity of some relative.

In almost every New England home could be found one or more of these women, sometimes welcome, more often unwelcome, and leading joyless, and in many instances unsatisfactory, lives. The cotton-factory was a great opening to these lonely and dependent women. From a condition approaching pauperism they were at once placed above want; they could earn money, and spend it as they pleased; and could gratify their tastes and desires without restraint, and without rendering an account to anybody. . . .

Among the older women who sought this new employment were very many lonely and dependent ones, such as used to be mentioned in old wills as "incumbrances" and "relicts," and to whom a chance of earning money was indeed a new revelation. How well I remember some of these solitary ones! As a child of eleven years, I often made fun of them—for children do not see the pathetic side of human life—and imitated their limp carriage and inelastic gait. I can see them now, even after sixty years, just as they looked,—depressed, modest, mincing, hardly daring to look one in the face, so shy and sylvan had been their lives. But after the first pay-day came, and they felt the jingle of silver in their pockets, and had begun to feel its mercurial influence, their bowed heads were lifted, their necks seemed braced with steel, they looked you in the face, sang blithely among their looms or frames, and walked with elastic step to and from their work. And when Sunday came, homespun was no longer their only wear; and how sedately gay in their new attire they walked to church, and how proudly they dropped their silver fourpences into the contribution-box! It seemed as if a great hope impelled them, — the harbinger of the new era that was about to dawn for them and for all women-kind.

CHAPTER V.
CHARACTERISTICS (CONTINUED)

One of the first strikes of cotton-factory operatives that ever took place in this country was that in Lowell, in October, 1836. When it was announced that the wages were to be cut down, great indignation was felt, and it was decided to strike, *en masse*. This was done. The mills were shut down, and the girls went in procession from their several corporations to the "grove" on Chapel Hill, and listened to "incendiary" speeches from early labor reformers.

One of the girls stood on a pump, and gave vent to the feelings of her companions in a neat speech, declaring that it was their duty to resist all attempts at cutting down the wages. This was the first time a woman had spoken in public in Lowell, and the event caused surprise and consternation among her audience.

Cutting down the wages was not their only grievance, nor the only cause of this strike. Hitherto the corporations had paid twenty-five cents a week towards the board of each operative, and now it was their purpose to have the girls pay the sum; and this, in addition to the cut in wages, would make a difference of at least one dollar a week. It was estimated that as many as twelve or fifteen hundred girls turned out, and walked in procession through the streets. They had neither flags nor music, but sang songs, a favorite (but rather inappropriate) one being a parody on "I won't be a nun."

> Oh! isn't it a pity, such a pretty girl as I —
>   Should be sent to the factory to pine away and die?
> Oh! I cannot be a slave,
>   I will not be a slave,
> For I'm so fond of liberty
>   That I cannot be a slave.

My own recollection of this first strike (or "turn out" as it was called) is very vivid. I worked in a lower room, where I had heard the proposed strike fully, if not vehemently, discussed; I had been an ardent listener to what was said against this attempt at "oppression" on the part of the corporation, and naturally I took sides with the strikers. When the day came on which the girls were to turn out, those in the upper rooms started first, and so many of them left that our mill was at once shut down. Then, when the girls in my room stood irresolute, uncertain what to do, asking each other, "Would you?" or "Shall we turn out?" and not one of them having the courage to lead off, I, who began to think they would not go out, after all their talk, became impatient, and started on ahead, saying, with childish bravado, "I don't care what you do, *I* am going to turn out, whether any one else does or not"; and I marched out, and was followed by the others.[2]

As I looked back at the long line that followed me, I was more proud than I have ever been since at any success I may have achieved, and more proud than I shall ever be again until my own beloved State gives to its women citizens the right of suffrage.

The agent of the corporation where I then worked took some small revenges on the supposed ringleaders; on the principle of sending the weaker to the wall, my mother was turned away from her boarding-house, that functionary saying, "Mrs. Hanson, you could not prevent the older girls from turning out, but your daughter is a child, and *her* you could control."

It is hardly necessary to say that so far as results were concerned this strike did no good. The dissatisfaction of the operatives subsided, or burned itself out, and though the authorities did not accede to their demands, the majority returned to their work, and the corporation went on cutting down the wages.

And after a time, as the wages became more and more reduced, the best portion of the girls left and went to their homes, or to the other employments that were fast opening to women, until there were very few of the old guard left; and thus the *status* of the factory population of New England gradually became what we know it to be to-day.

2. I was then eleven years and eight months old. [Robinson's note.]

35

Life Under the Lash
Charles Ball et al.

One of the great efforts of the current generation of American historians has been to capture the African American experience of slavery directly rather than from sources written by whites. As a result of this work, not only have new documents been unearthed but a new appreciation has developed for those slave writings that had been long known to historians but that required verification of their reliability.

The authors of the more than one hundred extant book-length accounts of slavery were by no means typical ex-slaves. Most of them succeeded in gaining their freedom by escape or purchase, which was not the lot of their less fortunate brothers and sisters. Most were highly literate. Some had help in writing their accounts from abolitionists and other ghost writers and editors. Nevertheless, historians in recent decades have discovered how generally accurate — in fact how indispensable — their narratives are for any serious understanding of the institution of American slavery.

The sampling of the literature presented here provides insight into the work regimen of a plantation, living conditions of slaves, and the agonizing limits slavery set on parental authority.

BEFORE YOU READ

1. How did Charles Ball explain the differences among the work regimes under which he labored as a slave?

2. What, according to Josiah Henson and Francis Henderson, were living conditions under slavery?

3. What was Francis Henderson's view of white Southerners?

4. What effect, as Jacob Stroyer described it, did slavery have on family relationships?

CHARLES BALL[1]

The Work Regimen of a Tobacco Plantation

In Maryland and Virginia, although the slaves are treated with so much rigour, and oftimes with so much cruelty, I have seen instances of the greatest tenderness of feeling on the part of their owners. I, myself, had three masters in Maryland, and I cannot say now, even after having resided so many years in a state where slavery is not tolerated, that either of them (except the last, who sold me to the Georgians, and was an unfeeling man,) used me worse than they had a moral right to do, regarding me merely as an article of property, and not

Steven Mintz, ed., *African-American Voices: The Life Cycle of Slavery* (New York: Brandywine Press), pp. 73–75, 78–79, 87–89, 111–13.

1. Ball had been a slave in Maryland, South Carolina, and Georgia.

entitled to any rights as a man, political or civil. My mistresses, in Maryland, were all good women; and the mistress of my wife, in whose kitchen I spent my Sundays and many of my nights, for several years, was a lady of most benevolent and kindly feelings. She was a true friend to me, and I shall always venerate her memory. . . .

If the proprietors of the soil in Maryland and Virginia, were skillful cultivators—had their lands in good condition—and kept no more slaves on each estate, than would be sufficient to work the soil in a proper manner, and kept up the repairs of the place—the condition of the coloured people would not be, by any means, a comparatively unhappy one. I am convinced, that in nine cases in ten, the hardships and suffering of the coloured population of lower Virginia, are attributable to the poverty and distress of its owners. In many instances, an estate scarcely yields enough to feed and clothe the slaves in a comfortable manner, without allowing anything for the support of the master and family; but it is obvious, that the family must first be supported, and the slaves must be content with the surplus—and this, on a poor, old, worn out tobacco plantation, is often very small, and wholly inadequate to the comfortable sustenance of the hands, as they are called. There, in many places, nothing is allowed to the poor Negro, but his peck of corn per week, without the sauce of a salt herring, or even a little salt itself. . . .

The general features of slavery are the same everywhere; but the utmost rigour of the system, is only to be met with, on the cotton plantations of Carolina and Georgia, or in the rice fields which skirt the deep swamps and morasses of the southern rivers. In the tobacco fields of Maryland and Virginia, great cruelties are practiced—not so frequently by the owners, as by the overseers of the slaves; but yet, the tasks are not so excessive as in the cotton region, nor is the press of labour so incessant throughout the year. It is true, that from the period when the tobacco plants are set in the field, there is no resting time until it is housed; but it is planted out about the first of May, and must be cut and taken out of the field before the frost comes. After it is hung and dried, the labor of stripping and preparing it for the hogshead in leaf, or of manufacturing it into twist, is comparatively a work of leisure and ease. Besides, on almost every plantation the hands are able to complete the work of preparing the tobacco by January, and sometimes earlier; so that the winter months, form some sort of respite from the toils of the year. The people are obliged, it is true, to occupy themselves in cutting wood for the house, making rails and repairing fences, and in clearing new land, to raise the tobacco plants for the next year; but as there is usually time enough, and to spare, for the completion of all this work, before the season arrives for setting the plants in the field; the men are seldom flogged much, unless they are very lazy or negligent, and the women are allowed to remain in the house, in the very cold, snowy, or rainy weather. . . .

In Maryland I never knew a mistress or a young mistress, who would not listen to the complaints of the slaves. It is true, we were always obliged to approach the door of the mansion, with our hats in our hands, and the most subdued and beseeching language in our mouths — but, in return, we generally received words of kindness, and very often a redress of our grievances; though I have known very great ladies, who would never grant any request from the plantation hands, but always referred them and their petitions to their master, under a pretence, that they could not meddle with things that did not belong to the house. The mistresses of the great families, generally gave mild language to the slaves; though they sometimes sent for the overseer and had them severely flogged; but I have never heard any mistress, in either Maryland or Virginia, indulge in the low, vulgar and profane vituperations, of which I was myself the object, in Georgia, for many years, whenever I came into the presence of my mistress. Flogging — though often severe and excruciating in Maryland, is not practiced with the order, regularity and system, to which it is often reduced in the South. On the Potomac, if a slave gives offence, he is generally chastised on the spot, in the field where he is at work, as the overseer always carried a whip — sometimes a twisted cow-hide, sometimes a kind of horse-whip, and very often a simple hickory switch or gad, cut in the adjoining woods. For stealing meat, or other provisions, or for any of the higher offences, the slaves are stripped, tied up by the hands — sometimes by the thumbs — and whipped at the quarter — but many times, on a large tobacco plantation, there is not more than one of these regular whippings in a week — though on others, where the master happens to be a bad man, or a drunkard — the back of the unhappy Maryland slaves, is seamed with scars from his neck to his hips.

JOSIAH HENSON[2]

"We Lodged in Log Huts"

My earliest employments were, to carry buckets of water to the men at work, and to hold a horse-plough, used for weeding between the rows of corn. As I grew older and taller, I was entrusted with the care of master's saddle-horse. Then a hoe was put into my hands, and I was soon required to do the day's work of a man; and it was not long before I could do it, at least as well as my associates in misery.

A description of the everyday life of a slave on a Southern plantation illustrates the character and habits of the slave and the slaveholder, created and perpetuated by their relative position. The principal food of those upon my master's plantation consisted of corn-meal and salt herrings; to which was added in summer a little buttermilk, and the few vegetables which each might raise for himself and his family, on the little piece of ground which was assigned to him for the purpose, called a truck-patch.

In ordinary times we had two regular meals in a day: breakfast at twelve o'clock, after laboring from daylight, and supper when the work of the remainder of the day was over. In harvest season we had three. Our dress was of

2. Henson had been a slave in Maryland before he escaped.

tow-cloth; for the children, nothing but a shirt; for the older ones a pair of pantaloons or a gown in addition, according to the sex. Besides these, in the winter a round jacket or overcoat, a wool-hat once in two or three years, for the
males, and a pair of coarse shoes once a year.

We lodged in log huts, and on the bare ground. Wooden floors were an unknown luxury. In a single room were huddled, like cattle, ten or a dozen persons, men, women, and children. All ideas of refinement and decency were, of
course, out of the question. We had neither bedsteads, nor furniture of any description. Our beds were collections of straw and old rags, thrown down in the
corners and boxed in with boards; a single blanket the only covering. Our
favourite way of sleeping, however, was on a plank, our heads raised on an old
jacket and our feet toasting before the smouldering fire. The wind whistled and
the rain and snow blew in through the cracks, and the damp earth soaked in
the moisture till the floor was miry as a pig-sty. Such were our houses. In these
wretched hovels were we penned at night, and fed by day; here were the children born and the sick—neglected.

FRANCIS HENDERSON[3]

Living Conditions on the Plantation

Our houses were but log huts—the tops partly open—ground floor—rain
would come through. My aunt was quite an old woman, and had been sick several years; in rains I have seen her moving from one part of the house to the
other, and rolling her bedclothes about to try to keep dry—everything would
be dirty and muddy. I lived in the house with my aunt. My bed and bedstead
consisted of a board wide enough to sleep on—one end on a stool, the other
placed near the fire. My pillow consisted of my jacket—my covering was whatever I could get. My bedtick was the board itself. And this was the way the single men slept—but we were comfortable in this way of sleeping, being used
to it. I only remember having but one blanket from my owners up to the age
of nineteen, when I ran away.

Our allowance was given weekly—a peck of sifted corn meal, a dozen
and a half herrings, two and a half pounds of pork. Some of the boys would
eat this up in three days—then they had to steal, or they could not perform
their daily tasks. They would visit the hog-pen, sheep-pen, and granaries. I
do not remember one slave but who stole some things—they were driven to
it as a matter of necessity. I myself did this—many a time have I, with others, run among the stumps in chase of a sheep, that we might have something
to eat. . . . In regard to cooking, sometimes many have to cook at one fire,
and before all could get to the fire to bake hoe cakes, the overseer's horn
would sound: then they must go at any rate. Many a time I have gone along
eating a piece of bread and meat, or herring broiled on the coals—I never
sat down at a table to eat except at harvest time, all the time I was a slave. In

3. Henderson escaped from slavery at the age of nineteen.

harvest time, the cooking is done at the great house, as the hands they have are wanted in the field. This was more like people, and we liked it, for we sat down then at meals. In the summer we had one pair of linen trousers given us—nothing else; every fall, one pair of woolen pantaloons, one woolen jacket, and two cotton shirts.

My master had four sons in his family. They all left except one, who remained to be a driver. He would often come to the field and accuse the slave of having taken so and so. If we denied it, he would whip the grown-up ones to make them own it. Many a time, when we didn't know he was anywhere around, he would be in the woods watching us—first thing we would know, he would be sitting on the fence looking down upon us, and if any had been idle, the young master would visit him with blows. I have known him to kick my aunt, an old woman who had raised and nursed him, and I have seen him punish my sisters awfully with hickories from the woods.

The slaves are watched by the patrols, who ride about to try to catch them off the quarters, especially at the house of a free person of color. I have known the slaves to stretch clothes lines across the street, high enough to let the horse pass, but not the rider; then the boys would run, and the patrols in full chase would be thrown off by running against the lines. The patrols are poor white men, who live by plundering and stealing, getting rewards for runaways, and setting up little shops on the public roads. They will take whatever the slaves steal, paying in money, whiskey, or whatever the slaves want. They take pigs, sheep, wheat, corn—anything that's raised they encourage the slaves to steal: these they take to market next day. It's all speculation—all a matter of self-interest, and when the slaves run away, these same traders catch them if they can, to get the reward. If the slave threatens to expose his traffic, he does not care—for the slave's word is good for nothing—it would not be taken.

JACOB STROYER

Parents and Children

Gilbert was a cruel [slave] boy. He used to strip his fellow Negroes while in the woods, and whip them two or three times a week, so that their backs were all scarred, and threatened them with severer punishments if they told; this state of things had been going on for quite a while. As I was a favorite with Gilbert, I always managed to escape a whipping, with the promise of keeping the secret of the punishment of the rest. . . . But finally, one day, Gilbert said to me, "Jake," as he used to call me, "you am a good boy, but I'm gwine to wip you some to-day, as I wip dem toder boys." Of course I was required to strip off my only garment, which was an Osnaburg linen shirt, worn by both sexes of the Negro children in the summer. As I stood trembling before my merciless superior, who had a switch in his hand, thousands of thoughts went through my little mind as to how to get rid of the whipping. I finally fell upon a plan which I hoped would save me from a punishment that was near at hand. . . . I commenced reluctantly to take off my shirt, at the same time pleading with Gilbert, who paid no attention to my prayer. . . . Having satisfied myself that no mercy was to be found with Gilbert, I drew my shirt off and threw it over his head, and bounded forward on a run in the direction of the sound of the [nearby] carpenters. By the time he got from the entanglement of my garment, I had quite a little start of him. . . . As I got near to the carpenters, one of them ran and met me, into whose arms I jumped. The man into whose arms I ran was Uncle Benjamin, my mother's uncle. . . . I told him that Gilbert had been in the habit of stripping the boys and whipping them two or three times a week, when we went into the woods, and threatened them with greater punishment if they told. . . . Gilbert was brought to trial, severely whipped, and they made him beg all the children to pardon him for his treatment to them.

[My] father . . . used to take care of horses and mules. I was around with him in the barn yard when but a very small boy; of course that gave me an early relish for the occupation of hostler,[4] and I soon made known my preference to Col. Singleton, who was a sportsman, and an owner of fine horses. And, although I was too small to work, the Colonel granted my request; hence I was allowed to be numbered among those who took care of the fine horses and learned to ride. But I soon found that my new occupation demanded a little more than I cared for. It was not long after I had entered my new work before they put me upon the back of a horse which threw me to the ground almost as soon as I had reached his back. It hurt me a little, but that was not the worst of it, for when I got up there was a man standing near with a switch in hand, and he immediately began to beat me. Although I was a very bad boy, this was the first time I had been whipped by anyone except father and mother, so I cried out in a tone of voice as if I would say, this is the first and last whipping you will give me when father gets hold of you.

When I had got away from him I ran to father with all my might, but soon found my expectation blasted, as father very coolly said to me, "Go back to your work and be a good boy, for I cannot do anything for you." But that did not satisfy me, so on I went to mother with my complaint and she came out to the man who had whipped me; he was a groom, a white man master had hired to train the horses. Mother and he began to talk, then he took a whip and started for her, and she ran from him, talking all the time. I ran back and forth between mother and him until he stopped beating her. After the fight between the groom and mother, he took me back to the stable yard and gave me a severe flogging. And, although mother failed to help me at first, still I had faith that when he had taken me back to the stable yard, and commenced whipping me, she would come and stop him, but I looked in vain, for she did not come.

Then the idea first came to me that I, with my dear father and mother and the rest of my fellow Negroes, were doomed to cruel treatment through life, and was defenseless. But when I found that father and mother could not save me from punishment, as they themselves had to submit to the same treatment,

4. **hostler:** a person who takes care of horses.

I concluded to appeal to the sympathy of the groom, who seemed to have full control over me; but my pitiful cries never touched his sympathy. . . .

One day, about two weeks after Boney Young [the white man who trained horses for Col. Singleton] and mother had the conflict, he called me to him. . . . When I got to him he said, "Go and bring me the switch, sir." I answered, "yes, sir," and off I went and brought him one . . . [and] . . . he gave me a first-class flogging. . . .

When I went home to father and mother, I said to them, "Mr. Young is whipping me too much now, I shall not stand it, I shall fight him." Father said to me, "You must not do that, because if you do he will say that your mother and I advised you to do it, and it will make it hard for your mother and me, as well as for yourself. You must do as I told you, my son: do your work the best you can, and do not say anything." I said to father, "But I don't know what I have done that he should whip me; he does not tell me what wrong I have done, he simply calls me to him and whips me when he gets ready." Father said, "I can do nothing more than to pray to the Lord to hasten the time when these things shall be done away; that is all I can do. . . ."

36

Pioneers for Women's Rights
Elizabeth Cady Stanton and
Susan B. Anthony

*The women's movement before the Civil War was among the most intensely un-
popular of all the reform efforts of that era. The ideal of domesticity, which assigned
to women a separate and less-powerful role in the family, made the reformists'
claims for equal rights, especially the right to vote, a violation of both social convention and religious belief. Friendships were enormously important in providing the
courage and emotional support women needed to oppose the oppressive family, religious, and political institutions. Elizabeth Cady Stanton was inspired by Lucretia
Mott, whose Quaker practice had given her experience in public speaking that she
applied to the antislavery cause. The two had met in London in 1840 and, as Stanton was to recall later, "resolved to hold a convention as soon as we returned home,
and form a society to advocate the rights of women." Yet eight years elapsed before
this resolve bore fruit in the Seneca Falls Woman's Rights Convention. In the interim, Stanton had settled in three different locations, bore three children (she would
eventually have seven), and assumed all the other cares of a financially strapped,
middle-class household.*

*The friendship, beginning in 1851, that finally launched the women's rights move-
ment in the United States was that between Elizabeth Cady Stanton (1815–1902)
and Susan B. Anthony (1820–1906), who had been a teacher and then a temperance
reformer and was the only pioneer of women's rights who never married. The first
cause the two shared—discussed in some of the letters here—was an unsuccessful effort to get temperance reformers' support for a proposal to allow women to divorce husbands who were drunkards. Anthony's intensity and dedication and Stanton's wit, literary ability, and insistence on making suffrage the movement's major goal set the
direction for the women's rights movement nationally. Their lifelong friendship provided advice, help, and comfort that sustained their devotion over decades to a cause
that would not be achieved until after their lives were over.*

BEFORE YOU READ

1. Describe the relationship between Stanton and Anthony.
2. To what did each woman devote her time during the period of this correspondence?
3. Why did Anthony call some of the women within the movement "false"?
4. Where did Stanton say she wants to sit when she passes St. Peter? Why?

LETTERS TO SUSAN B. ANTHONY

Seneca Falls, April 2, 1852

My dear friend,

I think you are doing up the temperance business just right. But do not let the conservative element control. For instance, you must take Mrs. Bloomer's[1] suggestions with great caution, for she has not the spirit of the true reformer. At the first woman's rights convention, but four years ago, she stood aloof and laughed at us. It was only with great effort and patience that she has been brought up to her present position. In her paper, she will not speak against the fugitive slave law, nor in her work to put down intemperance will she criticize the equivocal position of the Church. . . .

I will gladly do all in my power to help you. Come and stay with me and I will write the best lecture I can for you. I have no doubt a little practice will make you an admirable speaker. Dress loosely, take a great deal of exercise, be particular about your diet and sleep enough. The body has great influence upon the mind. In your meetings, if attacked, be cool and good-natured, for if you are simple and truth-loving, no sophistry can confound you. As for my own address, if I am to be president it ought perhaps to be sent out with the stamp of the convention, but as anything from my pen is necessarily radical no one may wish to share with me the odium of what I may choose to say. If so, I am ready to stand alone. I never write to please any one. If I do please I am happy, but to proclaim my highest convictions of truth is always my sole object. . . .

I have been re-reading the report of the London convention of 1840. How thoroughly humiliating it was to us! . . . Men and angels give me patience! I am at the boiling point! If I do not find some day the use of my tongue on this question, I shall die of an intellectual repression, a woman's rights convulsion! Oh, Susan! Susan! Susan! You must manage to spend a week with me before the Rochester convention, for I am afraid that I cannot attend it; I have so much with all these boys on my hands. But I will write a letter. How much I do long to be free from housekeeping and children, so as to have some time to read, and think, and write. But it may be well for me to understand all the trials of woman's lot, that I may more eloquently proclaim them when the time comes. Good night.

[Elizabeth Cady Stanton]

Ellen Carol DuBois, ed., *Elizabeth Cady Stanton, Susan B. Anthony: Correspondence, Writings, Speeches* (New York: Schocken Books, 1981), pp. 54–56, 58–63, 68–69.
    1. **Mrs. Bloomer:** Amelia Bloomer (1818–1894), women's rights advocate and dress reformer.

Seneca Falls, March 1st [1853]

Dear friend,

I do not know that the world is quite willing or ready to discuss the question of marriage. I feel in my innermost [soul] that the thoughts I sent your convention are true. It is in vain to look for the elevation of woman, so long as she is degraded in marriage. I say it is a sin, an outrage on our holiest feelings to pretend that anything but deep, fervent love and sympathy constitutes marriage. The right idea of marriage is at the foundation of all reforms. How strange it is, man will apply all the improvements in the arts and sciences to everything about him animate and inanimate, but himself. A child conceived in the midst of hate, sin, and discord, nurtured in abuse and injustice cannot do much to bless the world or himself. If we properly understood the science of life—it would be far easier to give to the world, harmonious, beautiful, noble, virtuous children, than it is to bring grown-up discord into harmony with the great divine soul of all. I ask for no laws on marriage. I say . . . remove law and a false public sentiment and woman will no more live as wife with a cruel, beastly drunkard, than a servant in this free country will stay with a pettish, unjust mistress. If law makers insist upon exercising their prerogative in some way on this question, let them forbid any woman to marry until she is twenty one. Let them fine a woman fifty dollars for every child she conceive by a Drunkard. Women have no right to saddle the state with idiots to be supported by the public. Only look at the statistics of the idiot asylums, nearly all the offspring of Drunkards. Woman must be made to feel that the transmitting of immortal life is a most solemn responsible act and never should be allowed, except when the parents are in the highest condition of mind and body. Man in his lust has regulated this whole question of sexual intercourse long enough. Let the mother of mankind whose prerogative it is to set bounds to his indulgence rouse up and give this whole question a thorough fearless examination. . . . My letter . . . will call attention to that subject, and if by martyrdom I can advance my race one step I am ready for it. I feel this whole question of woman's rights turns on the point of the marriage relation, and sooner or later it will be the question for discussion. I would not hurry it on, neither would I avoid it. . . .

[Elizabeth Cady Stanton]

Peterboro, September 10, 1855

Dear Susan,

I wish that I were as free as you and I would stump the state in a twinkling. But I am not, and what is more, I passed through a terrible scourging when last at my father's. I cannot tell you how deep the iron entered my soul. I never felt more keenly the degradation of my sex. To think that all in me of which my father would have felt a proper pride had I been a man, is deeply mortifying to him because I am a woman. That thought has stung me to a fierce decision—

to speak as soon as I can do myself credit. But the pressure on me just now is too great. Henry sides with my friends, who oppose me in all that is dearest to my heart. They are not willing that I should write even on the woman question. But I will both write and speak. I wish you to consider this letter strictly confidential. Sometimes, Susan, I struggle in deep waters. . . . I have sent six articles to the *Tribune*, and three have already appeared. I have promised to write for the *Una*. I read and write a good deal, as you see. But there are grievous interruptions. However, a good time is coming and my future is always bright and beautiful. Good night. . . .

[Elizabeth Cady Stanton]

LETTERS TO ELIZABETH CADY STANTON

Rochester, May 26, 1856

Dear Mrs. Stanton,

Taking it for granted that you are at home more, I'll say a word to you by way of "exhortation and prayer." I ought to be more pious than formerly, since I traveled all the way from Seneca Falls to Schenectady in company with President Finney[2] and Lady and heard [William Lloyd] Garrison, [Theodore] Parker[3] and all of us Woman's Rights actors duly trounced as "*Infidels.*" I told him our cause *was Infidel* to the *popular Theology* and *popular interpretation* of the Bible. Mrs. Finney took me to another seat and with much earnestness enquired all about, what we were doing and the growth of our movement. Said she, you have the sympathy of a large proportion of the educated women with you. In my circle I hear the movement much talked of and earnest hopes for its spread expressed. But these women dare not speak out their sympathy. . . .

I attended the Anniversary of the "American Woman's Education Association" headed by Catherine E. Beecher.[4] . . . Some parts of the Secretary's report were very fine [but] I said [to her] I would rather see the weight of your influence exerted to open the doors of the existing colleges to woman. Far greater good would be done for woman by such work, than by the establishment of separate Colleges. Said she, that is my mind exactly. Isn't it strange that such women as these, Miss Beecher, Mrs. [Caroline] Kirckland,[5] Mrs. [Ann] Stevens, S[arah] J. Hale,[6] etc., etc., are so stupid. Yet so *false* as to work for any thing secondary, any thing other than their *highest* conviction. . . .

I am now just done with house fixing and ready to commence operations on that Report [to the New York State Teacher's Convention]. Don't you think it would be a good plan to first state *what* we mean by educating the sexes together, then go in to show how the few institutions that profess to give *equal* education fail in the Physical, Moral and Intellectual departments, and lastly

2. **Finney:** Charles G. Finney, Evangelist and president of Oberlin College.
3. **Parker:** Boston minister and abolitionist.
4. **Catherine E. Beecher:** Writer and editor of books and magazines for women.
5. **Mrs. [Caroline] Kirckland:** Novelist.
6. **S[arah] J. Hale:** Writer and editor of books and magazines for women.

that it is folly to talk of giving to the sexes, *equal advantages*, while you *withhold* from them equal motive to improve those advantages. Do you please mark out a plan and give me as soon as you can. Oh, that I had the requisite power to do credit to womanhood in this emergency. Why is nature so *sparing* of her gifts? When will you come to Rochester to spend those days, I shall be most happy to see whenever it shall be, only let me know a few days before that I may be as much at leisure as may be. Amelia [a domestic servant] and the two babies of course and as many more as convenient. With love.

[Susan B. Anthony]

Home-getting, along towards 12 o'clock
Thursday night, June 5, 1856

. . . And, Mrs. Stanton, not a *word written* on that Address for Teacher's Convention. *This* week was to be *leisure* to me and lo, our *girl*, a *wife*, had a *miscarriage*, . . . and the Mercy only knows when I can get a moment; and what is *worse*, as the *Lord knows full well*, is, if I *get all the time* the *world has*, I *can't get up* a *decent document*. So, for the love of me and for the saving of the *reputation* of *womanhood*, I beg you, with one baby on your knee and another at your feet, and four boys whistling, buzzing, hallooing *Ma, Ma*, set yourself about the work. It is of but small moment *who writes* the Address, but of *vast moment* that it be *well done*. I promise you to work hard, oh, how hard, and *pay you whatever you say* for your *time* and *brains*, but . . . *don't* say *No* nor *don't delay* it a moment; for I must have it all done and almost commit it to memory. . . . Now will *you load my gun*, leaving me only to pull the trigger and let fly the powder and ball?

Don't delay one mail to tell me what you *will do*, for I *must not* and *will not* allow these *schoolmasters* to say—See, these *women can't* or *won't* do anything when we do give them a chance. No, they sha'n't say that, even if I have to get a *man* to write it! But no man can write from *my standpoint*, nor no woman but *you*, for *all, all* would base their *strongest* argument on the *un*likeness of the *sexes*. Nette [Brown][7] wrote me that she should, were she to make the Address. And more than any other place does the *difference* of sex, if there is any, need to be *forgotten* in the school room. . . . Now do, I pray you, give heed to my prayer. Those of you who have the *talent* to do honor to poor—oh! how poor— womanhood, have all given yourself over to baby-making; and left poor brainless me to do battle alone. It is a shame. Such a body as I might be spared to rock cradles. But it is a crime for you and Lucy Stone[8] and Antoinette Brown to be doing it. . . .

[Susan B. Anthony]

---

7. **Nette [Brown]:** Antoinette Brown Blackwell, women's rights advocate and first American woman to become an ordained minister.
8. **Lucy Stone:** Women's rights advocate and first American woman not to change her name after marriage.

LETTERS TO SUSAN B. ANTHONY

Seneca Falls, June 10, 1856

Dear Susan,

Your servant is not dead but liveth. Imagine me, day in and day out, watching, bathing, dressing, nursing, and promenading the precious contents of a little crib in the corner of the room. I pace up and down these two chambers of mine like a caged lioness, longing to bring to a close nursing and housekeeping cares. I have other work on hand too. . . . Is your speech to be exclusively on the point of educating the sexes together, or as to the best manner of educating women? I will do what I can to help you with your lecture. Let Lucy and Antoinette rest awhile in peace and quietness and think great thoughts for the future. It is not well to be in the excitement of public life all the time; do not keep stirring them up or mourning over their repose. You need rest too, Susan. Let the world alone awhile. We cannot bring about a moral revolution in a day or year. Now that I have two daughters, I feel fresh strength to work. It is not in vain that in myself I have experienced all the wearisome cares to which woman in her best estate is subject. Good night.

[Elizabeth Cady Stanton]

Seneca Falls, December 23, 1859

Dear Susan,

Where are you? Since a week ago last Monday, I have looked for you every day. I had the washing put off, we cooked a turkey, I made a pie in the morning, sent my first-born to the depot and put clean aprons on the children, but lo! you did not come. Nor did you soften the rough angles of our disappointment by one solitary line of excuse. And it would do me such great good to see some reformers just now. The death of my father, the worse than death of my dear Cousin Gerrit, the martyrdom of that grand and glorious John Brown — all this conspires to make me regret more than ever my dwarfed womanhood. In times like these, every one should do the work of a full-grown man. When I pass the gate of the celestial city and good Peter asks me where I would sit, I shall say, "Anywhere, so that I am neither a negro nor a woman. Confer on me, good angel, the glory of white manhood so that henceforth, sitting or standing, rising up or lying down, I may enjoy the most unlimited freedom." Good night.

[Elizabeth Cady Stanton]

37

Ten Nights in a Bar-Room
Timothy Shay Arthur

From colonial days Americans had been heavy drinkers. Wine, hard cider, and whiskey were staples of both economic and social life. Before the advent of canals and railroads, farmers often sent their corn to market distilled in a jug or barrel: Whiskey cost less than corn to ship over long distances and found a ready market. In many places, it was safer to drink than water. An early nineteenth-century traveller in Ohio found the use of alcohol nearly universal: "A house could not be raised, a field of wheat cut down, nor could there be a log rolling, a husking, a quilting, a wedding, a sheepwashing, or a funeral without the aid of alcohol."

Antebellum reformers mounted a determined attack on the evils of drink and were remarkably successful in reducing American consumption of alcohol. In the late 1830s a million people belonged to temperance societies. Timothy Shay Arthur's Ten Nights in a Bar-Room: And What I Saw There, *published in 1854, was the most popular of all the attacks on the tavern and during the 1850s was a best-seller second only to* Uncle Tom's Cabin. *Like Harriet Beecher Stowe's antislavery novel,* Ten Nights *became a widely performed stage melodrama.*

As is true of Uncle Tom's Cabin, Ten Nights *is a far more shrewd work than is sometimes thought. Simon Slade, Judge Hammond, Judge Lyman, and young Willy are people with whom respectable Americans could easily identify. The book is not an evangelical tract about the sin of drinking but an often subtle account of a tavern that corrupts the republican virtue of the town of Cedarville.*

BEFORE YOU READ

1. Who is the owner of the Sickle and Sheaf? How does the town regard him?
2. What kind of people frequent the tavern?
3. According to the story of Willy Hammond, what does alcohol do to a man's ambition, career, and health?
4. How would you describe the effect of the tavern on the town of Cedarville?

The state of affairs in Cedarville, it was plain, from the partial glimpses I had received, was rather desperate. Desperate, I mean, as regarded the various parties brought before my observation. An eating cancer was on the community, and so far as the eye could mark its destructive progress, the ravages were fearful. That its roots were striking deep, and penetrating, concealed from view, in many unsuspected directions, there could be no doubt. What appeared

Timothy Shay Arthur, *Ten Nights in a Bar-Room: And What I Saw There* (Philadelphia: Henry Altemus, 1897), pp. 160–75.

on the surface was but a milder form of the disease, compared with its hidden, more vital, and more dangerous advances.

I could not but feel a strong interest in some of these parties. The case of young Hammond had from the first awakened concern; and now a new element was added in the unlooked-for appearance of his mother on the stage, in a state that seemed one of partial derangement. The gentleman at whose office I met Mr. Harrison on the day before—the reader will remember Mr. H. as having come to the "Sickle and Sheaf" in search of his sons—was thoroughly conversant with the affairs of the village, and I called upon him early in the day in order to make some inquiries about Mrs. Hammond. My first question, as to whether he knew the lady, was answered by the remark—

"Oh, yes. She is one of my earliest friends."

The allusion to her did not seem to awaken agreeable states of mind. A slight shade obscured his face, and I noticed that he sighed involuntarily.

"Is Willy her only child?"

"Her only living child. She had four; another son and two daughters; but she lost all but Willy when they were quite young. And," he added, after a pause— "it would have been better for her, and for Willy too, if he had gone to the better land with them."

"His course of life must be to her a terrible affliction," said I.

"It is destroying her reason," he replied, with emphasis. "He was her idol. No mother ever loved a son with more self-devotion than Mrs. Hammond loved her beautiful, fine-spirited, intelligent, affectionate boy. To say that she was proud of him, is but a tame expression. Intense love—almost idolatry—was the strong passion of her heart. How tender, how watchful was her love! Except when at school, he was scarcely ever separated from her. In order to keep him by her side, she gave up her thoughts to the suggestion and maturing of plans for keeping his mind active and interested in her society—and her success was perfect. Up to the age of sixteen or seventeen, I do not think he had a desire for other companionship than that of his mother. But this, you know, could not last. The boy's maturing thought must go beyond the home and social circle. The great world, that he was soon to enter, was before him; and through loopholes that opened here and there he obtained partial glimpses of what was beyond. To step forth into this world where he was soon to be a busy actor and worker, and to step forth alone, next came in the natural order of progress. How his mother trembled with anxiety as she saw him leave her side. Of the dangers that would surround his path, she knew too well; and these were magnified by her fears—at least so I often said to her. Alas! how far the sad reality has outrun her most fearful anticipations.

"When Willy was eighteen—he was then reading law—I think I never saw a young man of fairer promise. As I have often heard it remarked of him, he did not appear to have a single fault. But he had a dangerous gift—rare conversational powers, united with great urbanity of manner. Every one who made his acquaintance became charmed with his society; and he soon found himself surrounded by a circle of young men, some of whom were not the best companions he might have chosen. Still, his own pure instincts and honorable principles were his safeguard; and I never have believed that any social allurements would have drawn him away from the right path if this accursed tavern had not been opened by Slade."

"There was a tavern here before the 'Sickle and Sheaf' was opened," said I.

"Oh, yes. But it was badly kept, and the bar-room visitors were of the lowest class. No respectable young man in Cedarville would have been seen there. It offered no temptations to one moving in Willy's circle. But the opening of the 'Sickle and Sheaf' formed a new era. Judge Hammond—himself not the purest man in the world, I'm afraid—gave his countenance to the establishment, and talked of Simon Slade as an enterprising man who ought to be encouraged. Judge Lyman and other men of position in Cedarville followed his bad example and the bar-room of the 'Sickle and Sheaf' was at once voted respectable. At all times of the day and evening you could see the flower of our young men going in and out, sitting in front of the bar-room, or talking hand and glove with the landlord, who, from a worthy miller, regarded as well enough in his place, was suddenly elevated into a man of importance, whom the best in the village were delighted to honor.

"In the beginning Willy went with the tide, and in an incredibly short period was acquiring a fondness for drink that startled and alarmed his friends. In going in through Slade's open door he entered the downward way, and has been moving onward with fleet footsteps ever since. The fiery poison inflamed his mind at the same time that it dimmed his noble perceptions. Fondness for mere pleasure followed, and this led him into various sensual indulgences and exciting modes of passing the time. Every one liked him—he was so free, so companionable, and so generous—and almost every one encouraged, rather than repressed, his dangerous proclivities. Even his father for a time treated the matter lightly, as only the first flush of young life. 'I commenced sowing my wild oats at quite as early an age,' I have heard him say. 'He'll cool off, and do well enough. Never fear.' But his mother was in a state of painful alarm from the beginning. Her truer instincts, made doubly acute by her yearning love, perceived the imminent danger; and in all possible ways did she seek to lure him from the path in which he was moving at so rapid a pace. Willy was always very much attached to his mother, and her influence over him was strong; but in this case he regarded her fears as chimerical.[1] The way in which he walked was to him so pleasant, and the companions of his journey so delightful, that he could not believe in the prophesied evil; and when his mother talked to him in her warning voice, and with a sad countenance, he smiled at her concern and made light of her fears.

"And so it went on, month after month, and year after year, until the young man's sad declensions were the town talk. In order to throw his mind into a new channel—to awaken, if possible, a new and better interest in life—his father ventured upon the doubtful experiment we spoke of yesterday: that of

---

1. **chimerical:** the product of a wild imagination.

placing capital in his hands, and making him an equal partner in the business of distilling and cotton-spinning. The disastrous—I might say disgraceful result—you know. The young man squandered his own capital, and heavily embarrassed his father.

"The effect of all this upon Mrs. Hammond has been painful in the extreme. We can only dimly imagine the terrible suffering through which she has passed. Her present aberration was first visible after a long period of sleeplessness, occasioned by distress of mind. During the whole of two weeks, I am told, she did not close her eyes; the most of that time walking the floor of her chamber and weeping. Powerful anodynes,[2] frequently repeated, at length brought relief. But when she awoke from a prolonged period of unconsciousness, the brightness of her reason was gone. Since then she has never been clearly conscious of what was passing around her; and well for her, I have sometimes thought it was, for even obscurity of intellect is a blessing in her case. Ah me! I always get the heartache when I think of her."

"Did not this event startle the young man from his fatal dream, if I may so call his mad infatuation?" I asked.

"No. He loved his mother, and was deeply afflicted by the calamity; but it seemed as if he could not stop. Some terrible necessity appeared to be impelling him onward. If he formed good resolutions—and I doubt not that he did—they were blown away like threads of gossamer[3] the moment he came within the sphere of old associations. His way to the mill was by the 'Sickle and Sheaf;' and it was not easy for him to pass there without being drawn into the bar, either by his own desire for drink, or through the invitation of some pleasant companion who was lounging in front of the tavern."

The man was strongly excited.

"Thus it is," he continued; "and we who see the whole extent, origin, and downward rushing force of a widely sweeping desolation, lift our voices of warning almost in vain. Men who have everything at stake—sons to be corrupted and daughters to become the wives of young men exposed to corrupting influences—stand aloof, questioning and doubting as to the expediency of protecting the innocent from the wolfish designs of bad men, who, to compass their own selfish ends, would destroy them body and soul. We are called fanatics, ultraists, designing, and all that, because we ask our law-makers to stay the fiery ruin. Oh, no! we must not touch the traffic. All the dearest and best interests of society may suffer, but the rum-seller must be protected. He must be allowed to get gain, if the jails and poorhouses are filled and the graveyards made fat with the bodies of young men stricken down in the flower of their years, and of wives and mothers who have died of broken hearts. Reform, we are told, must commence at home. We must rear temperate children, and then we shall have temperate men. That when there are none to desire liquor, the

2. **anodyne:** something that allays pain, calms, or comforts.
3. **gossamer:** a thin, sheer fabric.

rum-seller's traffic will cease. And all the while society's true benefactors are engaged in doing this, the weak, the unsuspecting, and the erring must be left an easy prey, even if the work requires for its accomplishment a hundred years. Sir! a human soul destroyed through the rum-seller's infernal agency is a sacrifice priceless in value. No considerations of worldly gain can, for an instant, be placed in comparison therewith. And yet souls are destroyed by thousands every year; and they will fall by tens of thousands ere society awakens from its fatal indifference and lays its strong hand of power on the corrupt men who are scattering disease, ruin and death broadcast over the land!

"I always get warm on this subject," he added, repressing his enthusiasm. "And who that observes and reflects can help growing excited? The evil is appalling, and the indifference of the community one of the strangest facts of the day."

While he was yet speaking, the elder Mr. Hammond came in. He looked wretched. The redness and humidity of his eyes showed want of sleep, and the relaxed muscles of his face exhaustion from weariness and suffering. He drew the person with whom I had been talking aside, and continued in earnest conversation with him for many minutes—often gesticulating violently. I could see his face, though I heard nothing of what he said. The play of his features was painful to look upon, for every changing muscle showed a new phase of mental suffering.

"Try and see him, will you not?" he said, as he turned, at length, to leave the office.

"I will go there immediately," was answered.

"Bring him home, if possible."

"My very best efforts shall be made."

Judge Hammond bowed, and went out hurriedly.

"Do you know the number of the room occupied by the man Green?" asked the gentleman as soon as his visitor had retired.

"Yes. It is No. 11."

"Willy has not been home since last night. His father, at this late day, suspects Green to be a gambler. The truth flashed upon him only yesterday; and this, added to his other sources of trouble, is driving him, so he says, almost mad. As a friend, he wishes me to go to the 'Sickle and Sheaf' and try and find Willy. Have you seen anything of him this morning?"

I answered in the negative.

"Nor of Green?"

"No."

"Was Slade about when you left the tavern?"

"I saw nothing of him."

"What Judge Hammond fears may be all too true—that in the present condition of Willy's affairs, which have reached the point of disaster, his tempter means to secure the largest possible share of property yet in his power to pledge or transfer; to squeeze from his victim the last drop of blood that remains, and then fling him ruthlessly from his hands."

"The young man must have been rendered almost desperate, or he would never have returned as he did last night. Did you mention this to his father?"

"No. It would have distressed him the more without effecting any good. He is wretched enough. But time passes, and none is to be lost now. Will you go with me?"

I walked to the tavern with him, and we went into the bar together. Two or three men were at the counter, drinking.

"Is Mr. Green about this morning?" was asked by the person who had come in search of young Hammond.

"Haven't seen anything of him."

"Is he in his room?"

"I don't know."

"Will you ascertain for me?"

"Certainly. Frank,"—and he spoke to the landlord's son, who was lounging on a settee,—"I wish you would see if Mr. Green is in his room."

"Go and see yourself. I'm not your waiter," was growled back, in an ill-natured voice.

"In a moment I'll ascertain for you," said Matthew, politely.

After waiting on some new customers, who were just entering, Matthew went upstairs to obtain the desired information. As he left the bar-room, Frank got up and went behind the counter, where he mixed himself a glass of liquor, and drank it off, evidently with real enjoyment.

"Rather a dangerous business for one so young as you are," remarked the gentleman with whom I had come, as Frank stepped out of the bar and passed near where we were standing. The only answer to this was an ill-natured frown, and an expression of face which said, almost as plainly as words, "It's none of your business."

"Not there," said Matthew, now coming in.

"Are you certain?"

"Yes, sir."

But there was a certain involuntary hesitation in the barkeeper's manner which led to a suspicion that his answer was not in accordance with the truth. We walked out together, conferring on the subject, and both concluded that his word was not to be relied upon.

"What is to be done?" was asked.

"Go to Green's room," I replied, "and knock at the door. If he is there, he may answer, not suspecting your errand."

"Show me the room."

I went with him, and pointed out No. 11. He knocked lightly, but there came no sound from within. He repeated the knock; all was silent. Again and again he knocked, but there came back only a hollow reverberation.

"There's no one there," said he, returning to where I stood, and we walked downstairs together. On the landing, as we reached the lower passage, we met Mrs. Slade. I had not, during this visit at Cedarville, stood face to face with her before. Oh! what a wreck she presented, with her pale, shrunken countenance, hollow, lustreless eyes, and bent, feeble body. I almost shuddered as I looked at her. What a haunting and sternly rebuking spectre she must have moved, daily, before the eyes of her husband.

"Have you noticed Mr. Green about, this morning?" I asked.

"He hasn't come down from his room yet," she replied.

"Are you certain?" said my companion. "I knocked several times at the door just now, but received no answer."

"What do you want with him?" asked Mrs. Slade, fixing her eyes upon us.

"We are in search of Willy Hammond, and it has been suggested that he is with Green."

"Knock twice lightly, and then three times more firmly," said Mrs. Slade; and as she spoke she glided past us with a noiseless tread.

"Shall we go up together?"

I did not object, for, although I had no delegated right of intrusion, my feelings were so much excited in the case that I went forward, scarcely reflecting on the propriety of so doing.

The signal knock found instant answer. The door was softly opened, and the unshaven face of Simon Slade presented itself.

"Mr. Jacobs!" he said, with surprise in his tones. "Do you wish to see me?"

"No, sir; I wish to see Mr. Green," and with a quick, firm pressure against the door, he pushed it wide open. The same party was there that I had seen on the night before, — Green, young Hammond, Judge Lyman, and Slade. On the table at which the three former were sitting were cards, slips of paper, an inkstand and pens, and a pile of banknotes. On a side-table, or, rather, butler's tray, were bottles, decanters and glasses.

"Judge Lyman! Is it possible?" exclaimed Mr. Jacobs, the name of my companion; "I did not expect to find you here."

Green instantly swept his hands over the table to secure the money and bills it contained; but, ere he had accomplished his purpose young Hammond grappled three or four narrow strips of paper and hastily tore them into shreds.

"You're a cheating scoundrel!" cried Green, fiercely, thrusting his hand into his bosom as if to draw from thence a weapon; but the words were scarcely uttered ere Hammond sprung upon him with the fierceness of a tiger, bearing him down upon the floor. Both hands were already about the gambler's neck, and, ere the bewildered spectators could interfere, and drag him off, Green was purple in the face, and nearly strangled.

"Call me a cheating scoundrel!" said Hammond, foaming at the mouth as he spoke. "Me! whom you have followed like a thirsty bloodhound. Me! whom you have robbed, and cheated, and debased from the beginning! Oh! for a pistol to rid the earth of the blackest-hearted villain that walks its surface. Let me go, gentlemen! I have nothing left in the world to care for, — there is no consequence I fear. Let me do society one good service before I die!"

And with one vigorous effort he swept himself clear of the hands that were pinioning him, and sprung again upon the gambler with the fierce energy of a savage beast. By this time Green had got his knife free from its sheath, and, as Hammond was closing upon him in his blind rage, plunged it into his side. Quick almost as lightning the knife was withdrawn, and two more stabs inflicted ere we could seize and disarm the murderer. As we did so, Willy Hammond fell over with a deep groan, the blood flowing from his side.

In the terror and excitement that followed Green rushed from the room. The doctor, who was instantly summoned, after carefully examining the wound and the condition of the unhappy young man, gave it as his opinion that he was fatally injured.

Oh! the anguish of the father, who had quickly heard of the dreadful occurrence, when this announcement was made. I never saw such fearful agony in any human countenance. The calmest of all the anxious group was Willy himself. On his father's face his eyes were fixed as if by a kind of fascination.

"Are you in much pain, my poor boy?" sobbed the old man, stooping over him, until his long white hair mingled with the damp locks of the sufferer.

"Not much, father," was the whispered reply. "Don't speak of this to mother yet. I'm afraid it will kill her."

What could the father answer? Nothing! And he was silent.

Mathew Brady captured William Tecumseh Sherman's character in this May 1865 photograph: "All his features express determination," noted a contemporary, "particularly the mouth, which is wide and straight with lips shut tightly together . . . he believes in hard war."

PART SIX

Civil War and Reconstruction

The Price of War

During the thirty years leading to the Civil War, America underwent a shift from the nationalism of the earlier nineteenth century to antebellum sectionalism. Both northerners and southerners resolutely proceeded westward, but in economic and societal matters the rapidly growing Southwest, including Alabama, Mississippi, and Louisiana, differed greatly from the new Northwest of Ohio, Illinois, and Wisconsin. Though both regions supported mostly small farms, the South was distinctive in its large plantations. Slaves worked much of the South; free labor developed the North. One society produced a rural gentry, the other cities, entrepreneurs, and lawyers; one grew conservative and fearful of change, while the other spawned liberal religions and reforms. Beneath it all was a basic — and national — antipathy toward the black race that made southerners fearful of the abolition of slavery and northerners committed to halting its expansion into their own society, a commitment that in much of the North was reinforced by a genuine moral and humane abhorrence of the institution of slavery.

The readings in this section all reflect the crises the nation faced. Clara Barton's picture of the battlefield and the accounts by George Ward Nichols and Pauline DeCaradeuc Heyward of the devastation wrought by William Tecumseh Sherman's march through Georgia and the Carolinas graphically illustrate the impact of war. The Detroit anti-Negro riot exposes the dilemma of conflicting visions of the goals of the war. Victory for the Union did not answer all the major questions posed by the antislavery debate and the war.

"I have vowed that if I should have children — the first ingredient of the first principle of their education shall be uncompromising hatred & contempt of the Yankee," declared a white southerner toward the end of the Civil War. You will read a similar response from a white southerner, Caleb Forshey. "I'm free as a frog!" exulted one former slave, reacting like Felix Haywood and other

253

black southerners to the prospect of a future without slavery. Great hopes or extreme bitterness, more common than the philosophical resignation of Henry Ravenel—some of whose journal you will read—promised a painful future for the South.

In the months following Appomattox, the South was a landscape of abandoned fields, twisted rails, burned buildings, white men hobbling about on one leg or dangling an empty sleeve, and ex-slaves exploring their new freedom or searching for food, shelter, and work. Some things the war had settled: secession was impossible, slavery dead, and the South desperately impoverished, its pre-war economy gone with the wind. Other outcomes the region and the United States struggle with still. In particular, victory for the Union did not resolve questions about the role of African American men and women in American life. The first attempts to secure rights for the ex-slaves, known as Reconstruction, produced the Thirteenth, Fourteenth, and Fifteenth Amendments to the Constitution that provided only the legal basis for a revolutionary change in their place in American life. Beyond that, Reconstruction was largely defeated by determined opposition from white Southerners. Emerging from the era of Civil War and Reconstruction neither slaves nor fully free, African Americans faced a civil rights struggle that would consume the next century and beyond.

Points of View:
Sherman's "March to the Sea" (1863–65)

38

Marching with Sherman's Army
George Ward Nichols

In 1864 the Union organized for final victory. General Ulysses S. Grant, in overall command of the Union armies, led his troops against Robert E. Lee in the East while his trusted subordinate William Tecumseh Sherman pressed into Georgia from the West. As Grant made his slow, bloody way through Virginia, Sherman was changing the rules of war. Hacking his way through the lower South, slashing to bits much of what remained of the rebel heartland, his men burned and looted their way through Georgia and the Carolinas.

George Ward Nichol's The Story of the Great March *became one of the most popular accounts of Sherman's campaign. Within a year of its publication in 1865, the book sold sixty thousand copies, and it was reprinted in European newspapers. An aide-de-camp on the general's personal staff, Nichols depicted more the public side of*

Sherman as he met with with various groups—his field staff, his soldiers, and freed slaves. Nichols described as well Sherman's methods of warfare and the particular character of his famous march.

Nichols (1831–1885), who had been active in the antislavery struggles in Kansas in the 1850s, settled in Cincinnati after the war and became a leading figure in developing that city's museum, art school, and orchestra.

BEFORE YOU READ

1. What did Nichols think of General Sherman and his strategy?
2. What was the reason for destroying southern land and property?
3. What was Nichols's opinion of the Southerners he encountered along the way?
4. How intense was the fighting during the march? How would you generally characterize it?

PREPARATIONS FOR THE SEAWARD MARCH — THE BURNING OF ATLANTA

General Sherman at once made preparations to abandon all the posts south of Dalton [Georgia]. From Gaylesville and Rome he issued his orders concerning the new movement. The sick and wounded, noncombatants, the machinery, extra baggage, tents, wagons, artillery, ammunition stores, every person and every thing not needed in the future campaigns, were sent back to Chattanooga. The army was stripped for fighting and marching.

Let us for a moment look at General Sherman as he appeared at Gaylesville, seated upon a camp-stool in front of his tent, with a map of the United States spread upon his knees. . . . General Sherman's finger runs swiftly down the map until it reaches Atlanta; then, with unerring accuracy, it follows the general direction to be taken by the right and left wings, until a halt is made at Milledgeville. "From here," the general says, "we have several alternatives; I am sure we can go to Savannah, or open communication with the sea somewhere in that direction." After studying the map a while, tracing upon the tangled maze of streams and towns a line from Savannah north and east, at Columbia, South Carolina, General Sherman looks up at General Howard with the remark, "Howard, I believe we can go there without any serious difficulty. If we can cross the Salkahatchie, we can capture Columbia. From Columbia"—passing his finger quickly over rivers, swamps, and cities to Goldsboro, North Carolina—"that point is a few days' march through a rich country. When we reach that important railroad junction—when I once plant this army at Goldsboro—Lee must leave Virginia, or he will be defeated beyond

George Ward Nichols, *The Story of the Great March from the Diary of a Staff Officer* (New York: Harper & Brothers, 1865).

hope of recovery. We can make this march, for General Grant assures me that Lee can not get away from Richmond without his knowledge, nor without serious loss to his army."

To those who gazed upon the map, and measured the great distance to be traversed, from this quiet village away up in the mountains of Northern Alabama down to the sea, and thence hundreds of miles through a strange and impassable country away to the south again, and over wide rivers and treacherous bogs, the whole scheme, in the hands of any man but he who conceived it, seemed weird, fatal, impossible. But it was at that moment in process of operation. General Sherman at once communicated the first part of his plan to General Grant, subsequently receiving his hearty approval, with entire freedom to act as he should deem best. The army was at once set in motion; the numerous threads spreading over a wide field of operations were gathered up; out of confusion came exquisite order. Detachments guarding various dépôts were sent to their commands, outposts were withdrawn, the cavalry were concentrated in one division, under the lead of a gallant soldier. Compact, confident, and cheerful, this well-appointed host, guided by that master mind, moved grandly on to the fulfillment of its high mission. The field of operations now entered upon belonged, as has been said, to the genius of strategy. Those who have written of this campaign always date its commencement as from Atlanta. Inasmuch as we trod upon hitherto unconquered soil when we went out from Atlanta, this statement is true; but the march really began at Rome and Kingston, and it is from this point that we take up the diary of events which occurred within the experience and knowledge of the writer.

November 13th.—Yesterday the last train of cars whirled rapidly past the troops moving south, speeding over bridges and into the woods as if they feared they might be left helpless in the deserted land. At Cartersville the last communications with the North were severed with the telegraph wire. It bore the message to General Thomas, "All is well." And so we have cut adrift from our base of operations, from our line of communications, launching out into uncertainty at the best, on a journey whose projected end only the General in command knows. Its real fate and destination he does not know, since that rests with the goodness of God and the brave hearts and strong limbs of our soldiers. The history of war bears no similar example, except that of Cortés burning his ships. It is a bold, hazardous undertaking. There is no backward step possible here. Thirty days' rations and a new base: that time and those supplies will be exhausted in the most rapid march ere we can arrive at the nearest sea-coast; arrived there, what then? I never heard that manna[1] grew on the sand-beaches or in the marshes, though we are sure that we can obtain forage on our way; and I have reason to know that General Sherman is in the highest degree sanguine and cheerful—sure even of success.

---

1. **manna:** something of value that comes one's way.

As for the soldiers, they do not stop to ask questions. Sherman says "Come," and that is the entire vocabulary to them. A most cheerful feature of the situation is the fact that the men are healthful and jolly as men can be; hoping for the best, willing to dare the worst.

Behind us we leave a track of smoke and flame. Half of Marietta was burned up—not by orders, however; for the command is that proper details shall be made to destroy all property which can ever be of use to the Rebel armies. Stragglers will get into these places, and dwelling-houses are leveled to the ground. In nearly all cases these are the deserted habitations formerly owned by Rebels who are now refugees.

Yesterday, as some of our men were marching toward the Chattahoochee River, they saw in the distance pillars of smoke rising along its banks—the bridges were in flames. Said one, hitching his musket on his shoulder in a free and easy way: "I say, Charley, I believe Sherman has set the river on fire." "Reckon not," replied the other, with the same indifference; "if he has, it's all right." And so they pass along; obeying orders, not knowing what is before them, but believing in their leader.

From Kingston to Atlanta the rails have been taken up on the road, fires built about them, and the iron twisted into all sorts of curves; thus they are left, never to be straightened again. The Rebel inhabitants are in agony of wonder at all this queer manœuvring. It appears as if we intended evacuating Atlanta; but our troops are taking the wrong direction for the hopes and purposes of these people.

Atlanta is entirely deserted by human beings, excepting a few soldiers here and there. The houses are vacant; there is no trade or traffic of any kind; the streets are empty. Beautiful roses bloom in the gardens of fine houses, but a terrible stillness and solitude cover all, depressing the hearts even of those who are glad to destroy it. In the peaceful homes at the North there can be no conception how these people have suffered for their crimes.

Atlanta, Night of the 15th November. A grand and awful spectacle is presented to the beholder in this beautiful city, now in flames. By order, the chief engineer has destroyed by powder and fire all the store-houses, dépôt buildings, and machine-shops. The heaven is one expanse of lurid fire; the air is filled with flying, burning cinders; buildings covering two hundred acres are in ruins or in flames; every instant there is the sharp detonation or the smothered booming sound of exploding shells and powder concealed in the buildings, and then the sparks and flame shoot away up into the black and red roof, scattering cinders far and wide.

These are the machine-shops where have been forged and cast the Rebel cannon, shot and shell that have carried death to many a brave defender of our nation's honor. These warehouses have been the receptacle of munitions of war, stored to be used for our destruction. The city, which, next to Richmond, has furnished more material for prosecuting the war than any other in the

South, exists no more as a means for injury to be used by the enemies of the Union.

A brigade of Massachusetts soldiers are the only troops now left in the town: they will be the last to leave it. To-night I heard the really fine band of the Thirty-third Massachusetts playing "John Brown's soul goes marching on," by the light of the burning buildings. I have never heard that noble anthem when it was so grand, so solemn, so inspiring.

News came from General Howard that the advance of the 17th Corps had arrived, at nine o'clock that morning, at a point thirteen miles from Cheraw, and had found the enemy intrenched in their front. It was said that Beauregard, Johnston, Hardee, and Hampton, with the garrisons of Charleston, Wilmington, and other points, were in Cheraw, and that a great battle was probable. The Rebels had certainly gathered an array of talent, in the way of generals, enough to appal this little army! The presence of all these men and any large force is doubtless an exaggeration, although there can be no question but the delays of the last few days have given the enemy an intimation of our plans, which they have improved by guarding the important outlet at Cheraw.

We were inclined to believe that the Rebels, not liking our society, would not interfere with our movements; indeed, that they would assist our passage through the country. The care with which they have laid in plentiful supplies of corn, fodder, hams, beef on the hoof, and other supplies, would have indicated this. Again, our infantry have hardly seen a Rebel soldier since we left Columbia until this morning. Our route from the Catawba crossed several creeks where there were valuable bridges uninjured, the destruction of any one of which would have delayed our column a day or more. Certainly we had every reason to suppose that the Rebels wished us a good riddance, and offered no objections to our speedy passage to the sea, or wherever we chose to go. Only one other hypothesis remained, and the presence of an enemy in our front to-night is a cogent argument in its favor. It is that the Rebel leaders did not divine the real movement until the last moment, and are now throwing obstacles in the way of our passage over the Pedee. We estimate that, without assistance from Virginia, they can not concentrate more than twenty-five thousand men in our front, and we will undertake to start that force in two or three days. Within that time we shall have brought up all our troops, and it will go hard with the Rebels, but we will have a pontoon floating quietly from either bank of the Pedee. Of course the hope of saving the bridge at Cheraw must be abandoned, and we must depend upon other resources.

Although for the last three days we have not seen the sun, and the rain has fallen now and then, the left wing has made some fine marches. The 14th Corps yesterday traveled over eighteen miles of the road which had already been used by the 20th Corps, and to-day the 20th Corps has marched twenty-one miles since daylight. Fortunately the route has led along the high ridges and through the pine barrens, where the soil is sandy, and better for the light fall of rain. Thus we were able to reach this place early in the afternoon, driving before us, at a good marching pace, Butler's, or rather Hampton's cavalry, who opposed the advance.

During the skirmishing, one of our men, a forager, was slightly wounded; but the most serious accident of the day occurred to a negro woman in a house where the Rebels had taken cover. When I saw this woman, who would not have been selected as the best type of South Carolina female beauty, the blood was streaming over her neck and bosom from a wound in the lobe of her ear, which the bullet had just clipped and passed by.

"What was it that struck you, aunty?" I asked.

"Lor bress me, massa, I dun know; I just fell right down."

"Didn't you feel any thing, nor hear any sound?"

"Yes, now I 'member, I heerd a s-z-z-z-z-z, and den I just knock down. I drap on de groun'. I'se so glad I not dead, for if I died den de Bad Man would git me, cos I dance lately a heap."

To-day is the first time within a week when I have seen a household where the women are neatly dressed and the children cleanly. The people who have inhabited the houses along the roads for fifty miles behind us are among the most degraded specimens of humanity I have ever seen. Many of the families I now refer to do not belong to the class known as the "poor whites" of the South, for these are large landowners, and holders of from ten to forty slaves.

The peasantry of France are uneducated, but they are usually cleanly in their habits. The serfs of Russia are ignorant, but they are semi-barbarous, and have, until lately, been slaves. A large proportion of the working classes in England are debased, but they work. But the people I have seen and talked to for several days past are not only disgustingly filthy in their houses and their persons, but are so provokingly lazy, or "shiftless," as Mrs. Stowe[2] has it, that they appear more like corpses recalled to a momentary existence than live human beings, and I have felt like applying a galvanic battery to see if they could be made to move. Even the inroads of our foragers do not start them into life; they loll about like sloths, and barely find energy enough to utter a whining lamentation that they will starve.

During this campaign I have seen terrible instances of the horrors of slavery. I have seen men and women as white as the purest type of the Anglo-Saxon race in our army, who had been bought and sold like animals. I have looked upon the mutilated forms of black men who had suffered torture at the caprice of their cruel masters, and I have heard tales of woe too horrible for belief; but in all these cases I have never been so impressed with the degrading, demoralizing influence of this curse of slavery as in the presence of these South Carolinians. The higher classes represent the scum, and the lower the dregs of civilization. They are South Carolinians, not Americans.

The clean people whom I met this afternoon were a refreshing spectacle. Several of the young ladies—the men ran away at our approach—were attending school at this place, where a seminary has been situated for many

---

2. **Mrs. Stowe:** Harriet Beecher Stowe, author of *Uncle Tom's Cabin.*

years. One of these girls, in reply to my question why she had not gone to her home, forty miles down the river, answered:

"What is the use? Your people go every where; you overrun the state; and I am as well off here as at my father's house."

I acknowledged the wisdom of her action, for there is no doubting the fact that our presence is quite sensibly felt.

I happened to be present this afternoon at one of those interviews which so often occur between General Sherman and the negroes. The conversation was piquant and interesting; not only characteristic of both parties, but the more significant because, on the part of the General, I believe it a fair expression of his feelings on the slavery question.

A party of ten or fifteen negroes had just found their way through the lines from Cheraw. Their owners had carried them from the vicinity of Columbia to the other side of the Pedee, with the mules and horses which they were running away from our army. The negroes had escaped, and were on their way back to find their families. A more ragged set of human beings could not have been found out of the slave states, or, perhaps, Italy. The negroes were of all ages, and had stopped in front of the General's tent, which was pitched a few feet back from the sidewalk of the main street.

Several officers of the army, among them General Slocum, were gathered round, interested in the scene. General Sherman said to them:

"Well, men, what can I do for you—where are you from?"

"We's just come from Cheraw. Massa took us wid him to carry mules and horses away from youins."

"You thought we would get them; did you wish us to get the mules?"

"Oh yes, massa, dat's what I wanted. We knowed youins cumin, and I wanted you to hav dem mules; but no use; dey heard dat youins on de road, and nuthin would stop 'em. Why, as we cum along, de cavalry run away from de Yanks as if dey fright to deth. Dey jumped into de river, and some of dem lost dere hosses. Dey frightened at de berry name ob Sherman."

Some one at this point said: "That is General Sherman who is talking to you."

"God bress me! Is you Mr. Sherman?"

"Yes, I am Mr. Sherman."

"Dat's him, su' nuff," said one.

"Is dat de grre-aat Mr. Sherman dat we'se heard ob so long?" said another.

"Why, dey so frightened at your berry name dat dey run right away," shouted a third.

"It is not me that they are afraid of," said the General; "the name of another man would have the same effect with them if he had this army. It is these soldiers that they run away from."

"Oh no," they all exclaimed, "it's de name ob Sherman, su'; and we hab wanted to see you so long while you trabbel all roun' jis whar you like to go. Dey said dat dey wanted to git you a little furder on, and den dey whip all your soldiers; but, God bress me! you keep cumin' and a cumin', an' dey allers git out."

"Dey mighty 'fraid ob you, sar; dey say you kill de colored men too," said an old man, who had not heretofore taken part in the conversation.

With much earnestness, General Sherman replied:

"Old man, and all of you, understand me. I desire that bad men should fear me, and the enemies of the government which we are all fighting for. Now we are your friends; you are now free ('Tank you, Massa Sherman,' was ejaculated by the group). You can go where you please; you can come with us or go home to your children. Wherever you go you are no longer slaves. You ought to be able to take care of yourselves. ('We is; we will.') You must earn your freedom, then you will be entitled to it, sure; you have a right to be all that you can be, but you must be industrious, and earn the right to be men. If you go back to your families, and I tell you again you can go with us if you wish, you must do the best you can. When you get a chance, go to Beaufort or Charleston, where you will have a little farm to work for yourselves."

The poor negroes were filled with gratitude and hope by these kind words, which the General uttered in the kindest manner, and they went away with thanks and blessings on their lips.

39

A Southern Woman's Wartime Journal
Pauline DeCaradeuc Heyward

Pauline DeCaradeuc Heyward's Journal offers a spirited account of a slaveholding family's experience of Sherman's march. Union soldiers, in Heyward's account, were determined to penalize South Carolina, the original seat of secession, for starting the Civil War. That the DeCaradeuc women managed to limit the damage done to their plantation and property indicates that even angry Union troops approaching the end of a terrible war continued to pay some homage to the code requiring gentlemen to respect feminine gentility.

The war cost the DeCaradeuc family the lives of two sons as well as most of its wealth. After the war Pauline married Geurard Heyward. When he failed as a planter, Pauline, Geurard, and their growing family moved to Savannah, Georgia, where they established a modest prosperity and continued to enlarge their family. Until her death in 1914, Pauline maintained the role of a cultured, genteel southern wife and mother.

BEFORE YOU READ

1. What were the Union soldiers seeking at the Heyward plantation?
2. How did the DeCaradeuc women manage to keep possessions they valued and safeguard their virtue?
3. Why was Pauline DeCaradeuc Heyward so afraid for her father?

Feb. 14th, 1864

Carrie and I went over to Augusta yesterday, and really in spite of everything had a very amusing time. We bought several photographs of our most illustrious Gen's. I got Lee, Davis & Kirby Smith. John Cochran sent me word the other day that he had sent out to Richmond for Stonewall Jackson's for me, so that I'll have that too.

We visited Mr. Henry who is better, also Mrs. Foster, Mrs. Tubman & Mother's old friend, Mrs. Campbell. Then we tried to shop, but the only thing in the shape of a dress for myself that we saw, was a worsted stuff at $30.00 a yard.

I met Lieut. Col. Croft who stopped me & talked awhile on the street, he is most dreadfully, *agonizingly*, wounded in his right hand & looks very badly.

When we finished our business we sauntered round to the church yard & sat there 'till time to meet the train. When we reached the depot there was such a concourse of soldiers there that I begged an old lady who was going too, to let us remain with her. I was very uneasy as I never was in a crowd of men without a protector before, however, a young & handsome soldier came up & introduced himself, Major Beaufort of Va. and begged us to allow him to remain near us until the car was opened. When the doors were unlocked we got in & obtained good seats, some twenty-five ladies had to stand up & as many had to be left, & such crowds of soldiers!! An officer in front of us spread his blanket on the seat & begged us to keep it for him, but 'twas impossible & he couldn't even get in the car again. After a little while I heard a plaintive voice outside under the window, say: "Oh, Miss Pauline, ain't there any room in there for me?" I looked out & saw Col. Croft, of course, he couldn't get in our car; he asked me to look for his cousin in our car who was wounded & on crutches, but I couldn't even move, after talking a while he went into the conductor's car then I heard another voice say: "Miss Pauline, can't you get me a seat in front of you? I want to get in your car so much." What could I do? He was a very handsome Capt. I felt assured I knew him, his face & voice were perfectly familiar, but I could not remember his name, he conversed for awhile just like some old friend, seemed to know me well, but I don't yet remember who he is. Anyhow *he* too had to go off. Then our Va. Major came under the window to chat, & I gave him some cake I bought for the children, they would not allow soldiers to come in our car, without a lady; meanwhile a soldier on crutches stood near us looking sick & weak, he *stood* of course, & Carrie, noble as she always is rose & insisted on his taking her seat, but he would not hear of it, he then introduced himself, Captain Croft, the cousin, the Lieut. Col. asked me to look for, he remained with us the rest of the time & proved to be most agreeable.

After awhile we looked up & there was our kind Virginia Major standing by us, he pretended to the conductor that he had to see us out, & thus got into

Mary D. Robertson, ed., *A Confederate Lady Comes of Age; The Journal of Pauline DeCaradeuc Heyward, 1863–1888* (Charleston: University of South Carolina Press), pp. 36–37, 65–69.

our car from which he did not again move, he is really quite charming & entertained us very nicely, two more Captains spoke to us & offered to assist us in any way, but our Va. friend didn't give them a chance, he saw us to the carriage at Johnston's & all but cried when we got off the car. I think somehow we will hear of him again, he was 'mazin kind & attentive to us, should like to return it.

May 23, 1864

I have no heart to keep this Journal or tell of the dreadful, fatal battles in Va. Oh my God! my heart is too heavy, I am entirely miserable. Many whom I know are killed & wounded. Robert Taft and Col. Shooter are killed. Capt. Barnwell killed. George Lalane wounded. Wise's Brigade was subjected to a fearful firing from the enemy at Druery's Bluff. I suppose John Cochran is wounded, from the moment I saw him I felt that his life would be given to this devouring war; and I am assured that he is dead or wounded, for I *feel it.*

Feb. 18th, 1865

The Yankees have come & gone. On the 10th Feb. they encamped at Johnstons. The whole of Kilpatrick's forces, they were turned on the country for forage, plunder, & provisions. The first we saw of them was about a dozen of them, dashing thro the gate shouting: "Here come the Yankees, look out now you d——d rebels." A moment after they were in the house, Mother & Grandmother met them at the door, but they didn't listen to a word they tried to say, but said, "Come give us your keys, where is your liquor? get your gold, get your silver, you old women, hurry yourselves, I say." I had a belt on under my dress, with my revolver, and a bag of bullets, caps & powder in my pocket, they rushed into the room, where all of us ladies were sitting, saying, "Give me your revolvers, d——d you, if we find them, you'd better look out, where are your pistols, we know you've got 'em." I felt it wouldn't do for them to find mine on me, infuriated as they were, so I took Tante's arm, hurried upstairs & threw the revolver between her sheets, hardly I had finished when the door burst open & the room was filled with them, they pulled the bed to pieces, of course.

We all went into the parlor, and by this time there were hundreds of them, in the house, upstairs, in the garret, in every chamber, under the house, in the yard, garden, &c., &c., some singing, shouting, whistling, and Oh, my God, *such cursing.* Both pianos were going at the same time, with axes they broke open every door, drawer, trunk that was locked, smashed a large French mirror, broke pieces of furniture, and flung every piece of clothing, that they didn't carry off, all over the floors, they got some of Fa.'s prettiest paintings and broke bottles of catsup over them, they carried off every piece of silver, every knife, jewel, & particle of possessions in the house & negro houses, every paper, letter, receipt, &c., they flung to the winds, all the roads are strewn with them. Mother and G. M. went among them like brave women, trying to save some few things in vain, at one time a horrid looking ruffian came into the

parlor, seeing only women there, he entered shut both doors, & said in an un-
dertone, "You cursed rebels, now empty your pockets." Ah, mon Dieu, mine
had my bag of ammunition in it, I rose, & while he was grabbing Miss Hessie's
pocket book, I dropped my bag in a corner & flung an old bonnet over it, in
my pocket, he found my watch. "Ah," said he, "This is a pretty little watch,
now where is the key, & does it go good?" & the villain put his hand on my
shoulder, I rose & stood before him, with all possible dignity & he turned
away. Then after taking Tante's watch and everybody's money, he walked up to
Mother, grinding his teeth & looking her full in the face, said: "Now, you've
just *got* to tell me where your gold & silver is buried, I know you've got it, and
if you know what's good for yourself & all in this room, you'll tell me where it
is." "I have no gold, my silver you have all taken with every other valuable in
the house." "That's a d——d lie, now I'll burn your house this minute, if you
don't tell me." "I have nothing more to tell, do you think I'd tell a lie?" "I don't
know." Then he walked up & down the room cursing, swearing, threatening,
& spitting on every side, then finding he could do nothing with us, took
Solomon out, put a pistol to his head, saying he would blow his brains out, if
he didn't tell. Solomon is as true to us as steel, so are they all, all faithful &
friends to us.

About sundown, on the 10th they left off coming here. I then went to ascertain the fate of my revolver, there it was still rolled in the sheets, thrown on
the floor with the chaos of clothing. I of course, sent it off. They took every
blanket & pillow case & towel, the cases for bags to carry off what they took,
& towels for handkerchiefs, they even made the servants get our chemises &
tear them up into pocket handkerchiefs for them.

Well the next day, which was Saturday, they came just the same, hundreds
of them, one of our villianous neighbors told them that our boys fired the first
gun on Sumter, so they said this house was the root of the rebellion & burn it
they would, but our good servants & Mother and G. Mother entreated in such
a way that they desisted, then they said that they had to arrest and shoot every
influential citizen in S.C., every mover of secession, & from the accumulation
of wealth, the quantities of food, books & clothes in this house, the finest they
had seen in these parts, that they knew Father was wealthy, literary, & influential, & they had heard enough of him, to make an example of him & catch
him they would. We have no less than five large libraries of refugees, here, besides our own, & the accumulated clothing & valuables of four separate families, no wonder they found us so rich, & came here so often.

As to provisions, 'tis true, few was so bountifully supplied. We had 7 barrels
of fine flour, 300 bushels of corn, 1 barrel & 1 box of nice sugar, &c., &c.

Out of that we have 15 bushels corn, 1 bag flour, 3 hams, they took all the
wine & brandy. They had scouts out in every direction looking for Father.
Thus passed Saturday, on Sunday morning they burned Uncle & Daughter's
home *everything* & every building on their place, even the well, they are here
with nothing but their clothes on, in the world, they searched uncle's person.
After breakfast, 500 Yankees came here in a body & dispersed over the house

& place, carrying off everything they could, they attempted to get into Aiken Saturday morning but were repulsed by Wheeler.

Well, on Saturday night, Father who was encamped in the woods, with the mules, horses & some provisions & one or two of the servants, sent us word that he could not evade the scouts longer & he was going to give himself up to K.ptr. [Gen. Kilpatrick] & demand protection, as a Frenchman, for himself & household, I went down in the swamp to see him & when half way between there & the house saw four Yankees entering the gate, my goodness didn't I run, it was a regular tug between them & me to see who could get to the house first, but I beat in safety, but I never ran so in my life.

Well, after Father went, we were filled with anxiety about him, knowing their threats about him, Oh, we were so frightened for him, when the door opened & a Yankee rushed in with a lit candle, he looked all 'round then ran into every room in the house to look for "that d——d rebel," he then went out saying he'd return during the night to fire the house, — pleasant intelligence — then he & two others asked the servants if there were any young ladies in the house, how old they were & where they slept, during all this I had on blue spectacles & my face muffled up, Carrie too.

When I heard of their questions to the servants I thought that burning the house was nothing; I was almost frantic, I sat up in a corner, without moving or closing my eyes once the whole night. My God! I suffered agony, I trembled *unceasingly* till morning; about eleven o'clock that night, two men went up the back stairs, we heard them walking over head, they went into the room over the parlour (we were in the parlour, of course, all together) and went to bed there, they stayed there all night.

Well, none of us undressed or went to bed for six nights. On Sunday, Mother & Grandmother determined to go out to the camp, to Kilpatrick & ask for protection & for Father's release, they went in the cart with a little blind mule, the only animal they left us, with pieces of yarn for bridle, as they carried off all the harness, &c., during their absence, quantities of Yankees came here, and walked in *every direction* sticking the ground with their swords, feeling for buried things. Wherever the ground was soft they dug, they found all Tante's silver, bonds & jewels, a quantity of provisions, — barrel of wine, one of china, a box of Confederate money & bonds, &c.

Fortunately, the bulk of our silver was sent off.

Mother returned from the camp, bringing Father and William whom they had captured.

Monday morning only a few Yankees came, about ten, I suppose, and then the entire force fell back, not wishing to engage our troops, the R.R., of course, cut & we knew nothing more of them.

Our own soldiers have been coming here constantly, these last two or three days. My goodness, how different they are to the Yankees, the commonest one is as gentle & respectful to us as can be.

Sherman was at Johnstons on Sunday. One dashing looking young officer entered the room where we were sitting on Saturday & Mother said, "Are you an officer, sir?" "I am Madam." "Then, sir, I entreate your protection for my helpless household." "I will, Madam, God knows I am disgusted with all this." He left the room, *we hoped*, to try to check the pillage, he walked into Miss Hessie's room, broke open her trunk and began stuffing his pockets.

They threw a good many shells at this house.

FOR CRITICAL THINKING

1. Was Sherman's policy of total war against the Confederacy justified? Compare the picture of the South's circumstances presented by George Ward Nichols with that presented by Pauline DeCaradeuc Heyward and argue for one side or the other.

2. How sympathetic are you to Heyward's moral outrage over the treatment her household received from Union soldiers? Should they have left the family's property alone? Argue for either side.

40

Nursing on the Firing Line
Clara Barton

Clara Barton (1821–1912) was one of the most famous women in nineteenth-century America, indeed one of the most famous in the world. While her services to the suffering accorded with the Victorian concept of womanhood, she nevertheless broke many barriers, including that which prohibited women from going anywhere near active battle. Her initial fame derived from her nursing activities on the battlefields of the Civil War. Though the dominant image of her work, presented in a stream of children's books, is of ministering to the wounded, she in fact acted like a medical executive — raising funds, commandeering supplies, and organizing transportation and personnel — as well as personally serving the wounded and dying.

Barton created her image of "the angel of the battlefield" through carefully contrived letters, speeches, and gestures that appealed to the romantic sensibility of the age. But in a long career that spanned the Civil War, the Franco-Prussian War, and the Spanish-American War, she lived as fully adventurous a life as any man. Her writings express a haunting ambivalence about war: Recoiling with horror at its brutalities, Barton also found herself irresistibly drawn to war as an arena for both sacrifice and the display of personal courage.

BEFORE YOU READ

1. Why did Clara Barton go to the battlefields and become a nurse?
2. In what instances do you see Barton as a leader and organizer?
3. How was Barton able to get the wounded men of Fredericksburg shelter and provisions?

AT CEDAR MOUNTAIN

I was strong and thought I might go to the rescue of the men who fell. The first regiment of troops, the old 6th Mass. that fought its way through Baltimore, brought my playmates and neighbors, the partakers of my childhood; the brigades of New Jersey brought scores of my brave boys, the same solid phalanx; and the strongest legions from old Herkimer brought the associates of my seminary days. They formed and crowded around me. What could I do but go with them, or work for them and my country? The patriot blood of my father was warm in my veins. The country which he had fought for, I might at least work for, and I had offered my service to the government in the capacity of a double clerkship at twice $1400 a year, upon discharge of two disloyal clerks from its employ, — the salary never to be given to me, but to be turned back

Perry H. Epler, *Life of Clara Barton* (New York: Macmillan, 1915), pp. 31–32, 35–43, 59, 96–98.

into the U.S. Treasury then poor to beggary, with no currency, no credit. But there was no law for this, and it could not be done and I would not draw salary from our government in such peril, so I resigned and went into direct service of the sick and wounded troops wherever found.

But I struggled long and hard with my sense of propriety—with the appalling fact that I was only a woman whispering in one ear, and thundering in the other the groans of suffering men dying like dogs—unfed and unsheltered, for the life of every institution which had protected and educated me!

I said that I struggled with my sense of propriety and I say it with humiliation and shame. I am ashamed that I thought of such a thing.

When our armies fought on Cedar Mountain, I broke the shackles and went to the field. . . .

Five days and nights with three hours sleep—a narrow escape from capture—and some days of getting the wounded into hospitals at Washington brought Saturday, August 30. And if you chance to feel, that the positions I occupied were rough and unseemly for a *woman*—I can only reply that they were rough and unseemly for *men*. But under all, lay the life of the nation. I had inherited the rich blessing of health and strength of constitution—such as are seldom given to woman—and I felt that some return was due from me and that I ought to be there.

. . . Our coaches were not elegant or commodious; they had no windows, no seats, no platforms, no steps, a slide door on the side was the only entrance, and this higher than my head. For my manner of attaining my elevated position, I must beg of you to draw on your own imaginations and spare me the labor of reproducing the boxes, barrels, boards, and rails, which in those days, seemed to help me up and on in the world. We did not criticize the unsightly helpers and were only too thankful that the stiff springs did not quite jostle us out. This description need not be limited to this particular trip or train, but will suffice for all that I have known in Army life. This is the kind of conveyance by which your tons of generous gifts have reached the field with the precious freights. These trains through day and night, sunshine and rain, heat and cold, have thundered over heights, across plains, through ravines, and over hastily built army bridges 90 feet across the rocky stream beneath.

At 10 o'clock Sunday (August 31) our train drew up at Fairfax Station. The ground, for acres, was a thinly wooded slope—and among the trees on the leaves and grass, were laid the wounded who were pouring in by scores of wagon loads, as picked up on the field under the flag of truce. All day they came and the whole hillside was covered. Bales of hay were broken open and scattered over the ground like littering for cattle, and the sore, famishing men were laid upon it.

And when the night shut in, in the mist and darkness about us, we knew that standing apart from the world of anxious hearts, throbbing over the whole country, we were a little band of almost empty handed workers literally by ourselves in the wild woods of Virginia, with 3000 suffering men crowded upon the few acres within our reach.

After gathering up every available implement or convenience for our work, our domestic inventory stood 2 water buckets, 5 tin cups, 1 camp kettle, 1 stewpan, 2 lanterns, 4 bread knives, 3 plates, and a 2-quart tin dish, and 3000 guests to serve.

You will perceive by this, that I had not yet learned to equip myself, for I was no Pallas,[1] ready armed, but grew into my work by hard thinking and sad experience. It may serve to relieve your apprehension for the future of my labors if I assure you that I was never caught so again.

You have read of adverse winds. To realize this in its full sense you have only to build a camp fire and attempt to cook something on it.

There is not a soldier within the sound of my voice, but will sustain me in the assertion that go whichsoever side of it you will, wind will blow the smoke and flame directly in your face. Notwithstanding these difficulties, within fifteen minutes from the time of our arrival we were preparing food, and dressing wounds. You wonder what, and how prepared, and how administered without dishes.

You generous thoughtful mothers and wives have not forgotten the tons of preserves and fruits with which you filled our hands. Huge boxes of these stood beside that railway track. Every can, jar, bucket, bowl, cup or tumbler, when emptied, that instant became a vehicle of mercy to convey some preparation of mingled bread and wine or soup or coffee to some helpless famishing sufferer who partook of it with the tears rolling down his bronzed cheeks and divided his blessings between the hands that fed him and his God. I never realized until that day how little a human being could be grateful for and that day's experience also taught me the utter worthlessness of that which could not be made to contribute directly to our necessities. The bit of bread which would rest on the surface of a gold eagle was worth more than the coin itself.

But the most fearful scene was reserved for the night. I have said that the ground was littered with dry hay and that we had only two lanterns, but there were plenty of candles. The wounded were laid so close that it was impossible to move about in the dark. The slightest misstep brought a torrent of groans from some poor mangled fellow in your path.

Consequently here were seen persons of all grades from the careful man of God who walked with a prayer upon his lips to the careless driver hunting for his lost whip, — each wandering about among this hay with an open flaming candle in his hands.

The slightest accident, the mere dropping of a light could have enveloped in flames this whole mass of helpless men.

How we watched and pleaded and cautioned as we worked and wept that night! How we put socks and slippers upon their cold, damp feet, wrapped

1. **Pallas:** Another name for Athena, Greek goddess of war, fertility, arts, and wisdom.

your blankets and quilts about them, and when we had no longer these to give, how we covered them in the hay and left them to their rest!" . . .

The slight, naked chest of a fair-haired lad caught my eye, and dropping down beside him, I bent low to draw the remnant of his torn blouse about him, when with a quick cry he threw his left arm across my neck and, burying his face in the folds of my dress, wept like a child at his mother's knee. I took his head in my hands and held it until his great burst of grief passed away. "And do you know me?" he asked at length, "I am Charley Hamilton, who used to carry your satchel home from school!" My faithful pupil, poor Charley. That mangled right arm would never carry a satchel again.

About three o'clock in the morning I observed a surgeon with his little flickering candle in hand approaching me with cautious step far up in the wood. "Lady," he said as he drew near, "will you go with me? Out on the hills is a poor distressed lad, mortally wounded and dying. His piteous cries for his sister have touched all our hearts and none of us can relieve him but rather seem to distress him by our presence."

By this time I was following him back over the bloody track, with great beseeching eyes of anguish on every side looking up into our faces, saying so plainly, "Don't step on us."

"He can't last half an hour longer," said the surgeon as we toiled on. "He is already quite cold, shot through the abdomen, a terrible wound." By this time the cries became plainly audible to me.

"Mary, Mary, sister Mary, come,—O come, I am wounded, Mary! I am shot. I am dying—Oh come to me—I have called you so long and my strength is almost gone—Don't let me die here alone. O Mary, Mary, come!"

Of all the tones of entreaty to which I have listened, and certainly I have had some experience of sorrow, I think these sounding through that dismal night, the most heart-rending. As we drew near some twenty persons attracted by his cries had gathered around and stood with moistened eyes and helpless hands waiting the change which would relieve them all. And in the midst, stretched upon the ground, lay, scarcely full grown, a young man with a graceful head of hair, tangled and matted, thrown back from a forehead and a face of livid whiteness. His throat was bare. His hands, bloody, clasped his breast, his large, bewildered eyes turning anxiously in every direction. And ever from between his ashen lips pealed that piteous cry of "Mary! Mary! Come."

I approached him unobserved, and motioning the lights away, I knelt by him alone in the darkness. Shall I confess that I intended if possible to cheat him out of his terrible death agony? But my lips were truer than my heart, and would not speak the word "Brother," I had willed them to do. So I placed my hands upon his neck, kissed his cold forehead and laid my cheek against his.

The illusion was complete; the act had done the falsehood my lips refused to speak. I can never forget that cry of joy. "Oh Mary! Mary! You have come? I knew you would come if I called you and I have called you so long. I could not die without you, Mary. Don't cry, darling, I am not afraid to die now that you have come to me. Oh, bless you. Bless you, Mary." And he ran his cold, blood-wet hands about my neck, passed them over my face, and twined them in my hair, which by this time had freed itself from fastenings and was hanging damp and heavy upon my shoulders. He gathered the loose locks in his stiffened fingers and holding them to his lips continued to whisper through them "Bless you, bless you, Mary!" And I felt the hot tears of joy trickling from the eyes I had thought stony in death. This encouraged me, and wrapping his feet closely in blankets and giving him such stimulants as he could take I seated myself on the ground and lifted him on my lap, and drawing the shawl on my own shoulders also about his I bade him rest.

I listened till his blessings grew fainter and in ten minutes with them on his lips he fell asleep. So the gray morning found us. My precious charge had grown warm, and was comfortable.

Of course the morning light would reveal his mistake. But he had grown calm and was refreshed and able to endure it, and when finally he woke, he seemed puzzled for a moment but then he smiled and said:—"I knew before I opened my eyes that this couldn't be Mary. I know now that she couldn't get here but it is almost as good. You've made me so happy. Who is it?"

I said it was simply a lady, who hearing that he was wounded, had come to care for him. He wanted the name, and with childlike simplicity he spelled it letter by letter to know if he were right. "In my pocket," he said, "you will find mother's last letter, please get it and write your name upon it, for I want both names by me when I die."

"Will they take away the wounded?" he asked. "Yes," I replied, "the first train for Washington is nearly ready now." "I must go," he said quickly. "Are you able?" I asked. "I must go if I die on the way. I'll tell you why. I am poor mother's only son, and when she consented that I go to war, I promised her faithfully that if I were not killed outright, but wounded, I would try every means in my power to be taken home to her dead or alive. If I die on the train, they will not throw me off, and if I were buried in Washington, she can get me. But out here in the Virginia woods in the hands of the enemy, never. I *must* go!"

I sent for the surgeon in charge of the train and requested that my boy be taken.

"Oh impossible! Madam, he is mortally wounded and will never reach the hospital. We must take those who have a hope of life." "But you must take him." "I cannot."—"Can you, Doctor, guarantee the lives of all you have on that train?" "I wish I could," said he sadly. "They are the worst cases, nearly fifty per cent must die eventually of their wounds and hardships."

"Then give this lad a chance with them. He can only die and he has given good and sufficient reasons why he must go—and a woman's word for it, Doctor. You take him. Send your men for him." Whether yielding to argument or entreaty, I neither knew nor cared so long as he did yield nobly and kindly. And they gathered up the fragments of the poor, torn boy and laid him carefully on a blanket on the crowded train and with stimulants and food and a kind hearted attendant, pledged to take him alive or dead to Armory Square Hospital and tell them he was Hugh Johnson of New York, and to mark his grave.

Although three hours of my time had been devoted to one sufferer among thousands, it must not be inferred that our general work had been suspended or that my assistants had been equally inefficient. They had seen how I was engaged and nobly redoubled their exertions to make amends for my deficiencies.

Probably not a man was laid upon those cars who did not receive some personal attention at their hands, some little kindness, if it were only to help lift him more tenderly.

This finds us shortly after daylight Monday morning. Train after train of cars were rushing on for the wounded and hundreds of wagons were bringing them in from the field still held by the enemy, where some poor sufferers had lain three days with no visible means of sustenance. If immediately placed upon the trains and not detained, at least twenty-four hours must elapse before they could be in the hospital and properly nourished. They were already famishing, weak and sinking from loss of blood and they could ill afford a further fast of twenty-four hours. I felt confident that unless nourished at once, all the weaker portion must be past recovery before reaching the hospitals of Washington. If once taken from the wagons and laid with those already cared for, they would be overlooked and perish on the way. Something must be done to meet this fearful emergency. I sought the various officers on the grounds, explained the case to them and asked permission to feed all the men as they arrived before they should be taken from the wagons. It was well for the poor sufferers of that field that it was controlled by noble-hearted, generous officers, quick to feel and prompt to act.

They at once saw the propriety of my request and gave orders that all wagons would be stayed at a certain point and only moved on when every one had been seen and fed. This point secured, I commenced my day's work of climbing from the wheel to the brake of every wagon and speaking to and feeding with my own hands each soldier until he expressed himself satisfied.

Still there were bright spots along the darkened lines. Early in the morning the Provost Marshal came to ask me if I could use fifty men. He had that number, who for some slight breach of military discipline were under guard and useless, unless I could use them. I only regretted there were not five hundred. They came,—strong willing men,—and these, added to our original force and what we had gained incidentally, made our number something over eighty, and believe me, eighty men and three women, acting with well directed purpose will accomplish a good deal in a day. Our fifty prisoners dug graves and gathered and buried the dead, bore mangled men over the rough ground in their arms, loaded cars, built fires, made soup, and administered it. And I failed to discern that their services were less valuable than those of the other men. I had long suspected, and have been since convinced that a private soldier may be placed under guard, courtmartialed, and even be imprisoned without forfeiting his honor or manliness, that the real dishonor is often upon the gold lace rather than the army blue.

. . . The departure of this train cleared the grounds of wounded for the night, and as the line of fire from its plunging engines died out in the darkness, a strange sensation of weakness and weariness fell upon me, almost defying my utmost exertion to move one foot before the other.

A little Sibley tent had been hastily pitched for me in a slight hollow upon the hillside. Your imaginations will not fail to picture its condition. Rivulets of water had rushed through it during the last three hours. Still I attempted to reach it, as its white surface, in the darkness, was a protection from the wheels of wagons and trampling of beasts.

Perhaps I shall never forget the painful effort which the making of those few rods, and the gaining of the tent cost me. How many times I fell from sheer exhaustion, in the darkness and mud of that slippery hillside, I have no knowledge, but at last I grasped the welcome canvas, and a well established brook which washed in on the upper side at the opening that served as door, met me on my entrance. My entire floor was covered with water, not an inch of dry, solid ground.

One of my lady assistants had previously taken train for Washington and the other worn out by faithful labors, was crouched upon the top of some boxes in one corner fast asleep. No such convenience remained for me, and I had no strength to arrange one. I sought the highest side of my tent which I remembered was grass grown, and ascertaining that the water was not very deep, I sank down. It was no laughing matter then. But the recollection of my position has since afforded me amusement.

I remember myself sitting on the ground, upheld by my left arm, my head resting on my hand, impelled by an almost uncontrollable desire to lie completely down, and prevented by the certain conviction that if I did, water would flow into my ears.

How long I balanced between my desires and cautions, I have no positive knowledge, but it is very certain that the former carried the point by the position from which I was aroused at twelve o'clock by the rumbling of more wagons of wounded men. I slept two hours, and oh, what strength I had gained! I may never know two other hours of equal worth. I sprang to my feet dripping wet, covered with ridges of dead grass and leaves, wrung the water from my hair and skirts, and went forth again to my work.

AT FREDERICKSBURG

No one has forgotten the heart sickness which spread over the entire country as the busy wires flashed the dire tidings of the terrible destitution and suffering of the wounded of the Wilderness whom I attended as they lay in Fredericksburg. But you may never have known how many hundredfold of these ills were augmented by the conduct of improper, heartless, unfaithful officers in the immediate command of the city and upon whose actions and indecisions depended entirely the care, food, shelter, comfort, and lives of that whole city of wounded men. One of the highest officers there has since been convicted a traitor. And another, a little dapper Captain quartered with the owners of one of the finest mansions in the town, boasted that he had changed his opinion since entering the city the day before,—that it was in fact a pretty hard thing for refined people like the people of Fredericksburg to be compelled to open their homes and admit "these dirty, lousy, common soldiers," and that he was not going to compel it.

This I heard him say and waited, until I saw him make his words good—till I saw, crowded into one old sunken hotel, lying helpless upon its bare, wet, bloody floors, 500 fainting men hold up their cold, bloodless, dingy hands, as I passed, and beg me in Heaven's name for a cracker to keep them from starving (and I had none); or to give them a cup that they might have something to drink water from, if they could get it (and I had no cup, and could get none), till I saw 200 six-mule army wagons in a line, ranged down the street to headquarters, and reaching so far out on the Wilderness road that I never found the end of it; every wagon crowded with wounded men, stopped, standing in the rain and mud, wrenched back and forth by the restless hungry animals all night from four o'clock in the afternoon till eight next morning and how much longer I know not.—The dark spot in the mud under many a wagon, told only too plainly where some poor fellow's life had dripped out in those dreadful hours.

I remembered one man who would set it right, if he knew it, who possessed the power and who would believe me if I told him, . . . I commanded immediately conveyance back to Belle Plain. With difficulty I obtained it, and four stout horses with a light army wagon took me ten miles at an unbroken gallop, through field and swamp, and stumps and mud to Belle Plain and a steam tug at once to Washington. Landing at dusk I sent for Henry Wilson, Chairman of the Military Committee of the Senate. A messenger brought him at eight, saddened and appalled like every other patriot in that fearful hour, at the weight of woe under which the nation staggered, groaned, and wept.

He listened to the story of suffering and faithlessness, and hurried from my presence, with lips compressed and face like ashes. At ten he stood in the War Department. They could not credit his report. He must have been deceived by some frightened villain. No official report of unusual suffering had reached them. Nothing had been called for by the military authorities commanding Fredericksburg.

Mr. Wilson assured them that the officers in trust there were not to be relied upon. They were faithless, overcome by the blandishments of the wily inhabitants. Still the department doubted. It was then that he proved that my confidence in his firmness was not misplaced, as facing his doubters he replies: "One of two things will have to be done—either you will send someone tonight with the power to investigate and correct the abuses of our wounded men at Fredericksburg—or the Senate will send some one to-morrow."

This threat recalled their scattered senses.

At two o'clock in the morning the Quartermaster-General and staff galloped to the 6th Street wharf under orders; at ten they were in Fredericksburg. At noon the wounded men were fed from the food of the city and the houses were opened to the "*dirty, lousy* soldiers" of the Union Army.

Both railroad and canal were opened. In three days I returned with carloads of supplies.

No more jolting in army wagons! And every man who left Fredericksburg by boat or by car owes it to the firm decision of one man that his grating bones were not dragged 10 miles across the country or left to bleach in the sands of that city.

41

Detroit Anti-Negro Riot
Mr. Dale et al.

The Midwest, with its proximity to and many migrants from the slave states, was the region, after the South, most hostile to the aspirations of African Americans. Throughout the first six decades of the nineteenth century, midwestern states enacted a series of antiblack legislation. Even in the 1850s after the slavery debate began to dominate the national conscience, Michigan, Iowa, and Wisconsin resoundingly defeated proposals to grant suffrage to blacks. And the legislatures of Iowa, Indiana, and Illinois each adopted a law in that decade making it a crime for blacks to settle in the state.

The onset of war increased the racial animosity in the region. Unskilled workmen in particular feared that, as an editorial expressed it, an influx of "two or three million semi-savages" would threaten their livelihoods. The Emancipation Proclamation that went into effect on January 1, 1863, gave further edge to such fears. And the passage by Congress soon after of a military draft act that allowed wealthier people to "commute" their draft obligation upon payment of $300 further hardened resistance to the aims of the war. Many Northerners would have agreed with the conviction among Confederate soldiers that it had become "a rich man's war and a poor man's fight."

These fears fueled a major riot in Detroit, Michigan, on March 6, 1863, after a black named Faulkner was sentenced to life imprisonment for the rape of a nine-year-old white girl. A group of rowdies, said to be largely Irish and German, attempted to lynch the convicted rapist. Frustrated, they rushed into a black neighborhood, burned down a house, and killed its inhabitants. As the crowd grew, the mob randomly terrorized the neighborhood, setting fire to about thirty-five houses and beating dozens of bystanders until soldiers dispersed them. Numerous blacks fled across the river to Canada. Newspaper stories headlined the incident as "The Negro Riot in Detroit," although none of the accounts indicate that any blacks had in fact rioted.

BEFORE YOU READ

1. From the documents here, can you put together an account of the events of March 6, 1863?

2. How did the victims of the mob escape?

3. According to Solomon Houston, why did the German pursuing him not kill him?

4. How would you answer Frederick Wilson's questions: "What is the meaning of all of this? What nation of barbarians do these families live in?" What does the newspaper description of the event as "The Negro Riot in Detroit" suggest?

ACCOUNT OF MR. DALE

Thomas Faulkner, charged of committing the outrages upon Ellen Hover, a colored girl and also a white girl, was to all intents a white man. This is beyond doubt, for he was a regular voter, and the journals of the city that understood his politics state that he voted the Democratic ticket. And an old veteran of over one hundred years of age declares, that in conversing with F. he said: "If he thought he had one drop of colored blood in his veins, if he could, he would let it out." And this was the man that caused the mob on colored men!

On the 6th of March an organized mob made their way from the jail down Beaubien street. They were yelling like demons, and crying "kill all the d—d niggers." In the cooper shop, just below Lafayette street, were five men working, namely: Robert Bennette, Joshua Boyd, Solomon Houston, Lewis Houston, Marcus Dale. These men were busy at work in the shop until the mob made an attack upon the shop. The windows were soon broken and the doors forced open. The men in the cooper shop were determined to resist any that might attempt to come in. The mob discovered this, and did not attempt to come in, but stood off and threw stones and bricks into the windows, a perfect shower. There happened to be one old shot gun in the shop, a couple of discharges from which drove the mob back from the shop. The dwelling house was attached to the shop, in which were three women and four children, namely: Mrs. Reynolds, Mrs. Bonn and one child, Mrs. Dale and three children.

Some ten minutes after the mob had fallen back from the shop, they made a rush upon the house in which were the women and children. The men in the shop seeing this, rushed out of the shop into the house to protect the women and children. The windows of the houses were soon all broken in; stones and bricks came into the house like hail. The women and children were dodging from one room to another to escape the stones. The men frequently stood before the women and children to shield them from the stones. Very soon after the men went from the shop into the house, the shop was set on fire by the mob. There were plenty of shavings in the shop, which facilitated the burning. The flames soon reached the house in which were the women and children. The mob by this time had completely surrounded the building. Mrs. Reynold attempted to go out at the back door but could not get out, for hundreds of stones were flying at that part of the building. Mr. Dale, in shielding his wife, got a blow in the face with a stone, which his wife might have gotten had he not stood before her. Some person outside was heard to say "the women will be protected—no protection for the men." Hearing this, Mr. Dale told the women to go out at the front door. Mrs. Dale seeing the blood running from her husband's face, said my dear you are bleeding—you will be killed. Said he to her, go out with your children; they say there is protection for the women, but none for the men. I will look out for myself. Mrs. Bonn started for the

Anti-Negro Riots in the North, 1863 (New York: Arno Press, 1969), pp. 2–13.

door, with her child in her arms, followed by Mrs. Dale, with one child in her arms and two children hanging to her. Mrs. Reynolds next followed. When the women approached the door, some fiend in human shape drew back a large club to strike them, but some spectators, having within them a spark of humanity, rushed to the women and rescued them—drawn probably by the screams of Mrs. Bonn. After the women had got out, the men, one by one, made their way out—were knocked down with stones when they came out, and beaten. Father Clark happened to be in the house, was beaten after he came out. The last one who came out was Mr. Dale. When he came out into the back yard the heat was so intense that he came near being overcome by it— he had his face badly burned. When he came out of the door some twenty dirty-looking Irishmen rushed at him with clubs, crying "kill the nager." But being thoughtful enough to come out with something in his hands, and having a good deal of physical strength he made them get back, and he got out without receiving further injuries. Three families living in the building near the cooper shop, lost all they had; namely, Mr. Reynolds, Mr. Dale and Mr. Bonn.

The mob, not satisfied with burning the cooper shop, and building adjacent, proceeded up Fort and Lafayette streets, robbing and burning some fifteen houses belonging to colored people.

Of the men who were in the cooper shop one has died from wounds received; namely, Joshua Boyd.

ACCOUNT OF LOUISA BONN

I had gotten home from a funeral of a young woman, and, after changing my apparel, commenced to get supper. I heard a yelling up Beaubien street, and looking out saw a crowd of men and boys throwing at Mr. Buckner's house. My husband told me I had better go into my mother's, and he would shut up the house so that they would not think any one was home. I went in, and in a few moments they were down to my father's house.

They then commenced breaking in the front room windows, and the doors and windows of the cooper shop.

Myself and child, mother, and Mrs. Dale, and her three children and brother, kept in the back part of the house while they were throwing stones, and then some one broke the front door open with an axe. Then the dining room caught fire. I started to go out the front door with my babe in my arms, thinking that, as I had not done anything at all to those fiends in human form, they would let me pass. On going to the door, a man met me with a large boulder in his hand, and would have knocked me in the head, had his hand not been caught by another man! I then returned in the house, the sheets of flames approaching me and my babe. I then went to the front door and found it locked, but the top pannel of the door was all knocked out. Finding I could not get out I commenced screaming! At this a crowd rushed across the street to me And I feared it was some of the mob, and ran back into the house again. Two gentlemen ran to me and kicked the lower part of the door open — one taking hold of me and the other caught my child, and told me I should not be hurt. I could not then tell whether mother was burned up or not. So I commenced screaming for my mother. Dr. Calhoun told the gentlemen to take me on up street, and he would go in and get my mother out. A Dutchman went in with the Doctor and got Mrs. Dale out, and took her to Mr. McCutchens, and I went on up the street.

Before the house was fired, heard them say: "Let us surround the house and burn the niggers up." So I thought my mother was burned up! No tongue can describe the feelings of my mind on that occasion; everything that we had were in burning sheets of flame! My husband, mother and other friends were all exposed to murderous assaults from those fiends; and to all human appearance there was not a friend in all the thousands that thronged and gazed upon our ruins. Who can form an idea of a female's distress, under such circumstances?

After I escaped the mob, I went up to Mrs. R. Clark's, Lafayette street. I thought, of course, my mother was dead, and was gazing intensely to see if I could discover any one coming up from there, and while thus watching, I saw my dear mother coming up the street all wet, with a trunk in her hands. I ran out to meet her. I then took the trunk from her and went into Mr. C.'s, and told her to come after me. When we got in, I told her she had better break the trunk open and get out father's money. Mrs. Clark handed her a hammer, and just at that moment a rush of the mob approached, and hailed in a shower of bricks and other missiles, smashing in the doors and window. Mrs. Clark and all of us were frightened to desperation. She attempted to run up stairs, but Ma told her not to do that, but go out of the house. At this Ma opened the back door, and went down the yard, and jumped the fence, leaving the trunk and all its contents sitting behind the stove. My mother knew that the trunk had all my father's money in it; that he was then just preparing to lay in a large stock of cooper stuff. She had dragged it several squares from our dwelling, that the mob had destroyed, to be compelled to leave it in the house of Mrs. Clark to be seized by those vile fiends. The amount of money in the trunk was twelve hundred dollars, besides a large lot of valuable clothes. We then proceeded from there up the alley to St. Antoine street, and from thence on to Clinton street — as poor wanderers, not knowing where to go to seek an asylum from the coldness of the approaching night. My babe was entirely naked, with the exception of a little dress and skirt, having lost all his clothes, even to his bonnet, in the fire and trying to escape the mob.

Wandering up and down about eight o'clock at night, we got on Mullett street and found Mr. E. Harberd was not burned out. We went there and found a shelter from the mob and cold.

During all this time, myself and mother was out of doors without bonnet or shawl. My distress was indescribable, on account of the absence of my husband and father. The former I saw last when the dining room fell in. He advised me to stand aside as much as possible out of the flames, as he heard the bell ringing, and thought the guards would soon come, and I could get out. From this time I never saw him any more till three o'clock on Saturday morning, when he and Mr. Dale came to father Harberd's. Mr. Dale was much wounded in the flames.

My father had gone to the country to see about lumber, and told us that if he was not back by five o'clock, we need not feel uneasy about him, as he would not be back till morning. But still I had the grief and burden of mind for him; for we did not know but what he had come in and fallen into the hands of the mob; and this suspense of mind we had till about 9 o'clock the next morning, when he came home.

ACCOUNT OF MRS. REYNOLDS

I found, on my daughter going to the front door, she had to hasten back to save her life from the mob; so I returned into the room and gave up to be burned up; for I saw from all appearances that if I went out in such a shower of stones, I should be certainly killed, and I just gave myself up to the mercy of God.

I remained in this position and heard my daughter scream again, and then soon it was over. I could not tell whether herself and babe had fallen speechless at the foot of the bloody assassin, or fell in the flames!

Not long after this, a couple of gentlemen came in and helped me and Mrs. Dale and children out of the flames.

I had taken care of the trunk.

ACCOUNT OF WHITNEY REYNOLDS

I was out at Oakland that day, and on coming heard that my wife, daughter and her husband and child were all burned up, with all my property. This struck me with such force, that when I came home and found my family all safe it filled me with such satisfaction that I did not feel the loss of the property scarcely at all.

I have lost in cash $1,200, and in property over four thousand, and all swept away in an hour for no cause, only the wickedness of a class of men who hate the colored man.

ACCOUNT OF SOLOMON HOUSTON

We were working in Mr. Reynold's cooper shop, between Fort and Lafayette streets. An immense crowd came to the shop, and the first thing we knew they smashed in the front window and door, and said: "Come out ye sons of b——h." They came around in the alley and smashed in the back windows. We did not go out, but they seemed too cowardly to come in, and they continued to smash and break up Mr. R.'s house. Finding the mob directing their fury on the dwelling house where there were none but the wife of Mr. Reynolds, Mrs. Bonn and child, and Mrs. Dale and four children, all exposed to all kinds of missiles that could be thrown through the doors and windows, we all went to the house to try to defend the women. Then the mob set the shop on fire. During our stay in the shop, none of them dared to come in; but after we left it they then put the torch to it, and soon it was in flames! The mob then surrounded the house in every direction, as if determined to burn up the property and all the men, women and children that were therein; during which time they were throwing brickbats and missiles from every direction. I came to the front door of the house, and it was then partly consumed. A gentleman that I knew called me to come to him, and I made my way to him, and he forbade the mob interfering with me. He knew me well, and I was a peaceable man. Several laid hold of me and said they were intent on taking my life; that they saw me shoot. A German man rushed on me with a spade, and struck me twice with it over the head, inflicting a severe wound at each blow. A person who stood by him, as he raised the spade the third time, asked him what he intended to do? Said he, "I intend to kill him!"

The man said to him: "You ought to be ashamed to strike a man with such a weapon, whom you have never seen, nor has done you any harm!" At this, the assassin threw the spade down.

A gentleman, who I did not know at that time, being much excited, but I very well knew him afterwards, came to me and took me down Lafayette street to Mr. Thairs', and the mob surrounded me again, and prevented the friend from taking me on. Here they knocked me down again. Mr. T. then came out and bade them not to interfere with me any more, and came and took me in. He sent for a doctor to examine my wounds, and washed me and took care of me kindly, till the next day.

I suffered for a couple of weeks severely; but, thank the Lord, I am now recovering, but have not been able to do a stroke of work since the 6th of March, five weeks, with a helpless family depending on me for protection!

ACCOUNT OF LOUIS HOUSTON

Finding the house about being entirely consumed, as before stated, as I was one of the last that came out, I went to the back part of the lot to go through a hole in the fence. . . .

. . . I made my way out to get through the fence, and was knocked down with a stone or brick, I don't know which. . . .

After some time I came to myself, enough to get up, and I then went up the alley to St. Antoine street; here the mob overtook me again. They commenced on me again, and with all kinds of weapons they beat me in the most cruel manner over the head till I heard some one say, "he is dead!" then they left me alone. I can't say how long I lay in the position they left me, but after some time, near night, I came to enough to rise from the place and try to get home. As I was coming on, a young white man overtook and asked me if would not rather go to jail? He advised me to go to jail, and I concluded it would be best, as I feared the mob might follow me home. The young man hurried on, and by the time I got there he had the door open; but I don't think the keeper was there. When the jailor came I found myself sadly disappointed, as he ordered me out, and told me to go over to Mr. Steward's, and asked me "what I came in there for." Humanity sickens at such cruelty! Here I had lived and paid my taxes for the last ten or twelve years, and it was the first time I had ever been in prison; and then when a most brutal mob was raging through the city, the civil authorities doing not one thing to defend me; and when I went to the prison for protection of my life, was turned out to the exposure of the mob! . . .

ACCOUNT OF FREDERICK WILSON

I reside on the corner of Fort and Beaubien streets, and about half-past four or five o'clock on Friday, March the 6th, 1863, I was aroused by the cry of "A mob! a mob!" On hastening to the door, I saw thousands of men and boys coming down Beaubien street, yelling in a most hideous manner, as if all Pandemonium were turned loose. They let loose a perfect volley of all kinds of missiles at Mr. Buckner's dwelling, on the corner of Beaubien and Croghan streets.

From this they came on down to Mr. W. Reynolds' residence and cooper shop. Here they made a general halt, as if determined to make a total destruction of every thing.

The several parts of the house and shop were attacked with indescribable fury! Doors, windows, and every part were under a shower of missiles. Axes, spades, clubs and stones, and whatever they could lay hands on to do mischief with, were freely used. It was heart appalling to see the fury with which they made their attack. No warning was given to the men engaged in their lawful avocations in the shop, till they were set upon in that murderous assault.

The workmen in the shop seemed to defend it from within; as I could see the mob falling back from the door, when they rushed as if they were going to enter. A single shot from a gun seemed to make all retreat. A short time after, I saw the flames rising from the shop. Some wretch had set it on fire!

Here I was compelled to pause, in wild astonishment, and ask myself the question: "What is the meaning of all this? What nation of barbarians do those families live in?"

But it was but a few moments, and I was called from my vision of the wrongs of my friends to witness my own outrages.

Having completed the work of destruction at the last named place, they came on to Mr. Morton's, who was a huckster in the market. It seemed as if they took great pleasure in doing all they could to such men as were about there doing business for themselves. And soon his house was in flames. They then let loose on my residence, and smashed in some windows and passed on.

I gathered up my family and part of my things, and a friend of mine went with them to go over to Canada. When the two draymen got down to the ferry, they made my friend pay them; and when I came down they demanded of me full pay again. It is plain to any honest man that the great purpose of the mob was to rob and plunder; so I had to give it or subject myself to the cruel treatment of many others who were suffering as innocently as I could possibly be! I hope never to see another such a scene.

ACCOUNT OF BENJAMIN SINGLETON

I lived at the corner of Fort and Beaubien streets, and have been sick for the last two years. I am so afflicted with blindness, that while I stand right up to you I can't discern the eyes in your head. All I could hear or understand were the yells and curses of, "Kill the Niggers," &c. A shower of stones, &c." made me understand that I was not to escape. They set fire to my house, and I was not able to get out; but some white ladies came to my relief. They broke a board off my fence, and came through the back way and dragged me out, or I should have been burned up with my house and all that I had. . . .

ACCOUNT OF WILLIAM JONES

I reside in Canada, and just had entered into the city of Detroit. In passing Mr. Reynold's house I was spoken to by Mrs. Dale. I then went in; and when I went in, I saw nor heard anything to cause me any fear of danger.

The people were then at the jail as I heard. A few minutes after I got in, I was sitting in the room, and the first intimations I had, was some one yelled out: "Here is the coopershop"; and at that moment a shower of clubs and stones came through the windows.

In a short time, we saw the shop was on fire, and the flames soon extended to the dwelling. The women screaming and almost distracted to get out of the house; the flames rolling in sheets nearer and nearer, and the mob all around the entire premises, with every kind of missiles, knocking and throwing to keep them in and burn up; the women crying for mercy's sake to let them out, for already a part of the roof of the house had fallen; but no entreaty, no appeal for sympathy, moved the mob. They seemed to be as deaf as the adder, and vile as the rattlesnake, determined to burn them all up.

We then made an attempt to force our way out of the house, from the back door, but was met by United States soldiers and others, with stones, bricks and billets of wood! I then rushed to the front door, and was met in a similar manner. With all the fury of demons did they fall on me, but through it all, I made my way through them, several times being knocked down upon my knees, inflicting severe wounds on my head, shoulder and side, and one stab in the neck.

I was still pursued by the mob, till I got to Ingersoll's Machine shop, crying: "Kill the nigger;" "kill the nigger." On arriving at the back part of the shop, Mr. Ingersoll told me to go into his shop in the upper story, where two others were.

It was to the humanity of Mr. and Mrs. Ingersoll, through the mercy of God, that my life was spared. She rushed into the mob saying: "You scoundrels are you going to kill that man!"

I heard one fellow say: "She ought to be shot for protecting the nigger." Finding a shelter, stayed there till dark before I could get to the dwelling house, where he sent after Dr. Gorton, who dressed my wounds; and in the morning they gave me breakfast, and desired me to stay longer, but I came over home. May the blessing of heaven rest upon those generous hearted persons who protected us.

42

A Slaveowner's Journal at the End of the Civil War

Henry William Ravenel

In a letter of August 26, 1865, Henry William Ravenel summarized the immediate effects of the collapse of the Confederacy as well as anyone ever has:

> A new era opens before us, but alas! with what great changes. Our country is in ruins, and our people reduced to poverty. . . . We had no money but Confederate and that is now worthless . . . all our securities and investments are bankrupt. . . . There is little money in the country, little cotton and other produce, so there is no business or employment for those who are anxiously seeking to make a living. . . .

Emancipation had altered social relations; the collapse of the Confederacy and then Reconstruction were transforming southern politics; the war and emancipation had upset every economic arrangement making currency worthless, land unsalable, and credit—previously based on chattel mortgages on slave "property"—scarcely to be obtained.

Ravenel was born in 1814 to a prominent South Carolina slaveholding family. In addition to managing a plantation, he was also to become an important self-trained naturalist whose studies of American fungi achieved international renown. After the war he supported his family by selling seeds and parts of his collections of fungi to collectors and later worked as a naturalist for the U.S. Department of Agriculture. After his death, Ravenel's botanical collections were sold to the British Museum.

Ravenel began his journal in 1859 and continued it to within weeks of his death in 1887. The journal shows how one thoughtful and well-placed member of the southern elite struggled to understand the collapse of his familiar world.

BEFORE YOU READ

1. How did Ravenel interpret the causes and outcome of the Civil War?
2. What did he expect to happen to the ex-slaves and how did he explain their behavior?
3. Are his reactions what you expected of a slaveholder or are there any surprises in what he writes in his journal?

November [1864]

F. 18   The Augusta paper of this morning has startling intelligence from Atlanta. There is no doubt that Sherman has burned Rome, Decatur & Atlanta, & has commenced a move with 4 or 5 army corps (40 to 50000) in the direction of

Arney Robinson Childs, ed., *The Private Journal of Henry William Ravenel, 1859–1887* (Columbia: University of South Carolina Press, 1947), pp. 202–03, 206–07, 210–21 passim, 228–29, 237, 239–40.

Macon & Augusta. The Northern papers say his intention is to move through to Charleston & Mobile, destroy the rail road & bridges behind him & feed his army from the country. I have been apprehending just such a move since Hood's army was withdrawn. It is a bold stroke, & if successful, would bring untold evils upon us, in the destruction of property & the means of subsistance. . . .

Sunday 20 Beauregard telegraphs the people to be firm & resolute—to obstruct his passage by cutting the woods in his front & flank—to destroy all provisions which cannot be carried away—to remove all negroes, horses & cattle, & leave a scene of desolation in his front, instead of in his rear as it would be if he passed. . . . Should Sherman succeed in taking Augusta, his march will be onward toward Charleston, & his track will be a scene of desolation. I await the developments of the next few days with anxiety, chiefly on account of my negroes. If I send them away & the farm & house is left without protection, my house will be robbed & despoiled of every thing, whether the enemy passes here or not. I must wait before removing them, until I am very sure the enemy will succeed in his designs upon Augusta—& then perhaps it may be too late.

M. 21 I have had a talk with my negroes on the subject, & explained to them the true state of affairs—that should the enemy pass through this place they must escape & take care of themselves for a while until the danger is passed. I am well satisfied from their assurances, that they are really alarmed at the idea of being seized & taken off by the Yankees, & that they will not desert me.

F. 25 We are now at the gloomiest period of the war which for nearly four years has afflicted our land. I cannot conceal from myself the many discouraging features of our situation & the perilous straits in which we stand.

1st Our Finances are in such a condition that universal discontent & real suffering exists. The currency is so much depreciated, that for the ordinary & necessary articles of subsistance, it requires an outlay beyond the means of most people. This involves privation & suffering. There is a want of confidence in the ability of the Govt. to redeem its credits, founded partly on their great amount & partly on the precarious condition of our affairs. If our cause fails the whole Govt. credits are lost, & doubtless this consideration has its weight among capitalists in producing distrust.

Sunday 8 Samuel Ravenel at home on furlough from Measles was here this morning. He told me that the Post Surgeon had offered Harry & himself & three other boys, exemptions on account of their age & size, & that two had accepted. He & Harry & another had declined. I was gratified to hear that our boys took such high views of their duty. Sam says they have no tents, & have to lie on the bare ground, or with such protection as a few bushes or straw can give. They do picket & *vidette* duty in sight & hearing of the enemy, see them drill & enjoy the music from their bands every day. . . .

M. 9 Sent off two boxes bacon today to the Depot for Aiken via Charleston. I hope these supplies may not be caught in Charleston or intercepted by the enemy on the way. We are in a quandary what to do. I am buying hogs down here, & at the same time sending supplies hurriedly to Aiken. . . .

January [1865]

Sunday 15 My claim for compensation for slave (Jim) lost in Confed. service, has passed the Legislature & $2000 are allowed. I am to send James Wilson a power of attorney to receive it. They have commenced to fortify Columbia. . . .

M. 23 Our currency still continues to depreciate, as is shown by the increasing prices of all articles. . . .

February [1865]

S. 18 It is reported that Columbia has fallen - - - - No mail from Charleston. We are now closed in & cut off from all news from the outside world. . . . We are now virtually in the enemy's lines. I am in doubt what to do with Harry. He is very weak & just able to walk about. If he remains, he may be captured as prisoner of war — if I undertake to carry him away, I then leave my family never to see them until the war is over. I would not hesitate about leaving my family if they were in a region where they needed no protection & could get subsistance — but the thoughts of deserting them here is very distressing to me.

Sunday 19 Dr. Frank Porcher dined here today. He thinks we should remain where we are. The upper country is in danger of famine, & will soon be without salt, now the coast is given up. . . . Charleston was occupied by the enemy yesterday at 10 A.M. — Columbia has been captured. We hear of a great fire in Charleston yesterday, but no particulars yet. Exciting times!

M. 20 In a few days the last of our army will have crossed the Santee, the bridge burnt behind them — & we then become an evacuated & conquered region. We fall under Yankee rule & the laws & authority of the U. States are established during the continuance of the war. What new relations between us & our negroes will be established we cannot tell but there is no doubt it will be a radical change. I do not apprehend destructive raids, or personal violence to citizens who remain, but we will be compelled to conform to the new conditions under which we are placed, as a conquered people. I suppose all the cotton will be seized & confiscated to the use of the U. S. govt, — & probably a system of culture will be adopted & enforced the profits from which will accrue to them. I think it the duty of all slave owners & planters who remain, to be with their negroes. They have been faithful to the last, & they deserve in turn, confidence from him, protection, attention & care. . . .

T. 21 I think masters who are within these lines of the enemy, should remain on their plantations among their negroes; — the first change of conditions should not be volunteered by us. We have always believed we were right in maintaining the relation of master & slave for the good of the country & also for the benefit of the negro. If we have believed firmly in the Divine sanction which the Bible affords to this relation, we should not be the first to sever it, by abandoning them. They have grown up under us, they look to us for support, for guidance & protection—They have faithfully done their duty during this trying time, when the great temptations were offered to leave us. In the sight of God, we have a sacred duty to stand by them as long as they are faithful to us. We know that if left to themselves, they cannot maintain their happy condition. We must reward their fidelity to us by the same care & consideration we exercised when they were more useful. . . .

T. 28   David returned with a cart from PineVille last night, & said Rene told him the Yankees had been, or were, in PineVille, taking poultry & whatever they wanted. The negroes on many places have refused to go to work. . . . I have spoken to some of them here & intend to give them advice as a friend to continue on the plantation, & work—Of course there must be great care & judgement used in preserving discipline & I have advised with the overseer. I think for their own good & the good of the country, it would be best for the present organization of labor to go on, so that all may get a subsistance, the old & young, the sick & disabled, & the other non producers. . . . The freed & idle negroes who are not kept now under discipline or fear will give us trouble. I feel great anxiety for the future. . . .

March [1865]

Th. 2   Half past two o'clock A.M. Night of horrors! How can I describe the agonizing suspense of the past six hours! Thank God who has protected us all we are still alive & have lost nothing but property.—About half past 8 oclock I was standing in the back piazza, when I heard the discharge of 3 or 4 fire arms. The negroes soon came running up to inform us that the Yankees were in the negro yard. They soon after entered the house, (4 or 5 colored men) armed & demanded to see the owner of the house. I called to Pa & he walked up to the back door where they were. They told him that they had come for provisions, corn, bacon, poultry & whatever they wanted—demanded his horses & wagons, his guns, wine &c. That they had come to tell the negroes they were free & should no longer work for him. They used very threatening language with oaths & curses. They then proceeded to the stable & took my pair & Renes horse—Took the 2 sets harness & put in the horses, into the two wagons & Lequeax buggy. They then emptied the smoke house, store room & meat house, giving to the negroes what they did not want. They then took from the fowl house what poultry they wanted, took the two plantation guns, & used great threats about the wine & brandy. To our great relief they did not enter the house again, & at 1.30 A.M. drove off. They told the negroes if they worked for their master again they would shoot them when they came back. What the future is to be to us God only knows. I feel that my trust is still unshaken in his all protecting Providence. I have all confidance in the fidelity of the negroes & their attachment to us if they are not restrained from showing it. We are all up for the night as the excitement is too great to permit sleep - - - - - 9 A M at the usual hour this morning the house negroes came in— They seemed much distressed & said the troops told them last night if they came to the yard or did anything for us, they would shoot them—That a large troop would come today. We told them to go back & not bring trouble upon themselves, until we could see the Commanding officer. The fidelity & attachment of some who have come forward is very gratifying. The girls have been cooking our simple breakfast & we have taken our first meal under the new regime. I long for a visit from some officer in authority, that we may know our future condition & whether the negroes will be allowed to hire themselves to us or not. I know if they are not restrained there are many who would willingly & gladly help us. I had heard often of insurrectionary feelings among the negroes, but I never believed they would be brought to it of their own accord. The experience of this war, & especially of last night all tend to confirm that conviction. Even when compelled by intimidation, & fear of the consequences to their lives, many of them evince real distress, & not one has yet joined in any language or act of defiance. Their fidelity & attachment is amazing with the temptations before them. Those who were engaged in the sacking of the store room & meat house, did so stealthily & I believe not until they were commanded to help themselves.

S. 4 Inauguration of Presdt. Lincoln today for his 2d term of 4 years. Will any thing come out of it in respect to the war? The negroes are completely bewildered at the change of their condition. Many are truly distressed, some of the younger ones delirious with the prospect of good living & nothing to do. Some are willing to remain & work, but object to gang work,—all is in a chaotic state. When they were told that they were free, some said they did not wish to be free, & they were immediately silenced with threats of being shot. I fear this region will be a desolate waste in one year hence, if this state of things continue - - On Thursday night when the army was camped here, their troops were among our negroes, distributing sugar, coffee, meats & bread in profusion—they killed 8 or 10 of the sheep & had them cooked in the negro yard. This was all intended as an earnest of the good things which followed their freedom. . . .

M. 6 The events of the past week have brought up vividly before us the horrors of the French Revolution—& those startling scenes which Dickens describes in his "Tale of two cities". We are in a fearful & trying crisis. If those who had unsettled the present order of things in the name of Humanity, were consistent, they would make some effort to order the freed negroes for their good, & ought to take some steps toward restoring order & recommanding & enforcing some plan by which such a large number may escape the horrors of insubordination, violence & ultimately starvation. The negroes are intoxicated with the idea of freedom. Many of them are deluded into the hope that their

future is to be provided for by the U S. Govt.—& hence they do not feel the
necessity of work. Many are disposed to remain, but perhaps will insist on
terms which are incompatable with discipline & good management. It is a
fearful crisis.

T. 7   No disposition evinced among the negroes to go to work. There
seems to be sullenness which I dislike to see. I think those who are disposed to
work or to do for us, are restrained. I hear that many of the negroes are armed
with pistols & guns. Some were at Black Oak last night firing off pistols. This
is a bad feature in this fearful period.—Oh, Humanity! what crimes are committed in thy name. One week ago we were in the midst of a peaceful, contented & orderly population—now all is confusion, disorder, discontent, violence, anarchy. If those who uprooted the old order of things had remained
long enough to reconstruct another system in which there should be order restored, it would have been well, but they have destroyed our system & left us
in the ruins—"God is our refuge & strength, a very present help in trouble"
- - - - The negroes are rambling about the country. This morning 4 mounted
on horses & mules rode through the negro yard, stopping for a while, & some
have passed through in vehicles. It is said they were told to go to St Stephens
for horses which the army left behind.

W. 8   We heard guns again last night, but cannot learn from the negroes
who fired them. The disordered state of affairs keeps us anxious. . . . On this
day a week ago the old system of slave labour was in peaceful operation. The
breath of Emancipation has passed over the country, & we are now in that transition state between the new & the old systems—a state of chaos & disorder.
Will the negro be materially benefitted by the change? Will the condition of
the country in its productive resources, in material prosperity be improved?
Will it be a benefit to the landed proprietors? These are questions which will
have their solution in the future. They are in the hands of that Providence
which over-ruleth all things for good. It was a strong conviction of my best
judgement that the old relation of master & slave, had received the divine
sanction & was the best condition in which the two races could live together
for mutual benefit. There were many defects to be corrected & many abuses
to be remedied, which I think would have been done if we had gained our independence & were freed from outside pressure. Among these defects I will
enumerate the want of legislation to make the marriage contract binding—to
prevent the separation of families, & to restrain the cupidity of cruel masters.
Perhaps it is for neglecting these obligations that God has seen fit to dissolve
that relation. I believe the negro must remain in this country & that his condition although a freed-man, must be to labour on the soil. Nothing but necessity will compel him to labour. Now the question is, will that necessity be
so strong as to compel him to labour, which will be profitable to the landed
proprietors. Will he make as much cotton, sugar, rice & tobacco for the world
as he did previously? They will now have a choice *where* to labour. This will
ensure good treatment & the best terms. The most humane, the most ener-

getic & the most judicious managers have the best chances in the race for success. I expect to see a revolution in the ownership of landed estates. Those only
can succeed who bring the best capacity for the business. Time will show. . . .

Sunday 12   Some of the very peculiar traits of negro character are now exhibited. John & Solomon left Morefield on Thursday with the black troops
wild with excitement & probably drunk—In all this reign of disorder & anarchy I have not seen or heard of any violence or even of rudeness or incivil-
ity from the plantation negroes. Docility & submissiveness still prevail. There
are two exhibitions of character which have surprised us, & which were never
anticipated. 1st. On many places where there was really kind treatment & mutual attachment, the exciting events of the last week or two, & the powerful
temptations brought to bear upon them, have seemed to snap the ties suddenly. Some have left their comfortable homes & kind masters & friends, &
gone off with the army, thinking to better their conditions. We must be patient
& charitable in our opinions—They are ignorant of what they have to encounter, mere children in knowledge & experience, excitable, impulsive &
have fallen under the tempting delusions presented to them in such glowing
terms—Some who are disposed to take a proper view of their condition, & to
return to work, are intimidated & kept back by threats from the more strong
& overbearing. They do not clearly comprehend this situation—they have
been told they are free, & their idea of freedom is associated with freedom
from work & toil. In many places there was bad discipline & little care for the
negroes. These are generally the foremost in all the acts of disorder,—& their
example & word keep back others. We are astonished at this defection when
we do not expect it, but on reflection the causes at work are sufficient to account for it. 2nd. Had we been told four years ago, that our negroes would
have withstood the temptation to fidelity which have been constantly before
them during the war, we would have doubted the possibility—& had we been
told further of the events of the last two weeks, the incitements to acts of violence both by the example & the precepts of the black troops all throughout
this region, we would have shuddered for the consequences. Except from the
black soldiers, I have not heard of a single act of violence, or even of rude or
uncivil language. Their behaviour is perfectly civil so far, & I believe, with a
judicous course on the part of the whites, will continue so. This whole revolution from its commencement has developed in its progress, a course of
events which no human sagacity on either side, ever foresaw. We are carried
along by an inscrutable providence to the consummation of great & radical
changes,—we are the actors in a Great Revolution where, not civil institutions
only, but social polity, must be reconstructed & re-organized. . . .

May [1865]

May M. 1   Gen Lees surrender took place on the 9th.ult, but it only
reached us through our papers & the returning prisoners about a week ago. . . .
[This] means the loss of our Independence for which we have been struggling

for four years with immense loss of life & property. But the fate of nations is controlled & over-ruled by a wise Providence, which sees the end from the beginning, & orders all things in the highest wisdom. Whatever therefore may be the will of God regarding our destiny, I accept His decision as final & as eminently good. I have honestly believed we were right in our revolution, & would receive the divine sanction—if I have erred, I pray God to forgive me the error, & I submit with perfect satisfaction to His decree, knowing that He cannot err.

M. 22.   We begin now to realize the ruin to property which the war has entailed upon us. All classes & conditions of men will suffer who had property, except the small farmers who owned no negroes. Confederate securities, I consider a total loss. Bank stock, confederation & private bonds, are all more or less dependent for their availability upon Confed securities, & upon the value of negro property; both of which are lost. The Rail road companies are nearly all ruined by the destruction of their roads & the heavy debt they must incur to rebuild. The only money now in possession of our people is coin in small quantities which had been hoarded through the war, & some bills of the local banks. There will be but little means of increasing this amount for some time to come, as provisions are scarce, & the cotton has been mostly burnt, captured or sold. The financial prospect is a gloomy one, & there will be much distress before our conditions can improve. . . .

M. 29   I went in to Aiken this morning & called at the hotel to inquire if any officer in Aiken was authorized to administer the Oath of Allegiance. They expected in a day or two to have it done here. It is necessary now in order to save property, have personal protection, or exercise the rights of citizenship, or any business calling. Every one who is allowed, is now taking the oath, as the Confederate govt. is annulled, the state govt. destroyed, & the return into the Union absolutely necessary to our condition as an organized community. As Gen. Gillmore's order based upon Chief Justice Chase's opinion announces the freedom of the negroes there is no further room to doubt that it is the settled policy of the country. I have today formally announced to my negroes the fact, & made such arrangements with each as the new relation rendered necessary. Those whose whole time we need, get at present clothes & food, house rent & medical attendance. The others work for themselves giving me a portion of their time on the farm in lieu of house rent. Old Amelia & her two grandchildren, I will spare the mockery of offering freedom to. I must support them as long as I have any thing to give.

T. 30   My negroes all express a desire to remain with me. I am gratified at the proof of their attachment. I believe it to be real & unfeigned. For the present they will remain, but in course of time we must part, as I cannot afford to keep so many, & they cannot afford to hire for what I could give them. As they have always been faithful & attached to us, & have been raised as family servants, & have all of them been in our family for several generations, there is a feeling towards them somewhat like that of a father who is about to send out his children on the world to make their way through life. Those who have brought the present change of relation upon us are ignorant of these ties. They have charged us with cruelty. They call us, man stealers, robbers, tyrants. The indignant denial of these changes & the ill feelings engendered during 30 years of angry controversy, have culminated at length in the four years war which has now ended. It has pleased God that we should fail in our efforts for independance—& with the loss of independance, we return to the Union under the dominion of the abolition sentiment. The experiment is now to be tried. The negro is not only to be emancipated, but is to become a citizen with all the right & priviledges! It produces a financial, political & social revolution at the South, fearful to contemplate in its ultimate effects. Whatever the result may be, let it be known & remembered that neither the negro slave nor his master is responsible. It has been done by those who having political power, are determined to carry into practice the sentimental philanthropy they have so long & angrily advocated. Now that is fixed. I pray God for the great issues at stake, that he may bless the effort & make it successful—make it a blessing & not a curse to the poor negro.

43

African Americans During Reconstruction
Felix Haywood et al.

The Thirteenth, Fourteenth, and Fifteenth Amendments to the U.S. Constitution decreed an equality between the races that did not become a reality in African Americans' daily lives. At first the federal government through the Freedman's Bureau and support for Reconstruction governments in southern states made vigorous efforts to help the freed slaves gain education, legal and medical services, reasonable employment contracts, and a measure of political power. But within about a decade those efforts were abandoned as the northern public, tired of disorder in the South and wary of government intervention, abandoned the ex-slaves to their ex-masters. The newly freed African Americans were soon left to respond however they could to the social revolution brought about by emancipation, the war's impoverishment of the South, and the violence of groups like the Ku Klux Klan. Historians have pieced together the story of their actions from a multiplicity of sources. Interviews with ex-slaves collected in the 1930s, of which you will here read a sample, are one important source.

BEFORE YOU READ

1. What, judging from these accounts, were the major problems the ex-slaves faced after the war?
2. What did these ex-slaves expect of freedom?
3. What role did the Ku Klux Klan play in ex-slaves' lives?
4. Why did some freedmen continue to work for their former masters?

FELIX HAYWOOD

San Antonio, Texas. Born in Raleigh,
North Carolina. Age at interview: 88.

The end of the war, it come just like that—like you snap your fingers. . . . How did we know it! Hallelujah broke out—

> Abe Lincoln freed the nigger
>   With the gun and the trigger;
> And I ain't going to get whipped any more.
>   I got my ticket,
> Leaving the thicket,
>   And I'm a-heading for the Golden Shore!

"African Americans React to Reconstruction" from B. A. Botkin, ed., *Lay My Burden Down: A Folk History of Slavery* (Chicago: The University of Chicago Press, 1945), pp. 65–70, 223–24, 241–42, and 246–47.

Soldiers, all of a sudden, was everywhere—coming in bunches, crossing and walking and riding. Everyone was a-singing. We was all walking on golden clouds. Hallelujah!

> Union forever,
>   Hurrah, boys, hurrah!
> Although I may be poor,
>   I'll never be a slave—
> Shouting the battle cry of freedom.

Everybody went wild. We felt like heroes, and nobody had made us that way but ourselves. We was free. Just like that, we was free. It didn't seem to make the whites mad, either. They went right on giving us food just the same. Nobody took our homes away, but right off colored folks started on the move. They seemed to want to get closer to freedom, so they'd know what it was— like it was a place or a city. Me and my father stuck, stuck close as a lean tick to a sick kitten. The Gudlows started us out on a ranch. My father, he'd round up cattle—unbranded cattle—for the whites. They was cattle that they belonged to, all right; they had gone to find water 'long the San Antonio River and the Guadalupe. Then the whites gave me and my father some cattle for our own. My father had his own brand—7 B)—and we had a herd to start out with of seventy.

We knowed freedom was on us, but we didn't know what was to come with it. We thought we was going to get rich like the white folks. We thought we was going to be richer than the white folks, 'cause we was stronger and knowed how to work, and the whites didn't, and they didn't have us to work for them any more. But it didn't turn out that way. We soon found out that freedom could make folks proud, but it didn't make 'em rich.

Did you ever stop to think that thinking don't do any good when you do it too late? Well, that's how it was with us. If every mother's son of a black had thrown 'way his hoe and took up a gun to fight for his own freedom along with the Yankees, the war'd been over before it began. But we didn't do it. We couldn't help stick to our masters. We couldn't no more shoot 'em than we could fly. My father and me used to talk 'bout it. We decided we was too soft and freedom wasn't going to be much to our good even if we had a education.

WARREN McKINNEY

Hazen, Arkansas. Born in South Carolina.
Age at interview: 85.

I was born in Edgefield County, South Carolina. I am eighty-five years old. I was born a slave of George Strauter. I remembers hearing them say, "Thank God, I's free as a jay bird." My ma was a slave in the field. I was eleven years old when freedom was declared. When I was little, Mr. Strauter whipped my ma. It hurt me bad as it did her. I hated him. She was crying. I chunked him with rocks. He run after me, but he didn't catch me. There was twenty-five or thirty hands that worked in the field. They raised wheat, corn, oats, barley, and cotton. All the children that couldn't work stayed at one house. Aunt Mat kept the babies and small children that couldn't go to the field. He had a gin and a shop. The shop was at the fork of the roads. When the war come on, my papa went to built forts. He quit Ma and took another woman. When the war close, Ma took her four children, bundled 'em up and went to Augusta. The government give out rations there. My ma washed and ironed. People died in piles. I don't know till yet what was the matter. They said it was the change of living. I seen five or six wooden, painted coffins piled up on wagons pass by our house. Loads passed every day like you see cotton pass here. Some said it was cholera and some took consumption. Lots of the colored people nearly starved. Not much to get to do and not much houseroom. Several families had to live in one house. Lots of the colored folks went up North and froze to death. They couldn't stand the cold. They wrote back about them dying. No, they never sent them back. I heard some sent for money to come back. I heard plenty 'bout the Ku Klux. They scared the folks to death. People left Augusta in droves. About a thousand would all meet and walk going to hunt work and new homes. Some of them died. I had a sister and brother lost that way. I had another sister come to Louisiana that way. She wrote back.

I don't think the colored folks looked for a share of land. They never got nothing 'cause the white folks didn't have nothing but barren hills left. About all the mules was wore out hauling provisions in the army. Some folks say they ought to done more for the colored folks when they left, but they say they was broke. Freeing all the slaves left 'em broke.

That reconstruction was a mighty hard pull. Me and Ma couldn't live. A man paid our ways to Carlisle, Arkansas, and we come. We started working for Mr. Emenson. He had a big store, teams, and land. We liked it fine, and I been here fifty-six years now. There was so much wild game, living was not so hard. If a fellow could get a little bread and a place to stay, he was all right. After I come to this state, I voted some. I have farmed and worked at odd jobs. I farmed mostly. Ma went back to her old master. He persuaded her to come back home. Me and her went back and run a farm four or five years before she died. Then I come back here.

LEE GUIDON

South Carolina. Born in South Carolina.
Age at interview: 89.

Yes, ma'am, I sure was in the Civil War. I plowed all day, and me and my sister helped take care of the baby at night. It would cry, and me bumping it [in a straight chair, rocking.] Time I git it to the bed where its mama was, it wake up and start crying all over again. I be so sleepy. It was a puny sort of baby. Its papa was off at war. His name was Jim Cowan, and his wife Miss Margaret

Brown 'fore she married him. Miss Lucy Smith give me and my sister to them. Then she married Mr. Abe Moore. Jim Smith was Miss Lucy's boy. He lay out in the woods all time. He say no need in him gitting shot up and killed. He say let the slaves be free. We lived, seemed like, on 'bout the line of York and Union counties. He lay out in the woods over in York County. Mr. Jim say all the fighting 'bout was jealousy. They caught him several times, but every time he got away from 'em. After they come home Mr. Jim say they never win no war. They stole and starved out the South. . . .

After freedom a heap of people say they was going to name theirselves over. They named theirselves big names, then went roaming round like wild, hunting cities. They changed up so it was hard to tell who or where anybody was. Heap of 'em died, and you didn't know when you hear about it if he was your folks hardly. Some of the names was Abraham, and some called theirselves Lincum. Any big name 'cepting their master's name. It was the fashion. I heard 'em talking 'bout it one evening, and my pa say, "Fine folks raise us and we gonna hold to our own names." That settled it with all of us. . . .

I reckon I do know 'bout the Ku Kluck. I knowed a man named Alfred Owens. He seemed all right, but he was a Republican. He said he was not afraid. He run a tanyard and kept a heap of guns in a big room. They all loaded. He married a Southern woman. Her husband either died or was killed. She had a son living with them. The Ku Kluck was called Upper League. They get this boy to unload all the guns. Then the white men went there. The white man give up and said, "I ain't got no gun to defend myself with. The guns all unloaded, and I ain't got no powder and shot." But the Ku Kluck shot in the houses and shot him up like lacework. He sold fine harness, saddles, bridles — all sorts of leather things. The Ku Kluck sure run them outen their country. They say they not going to have them round, and they sure run them out, back where they came from. . . .

For them what stayed on like they were, Reconstruction times 'bout like times before that 'cepting the Yankee stole out and tore up a scandalous heap. They tell the black folks to do something, and then come white folks you live with and say Ku Kluck whup you. They say leave, and white folks say better not listen to them old yankees. They'll git you too far off to come back, and you freeze. They done give you all the use they got for you. How they do? All sorts of ways. Some stayed at their cabins glad to have one to live in and farmed on. Some running round begging, some hunting work for money, and nobody had no money 'cepting the Yankees, and they had no homes or land and mighty little work for you to do. No work to live on. Some going every day to the city. That winter I heard 'bout them starving and freezing by the wagon loads. I never heard nothing 'bout voting till freedom. I don't think I ever voted till I come to Mississippi. I votes Republican. That's the party of my color, and I stick to them as long as they do right. I don't dabble in white folks' business, and that white folks' voting is their business. If I vote, I go do it and go on home.

I been plowing all my life, and in the hot days I cuts and saws wood. Then when I gets outa cotton-picking, I put each boy on a load of wood and we sell wood. The last years we got $3 a cord. Then we clear land till next spring. I don't find no time to be loafing. I never missed a year farming till I got the Bright's disease [one of several kinds of kidney ailments] and it hurt me to do hard work. Farming is the best life there is when you are able. . . .

When I owned most, I had six head mules and five head horses. I rented 140 acres of land. I bought this house and some other land about. The anthrax killed nearly all my horses and mules. I got one big fine mule yet. Its mate died. I lost my house. My son give me one room, and he paying the debt off now. It's hard for colored folks to keep anything. Somebody gets it from 'em if they don't mind.

The present times is hard. Timber is scarce. Game is about all gone. Prices higher. Old folks cannot work. Times is hard for younger folks too. They go to town too much and go to shows. They going to a tent show now. Circus coming, they say. They spending too much money for foolishness. It's a fast time. Folks too restless. Some of the colored folks work hard as folks ever did. They spends too much. Some folks is lazy. Always been that way.

I signed up to the government, but they ain't give me nothing 'cepting powdered milk and rice what wasn't fit to eat. It cracked up and had black something in it. A lady said she would give me some shirts that was her husband's. I went to get them, but she wasn't home. These heavy shirts give me heat. They won't give me the pension, and I don't know why. It would help me buy my salts and pills and the other medicines like Swamp Root. They won't give it to me.

TOBY JONES

Madisonville, Texas. Born in South Carolina.
Age at interview: 87.

I worked for Massa 'bout four years after freedom, 'cause he forced me to, said he couldn't 'ford to let me go. His place was near ruint, the fences burnt, and the house would have been, but it was rock. There was a battle fought near his place, and I taken Missy to a hideout in the mountains to where her father was, 'cause there was bullets flying everywhere. When the war was over, Massa come home and says, "You son of a gun, you's supposed to be free, but you ain't, 'cause I ain't gwine give you freedom." So I goes on working for him till I gits the chance to steal a hoss from him. The woman I wanted to marry, Govie, she 'cides to come to Texas with me. Me and Govie, we rides the hoss 'most a hundred miles, then we turned him a-loose and give him a scare back to his house, and come on foot the rest the way to Texas.

All we had to eat was what we could beg, and sometimes we went three days without a bite to eat. Sometimes we'd pick a few berries. When we got cold we'd crawl in a brushpile and hug up close together to keep warm. Once in a while we'd come to a farmhouse, and the man let us sleep on cottonseed in his barn, but they was far and few between, 'cause they wasn't many houses in the country them days like now.

When we gits to Texas, we gits married, but all they was to our wedding am we just 'grees to live together as man and wife. I settled on some land, and we cut some trees and split them open and stood them on end with the tops together for our house. Then we deadened some trees, and the land was ready to farm. There was some wild cattle and hogs, and that's the way we got our start, caught some of them and tamed them.

I don't know as I 'spected nothing from freedom, but they turned us out like a bunch of stray dogs, no homes, no clothing, no nothing, not 'nough food to last us one meal. After we settles on that place, I never seed man or woman, 'cept Govie, for six years, 'cause it was a long ways to anywhere. All we had to farm with was sharp sticks. We'd stick holes and plant corn, and when it come up we'd punch up the dirt round it. We didn't plant cotton, 'cause we couldn't eat that. I made bows and arrows to kill wild game with, and we never went to a store for nothing. We made our clothes out of animal skins.

WHY ADAM KIRK WAS A DEMOCRAT

(House Report No. 262, 43 Cong., 2 Sess., p. 106.
Statement of an Alabama Negro [1874].)

A white man raised me. I was raised in the house of old man Billy Kirk. He raised me as a body servant. The class that he belongs to seems nearer to me than the northern white man, and actually, since the war, everything I have got is by their aid and their assistance. They have helped me raise up my family and have stood by me, and whenever I want a doctor, no matter what hour of the day or night, he is called in whether I have got a cent or not. And when I want any assistance I can get it from them. I think they have got better principles and better character than the republicans.

44

White Southerners'
Reactions to Reconstruction

Caleb G. Forshey
and Reverend James Sinclair

The Congressional Joint Committee of Fifteen, assembled to examine Southern represen-
tation in Congress, was named in December 1865 as part of the Republican Congress's
response to President Andrew Johnson's plan of Reconstruction. In 1866, the committee held
hearings as part of its effort to develop the Fourteenth Amendment. Despite the president's
veto, Congress had already enlarged the scope of the Freedmen's Bureau to care for dis-
placed ex-slaves and to try by military commission those accused of depriving freedmen of
civil rights. Republicans in Congress, in opposition to the Johnson administration, would
continue to evolve a Reconstruction policy that attempted to protect the ex-slaves' rights.

Of the two white Southerners whose interviews with the committee you will read
here, Caleb G. Forshey had supported secession while James Sinclair, although a slave-
holder, had opposed it. A Scottish-born minister who had only moved to North Car-
olina in 1857, Sinclair's Unionist sentiments had led to the loss of his church and then
to his arrest during the war. In 1865 he served on the Freedmen's Bureau.

BEFORE YOU READ

1. What effect did Caleb Forshey anticipate from military occupation of southern states?
2. What was his evaluation of the Freedmen's Bureau?
3. What were Forshey's beliefs about African Americans?
4. What were the strengths and weaknesses of the Freedmen's Bureau according to James Sinclair?
5. How does Sinclair's view of southern opinion differ from Forshey's?

CALEB G. FORSHEY

Washington, D.C., March 28, 1866

Question: Where do you reside?
Answer: I reside in the State of Texas.
Question: How long have you been a resident of Texas?
Answer: I have resided in Texas and been a citizen of that State for nearly thirteen years.

The Report of the Committees of the House of Representatives Made During the First Session, Thirty-Ninth
Congress, 1865–1866. Volume II. (Washington, D.C., Government Printing Office, 1866), Forshey: pp. 129 32; Sinclair: pp. 168–71.

Question: What opportunities have you had for ascertaining the temper and disposition of the people of Texas towards the government and authority of the United States?

Answer: For ten years I have been superintendent of the Texas Military Institute, as its founder and conductor. I have been in the confederate service in various parts of the confederacy; but chiefly in the trans-Mississippi department, in Louisiana and Texas, as an officer of engineers. I have had occasion to see and know very extensively the condition of affairs in Texas, and also to a considerable extent in Louisiana. I think I am pretty well-informed, as well as anybody, perhaps, of the present state of affairs in Texas.

Question: What are the feelings and views of the people of Texas as to the late rebellion, and the future condition and circumstances of the State, and its relations to the federal government?

Answer: After our army had given up its arms and gone home, the surrender of all matters in controversy was complete, and as nearly universal, perhaps, as anything could be. Assuming the matters in controversy to have been the right to secede, and the right to hold slaves, I think they were given up tee-totally, to use a strong Americanism. When you speak of feeling, I should discriminate a little. The feeling was that of any party who had been cast in a suit he had staked all upon. They did not return from feeling, but from a sense of necessity, and from a judgment that it was the only and necessary thing to be done, to give up the contest. But when they gave it up, it was without reservation; with a view to look forward, and not back. That is my impression of the manner in which the thing was done. There was a public expectation that in some very limited time there would be a restoration to former relations. . . . It was the expectation of the people that, as soon as the State was organized as proposed by the President, they would be restored to their former relations, and things would go on as before.

Question: What is your opinion of a military force under the authority of the federal government to preserve order in Texas and to protect those who have been loyal, both white and black, from the aggressions of those who have been in the rebellion?

Answer: My judgment is well founded on that subject: that wherever such military force is and has been, it has excited the very feeling it was intended to prevent; that so far from being necessary it is very pernicious everywhere, and without exception. The local authorities and public sentiment are ample for protection. I think no occasion would occur, unless some individual case that our laws would not reach. We had an opportunity to test this after the surrender and before any authority was there. The military authorities, or the military officers, declared that we were without laws, and it was a long time before the governor appointed arrived there, and then it was sometime before we could effect anything in the way of organization. We were a people without law, order, or anything; and it was a time for violence if it would occur. I think it is a great credit to our civilization that, in that state of affairs, there was nowhere any instance of violence. I am proud of it, for I expected the contrary; I expected that our soldiers on coming home, many of them, would be dissolute, and that many of them would oppress the class of men you speak of; but it did not occur. But afterwards, wherever soldiers have been sent, there have been little troubles, none of them large; but personal collisions between soldiers and citizens.

Question: What is your opinion as to the necessity and advantages of the Freedmen's Bureau, or an agency of that kind, in Texas?

Answer: My opinion is that it is not needed; my opinion is stronger than that—that the effect of it is to irritate, if nothing else. While in New York city recently I had a conversation with some friends from Texas, from five distant points in the State. We met together and compared opinions; and the opinion of each was the same, that the negroes had generally gone to work since January; that except where the Freedmen's Bureau had interfered, or rather encouraged troubles, such as little complaints, especially between negro and negro, the negro's disposition was very good, and they had generally gone to work, a vast majority of them with their former masters. . . . The impression in Texas at present is that the negroes under the influence of the Freedmens's Bureau do worse than without it.

I want to state that I believe all our former owners of negroes are the friends of the negroes; and that the antagonism paraded in the papers of the north does not exist at all. I know the fact is the very converse of that; and good feeling always prevails between the masters and the slaves. But the negroes went off and left them in the lurch; my own family was an instance of it. But they came back after a time, saying they had been free enough and wanted a home.

Question: Do you think those who employ the negroes there are willing to make contracts with them, so that they shall have fair wages for their labor?

Answer: I think so; I think they are paid liberally, more than the white men in this country get; the average compensation to negroes there is greater than the average compensation of free laboring white men in this country. It seems to have regulated itself in a great measure by what each neighborhood was doing; the negroes saying, "I can get thus and so at such a place." Men have hired from eight to fifteen dollars per month during the year, and women at about two dollars less a month; house-servants at a great deal more.

Question: Do the men who employ the negroes claim to exercise the right to enforce their contract by physical force?

Answer: Not at all; that is totally abandoned; not a single instance of it has occurred. I think they still chastise children, though. The negro parents often neglect that, and the children are still switched as we switch our own children. I know it is done in my own house; we have little house-servants that we switch just as I do our own little fellows.

Question: What is your opinion as to the respective advantages to the white and black races, of the present free system of labor and the institution of slavery?

Answer: I think freedom is very unfortunate for the negro; I think it is sad; his present helpless condition touches my heart more than anything else I ever contemplated, and I think that is the common sentiment of our slaveholders. I have seen it on the largest plantations, where the negro men had all left, and where only women and children remained, and the owners had to keep them and feed them. The beginning certainly presents a touching and sad spectacle. The poor negro is dying at a rate fearful to relate.

I have some ethnological theories that may perhaps warp my judgment; but my judgment is that the highest condition the black race has ever reached or can reach, is one where he is provided for by a master race. That is the result of a great deal of scientific investigation and observation of the negro character by me ever since I was a man. The labor question had become a most momentous one, and I was studying it. I undertook to investigate the condition of the negro from statistics under various circumstances, to treat it purely as a matter of statistics from the census tables of this country of ours. I found that the free blacks of the north decreased 8 per cent.; the free blacks of the south increased 7 or 8 per cent , while the slaves by their sides increased 34 per cent. I inferred from the doctrines of political economy that the race is in the best condition when it procreates the fastest; that, other things being equal, slavery is of vast advantage to the negro. I will mention one or two things in connexion with this as explanatory of that result. The negro will not take care of his offspring unless required to do it, as compared with the whites. The little children will die; they do die, and hence the necessity of very rigorous regulations on our plantations which we have adopted in our nursery system.

Another cause is that there is no continence among the negroes. All the continence I have ever seen among the negroes has been enforced upon plantations, where it is generally assumed there is none. For the sake of procreation, if nothing else, we compel men to live with their wives. The discipline of the plantation was more rigorous, perhaps, in regard to men staying with their wives, than in regard to anything else; and I think the procreative results, as shown by the census tables, is due in a great measure to that discipline. . . .

Question: What is the prevailing inclination among the people of Texas in regard to giving the negroes civil or political rights and privileges?

Answer: I think they are all opposed to it. There are some men—I am not among them—who think that the basis of intelligence might be a good basis for the elective franchise. But a much larger class, perhaps nine-tenths of our people, believe that the distinctions between the races should not be broken down by any such community of interests in the management of the affairs of the State. I think there is a very common sentiment that the negro, even with education, has not a mind capable of appreciating the political institutions of the country to such an extent as would make him a good associate for the white man in the administration of the government. I think if the vote was taken on the question of admitting him to the right of suffrage there would be a very small vote in favor of it—scarcely respectable: that is my judgment.

REVEREND JAMES SINCLAIR
Washington, D.C., January 29, 1866

Question: What is generally the state of feeling among the white people of
North Carolina towards the government of the United States?

Answer: That is a difficult question to answer, but I will answer it as far as
my own knowledge goes. In my opinion, there is generally among the white
people not much love for the government. Though they are willing, and I believe determined, to acquiesce in what is inevitable, yet so far as love and affection for the government is concerned, I do not believe that they have any
of it at all, outside of their personal respect and regard for President Johnson.

Question: How do they feel towards the mass of the northern people — that
is, the people of what were known formerly as the free States?

Answer: They feel in this way: that they have been ruined by them. You can
imagine the feelings of a person towards one whom he regards as having ruined him. They regard the northern people as having destroyed their property
or taken it from them, and brought all the calamaties of this war upon them.

Question: How do they feel in regard to what is called the right of secession?

Answer: They think that it was right . . . that there was no wrong in it.
They are willing now to accept the decision of the question that has been
made by the sword, but they are not by any means converted from their old
opinion that they had a right to secede. It is true that there have always been
Union men in our State, but not Union men without slavery, except perhaps
among Quakers. Slavery was the central idea even of the Unionist. The only
difference between them and the others upon that question was, that they desired to have that institution under the aegis of the Constitution, and protected by it. The secessionists wanted to get away from the north altogether.
When the secessionists precipitated our State into rebellion, the Unionists
and secessionists went together, because the great object with both was the
preservation of slavery by the preservation of State sovereignty. There was
another class of Unionists who did not care anything at all about slavery, but
they were driven by the other whites into the rebellion for the purpose of preserving slavery. The poor whites are to-day very much opposed to conferring
upon the negro the right of suffrage; as much so as the other classes of the
whites. They believe it is the intention of government to give the negro rights
at their expense. They cannot see it in any other light than that as the negro
is elevated they must proportionately go down. While they are glad that slavery is done away with, they are bitterly opposed to conferring the right of suffrage on the negro as the most prominent secessionists; but it is for the reason
I have stated, that they think rights conferred on the negro must necessarily be
taken from them, particularly the ballot, which was the only bulwark guarding
their superiority to the negro race.

Question: In your judgment, what proportion of the white people of North
Carolina are really, and truly, and cordially attached to the government of the
United States?

Answer: Very few, sir; very few. . . .

Question: Is the Freedmen's Bureau acceptable to the great mass of the white people in North Carolina?

Answer: No, sir; I do not think it is; I think the most of the whites wish the bureau to be taken away.

Question: Why do they wish that?

Answer: They think that they can manage the negro for themselves: that they understand him better than northern men do. They say, "Let us understand what you want us to do with negro—what you desire of us; lay down your conditions for our readmission into the Union, and then we will know what we have to do, and if you will do that we will enact laws for the government of these negroes. They have lived among us, and they are all with us, and we can manage them better than you can." They think it is interfering with the rights of the State for a bureau, the agent and representative of the federal government, to overslaugh the State entirely, and interfere with the regulations and administration of justice before their courts.

Question: Is there generally a willingness on the part of the whites to allow the freedmen to enjoy the right of acquiring land and personal property?

Answer: I think they are very willing to let them do that, for this reason; to get rid of some portion of the taxes imposed upon their property by the government. For instance, a white man will agree to sell a negro some of his land on condition of his paying so much a year on it, promising to give him a deed of it when the whole payment is made, taking his note in the mean time. This relieves that much of the land from taxes to be paid by the white man. All I am afraid of is, that the negro is too eager to go into this thing; that he will ruin himself, get himself into debt to the white man, and be forever bound to him for the debt and never get the land. I have often warned them to be careful what they did about these things.

Question: There is no repugnance on the part of the whites to the negro owning land and personal property?

Answer: I think not.

Question: Have they any objection to the legal establishment of the domestic relations among the blacks, such as the relation of husband and wife, of parent and child, and the securing by law to the negro the rights of those relations?

Answer: That is a matter of ridicule with the whites. They do not believe the negroes will ever respect those relations more than the brutes. I suppose I have married more than two hundred couples of negroes since the war, but the whites laugh at the very idea of the thing. Under the old laws a slave could not marry a free woman of color; it was made a penal offence in North Carolina for any one to perform such a marriage. But there was in my own family a slave who desired to marry a free woman of color, and I did what I conceived to be my duty, and married them, and I was presented to the grand jury for doing so, but the prosecuting attorney threw out the case and would not try it. In former times the officiating clergyman marrying slaves, could not use the usual formula: "Whom God has joined together let no man put asunder"; you could not say, "According to the ordinance of God I pronounce you man and wife; you are no longer two but one." It was not legal for you to do so.

Question: What, in general, has been the treatment of the blacks by the whites since the close of hostilities?

Answer: It has not generally been of the kindest character, I must say that; I am compelled to say that.

Question: Are you aware of any instance of personal ill treatment towards the blacks by the whites?

Answer: Yes, sir.

Question: Give some instances that have occurred since the war.

Answer: [Sinclair describes the beating of a young woman across her buttocks in graphic detail.]

Question: What was the provocation, if any?

Answer: Something in regard to some work, which is generally the provocation.

Question: Was there no law in North Carolina at that time to punish such an outrage?

Answer: No, sir; only the regulations of the Freedmen's Bureau; we took cognizance of the case. In old times that was quite allowable; it is what was called "paddling."

Question: Did you deal with the master?

Answer: I immediately sent a letter to him to come to my office, but he did not come, and I have never seen him in regard to the matter since. I had no soldiers to enforce compliance, and I was obliged to let the matter drop.

Question: Have you any reason to suppose that such instances of cruelty are frequent in North Carolina at this time—instances of whipping and striking?

Answer: I think they are; it was only a few days before I left that a woman came there with her head all bandaged up, having been cut and bruised by her employer. They think nothing of striking them.

Question: And the negro has practically no redress?

Answer: Only what he can get from the Freedmen's Bureau.

Question: Can you say anything further in regard to the political condition of North Carolina—the feeling of the people towards the government of the United States?

Answer: I for one would not wish to be left there in the hands of those men; I could not live there just now. But perhaps my case is an isolated one from the position I was compelled to take in that State. I was persecuted, arrested, and they tried to get me into their service; they tried everything to accomplish their purpose, and of course I have rendered myself still more obnoxious by accepting an appointment under the Freedmen's Bureau. As for myself I would not be allowed to remain there. I do not want to be handed over to these people. I know it is utterly impossible for any man who was not true to the Confederate States up to the last moment of the existence of the confederacy, to expect any favor of these people as the State is constituted at present.

Question: Suppose the military pressure of the government of the United States should be withdrawn from North Carolina, would northern men and true Unionists be safe in that State?

Answer: A northern man going there would perhaps present nothing obnoxious to the people of the State. But men who were born there, who have been true to the Union, and who have fought against the rebellion, are worse off than northern men. . . .

Question: In your judgment, what effect has been produced by the liberality of the President in granting pardons and amnesties to rebels in that State — what effect upon the public mind?

Answer: On my oath I am bound to reply exactly as I believe; that is, that if President Johnson is ever a candidate for re-election he will be supported by the southern States, particularly by North Carolina; but that his liberality to them has drawn them one whit closer to the government than before, I do not believe. It has drawn them to President Johnson personally, and to the Democratic party, I suppose.

(Acknowledgments continued from page iv)

[18] "Secret Correspondence of a Loyalist Wife" from H. O. H. Vernon-Jackson, ed., "A Loyalist Wife: Letters of Mrs. Philip Van Cortlandt, December 1776–February 1777" from *History Today* 14 (1964): 574–80. Reprinted with the permission of *History Today*.

[19] "War in the South" from Jack P. Greene, ed., *The Diary of Colonel Landon Carter of Sabine Hall, 1752–1778, 2 vols.* (Charlottesville: The University Press of Virginia for the Virginia Historical Society, 1965), pp. 1051–52, 1054–56, 1064, 1084–95, and 1109–10. Reprinted with the permission of the Virginia Historical Society.

[23] "A Mexican Perspective" from José Enrique de la Peña, *With Santa Anna in Texas: A Personal Narrative of the Revolution*, translated and edited by Carmen Perry, pp. 44–56. Copyright © 1975. Reprinted with the permission of Texas A & M University Press.

[25] "Crossing the Great Divide" from Bernard DeVoto, ed., *The Journals of Lewis and Clark*, pp. 202–06, 207–11, and 213–14. Copyright 1953 by Bernard DeVoto, renewed © 1981 by Avis DeVoto. Reprinted by permission of Houghton Mifflin Company. All rights reserved.

[27] "The Trail of Tears" from Gary E. Moulton, ed., *The Papers of Chief John Ross: Volume I, 1807–1839*, pp. 470–74, 678–80, and 704–05. Copyright © 1985 by the University of Oklahoma Press. Reprinted with the permission of the publishers.

[29] "Pulling a Handcart to the Mormon Zion" by Priscilla Merriman Evans, from *Hearts of the West*, Volume 9, pp. 8–13, compiled by Kate B. Carter. Reprinted by permission of the International Society Daughters of Utah Pioneers.

[30] "A Railroad Town" by Frithjof Meidell, from *Norwegian-American Studies and Records* 9 (1936): 48–53. Reprinted with the permission of the Norwegian-American Historical Association.

[39] "A Southern Woman's Wartime Journal" from Mary D. Robertson, ed., *A Confederate Lady Comes of Age: The Journal of Pauline DeCaradeuc Heyward, 1863–1888* (Columbia: The University of South Carolina Press, 1992), pp. 36–37 and 65–69. Reprinted by permission of the publishers.

[42] "A Slaveholder's Journal at the End of the Civil War" from Arney Robinson Childs, ed., *The Private Journal of Henry William Ravenal, 1859–1887* (Columbia: The University of South Carolina Press, 1947), pp. 202–03, 206–07, 210–21 *passim*, 228–29, 237, and 239–40. Reprinted with the permission of the publishers.

[43] "African Americans React to Reconstruction" from B. A. Botkin, ed., *Lay My Burden Down: A Folk History of Slavery* (Chicago: The University of Chicago Press, 1945), pp. 65–70, 223–24, 241–42, and 246–47. Copyright 1945 by B. A. Botkin. Reprinted by permission of Curtis Brown, Ltd.